EAGLE
FORGOTTEN

EAGLE
FORGOTTEN

The Life of John Peter Altgeld

HARRY BARNARD

LYLE STUART, INC.　•　Secaucus, New Jersey

THE EAGLE THAT IS FORGOTTEN

(John P. Altgeld. Born December 30, 1847 ; died March 12, 1902)

Sleep softly . . . eagle forgotten . . . under the stone.
Time has its way with you there, and the clay has its own.

"We have buried him now," thought your foes, and in secret rejoiced.
They have made a brave show of their mourning, their hatred unvoiced.
They had snarled at you, barked at you, foamed at you, day after day.
Now you were ended. They praised you, . . . and laid you away.

The others that mourned you in silence and terror and truth,
The widow bereft of her pittance, the boy without youth,
The mocked and the scorned and the wounded, the lame and the poor
That should have remembered forever, . . . remember no more.

Where are those lovers of yours, on what name do they call
The lost, that in armies wept over your funeral pall?
They call on the names of a hundred high-valiant ones,
A hundred white eagles have risen, the sons of your sons,
The zeal in their wings is a zeal that your dreaming began,
The valor that wore out your soul in the service of man.

Sleep softly, . . . eagle forgotten, . . . under the stone,
Time has its way with you there, and the clay has its own.
Sleep on, O brave-hearted, O wise man, that kindled the flame—
To live in mankind is far more than to live in a name,
To live in mankind, far, far more . . . than to live in a name.

—Vachel Lindsay

Reprinted by permission of the publishers, The Macmillan Company,
from *Collected Poems* by Vachel Lindsay.

CONTENTS

CONTENTS—Concluded

BOOK ONE

THE STRUGGLE

CHAPTER ONE

Beginnings

1

In the spring of 1848 a young German couple named Altgeld came to America from the tiny village Nieder Selters in the province of Nassau in Southern Germany. With them they brought their three-months-old son,[1] who was born on December 30, 1847, and was christened John Peter after his father. Their destination was Ohio.

Later it would be said of their baby that he was in America because he had been one of "those German revolutionists of 1848." This was not even true of the father. Probably the father never realized that others left Germany that year for any reason except to seek a better living. Had anyone mentioned the word socialism to him, he would have had to ask what it meant. Perhaps he would not even have asked. Such things held no interest for him.

They were peasant folk. In Nieder Selters, from which seltzer water gets its name, the young father had combined farming with the trade of wagon-making. But it had become increasingly difficult for him to earn a living there, especially after a series of crop failures had impoverished the working classes in all the Central European states. There was little money for the barest necessities and the services of the wagon-maker Altgeld were needed least. And so the Altgelds decided to join the stream of hundreds and indeed thousands of other Germans who that year made the hard voyage to America.

They reached Ohio by following the directions furnished by the brothers of the young mother. One of her brothers, Peter Lanehart (originally spelled Lehnhart), had been in Ohio since 1843 and another, William, since 1847. Already they were prospering and it was probably their money that made it possible for their sister, Mary, and her stolid, dull-headed husband to make the trip from Nieder Selters. The elder Altgeld may have resented this, for he never had much to do with the Laneharts afterward. Moreover, he did not like the ideas held by his wife's people. They talked of sending their sons to high schools and then to colleges. He felt that education spoiled a person.

15

It was better to stick to the land, and hard, manual labor. It annoyed him to think that perhaps his wife shared her brothers' ideas for their son.

2

The wagon-maker Altgeld rented a farm in the hilly section near the little village of Newville, not far from Mansfield, Ohio. Dominating the county, Richland, was Mansfield, home of John Sherman, who later came to be known as the United States senator responsible for the Free Silver movement of 1896. Mansfield in the 'forties already gave promise of becoming a bustling little warehouse and railroad center. But the rest of the county was still half wilderness, out of which farm lands had been carved, with here and there little clusters of houses—villages such as Newville.

The first settlers in the region were New Englanders. Then came large numbers from Pennsylvania, including many Germans, and finally an increasing number of immigrants direct from the old world, Germans like the Altgelds and Laneharts, and many Irish. Yet it could not be called a foreign community in which the Altgelds settled with their son. It was typically American. That should be remembered.

As early as the 'forties Richland County already had a local history rich with legend. It was widely believed that a certain white man who grew up among the Indians and wandered over the hills there was really the Lost Dauphin, Louis XVII, King of France. Many were the tales told of this man, Lazarre. Then there was Johnny Appleseed, born John Chapman. Richland County was the home of that vague, half-demented, half-inspired figure who planted apple seeds wherever he wandered and also distributed Swedenborgian tracts.

Here, then, in Johnny Appleseed's country, John Peter Altgeld grew from infancy to young manhood. From the hills and forests of Ohio he received the first impressions to be made on his mind.[2] His next impressions were of poverty.

3

For twelve years the Altgelds struggled to win a living from the Newville farm. The land was poor, and eight more children came in rapid succession, three other sons and five girls. Two girls and a boy died in infancy, leaving John Peter, Mina, William, Mary, Amelia and Louis. However, only scant attention need be paid to these brothers and sisters. William might in time have left his mark, for he was thought to be "even brighter than John Peter." But he succumbed to tuberculosis while in his twenties. The other brother, Louis, "cared nothing for schooling and it was finally decided to make him a plumber." He, too, died young. The girls married and lived quiet and uneventful lives. They exerted no influence upon John Peter.[3]

In 1860 the family moved to a larger farm, 140 acres, on the Diamond Street road near Little Washington, about six miles southeast of Mansfield. This was made necessary by the growing family. Now the father did not rent, but purchased, the land. The mortgage was large—and pressing. But by then he had the assistance of his eldest son at plowing, seeding and harvesting. Young Pete—so he was called for many years—was "taught to work from daylight until dark—and do the chores afterward," so he recalled.[4] When there was no work for him on the father's place, he was hired out to the neighbors. At other times he was sent to Mansfield to peddle butter and eggs and the vegetables his mother raised. His father was known as strict, given to beating his children when disobeyed.

Before the family moved to the new farm, young Pete was permitted to attend the district school—for two summers and a winter. There he learned to speak and read in English. For a time, too, he attended an English Sunday School of the Methodist Church at Newville, although his parents belonged to the German-speaking Lutheran Church.[5] But when he was twelve, the father felt that he had had enough education.

The boy did not object. He had not displayed any special brilliance in school. Learning was not easy for him, even though he did have a tremendous curiosity and there is a picture of his raiding all of the neighbors' bookshelves. Then, too, his school days were far from happy. "In school, the boys all picked on me. No one of them ever thought of protecting me from abuse. It was the crowd on one side and John Peter Altgeld on the other." So Altgeld to an intimate some forty years later.[6]

Then it was Altgeld—derisively they called him "the little Dutchman"—who was the under-dog. He never forgot what this meant.

4

His own explanation for the abuse that he suffered in those days was: "I have thought there must be something about me that repels others."[7] In a sense, this was always true until his character was appreciated.

His appearance must have been quite wretched in those days. Although slightly under average height because of noticeably short legs, he was big-boned, like his father, and this gave his looks a quality that is described suggestively, if not accurately, as "foreign." It was a quality that years later caused Professor Harry Thurston Peck to write, thoughtlessly, that Altgeld "in appearance resembled a typical German anarchist, fanatical and intense." Altgeld himself, in a joking mood, once said: "Hell, if I had to depend on my looks I'd have been hung long ago!"[8]

Actually, there was nothing more sinister or displeasing in his appearance than might be expected from peasant stock. His nose was large, with distended nostrils, and only partially regular in contour. He had a severely rugged, heavy jaw. Then, there was his hair. It seemed to be affixed to his skull as if it were a mat. It was always short and grew straight up, like a stubble. There was no parting it and it had to be combed either straight up or down. "I never saw hair worn in just [his] style, except by boys who had gone swimming and had no comb when they came back." So Nellie Bly, the famous "girl reporter" of the New York World, would write when she saw him years later.[9]

And he had a slight harelip, which impeded his speech a trace, emphasizing the peculiar roughness of his general appearance. Only his eyes, which Nellie Bly found to be of "deep indigo blue," were a redeeming feature. They softened an effect that otherwise "marked him peculiarly as the caricaturist's prey." Many persons would be won over by those eyes, and Edgar Lee Masters would catch their quality in his Spoon River Anthology.

Consider such features, excepting the eyes, in combination with a heavy Teutonic accent. Add to the general effect coarse, homespun and home-sewn clothes. It is easy, then, to realize why the wagon-maker's son would be an object of scorn and ridicule. Moreover, it was a time in America—and this would happen repeatedly afterward—when the popular thing was to torment "foreigners" and Catholics. When Pete was eight or nine, this anti-foreign fanaticism caused blood to flow in Cincinnati and Louisville, both cities near at hand. The agitation was so shocking that an ex-congressman in Illinois, a politician not yet given to speaking out vigorously on many issues, exclaimed that if Know-nothingism was triumphant he "would prefer emigrating to some country where they make no pretence at loving liberty—to Russia, for instance, where despotism can be taken pure. . . ."[10] The ex-congressman was Abraham Lincoln.

Undoubtedly, this Know-nothingism played a part in the unhappiness of young Altgeld's school days. It could have had the effect, too, of inspiring an ambition to rise in the world, an urge for power.

5

In the spring of 1857, when Pete was nine, Chief Justice Roger Taney read a Supreme Court decision in the case of a Negro called Dred Scott. The decision, involving the slavery issue, had repercussions even in the isolated Little Washington community, for a new political group styling itself Republican hastened to martyrize Dred Scott and heap abuse upon the Supreme Court. The court, said the Republicans, was in the control of slave-owners. Its decisions deserved no more respect than if made by persons congregated in any Washington saloon.[11] Pete undoubtedly heard some of that talk and remembered it when the day came when these same Republicans would profess to view even slight disagreement with the Supreme Court as "alienism" and "radicalism."

When the news reached Richland County that Fort Sumter had been fired on, ushering in the War between the States, Pete was thirteen, going on fourteen. He saw neighbors, men and boys, march off to answer President Lincoln's calls for volunteers. Troops drilled in near-by Mansfield. All of Richland County seethed with war activity and war talk. To use his own expression, he was infected like any American youth "with the enthusiasm of those days, the drums, and flags and all the rest of it."[12] He wanted to go, for he was husky and broad-shouldered. But he was too young.

The war dragged on. When he was sixteen, there came a call for members of the Ohio Home Guards to volunteer for one hundred days of war service. Pete hunted up a member of the Guard who preferred to stay home, and arranged to go as a substitute. The county gave a hundred-dollar bounty to volunteers, and probably that was a factor persuading his father to let Pete go to war. Pete turned over to his father all but ten dollars of that windfall, and on May 12, 1864, marched off with the Forty-eighth Regiment of the Ohio National Guard, later the One Hundred and Sixty-third Ohio Volunteer Infantry.[13]

Up to then, Mansfield had been the wide world to Pete Altgeld.

Now he saw Washington, D. C. and all the other cities between Mansfield and the Capital.

6

After a short training period at Camp Chase, he went with his regiment to Virginia, where General Ulysses S. Grant was jockeying for a final smash at Lee. On June 12, 1864, Altgeld's regiment reported to the command of General Benjamin F. Butler at Point of Rocks, Virginia.

Probably, it was fortunate for Altgeld that Ben ("The Beast") Butler, half adventurer, half idealist, was in command. Another commander might have obeyed Grant's orders explicitly, and plunged the regiment into a vicious battle at Bermuda Hundred. As it was, the unpredictable Ben Butler chose to do his own thinking, and kept the regiment on the safe side of the James River during the battle there. Hence, aside from a few reconnoitering skirmishes, the Ohio Volunteers were kept at the relatively mild activity of patrolling the swamp land.

There is a story that in some of those James River skirmishes Altgeld exhibited bravery which, "for one so young, attracted notice," and that only "his youthful appearance kept him from a lieutenant's position after his second battle."[14] This, however, appears to have been romanticism. "My war experience was nothing of consequence,"[15] he said himself. In a speech in which it might have been the political thing to wax eloquent about his soldiering, he summed up this phase of his life by saying he "did not bleed and did not die, but was there; always reported for duty, was always on deck and never shirked and never ran away."[16] Yet one thing happened which left a lasting effect.

He came down with a fever—it was called "Chickahominy fever," probably a local name for the ague. Many of the Richland County boys died of it, as he nearly did. Doubtless he could have returned home then, "but he insisted on remaining with the regiment and after a couple of weeks in the field hospital, returned to duty." He thought he was cured. The fever was to plague him all through his life.

In September the Ohio boys were released from service and sent marching home. They were given a dinner in Mansfield and subjected to a speech by John Sherman, who told them how brave they were. Then it was back to the farm. But for Pete Altgeld, the farm would not be the same. "He had seen something of the world—and new aspirations and ambitions had been awakened."[17]

7

As a reflection of his new ambitions, Pete made an announcement a few weeks after his return from the war that produced something of a crisis in his relations with his father. He intended to enroll in the high school at Mansfield. Old Pete objected strongly. If the boy persisted in such notions, he could expect no help—neither money nor food nor clothes. But young Pete proved stubborn—a trait to be remembered.

Secretly, he had his mother on his side. And so that fall term of the "Old First High School" in Mansfield found him a student. With two other boys, W. E. Ford and Robert McKee, he lived during the school term in a little room above a carpenter shop and tannery known as Ritter's. The boys cooked their own meals, with Pete's share of the common larder smuggled to him by his mother. On the excuse of peddling vegetables in Mansfield, she regularly managed to bring him baskets containing potatoes, cabbages, meat, butter and eggs. When she could not go herself, she persuaded her neighbor, Mrs. Pollock, to take the food to Pete.

Thus he got along. But clothing was a vexing problem. One evening Neighbor Bill Pollock found him walking about Mansfield in a dejected mood. He needed a suit. Farmer Pollock took him to a store and fitted him with a suit and overcoat. That night Pete did a thing which Farmer Pollock's daughter felt ought not be told about Altgeld. He went to his father's granary and transferred to the Pollock barn enough wheat to pay for the clothes. Farmer Pollock protested that the repayment was not necessary.

"It's right!" said Pete.[18]

He would use that phrase again.

8

Yet, for all his willingness to endure hardship to attend school, Pete's scholastic record was not striking. His roommate, Ford, thought him "a bit stupid." He was especially poor in arithmetic, and Ford had to help him do his sums.[19] But he showed keen interest in everything. He and his roommates discussed all subjects, including politics. Most of the poor folk in that district, including Altgeld's father, were Democrats. The father was a Democrat "because his neighbors were." Pete was a Democrat, presumably, because his father was. Some of the political discussions were rather heated, because his roommates were Republicans. Pete read all he could find about Thomas Jefferson, came to believe him "a greater man even than George Washington."[20] Thus his political leanings began.

His immediate ambition was to become a schoolteacher. That seemed the best way to get away from the farm. On finishing the high school term, he enrolled at a "select school" maintained by the Reverend Mr. Gailey, in near-by Lexington.[21] After three months he felt confident enough to apply for a teacher's certificate. Luckily, the district school board placed less emphasis upon scholarship than upon "good moral quality." He began teaching at Woodville, near Mansfield, when he was nineteen, earning thirty-five dollars a month, all of which went toward paying for his father's farm.

At the Woodville school there was another teacher, a young lady with "soft, dark, rather languid eyes and heavy black hair." Emma Ford was, relatively, a rich girl. Her family lived in a large brick home on a fine farm just out of Little Washington and had been able to send her to Oberlin College to study music. Emma was the belle of the district—and Pete Altgeld fell in love with her. For all his rough appearance, Emma Ford responded, if not with love, then certainly with interest. This subjected her to gibes by her family, who talked about "that little Dutchman from down in the hills." Such a queer-looking boy! And she defended him. But when the affair began to seem serious, her father, proud John Ford, put his foot down. Once more he was made to feel that "it was the crowd on one side and John Peter Altgeld on the other." Well, he would show them! Fortunately, he would soon be twenty-one. That meant freedom from his father's authority. He could strike out for a new country. The West!

In the spring of 1869 he was on his way.

CHAPTER TWO

WANDERJAHRE

1

WHEN Pete Altgeld, ten dollars in his pocket, turned his back upon the Ohio farm of his father and set his face westward, he was exactly in tune with the national direction then of America itself. For after the war, America too was footloose—and facing westward. And from tens of thousands of farms and villages, youths like Altgeld, uprooted by the conflict, were making the same trek.

Not a few of these same youngsters, then walking so bravely, would tramp eastward again, twenty-five years later. And when that time came, people talked of them derisively as the wild men of "General" Coxey's Army of the Commonweal of Christ. They would be disillusioned and embittered because Eldorado had eluded them and Mr. Greeley's advice "Go west, young man!" turned sour. But that was a quarter of a century hence.

Many things lured them, besides their own war-generated restlessness. There was the Homestead Act, passed under Lincoln. It promised free land for the taking, acres and acres of government-owned land. True, much of this empire which Lincoln intended for the poor would find itself, mysteriously, in the hands of great corporations and feudal stock-raisers. But that would not appear until later. The belief was that land was available to everyone, particularly to the soldiers of the war. They had a song about it.

> "Come along, come along; make no delay;
> Come from every nation, come from every way;
> Come along, come along; don't be alarmed,—
> Uncle Sam is rich enough to give us all a farm!"

Something else was happening too, to lure America's youth from eastern farms and towns. With the warring done, the Iron Horse snorted its way across and up and down the continent in earnest. It was a horse upon which astute financiers rode; men who, in a later

23

generation, would be known as "the robber barons," and would be symbolized by the phrase "the public be damned!" The imperial Commodore Cornelius Vanderbilt, scheming Jay Gould, crafty James Fisk, Jr., ruthless James J. Hill and E. H. Harriman, and the shrewd Leland Stanford—these were some of the iron horsemen. In the main they amassed their astounding fortunes by using the railroads for stock schemes, and government contract manipulations, with such men as Lawyer Chauncey M. Depew supplying the legal finesse to cover up their ruthlessness. But they did have the railroads built. And because it took labor as well as gilt-edge bonds to build them, the cry went up for more and still more men to wield picks and to heave shovels. Pete would be among those to answer.

2

However, there is nothing to indicate that at first he had any special destination, unless it was vaguely St. Louis. He was merely "going west," trusting to luck and to circumstance to shape his ultimate course. Already, it seems, he was nourishing an idea of becoming a lawyer. How he would get the opportunity to read law was vague. But he had no cause to worry. The copybook maxims were true then. Ambition, industry and perseverance would win out. Self-reliance was not only a quality to be drilled into young minds. It was a philosophy that worked. And, of self-reliance, young Altgeld had an abundance. "Nothing appalled him, nothing turned him back. . . . His self-reliance was superb,"[1] a friend related. So he pushed on, hopeful, eager.

From his father's place he walked the familiar stretch to Mansfield, from there to Cincinnati. He stayed a while in Cincinnati,[2] then moved on through southern Indiana. Along the way he solicited work on farms. Sometimes he was successful. But most of the nights found him sleeping in the open, near some barn or haystack, under the stars. He was fond, in later life, of speaking or writing of the stars. "Ask no man! Go out into the night and look straight up to the stars. Take counsel and comfort from them."[3]

Tramping across Indiana, he entered upon the southern tip of Illinois. Not far away, to the north, was the city of Springfield. Here Lincoln had been but lately interred and here this wayfarer was destined also to play a part in history. But he gave Springfield not a second thought. Still farther north was bustling, ribald Chicago, already being called "the wickedest city of the world." It was fast becoming the railroad center of the West. The beginnings of great factories came with this development—also the beginnings of friction between capital and labor. George Pullman was then perfecting his first palace cars in Chicago. Altgeld would have reason to remember that name. At this time, too, the seeds of socialist agitation were being sown in Chicago, carried on the tide of German immigration that poured into the city since '48. Wild-eyed anarchism would spring out of this. Note, too, another movement, already well-entrenched in Chicago: the resurgence of nativistic Know-nothingism, making a cleavage between "foreigners" and "Americans." Voicing the slogan "Put None but Americans on Guard," the nativists elected a mayor of Chicago, one Levi Daniel Boone, and produced riots.

But as Chicago in these late 'sixties surged toward its own destiny, also his, Altgeld snubbed it. Conceivably, as he reached Illinois, he debated the question: Chicago or St. Louis? Both represented the kind of life in which he wished to participate. Both were growing, alive with activity. But St. Louis, fattened by the wealth that flowed to it from the Mississippi, was then ahead of Chicago in wealth and population. Not perceiving that Chicago was destined to win the race with St. Louis for supremacy, Altgeld headed south and west, instead of north. It would be six years before he realized that he had decided wrong and came to speak of St. Louis as "that respectable but sleepy town."[4]

3

When he reached the Mississippi, within sight of St. Louis, he had fifteen cents left, and he had joined forces with another young man, unidentified, who had no money at all, the net upshot of which was to render Altgeld totally penniless after he had crossed the river to St. Louis. "He paid five cents ferryboat fare, and a like sum for [the] still more unfortunate traveler, and then balanced and closed his account by buying writing paper and a postage stamp with the remainder to write home."

If St. Louis was "journey's end" for Altgeld, it proved disappointing. He seems to have made no contacts there, nor to have found any sympathetic acquaintances such as he made so consistently in other places later. Strange, this, in view of the large German-born population. That same year another German-born American, Carl Schurz, was elected United States senator from Missouri, largely because of the St. Louis Germans. Undoubtedly Altgeld noted that name.

Yet in '69 the St. Louis that elevated Schurz to the heights of national prominence had scarcely any place for Altgeld. He tramped the streets. Cash was his desperate need. Finally, his perseverance was rewarded with a job in a chemical plant.[5] It involved unrelieved menial labor at a meager wage. But it was a job.

4

He might have stayed on in St. Louis except for the clamor for railroad laborers. Wages of three dollars and fifty cents a day, probably three or four times what he was earning at the chemical plant, were offered to laborers by the Missouri, Kansas and Texas Railroad. Anyone capable of swinging a pick was being hired. Altgeld signed up and was set working with section hands near Fort Scott, Kansas, and in Arkansas. For a time he was able to hold his own with the other laborers. But, under the broiling southwestern sun, the fever that struck him in '64 at Wilson's Landing came back on him. One afternoon the cry ran through the construction camp that "the Dutchman," so the Irish workers affectionately called him, had collapsed on the job. They carried him to a hospital shack and there he "lay for some weeks while the fever ran its course." For a time it was doubtful if he would recover. He knew this. But when asked to give the address of his parents so that they might be notified, he refused. If he died he should be buried in the neighborhood "with the least possible bother to anyone." Emphatically he did not wish to "bother" his parents.[6]

When the fever at last abated, the camp doctor warned that he must go to a northern climate. Particularly was he cautioned against attempting to resume work with the section gang. Yet he tried to go on working, for all the money he had saved was now gone for medicines and doctors. Soon he had to quit, and then, on foot, he started north for Topeka, Kansas. From there he intended to head for Iowa.[7] Along the way, the fever came back on him. Still he kept on.

Three miles south of Topeka, he stopped at a farmhouse and asked to be put up for the night. He would work, he said, to pay for the trouble, although it was plain that he was in no condition to do so. Impressed by the boy's "modesty," the farmer took him in. He remained, not one night, but three weeks, for his hosts had not the heart to turn him out. But when he continued to ail, it was determined that he should be placed in a public hospital in Topeka. This matter was discussed with the neighbors and there was general agreement that the young stranger should be in an institution. Some felt he was "weakened in brain as well as body." Altgeld "hotly opposed the wishes of his new friends on this point." Fearing they would send him away without his consent, he quit the farmhouse late one night.[8]

5

Early one morning in St. Joseph, Missouri, there appeared a wretched creature, more like some kind of apparition than a human being. His feet were bound up in rags, his clothes were in tatters. "From place to place, from one man to another, he went about telling his hard-luck story." But "he failed to impress anyone to whom he appealed."[9] Life doubtless was then at its lowest ebb for Pete Altgeld. He was depressed mentally, stunned and bewildered by what he had been through. No wonder the farmers with whom he had stayed near Topeka believed that his "brain was weakened." He had walked a hundred miles, through open prairies, on bare feet.[10] And the effects of the fever continued to plague him. His cool reception in St. Joseph did not help.

He dragged himself on. In the north, beyond the rolling Missouri country, lay Iowa. That was his goal and he intended to make it. Iowa meant release, perhaps, from the fever. It is certain that no thought of giving up and returning to his father's farm occurred to him. He had cut himself off from that completely. Some years later he philosophized to a friend that if young men of poor families sought success, they must cut themselves away from their people, ruthlessly if necessary, and place their ambitions above everything else.[11] Perhaps no Mark Hanna, George Pullman or Marshall Field worshiped more devoutly at the shrine of personal success than this Altgeld, now and later. In a little while he would be saying: "I commend you to the goddess of ambition. She teaches the great virtues of labor, aggression and perseverance." He was trying to practice those virtues now. So he tramped on from St. Joseph.

6

He did not get to Iowa, for ten miles out of St. Joseph was the little town of Savannah and there his tramping came to an end. "Savannah is pleasantly situated on an elevation which affords a fine view of the surrounding country. It has an excellent courthouse and other fine county buildings." The writer of that had put down nearly all of a remarkable nature that could be said about the seat of Andrew County. Its population then was about 3,000, never to be exceeded.

Here then, in a town almost completely insulated from the world by the wooded hills and acres of shady groves which surrounded it, was the setting in which Altgeld was to mature. Here his political views were shaped, if not crystallized, and here he spent some of the few really happy years of his life. Yet, when he reached Savannah, he nearly passed it by.

He was hurrying farther north, and with good reason. Again he was assailed by the fitful chills of the fever. That afternoon, a few miles beyond Savannah, near a group of farm homes which made up a village called Flag Springs, a violent sick spell came upon him. He sank to the ground near a spring. He crawled to it to refresh himself and to overcome his nausea. But he did not quite reach it. A paroxysm seized him, and he suffered a vomiting spell.[12] For hours he lay there, agonized by the nausea, the chills and his weakness. Not until dusk was he able to rouse himself.

7

As darkness was falling, a farmer beheld at his door "a strange young man, poorly clad, sick and penniless."[13] The young man spoke "with a strong German accent," an unfamiliar thing in those parts. Probably the farmer was as fascinated by the strange spectacle Altgeld presented as moved by feelings of compassion. And if Altgeld was strange in appearance, strange also must have seemed to the farmer his manner of asking assistance—Altgeldian in its self-reliance even then. "He had no money and was sick, but if he got well he would work and pay for what they did for him. But if he died, it would be an act of charity on their part."[14] It was an effective appeal.

"Just what particular quality of individuality attracted him to Altgeld, the Andrew County farmer was unable to decide, but his sympathy was aroused and he made him a member of the family circle," even though he could not afford a helper.[15] When Altgeld's new employer, Cam Williams, advanced the opinion that it was unnecessary for him to go to Iowa, suggesting that Savannah was far enough north, Altgeld decided to stay on.

Williams related that he "never had a better farm hand about the place." And when he had to let his new helper go after a few months, Pete had little difficulty in finding work at other farms in the neighborhood. Descendants of a half-dozen families in the Savannah district have recalled that Pete worked on their farms.

His wanderings were over. The melancholia was lifting, and he was regaining his health.

CHAPTER THREE

"J. P. ALTGELD, ESQ."

1

HE GAINED something else, too—the friendly interest of one of the richest families of the district, that of Benjamin Holt. With Ben Holt, Junior, whose own son, Elmer, became governor of Montana in 1935, Altgeld struck up a comradely relationship that was important in helping him to regain his courage and confidence. The two young men were inseparable when Pete had any leisure, and Ben Holt's father once joked: "It looks like Ben and Pete Altgeld would get married." The Holts had a large library for a country home, and Pete read most of the books in it, young Holt's interest in books spurring his. Yet he and young Ben were far from bookworms. They hunted, indulged in other sports together and joked a good deal. They shared a dry kind of humor of their own. "Pete Altgeld would get a crowd in stitches, while himself keeping a straight face," one who knew him then recalled.[1]

Pete's accent amused his Savannah friends. And certain of his expressions "sounded funny." "Horse" was one word hard for him to pronounce properly. He would say "stand the bucket down" for "put the bucket down." Once this caused so much amusement that he attempted to prove he was right by "standing down" a pail of milk. He spilled the milk and got a severe scolding from the Holt's cook for his effort. But he accepted teasing about his speech good-naturedly. Young Ben Holt worked with him to improve his pronunciation. He listened and corrected as Pete repeated words and phrases from a book as they sprawled under a tree.

2

That winter the teacher at the Republican school at Bedford Chapel, near Savannah, left in mid-term. Altgeld determined to seek the vacancy.

The first of three school trustees whose approval he needed hedged.

He would approve if either of the others did. Then Pete interviewed Trustee Alexander Bedford. Bedford was a hard nut to crack, for he set store by a man's personal appearance. And he was bitter against anyone who had served in the Union army during the Civil War.[2] What chance, then, did the "greenest looking, most awkward and homely young man in Savannah,"[3] a northern soldier boy to boot, have with Bedford? Yet Bedford did not turn down Altgeld flatly. Presumably he wished to have some sport with the third trustee, Josiah Kent. "If Joe Kent says yes, I will too," he told Pete. He believed Kent would reject Altgeld and also be annoyed. But Josiah Kent, busy in his potato patch when Altgeld approached him, instead was annoyed with Bedford. "He said that, did he? Listen, young man, if you can dig more 'taters than I can, you'll get that teaching position!"

Altgeld leaped a fence and set to work. When quitting time came, he had dug five bushels, and Joe Kent said the job was his.

After that, they called Pete Altgeld "the 'tater teacher."[4]

3

The " 'tater teacher" made good. He even won over Alexander Bedford, who, to the surprise of everyone, became one of his principal boosters and best friends. Soon he was boarding at the Bedford home and the erstwhile objector proudly predicted that "Altgeld would make his mark some day."[5] And it was through Bedford that Altgeld came in contact with the leading lawyer of the district, Judge David Rea of Savannah, afterward a member of Congress. It was the most important contact of Altgeld's youth, for Judge Rea, who had risen from a background not unlike Altgeld's, encouraged Pete in his ambition to become a lawyer and lent him law books.

Pete Altgeld was on his way in earnest now. He taught at the Republican school, worked on the Bedford farm and read law at night. "It was not unusual for him to keep the oil lamp burning in the southwest room, downstairs of the Bedford home, until after one o'clock."[6] One of the Bedford children, who was also his pupil, remembers him "copying law in his law books at night [while] we boys studied our lessons at the same time in the room with him." Bedford related that Altgeld nearly ruined his eyes by his midnight work.[7]

The next school session Pete changed schools for better pay, Judge Rea having recommended him to a brother, Joseph Rea, who was a school director at the Mount Craig district. He lived at the home of Joseph Rea that season. There, as with the Bedfords, he left a lingering impression of tremendous industry. "He always did the work of two men—gathering corn and other work on Saturdays and did other work about the farm mornings and evenings. . . . He studied evenings, mended and patched his own clothes, knitted his own socks."[8]

The Mount Craig term was the last that Altgeld served as school teacher, for Judge Rea, "noting in him both ambition and ability," took him in his office as a clerk.[9] In April, 1871, another shingle went up on the door of the two-story red-brick building, across from the courthouse square, that housed the law firm of David Rea and William Heren. Gone, now, was the farmer and the " 'tater teacher." Gone, too, except to his most intimate acquaintances, was the youth called Pete. There had arrived "J. P. Altgeld, Att'y."

4

There was no dearth of native legal talent in Savannah, yet out of all the lawyers there, Altgeld was appointed city attorney in 1872, less than a year after he had been admitted to the bar. It has been suggested that this appointment, marking the beginnings of a public career, resulted because his "ability and energy seem to have won almost immediate local recognition."[10] Perhaps, but doubtful. A more plausible explanation reveals the hand of his patron, for Judge Rea had the political prestige necessary to persuade the town council to make the job Altgeld's. Now Altgeld was a personage, referred to in the weekly newspaper as "J. P. Altgeld, Esq." This nourished his ego and proved an attraction for bringing him private clients. Within a year he was able to resign the city position and devote himself to his own cases.

Although there could be some doubt as to the importance of this litigation, he took a surprising number of cases to the Supreme Court of Missouri. But he waged no legal crusades and championed no lost causes—a typical country lawyer with a country lawyer's practice. One farmer retained him because another had "wrongfully, forcibly and unlawfully seized, took into his possession, drove, rode and carried away—one black mare with a blaze face, and one bay mare." A Mr. Munkers hired him to sue a railroad that crossed his land, because of damage from a flood. He represented a livery-keeper because a horse fell dead supposedly "in consequence of the defendant driving . . . rapidly and without exercising the proper care on a warm day." An unscrupulous guardian was found to have mulcted his ward of a $2,600 estate in a shady land deal, and Altgeld, with Lawyer Heren, Judge Rea's partner, defended the wronged youngster. Another case was

notable for the sheer multiplicity of clients joined in it. It involved
thirteen plaintiffs, each with separate complaints against a railroad and
all represented by "J. P. Altgeld." He took this to the Supreme Court
of Missouri from a justice of peace. And there was a case revealing
how close the time was to the Civil War and slavery, the issue being
joined on whether a Negro woman was "property." Altgeld said she
was, under the law.[11]

Such were samples of Altgeld's legal business in Savannah. If he
demonstrated any special legal brilliance, the records do not show it.
However, they do reveal his demonstrating a marked shrewdness. In
one case, he permitted the opposition to argue for days, then had the
matter thrown out of court on the showing that, after all, the judge
had no jurisdiction. He was determined and tenacious, taking justice
of peace matters to the highest court in the state when other lawyers
might have let them go. But he was far from sensational as a winning
lawyer. Out of seven Supreme Court cases, he scored victories in only
two. But in one of these victories the opposing counsel was Judge
Rea, who had confided to friends that his pupil "was better grounded
in the principles of elementary law than his teacher."[12]

5

Personal changes were now taking place in him, the rough edges
being polished off. He nursed a mustache, later to be joined by a
clipped beard. It would soften his features and give him a lawyer's
"dignity"; also it would serve to hide the harelip about which he was
sensitive. By then, too, he had taken to wearing "store clothes." He
was very particular about his clothes, testified the town clothier. "His
shirts, especially, had to be just so."[13] Years later, it would be discovered that he left Savannah owing a clothing bill which never was
paid—perhaps evidence that he dressed beyond his means.

He was a "mixer," too, taking an interest in girls. More than one
Savannah lady recalls that she was squired by Lawyer Altgeld. "Altgeld liked Rebecca Holt," is one reminiscence. Another, by Mrs.
Lizzie Farley: "I might have had Altgeld." And if certain compelling
testimony is to be believed, he had at least one serious love affair, the
effects of which will be noted later. Judging from the social column
of the local newspaper, scarcely a social affair in the community was
held without his being in attendance. He went to an oyster supper
"gotten up in Shedrick's best style" in April, 1874. The following

month he was a leading figure at a farewell dinner honoring another lawyer. He made one of the speeches of the evening.[14]

In July, 1874, he made a trip. "J. P. Altgeld, Esq., returned from an extended trip to St. Louis, through Illinois, Chicago, &c., on Wednesday. He was none the worse for the jaunt." So the Andrew County Republican reported. Did his visit to Chicago that summer start him thinking of settling there? Perhaps. But another full—and vital—year of his story in Savannah remained. It would be a year which, perhaps more than any so far, shaped things to be for him. For that was the year of the great Granger revolt in the American hinterlands. And out of that agrarian political phenomenon emerged, for the first time, Altgeld the politician.

6

The Granger revolt began in the fall of '73 after the collapse of Jay Cooke and Sons, the banking house to the Government during the Civil War. A chain of banking catastrophes followed which left the country's financial and commercial structure almost a ruin. Credit tightened. Mortgages were foreclosed by the thousands. Suffering more keenly than any other class were the farmers of the West. Enraged at the financiers, at the politicians and at "the East," the farmers reached for a weapon. They found it in their granges, originally conceived as merely educational and social associations. Drive out the rascals in both parties! This was the idea which apparently came to the farmers all at once as they sensed the power of their granges. Down with the railroads! Down with monopolists! Lincoln's old partner, William Herndon, expressed the spirit in an article in the Illinois State Register for February 19, 1873.

"They are down on railroads and rings, conspiracies and monopolies, and treason against the public welfare. They say: If the War lasts for ages, they intend to fight it out to the bitter end, and woe be to the politician who stands in their way to the end fought for."[15]

Some politicians went along or even fanned the flames. Governor Austin of Minnesota cried: "It is time to take these robber corporations by the scruff of the neck and shake them over hell!"[16] The farmers cheered. The ordinary politicians rubbed their eyes, then quaked.

Altgeld watched this movement closely, both as a student and as a rising political leader in a farm community. He saw the Grange fever spread with amazing rapidity in Missouri, and in Andrew County. Indeed, Missouri was one of the strongest Grange states in the country.[17] This gave him a problem. If his sympathies were with the Grangers, he had to give thought to his political connections. The Granger movement in Missouri, with Andrew County no exception, had a decided Republican complexion because the Republicans, out of power locally and hungry for places, schemed to take over the movement. And Altgeld was a Democrat—a "Bourbon Democrat" at that, as the local paper called him.[18] Should he stick with the local Democracy, the statehouse crowd of the Bourbon Democracy, or join in the protest? He would have to decide shortly, for there had already emerged in Andrew County a "People's Party," by which name the Granger political units were known.

When the Andrew County Democratic Convention assembled that August in the courthouse at Savannah, the People's Party development was uppermost in the minds of the Andrew County Democracy. But it was too fearful a matter to be discussed much in the open. It was Altgeld—"J. P. Altgeld, Esq."—who finally brought it up. He was then only twenty-six, had lived in that community only four years, yet, amazingly enough, he appeared in that convention in the rôle of leading spokesman for the party. The convention, in fact, turned out to be pretty largely dominated by Altgeld. "Mr. Altgeld moved," "Mr. Altgeld thought," "Mr. Altgeld suggested'" . . . so ran the report of the proceedings in the town newspaper. It was his nominee who was designated as delegate to the state convention. Moreover, the gathering wished to pick him as an alternate delegate, refraining only because "he said he couldn't possibly go."

And already he had a reputation for political shrewdness. The editor of the Andrew County *Republican* chided him for starting a speech by saying he was "not posted on politics as they now existed— in fact, he paid no attention to them." A "startling statement from Mr. Altgeld," the editor wrote. Of course, he had "just dropped in, some thing like Paul Pry." And the People's Party business? "Mr. Altgeld did not know whether the Democrats here would take part in that, as a party. . . . It depended greatly on the ticket nominated by the people."[19]

Before the following month was out, "Mr. Altgeld" did know whether he would take part. When the county convention of the People's Party gathered in September none other than the Bourbon Democrat, Altgeld, was being boomed as the People's choice for prosecuting attorney of Andrew County. On the second ballot he won the nomination, but he had a fight on his hands to keep it. "A motion was made to take the vote over," related the Andrew County *Republican* for September 18, 1874, "it having been learned by some of the delegates that Mr. Altgeld took his Bourbon (Democracy) straight." One delegation walked out of the convention in disgust. Altgeld took the floor, and made a speech. It was true, he said, that he had "attended the Bourbon convention recently." But he had said at that time that he would not support the full Bourbon ticket. He had learned some of the nominations to be made by the People's Party, and, as most of them were Democrats, he thought he could support the People's ticket "in the main."[20] Weasel words, of course. But they saved the day for him. The next and final ballot showed him again the nominee, 48 to 43.

The St. Joseph *Gazette* took notice of the incident. With evident amusement, it observed that the People's candidate for prosecuting attorney of Andrew County "had to be nominated twice before it would be counted." But this attention by a "metropolitan newspaper" could not have flattered Altgeld too much, for the story identified him as "Al Gelt."[21]

7

He had another fight on his hands before the campaign started for the regular Democrats felt that Altgeld, and other Democrats who accepted nominations on the Granger ticket, had committed treason. A mass meeting was called to denounce the renegades. Altgeld attended, prepared to argue that the People's Party was not a party but a "movement," hence there was no inconsistency in a Democrat being on its ticket. More weasel words. But he changed his mind when he heard the speech of Lawyer Charles Booher, who presided. Booher charged that the Democrats on the People's ticket "were truckling and scheming with the enemy for the sake of paltry office, and in so doing, forsaking 'Democratic principles.' "

"This reference to selling out principle for office brought Mr. Altgeld to his feet. He was excited and assumed a forced, calm demeanor." Then he went after Booher, who was, incidentally, a friend. "His 'young friend's' remarks had the same effect upon him as the barking of a small dog had on a passing ox." And what was the effect? "The ox went on its way as though nothing was the matter. So far as the 'great, imperishable principles of the Democracy'—well, the Democratic platform principles were very high-sounding . . . [but] they glit-

tered with meaningless generalities. They began and ended in sound—
they accomplished nothing. The new political party (rather, movement) was going to take things in its own hands, and do something!"[22]

Altgeld the dissenter had emerged.

8

In striking respects, that political campaign, Altgeld's first, was the
original of which his later ones would be carbon copies.

His opponent, W. W. Caldwell, a lawyer, wealthy and formerly
mayor of Savannah, was no mean contestant. Caldwell had sought
the People's endorsement for himself, but on being defeated by Altgeld became the candidate for a so-called "Independent Party" and
then characterized the People's party as "the cheapest kind of Know-
nothingism . . . it is worse."[23] Lawyer Caldwell talked, not about the
issues which the farmers so eagerly desired discussed, but about Altgeld.

"Mr. Altgeld is a great People's man! He was in the Bourbon convention to elect delegates to the state [Democratic] convention; even
had himself elected as a delegate and only declined because he would
not pay his expenses there and back. . . . He was very well pleased
with . . . the whole Bourbon ticket—until the People's convention
nominated him for office. He has adopted the rôle very suddenly of
public sympathizer. He says the people are ground down by oppression, and says therefore they ought to elect him. But he offers no
remedy. He takes no stand on anything."[24]

Shrewdly, Altgeld conducted an aggressive fight on principles—and
ignored his opponent. He made out-and-out Granger speeches.

". . . While labor is the very foundation of the wealth and prosperity
of the country, those who administer the laws have been taken from
classes of citizens who live off the farmers and who profit by the distress of the farmers. . . . Is it to be wondered at, then, that the large
corporations grow rich when favored by the laws, to the detriment
of the farming community?

"Farmers have been ground down under the heel of monopoly and
tyranny until they can no longer bear it. They have got to rise sometime and assert their rights, and now is the opportunity. [Applause]
If they do not [rise] before long, ruin will stare them in the face, begging will be their allotted portion and the farmers will bewail the time

when they brought desolation upon themselves by failing to elect the farmers' ticket!"[25]

So Altgeld in October, 1874, to the farmers of Missouri, at the age of twenty-six. If he lacked oratorical finish, he made up the deficiency by his earnestness. Did he believe his dire prophecy if the farmers failed to "rise?" Probably not, but the farmers liked it. "Nobody went to sleep when he talked," recalled one who heard him at Flag Springs.[26]

The vote was: Caldwell, 1,087; Altgeld, 1,462. He had won his spurs as a campaigner for public office. The Savannah weekly newspaper carried an editorial suggesting he had won against newspaper opposition in the bargain. "John P. Altgeld, whom we are sorry to say, thinks *The Republican* has acted unfairly with him, can possibly forgive us now. His majority over W. W. Caldwell is 375, and if that don't make him feel in good humor, with everybody, it is hard to say what would."[27]

9

It was true that he then had every reason to be in "good humor." He was riding the crest of political prestige in his own right. His patron, Judge Rea, in the same campaign had been elected to Congress. With the large German population in Missouri, it would appear that he had reason to count upon a real career in the state. Governor? United States senator? Who could say? That other German immigrant, Schurz, did it. But within eleven months after his election as prosecuting attorney, he resigned, giving no adequate reason to anyone, and packed his bags for Chicago. He knew no one there. That meant starting all over again. There are conflicting explanations for that move, none completely substantiated, and we can only take our choice.

It has been inferred that Altgeld relinquished the prosecuting attorneyship because of disgust for the processes of the penal machinery, that he did not relish prosecuting people. However, there is no evidence to indicate that Altgeld, while in Savannah, had arrived at any philosophy concerning crime and punishment. The prosecuting attorney of Andrew County did not have much experience with either crime or punishment. During Altgeld's incumbency only one case involving a prosecution by him is recorded in the State Supreme Court records—this an effort to have a youth kept in jail after two juries failed to agree on a verdict of murder. He lost the case and the prisoner went free.[28]

Sally Woodcock, granddaughter of Benjamin Holt, understood that Altgeld left Savannah because he had obtained an appointment of "some kind" in Chicago. She thought Altgeld told her that. Yet, no evidence at all exists to substantiate this idea, while much evidence is against it. Perhaps Altgeld gave out such a story to avoid questions. Thomas B. Rea, nephew of Judge Rea, has come forth with still another explanation. He understood that Altgeld, after his election, affiliated with the M. E. Church North. "From my knowledge of Altgeld's friends in Andrew County, none of them would look with favor on his affiliation with that particular church denomination (because of their Civil War antipathies). Altgeld may have noticed somewhat of a cooled ardor among his most strenuous supporters."[29] But this also lacks corroboration. Even if true, it hardly would represent a reason strong enough to cause him to leave as suddenly as he did. There is left a story of a love affair with more to support it than any of the others.

In 1902, the St. Louis *Republic* and other newspapers told that tale.

"One day in Savannah, Mo., Altgeld met Miss Anna Rohrer, daughter of George Rohrer, who was then president of the State Bank of Savannah and one of the wealthy men of town. To the young lawyer, the girl was the incarnation of his ideals. With characteristic decision he set to work to win her. His suit did not prosper, however, and the girl's father at last gave him to understand that his visits to their home must cease. This was a hard blow, not only to the affections, but to the pride of Altgeld. . . .

"Never did he lose sight of his intent, and later, when the situation became less strained, he visited her again. He made a formal proposal of marriage, but was refused by the young woman in obedience to the wishes of her father. Crushed with disappointment, he left the house. . . . He at once made an effort to get away from Savannah. . . ."[30]

How much fact and how much fancy exists in that story? It is difficult to judge. There was a girl named Annie Rohrer in Savannah, although her father was Upton, not George, Rohrer, and was a wealthy farmer, not a banker. Whether or not she was the romantically described "rich man's beautiful daughter" was a matter of opinion. To Sally Woodcock, at least, she was no beauty. Waldo Browne has said that he investigated the story and was told by "a man in Savannah who knew Altgeld there" that the tale was "pure bunk—Altgeld never had a love affair in Savannah."[31] Yet there are credible persons who support this tale.

Justice of Peace J. P. Burns of Savannah is one. "The Rohrers were active in the Presbyterian Church. . . . My wife was raised in that church, and was a girl friend of Miss Rohrer. I have heard her speak of Altgeld and Miss Anna, and she thought her refusal of his attentions caused him to leave here. . . . The Rohrers were what might be called aristocratic people, and Altgeld was anything but an aristocrat at that time. . . . There is no doubt but he, Altgeld, sought Miss Rohrer's hand. . . ."[32] George A. Schilling, who for a period was more intimate with Altgeld than any other man, also believed the story. "I had a talk with a man—who married the sister of the [girl] in Savannah, Mo., that Altgeld was supposed to have been in love with. He confirmed the story."[33]

The Mansfield, O., *Daily Shield* has added some detail. Altgeld had been neglecting his law practice because of his affair, according to this story. But after the collapse "he sat down one night and thought it all over." To a friend, he is supposed to have voiced a resolution. "Miss——does not think I am good enough for her. I know I have been neglecting my law on her account. But I am going to sail in now, and I'll show these people before I die whether I am any good or not."[34] That quotation has a sound ring. And so perhaps there is basis for concluding that a jilting did cause Altgeld to uproot himself from Missouri.

There was no other good reason. The only discoverable reference made by Altgeld himself to this was in the interview with Nellie Bly. "My head swelled. I wanted broader fields, so I went to Chicago."[35]

Whatever his real reason, sometime between October 1 and November 1, 1875, he sent his resignation as prosecuting attorney to the Governor of Missouri. He recommended the appointment of Charles F. Booher in his place, and Booher obtained the job, making it a stepping-stone to Congress. To him, Altgeld sold his office fixtures and library for $100, and entrained for Chicago.

He was then twenty-seven. All he had was the $100, although he hoped to collect some fees owing him in Savannah. That and a tenacity of spirit. But his period of immaturity and groping was now definitely finished. The real Altgeld was emerging.

BOOK TWO

THE MAN OF PROPERTY

CHAPTER FOUR

Chicago, 1875

1

THE Chicago toward which Altgeld headed in 1875 was a city impatient. Four years had passed since the "Great Fire." What had been destroyed by the flames had been, actually, an overgrown village. Now there had emerged a city, metropolitan, worldly. It squirmed restlessly on Lake Michigan's shore. Physically, Chicago offended. A bird's-eye view would reveal a confused, crowded mass of crate-like commercial buildings, endless regiments of smokestacks, vast slum areas. The streets were unpaved. Jagged wooden sidewalks rose and fell, emphasizing a composite, unsightly, crazy-quilt confusion. The atmosphere was heavy with dust, smoke, the smell of stockyards, and of the horses that pulled rattling cable-cars.

"An overwhelming pall of smoke; streets filled with busy, quick-moving people, a vast aggregation of railways, vessels and traffic of all kinds; and a paramount devotion to the Almighty Dollar are the prominent characteristics of Chicago." So a foreign visitor described the city. Not even the most fervently patriotic citizen could maintain that description was a libel. Only Lake Michigan, which the city skirted for a pace, then sprawled away from, furnished some relief, soothing the feverish metropolis a little.

But if Chicago failed to present a pretty picture, it did form an appropriate and challenging background for any man who wished to sink his teeth deep in the world—and bite hard, as Altgeld wished to do. Moreover, of all American cities, Chicago could be considered the most frankly American. Here the commercial East and the agricultural West met and clashed. Here were concentrated the railroads, the reaper works, the processing establishments, the granaries and the packing plants, all the great outward manifestations of the new era. Here intensely "capitalistic" titans of industry faced just as intense advocates of labor's "rights." Here, too, the "native Americans" and the "foreigners" lived in almost equal numbers, struggling for the amalgamation which was supposed to occur, but not always did.

43

2

It was a city curiously attuned in spirit to the young lawyer from Missouri. If Chicago was ruthless in its way (and it was), Altgeld, too, could be ruthless in his way. He knew what he wanted and possessed the tenacity and drive to get it, given half a chance. The quest for success—material success—epitomized the Chicago spirit, one attested conspicuously by such first citizens as George Pullman, Cyrus McCormick, Marshall Field, the Armours and the Swifts. Altgeld was fired by that spirit no less than they. Chicago was daring, given to defying precedents. It would think seriously of causing its river to flow backward—and carry out the plan. Altgeld would prove as daring. Chicago was ruggedly capitalistic to the core. Yet, more than any other city in that period, it would mother and nurture movements and ideas running counter to the current of the times. This contradiction also would prove a common denominator of the city and the new resident.

By 1875, because of its fire, its riots, its seemingly volcanic rise to fabulous wealth and its general boisterousness and downright wickedness, Chicago had developed a reputation. It was one which fascinated the world. According to *Scribner's Monthly* of that year, the name Chicago was "familiar in the remotest villages of Europe" and the city the "best advertised of any in America." The great Bismarck had exclaimed a short time before: "I wish I could go to America if only to see that Chicago!"[1] Many of Bismarck's subjects did go, attracted by Chicago's reputation and also the opportunity to escape Bismarck and his restrictions against socialists. Streams from Ireland and from the Slavic and Bohemian states joined the exiled Germans to form a flood tide of immigration into Chicago. And so the city grew— from less than 170,000 when the Civil War ended, to nearly 400,000 by the time Altgeld arrived.

3

This flow of immigration caused elation among Chicago's numerous, highly vocal "boosters," who were anxious for it to overtake Philadelphia and even New York in the census. They worshiped bigness, and also, perhaps, gave some thought to rising values in real estate, which most of them owned for speculative purposes. True, there was ill-concealed grumbling among Know-nothing diehards. But even these conceded that the Germans, Irish and Bohemians were needed—

for George Pullman's palace car company, for Cyrus McCormick's reaper works, the packing plants and the railroad shops. But the immigrants would bear watching. They might go in for unionism or demand that foolishness called "the eight-hour day" of which talk was being heard. Worse still, there was the menace of socialism. Had not sound Americans such as Horace Greeley been attracted by that alien nonsense? He had even engaged a German named Karl Marx to write about it for his New York Tribune.[2] Well, Chicago knew how to deal with such things when the time came.

At least certain spokesmen did. How one influential element of the city might meet such agitation seemed indicated clearly enough by an editorial that Altgeld probably read in the Chicago Tribune of November 23, 1875. It was headed "Warnings to Communists."

"If the Communists in this country are counting upon the looseness of our police system and the tendency to proceed against criminals by due process of law, and hope on that account, to receive more leniency than in Europe, they have ignored some of the most significant episodes in American history. There is no people so prone as the American to take the law into their own hands when the sanctity of human life is threatened and the rights of property invaded in a manner that cannot be adequately reached and punished by the tortuous course of the law. Judge Lynch is an American by birth and character. The Vigilance Committee is a peculiarly American institution. . . . Every lamp-post in Chicago will be decorated with a communistic carcass if necessary to prevent wholesale incendiarism or prevent any attempt at it."

The cause for this outburst by "the greatest newspaper of the Northwest"? Some fifty "malcontents" had staged a "mass meeting" on the Lake Front, to protest against the policies of the Relief and Aid Society in distributing doles to the unemployed. According to the Tribune, there had been talk of "burning Chicago."[3]

4

Thoughtful citizens, men who remembered the extravagances of the old Abolitionist organs, doubtless shook their heads in dismay over the implications in that editorial and others like it. That the wretched orators on the Lake Front indulged in fantastically ugly rantings was true enough. Willis J. Abbott, who became a friend of Altgeld's and later the editor of the Christian Science Monitor, heard

some of these talks as a boy. He recalled "turning away from one of
the stands with a sense that what was being preached was not precisely
a doctrine of general good will. The speaker, after pointing out the
necessity for doing away with the capitalists, . . . went on to assure his
hearers that it was particularly necessary that the children likewise be
slain, since the curse of capitalism was in their blood. . . ."[4] Talk like
that would cause trouble. No doubt of it.

Yet there were citizens who questioned if matching it with editorial
paragraphs just as wild was the way to meet a condition which probably
would disappear anyway. They looked askance at the *Tribune*, worried.
Others who knew the paper's new publisher might have passed the editorials off as further evidence of Joseph Medill's perhaps harmless idio-
syncracies. He had many eccentricities, that really great journalist and
spirited Chicagoan who had done much, in his way, to build Chicago.
He had served as the city's "fireproof" mayor after the fire. Naturally
he would not want the town burned again, especially not by "communists." Likely as not, the next day Medill would let loose a blast
at businessmen who were violating the city's new fire ordinances. He
was that way. It was said of Medill that, as an editor, "his passion for
interlineations was so great that he had been known to interpolate
matter of his own in the letter of an angry or carping subscriber and
then in a trenchant editorial demolish the views which he himself had
ascribed to the hapless correspondent."[5] Probably apocryphal, but
nonetheless revealing.

Joseph Medill was a Chicagoan to keep an eye on in connection with
Altgeld.

5

It is well, too, to keep an eye on the immigrants in the mass. They
crowded into squalid districts near the packing houses and the railroad shops, ghetto-like communities, isolated pitifully from the normal
currents of the city. They were suspected and suspicious. In articles
about them, the *Tribune* would be generous with such information as
"the men are either day laborers or loafers" . . . "communists who
would like nothing better than to incite an open riot . . . in the poor
pretense they are the downtrodden and oppressed."[6] And so, the rest
of Chicago, instead of being sympathetic, resented these people.

Understanding would have to wait until there arrived such persons
as Jane Addams, then a "slender . . . rather quaint" girl of thirteen in
Cedarville, Illinois,[7] and until a great tragedy occurred near Haymarket Square.

There were, of course, some bright spots in the scene which high-lighted grim economic aspects. An Academy of Music sponsored Sunday night concerts. The winter of 1875 saw an Italian opera company in the city with *La Traviata*, *Lucia*, and *Faust* in its repertoire. Sir Henry Irving thrilled the matinee-goers in tragedies. He was Altgeld's favorite.[8] Beer gardens, with gay music, dotted the city. For the intellectuals and mentally curious, there were scores of literary societies and lectures. Yet over it all the pressure of "sociological forces" was outstanding and emphatic. And there were tenseness and suspense. Chicagoans were assured from a pontifical source—the *Tribune* again—that "We are fallen upon a time of agitation. There is a general shaking up of the virtues, and the vices, and the pools of society are being vigorously stirred by the angels of reform."[9]

6

This was the scene into which young Lawyer Altgeld stepped, dusty and cindery from the trip which ended in a smoke-filled Chicago train-shed. If he gave little or no thought to the forces which were operating to produce a time of agitation, he had sufficient reason. The hundred dollars in his wallet was a personal fact, transcending social facts. He may have pondered that the sum would not last forever, as he appraised with intent eyes the visible aspects of this new province to be conquered. In his twenty-eight years, he had overcome some obstacles. Back there in Savannah, now very far away indeed, he had come to be "somebody." But here, in this Chicago, unknown and un-welcomed, doubtless assailed by some uneasiness, he faced—what?

The city gave no sign.

CHAPTER FIVE

The New Career in the New Era

1

His first act was a bold one. He paid out nearly all of his capital in advance rent for an office in the Reaper Block, then one of the finest buildings in town. Thus he assured himself of a site for professional operations. And he was anchored. Separate living quarters were out of the question because of his boldness, and so, partitioning off a part of the office, he installed a bed for himself. He was "happy," we are told, "because he knew he could make enough out of his law practice to live and he was assured of a roof over his head."[1]

His cocksureness, however, was not soon justified. Chicago was well supplied with legal talent. Moreover, young Lawyer Altgeld did not, at first meeting, inspire strangers with confidence in his ability. "He was not . . . an attractive or graceful personality."[2] Such was the first recorded impression that he left.

The times were against him, too. For all its noisy activity, the talk of its "boosters," Chicago with the rest of the country was deep in a business depression. It was the slump which had begun in '73, rolling across the continent in the wake of the Jay Cooke and Sons collapse; the same that had produced the Granger "rebellion" which served as a springboard for Altgeld in his political career at Savannah. The city government had difficulty paying its schoolteachers and other employees, and there was talk of municipal bankruptcy. Mass unemployment, intensified because of the thousands of mechanics who had come here to rebuild the city after the Great Fire of '71, was a problem. A regular duty of the police was to meet all trains and turn away the job-hunters. There were sporadic strikes, feeble stirrings of militancy by the distressed workers. But the strikes failed and even lower wage scales resulted because "ten pairs of hands [were] ready and willing to take the place of every single pair that quit work."[3]

And so, Chicago kept Altgeld in suspense. Perhaps a little hungry too. If it had occurred to him to try to get employment as a clerk in an established lawyer's office, he must have vetoed the thought immediately. "Hang out your shingle and build up your own business. If you make only fifteen dollars a month, live on it. Never ask another lawyer what the law is on any subject. Look it up yourself. It will make you more self-reliant and a better lawyer in the end." That was the advice he gave to another young lawyer.[4] That was his own policy when he started out.

At least once, serious misgivings gripped him about his future in the city. "I think," he wrote back to his chum, Ben Holt in Savannah, "I made a mistake in leaving Northwest Missouri. I should have stayed with you. . . ."[5] But he persevered.

2

In time he made a few contacts important then and later. Through repeated borrowing of a dictionary, he met Edward Osgood Brown, a young lawyer in the suite across the corridor. "There was something about him," Brown recalled, speaking for himself and his partner, Orville Peckham, "that instantly arrested our attention and invited a respect and friendship. It was only a little while thereafter that he commanded our admiration as well."[6]

One conversation in particular impressed his new acquaintance. Brown had made a joking reference to Altgeld's frequent calls for the dictionary, then apologized for the remark.

"I have to look at the dictionary for one word in every five to know that I have spelled it right," said Altgeld.

"Oh, take the chance!" laughed Brown, who was a university graduate.

"That will do for you," said Altgeld. "But not for me. I have to get, while I do my work, those means of doing it accurately which you were fortunate enough to get in preparation for your work."[7] But he added, "I do not have to look up the same word a second or a third time."[8]

The two lawyers across the hall, both of old Anglo-Saxon families which had settled in America generations before, began finding the German-looking young man a fascinating personality, for all the social gap between him and them. His earnestness interested them. And one day when they were retained in a complicated bit of litigation, involving tedious research, they asked their new acquaintance to help out. The work assigned to him required much delving into musty records in stifling vaults of public offices. Judge Brown recalled that "his industry and conscientiousness were phenomenal through it all." Moreover, when the research grubbing was done, his new friends determined to have him appear in court with them to add his "ability . . . in the forensic part of the business also."[9] He was practicing law in Chicago at last! Not that it was a profitable beginning. "I am afraid [we] put too much of that work on him and gave him too little fees," Judge Brown related on this point. But Altgeld was started.

3

Merest chance brought him what may have been the first law business of his own. He was sitting at his desk, facing the opened door of the office. A woman paced the corridor, obviously waiting for someone, and not too patiently. Altgeld invited her to wait in his office. She accepted his invitation. Passing the time of day, they exchanged some German phrases and thereby established a common bond. Soon she was explaining that she had some trouble over property owned by her. This was what had brought her to the Reaper Block to consult her attorney. The thought occurred to her, Why wait longer for her attorney? Why not entrust the matter to this polite, earnest-looking young lawyer? As a result Altgeld had what Attorney Henry M. Walker, son of the woman, was told was his first case in Chicago.[10]

He threw all his energies into the case, so that he made a deep impression upon his client's brother-in-law, Cornelius McGinnis. In Pittsburgh, McGinnis had owned a foundry that did an extensive credit business in the Middle West. He had sold the business before moving to Chicago and the company was having difficulty just then collecting its accounts. A Chicago lawyer was wanted for this work. McGinnis recommended Altgeld. Thus, only a year after his arrival in Chicago, he found himself suddenly possessed of a sizeable portfolio of collection business.[11]

But not all his cases involved satisfactory financial results. Laborers and more than one legal "pauper" were among his early clients. The first case in which the name "John P. Altgeld, No. 39, 97 Clark St., solicitor for plaintiff" appears on the court records of Cook County, shows that he represented a discharged livery stable laborer, Jacob Themke, in a suit against George and Edward Eager, the stable owners. In a document dated June 29, 1876, Altgeld wrote out in his clumsy scrawl the complaint that Themke had $332 coming to him for "services and labor" and the brothers Eager refused to pay. Yet the case apparently was not very strong, for Altgeld agreed to dismissal just before it went to the jury. He probably earned no fee at all.[12]

He was more successful with an action brought the next month. According to Altgeld's bill of particulars, one George Lobsten "did wilfully and injuriously keep a certain dog . . . which he knew [was] accustomed to attack and bite mankind." It had bitten a boy, Patrick Garen, who was "greatly lacerated, hurt and wounded" and caused to be "sick, sore and lame." Damages of $6,000 were asked. After a jury heard Altgeld's appeal for the boy, it returned a verdict of $50.[13] But Altgeld was not through. Immediately afterward he filed another action for $6,000 in behalf of Patrick's father for the loss of the boy's "services." This time he obtained a verdict for $650. But, alas for Altgeld's fee, the other side threatened to appeal. The judgment was called excessive and so Altgeld advised his client to "remit" $450, leaving only $200 to be split between the client and counsel.[14]

He handled a divorce case in February, 1877, for one Mary V. Henry, who told a tale of domestic woe that must have chilled the bachelor lawyer. Her husband, James, (Altgeld recited) had sent her off to Philadelphia, then proceeded to pawn and sell all their household furnishings and also her clothes and her gold watch. He quit his job, refused to take another and permitted her to be evicted, making it necessary for her to sleep on a floor. Finally, he was caught with another woman. Altgeld averred that these acts entitled Mrs. Henry to a divorce, which she received. But as to his fee, the amount, if any, may be gathered from the fact that the unhappy wife was a "pauper."[15]

4

Despite such unprofitable cases, however, Altgeld, by the summer of 1877, was at least making a living. There is reason to believe that he sent considerable money to his parents in Ohio, enough eventually to redeem the mortgage on their farm. No longer needing to live in his office, he rented a room on the North Side, where many middle-class Germans resided. He was thinking then, too, of settling down, of marriage. At any rate, he had no thought of remaining faithful to the memory of Annie Rohrer of Savannah.

He had been seeing a good deal of his first client, the mother of Henry Walker. She was "tall and graceful and her intellect was such as would appeal to Altgeld." But she was already married. He learned however that she was extremely unhappy with her husband. According to evidence which appears credible, Altgeld took more than a professional interest in her troubles and proposed that she obtain a divorce and marry him.[16] But once again he was rejected.

It was about this time—the summer of 1877—that Altgeld went on

something of a spending spree, perhaps to recover from his new disappointment in love. "He took a two or three weeks' vacation . . .
visiting Newport and other fashionable Eastern resorts." A writer inclined to view Altgeld as wholly "sociological" relates that he took this
trip "to see how the leisure class lived." Perhaps. But it has been seen
that Altgeld was not merely "sociological." He liked gaiety—and the
society of women. He liked to dance, although he was never very
good at it.[17] He could, in short, enjoy a "good time" for its own sake.
And that alone, one guesses, took him to Newport.

5

That was the summer, in 1877, when there would occur events
more potent in their influence upon Altgeld than his jaunt to Newport. America's first major clash between labor and capital was at
hand: the bloody railroad strikes of 1877. They would jolt the nation—
and also Altgeld—into the first serious realization of the explosive nature of the new social problems of the industrial era.

At the time of the 1877 strikes, Altgeld may have been on his Newport trip. But he could not have escaped their import. The sudden
strife enveloped almost the entire nation. The press had for days
scarcely space for any other news. The country seemed to be tottering
on the brink of revolution,[18] and this from a seemingly harmless ten
per cent reduction in wages announced by the Baltimore and Ohio
Railroad, effective July sixteenth. In itself, that would have caused
ordinarily no more than mere grumbling. But there had been many
such wage cuts since the depression of '73. Looking at the cold financial figures, the railroads seemed forced to reduce labor costs. Scores
of systems were in bankruptcy or heading there, and all the lines were
"in the red." Yet the workers felt that the causes were to be found in
financial racketeering, stock watering and downright theft more than
in the general depression.

The match which set off the tinderbox was the feudalistic attitude
of the railroad managements. Union leaders were blacklisted. Members of grievance committees were discharged. Pinkerton detectives
were hired to set up a system of espionage. When committees representing the distressed Baltimore and Ohio workers sought to discuss
their wage condition, the managers refused to listen. Why should
they? Thousands of unemployed were ready to fill the places of any
dissatisfied employes.

And then it happened.

6

In the middle of the afternoon on July seventeenth, a crew of Baltimore and Ohio firemen and brakemen brought a train to a stop at a junction in Maryland, near Baltimore. They were on "strike." By evening, it was plain that no ordinary or local trouble was brewing. Within the space of twenty-four hours, the entire Baltimore and Ohio system was paralyzed. Soon workers in other trades joined the railroad men. The railroad asked for state troops at Martinsburg, West Virginia. The strikers massed in front of the militia. Shots were exchanged. A locomotive fireman fell dead. After that, there was bedlam. "Mobs of townspeople and farmers from the surrounding country joined the strikers, and finally two companies of militia deserted to the strikers' side." Terrorized, the Governor of West Virginia appealed to President Rutherford B. Hayes for Federal troops. They arrived and brought order. The trouble was over, it was thought. But it was only the beginning.[19]

An epidemic of strike spirit—and mob spirit—caught up other railroad lines and other cities. Nine workers were killed in Baltimore. Ten died in Cumberland, Maryland. There were clashes in Reading, Pennsylvania, and in Buffalo, New York, where Grover Cleveland then was practicing law. "Labor committees" forced the closing of nearly all industrial establishments in Columbus, Ohio. In Indianapolis, a distinguished member of the Federal judiciary left his law library to call out troops, assemble deputy marshals and order the arrest of strikers for contempt of court. He was Walter Q. Gresham. His legal theory was that, because the railroad involved was in receivership, the court and the government itself had the duty to break the strike.[20] "Government by injunction" was ahead.

7

For a full week, Chicago held its breath, wondering and fearful. Already it was known as "the most radical city in America." The city knew that its laboring men were dissatisfied. Early that year the Chicago Inter-Ocean, a Republican organ, had commented: "In Chicago, today, there are hundreds of well-born, well-bred, and well-informed men walking the streets without a cent, and without knowledge of where to get a dinner or a bed." Scarcely anything franker was being said by the group of "labor agitators" then active in Chicago.

As if conditions were not bad enough, the newspapers and influential citizens were constantly making statements calculated, if not designed, to stir the workers. For example, there was an item in the *Tribune* only four days before the walkout of the Baltimore and Ohio workers. A "suburban correspondent" had complained about being annoyed by tramps and asked the *Tribune* for the law. After explaining the legal steps for handling tramps, the *Tribune* indulged in some independent observations.

"The law . . . is not of much use for suburban districts where officers are scarce and justices of peace hard to find. The simplest plan, where one is not a member of the Humane Society, is to put a little strychnine or arsenic in the meat and other supplies furnished the tramp. This produces death within a comparatively short period of time, is a warning to other tramps to keep out of the neighborhood, puts the coroner in good humor, and saves one's chickens and other portable property from constant depredation."[21]

Undoubtedly that paragraph was intended to be humorous. But it was unfortunate humor at a time when distressed working people and involuntary "tramps" were easily stirred.

8

Very soon Chicago was confronted not merely by a railroad strike but by a general strike. Police squads and strikers clashed. Panic gripped the city. Leading citizens left town. Businessmen voiced a demand for 5,000 militiamen to subdue "the ragged commune wretches." The terror lasted until a regiment of Federal troops, led by Lieutenant-Colonel Frederick Dent Grant, the Civil War general's son, marched into the city. Before it was all over, Chicago had lived up to its reputation of doing things in a big way. At least nineteen strikers and rioters had been killed. Some counted thirty.

And the workers? They gained nothing. Their very fury had aroused the force which crushed the strike. Most of the strikers returned to their jobs at wages lower than before. But on both sides a reservoir of bitterness had been formed. Marshall Field organized a citizen's committee "to fight communists."[22] William Pinkerton, whose father had been an agitator in England and had guarded Lincoln, foresaw and prepared for profitable business ahead in strikebreaking and labor spying. The Chicago police force seriously considered conducting itself like an army. "The superintendent became a colonel, and wore shoulder straps . . . the men were drilled regularly, taught to handle guns, to go through street fight maneuvers and handle themselves like soldiers."[23]

Certain incidents produced extreme bitterness among the workers toward the Chicago police. There was, notably, the Turner Hall occurrence on July 26, after the general disorder had ended. A meeting in the hall of both furniture workers and employers, called, in fact, by the employers to discuss wage demands of the union, was being held.

"The attendants [at the meeting] were wholly unarmed, and the meeting was perfectly peaceable, and orderly, and while the people were sitting quietly, with their backs toward the entrance hall . . . a force of from fifteen to twenty policemen came suddenly into the hall, having a policeman's club in one hand and a revolver in the other, and making no pause to determine the character of the meeting, they immediately shouted : 'Get out of here, you damned sons of bitches,' and began beating the people with their clubs, and some of them actually fired their revolvers. One young man was shot through the back of the head.

"But to complete the atrocity of the affair on the part of the officers engaged in it, when the people hastened to make their escape from the assembly room, they found policemen stationed on either side of the stairway . . . who applied their clubs to them as they passed. . . . Mr. Jacob Beiersdorf, who was a manufacturer of furniture, employing some 200 men, had been invited to the meeting and came, but as he was about to enter the place where it was held, an inoffensive old man, doing nothing unlawful, was stricken down at his feet by a policeman's club."[24]

So Judge William K. McAllister described the Turner Hall affair in a court decision denouncing the police for violation of civil liberties guaranteed by the Constitution. It was an incident long remembered because of its wantonness. Unfortunately, it would not be the last such, from that time to Haymarket—and after.

9

A few appalled voices were raised for compromise and understanding, but pitifully few. Some tried to discern causes other than "the awful presence of socialism." The Chicago *Daily News*, while deploring mob violence, said editorially that the railroad owners shared blame. "The people have no sympathy with the rioters, but they have as little for the Vanderbilts, the Jay Goulds and the Jim Fisks. . . . It is simply nonsense to say that there are not two sides to the question."[25]

Yet "the moral of the whole business, as it appeared to the businessmen," observed Floyd Dell, after a study of that episode some forty years later, "was the need of a Gatling quick-firing gun which could sweep a street from side to side and mow down a thousand men in a few seconds." Accordingly, in 1878, the Citizens' Association presented one to the city.[26]

These events held fateful meaning for the lawyer making merry in Newport.

CHAPTER SIX

The Man of Property

1

While Altgeld undoubtedly had his thoughts sharply directed toward labor conditions by the events of that July, this was not to the exclusion of other topics—marriage, for instance. On his trip that summer, he had stopped off at the farm of his parents. The girl Emma Ford was still in Ohio, and unmarried. Moreover, her father had died a short time ago, so there were no more parental objections to her seeing "the little Dutchman." Between them, the old interest flamed anew. In November, 1877, young Lawyer Altgeld paid another visit to the Little Washington community, and on November twenty-first escorted Emma Ford to the courthouse in Mansfield to obtain a marriage license. On the same day, in a quiet ceremony at the Ford home, they were married by the Reverend Mr. F. M. Searles of Mansfield.[1]

"Theirs was one of the happiest marriages I have ever known," related one niece, and another, who lived with them many years: "Never an unkind word passed between them; they were the soul of consideration for each other."[2] In later years, he gave to a young friend his formula for a happy married life. "Never forget the small courtesies after your marriage. If, at the table, you want the salt, never forget to say please to your wife when you ask her to pass it to you, nor to say thanks when she does. Such little things keep harmony and happiness alive."[3]

2

Mrs. Altgeld was a handsome woman. "She is tall and lithe and her carriage is one of natural grace," wrote a newspaper reporter.[4] She "wore beautiful clothes and had excellent taste" and was "dignified, but friendly," a niece recalled.[5] Her dark eyes were soft, indicative of a calm, serene temperament. Possibly she could have had a career of her own in teaching music, or even literature, but she subordinated herself completely into her husband's life, without, however, losing

her own interests. A friend called her "the most sympathetic and devoted wife she ever knew. It is Mrs. Altgeld's own confession that she
is thoroughly wrapped up in her husband. . . . While she has views of
her own, they are in perfect harmony with his."[6]

She was unusually cultured, not only for the small community in
which she was reared but for the period. Her days at Oberlin College
gave her an uncommon knowledge and appreciation of music, and
she dabbled in writing. Several short stories by her were published,
also a romantic novelette called *Sarah's Choice; or, The Nortons.*"[7]
She painted a bit, too, and did a portrait in oils of her husband that
was hung prominently in the drawing room of their home.

No wonder, then, it would be noted that after his marriage young
Lawyer Altgeld was a changed man. The country bumpkin was gone
completely and in his place was a self-assured, polite, urbane gentleman. Mrs. Altgeld exerted a similar influence of refinement upon his
speeches and writings. "Justice requires me to state," he would write
in the preface to his final volume of *Live Questions,* "that I have been
greatly assisted by the unerring judgment and wise criticism of Mrs.
Altgeld. Through her influence, some of the articles were softened in
tone and others were changed in character." "Softened in tone"—
there was the great effect upon Altgeld of his marriage. He accepted
criticisms from her when he would not from others. "When changes
[in his speeches] were suggested, it always irritated him," recalled a
political associate.[8] But he really appreciated his wife's suggestions.

3

They set up housekeeping in what was then the Town of Lake, a
North Side suburb of Chicago, renting the ground floor of a two-
story frame home on Wellington Street, between Halsted and Clark
streets. For a time William Altgeld, who had come to Chicago to
study law and served as his brother's clerk, lived with them there, perhaps until he returned to Ohio to die of tuberculosis. Financially,
their beginning was not too happy, for Altgeld's business seems to
have gone into a slump at that time. He found it necessary to walk
to his office to save the fare of a horse-car ride. This turned out fortunately for him, however, for one morning Adolph Heile, a successful Chicago lawyer of German extraction, gave him a lift in his buggy.
On that ride with his new acquaintance he confided that he was considering giving up his office to take desk space only. Mr. Heile promptly invited him to take space with him in the Boyce Block.[9] Altgeld ac-

cepted, and soon Lawyer Heile was sending some business his way. In the same office was Henry M. Shepard. When Mr. Shepard became a judge, Altgeld purchased his practice.[10]

However, a year after his marriage, Altgeld's business was still so poor that he told Mr. Heile that he could not afford a turkey for their Thanksgiving dinner. He and his wife would have to be satisfied with roast beef. Once he was forced to ask Mr. Heile to advance him money for having "his boots halfsoled." Mrs. Altgeld related to a niece that she did her own housework and "wondered how they survived for she did not like to cook."[11]

4

But by 1879 Altgeld had discovered a way in which to win for himself some of Chicago's wealth: real estate. He had managed to save $500. "With this he made his first investment in real estate. Then, securing the assistance of friends, he made other investments in realty, subdividing and selling the properties acquired, and managing his affairs so judiciously that in a comparatively short time he was able to operate extensively on his own account."[12] In an amazingly few years he was well-to-do. Seemingly, that happened almost overnight, not a strange happening in Chicago for those who had foresight, luck and faith in the growing city.

Among the friends who assisted him in his real estate ventures was William C. Goudy. An interesting, as well as an extremely important, friendship for Altgeld began. For Goudy, first president of the Chicago Bar Association, was the Vanderbilt lawyer in Illinois. There was no more active "corporation lawyer" than Goudy in Chicago, nor one more powerful politically. On his say-so, legislation was killed, judges nominated, Supreme Court judges appointed—in short, he was a local Chauncey Depew. How Altgeld came to know him does not appear, but in the early '80's they were on intimate terms, and Goudy was passing on to the younger lawyer "inside" tips for realty buys.[13]

In addition, Altgeld demonstrated a flair for land values which amazed even persons specializing in the field. "He knew property values in Chicago better than any other man," said one expert.[14] Once started, he became a plunger. Early in this phase of his career he boldly entered into a $200,000 deal for seventy-five or more acres of lots in Lake View. All that was paid down was $30,000. He signed notes and gave mortgages for the rest.[15] He operated so extensively that, it has been said, at one time or another Altgeld owned most of the lots in the now densely built and fabulously valuable Lake View section of Chicago.[16] From residential property he branched into the business district. Real-estate experts shook their heads when, early in the '80's, he acquired some expensive lots in Market Street, between Jackson and Van Buren streets, and proceeded to contract for a seven-story office building. He would be ruined, they said. But the venture proved a success.

A Man of Property had replaced the struggling young lawyer.

5

There is a curious coincidence in the fact that Altgeld began making his fortune out of real estate in the year 1879. That was the year a handsome, luxuriously bearded forty-year-old printer-editor, a great flame of inspiration burning in his soul and brain, had finished a manuscript. This manuscript would bristle with many passages, seemingly apropos of Altgeld's activities at the time, such as this:

"The wide-spreading social evils which everywhere oppress men amid an advancing civilization spring from a great primary wrong— the appropriation, as the exclusive property of some men, of the land on which and from which all must live. From this fundamental injustice flow all the injustices which distort and endanger modern development, which condemn the producer of wealth to poverty and pamper the non-producer of wealth in luxury, which rear the tenement house with the palace, plant the brothel behind the church, and compel us to build prisons as we open new schools."[17]

Progress and Poverty was the title of that work. The author was Henry George.

Although after a few years Altgeld and Henry George will be found making common cause in politics, it cannot be gainsaid that Altgeld profited from the very system that George denounced. Yet Altgeld was no mere land speculator. After making his nest-egg, he became a builder. In one year alone he erected "five large blocks of buildings, costing over $500,000."[18] It became an obsession with him to create buildings. He was never happier than when consulting with architects and contractors or studying blueprints. As a hobby, he familiarized himself with every phase of building construction, learning about materials, tensile strengths and architecture. Even after he had amassed all the money he desired, he could not stop building. It had seeped into his blood. This would have potent effects upon him.

After a while his law practice became a sideline to his real estate and construction ventures. This may have been intentional. "He didn't like the law," according to Clarence Darrow.[19] Of a later period, Darrow would write: "He had come to despise that profession; he felt that its strongest men sold themselves to destroy people, to perpetuate and intensify the poverty of the oppressed and enlarge their burdens."[20] But some time would pass before that attitude became crystallized in him.

6

The standard of living of the Altgelds kept in step with his improving financial status. First they moved from the frame house near Halsted Street to a brick residence on Grace Street. Then he purchased a gray stone, two-story residence on fashionable Frederick Street, so tastefully furnished that the *Tribune* commented on its "refined atmosphere." He had a large study on the second floor, the walls lined with books. On one side of a mantle was a bust of Minerva, on the other a bust of Augustus Caesar: Wisdom and Power.[21]

He joined several clubs, including the Germania, the Sunset and the North Shore Club and, with Mrs. Altgeld, appeared at social functions, mingling with a well-to-do, if not wealthy, circle.[22] She became a member of the Chicago Woman's Club. They attended concerts and lectures, such as one given by the Women's Christian Temperance Union with Justin McCarthy speaking on the "Irish Question" and Joseph Medill presiding.[23] They spent pleasant evenings with the Heiles. The men sang and Altgeld joined the chorus, "especially if it was a German song." Frequently they took little trips. On a trip to Florida, Altgeld appears as a sportsman. "He came with an expensive new shotgun for hunting, and with all kinds of fishing tackle." But he was a failure both as fisherman and hunter.[24] On a horse, however, he was superb. He once boasted that he never saw a horse that he could not ride. Riding was his favorite recreation, and Mrs. Altgeld often accompanied him.

7

His was an easy-going existence in this period, but marred at times by illness. The fever which he had contracted at Wilson's Landing during the Civil War kept coming back. The files of a lawsuit he handled in March, 1881, reveal this notation: "It is hereby agreed that said cause shall be passed on the regular call . . . on account of sickness of plaintiff's counsel."[25] The plaintiff's counsel was Altgeld. Worse still for his peace of mind, Mrs. Altgeld was far from robust. Judge Brown once received a message from Altgeld to come to his home to discuss a lawsuit in which they were co-counsel. He found Mrs. Altgeld ill in one room and Altgeld "stretched helpless on a bed in another . . . alternating between a burning fever and wretched chills."[26]

To Mrs. Heile, Mrs. Altgeld confided that her illness was due, mainly, to the fact that she and Altgeld practiced birth control. So Dr. O. A. Paoli, a prominent Chicago physician who lived next door to the Altgelds, had told her. She had once witnessed the birth of a child and the experience had left her terror-stricken. "But I would gladly have a baby if John wanted one," she said.[27] In the middle '80's a son was born to them but he was either stillborn or succumbed immediately afterward. Few persons, not even some close friends, knew of this tragedy in the life of the Altgelds. It probably was too painful for them to mention, and in later years he brooded over his childlessness. To a niece, Ruth Ford Atkinson, Mrs. Altgeld once mused how different their lives would have been if this child had lived.[28] Altgeld himself felt that because he had no children he interested himself in a political career in Chicago more keenly than he might have otherwise. That phase of his career now begins.

CHAPTER SEVEN

The Return to Politics

1

The year of Grover Cleveland's first election as President of the United States marked Altgeld's emergence into the political arena in Chicago, a slight connection between Altgeld and Cleveland that is interesting to remember. This was 1884. By that time Altgeld had been in Chicago long enough to discover that politics there represented something different from what he had known in Savannah, Missouri. Certainly the political game in Chicago was more violent both in word and deed. Typical was this description of one Chicago political leader, as printed in the *Tribune*: "He has kissed and made up with the men whom, last April, he called thieves, pimps and ballot-box stuffers."[1] Election riots leading to fatalities were not uncommon. "Outrageous Performance of the Gang in the Twentieth Ward—Stabbing of the Challengers in the First Ward," read an election headline. In 1884, an alderman, Michael Gaynor, was murdered for political reasons. Ballot boxes were stolen from under the noses of officials and systematically stuffed. The "big boss" was Michael Cassius McDonald, "King Mike," who operated gambling houses in the heart of the town.

Thus, except for upsurging social and economic issues, which for the most part the leaders attempted to ignore, the political scene was not one that could have been expected to attract Altgeld. Especially was this so because, then and later, he possessed a deep-rooted contempt for the *homo politicus*. He expressed his credo in a newspaper interview published a few years later, declaring that he believed in "the private individual" because it is "the successful private individual who is the important factor in American society." As for the "office-holding class," he felt it to be a "cowardly hanging-on class, . . . a negative class." "It is difficult," he said, "to point out wherein it does anything that can be regarded as raising the standard of public morals, creating a healthy public sentiment or solving in a proper way any of the great questions, both economic and social, that are calling for solution. . . ."[2]

That statement was not ballyhoo. Yet he entered politics, associated himself with politicians and became, indeed, one of the most consummate politicians of his time. Was this because of an overwhelming desire to change the political picture, to solve "the great questions, both economic and social"? The answer is no—not in the beginning at least. "Politics has a strong fascination for me, just as gambling has for some men," he confided to a newspaper reporter to explain his interest in politics. To a friend he said: "Other men get recreation from playing cards. Or they bet on horse races. Or they have their children. Politics is my recreation."[3]

2

He was bored, too, at devoting his energies solely to making money, especially since making money had suddenly become so easy for him. And he had more leisure after he took into his office, about 1882, John W. Lanehart, who became his partner in the firm of Altgeld and Lanehart. By 1884 Lanehart was handling many of Altgeld's business affairs. In his association with Altgeld, Lanehart has been made to appear a "man of mystery." He looked the rôle, sporting a pair of dashing black mustachios, parting a heavy shock of black hair in the middle and always fashionably groomed, almost foppishly so, in marked contrast to Altgeld. "Mr. Lanehart had a peculiar personality," the *Daily News* would comment. "He was . . . reticent to the point of taciturnity . . . and inspired those who met him with the impression that he knew far more than he cared to tell. . . ."[4] It was asserted there was "considerable speculation" over his relationship to Altgeld, that "people who were supposed to be in a position to know" called him Altgeld's nephew, while others said he was a brother-in-law.[5] The simple fact is that John W. Lanehart was Altgeld's first cousin. His father was one of the brothers of Altgeld's mother who preceded her to America in the 'forties.

For Lanehart, Altgeld developed tremendous affection, even to the point of overlooking incidents which tended to reflect on himself. This was true despite—or perhaps because of—the fact that Lanehart was so opposite to him. He seems to have shared none of Altgeld's interest in social problems. Politics, for which he was admirably fitted by temperament and in which he played an important part locally, was neither recreation nor a medium for social service for Lanehart. It was a business proposition concerning such items as gas and electricity franchises. In a sense, Lanehart represented a personification of Altgeld's alter ego, the practical Altgeld. This may have been the strong bond between them.

3

By 1884, too, Altgeld had established contact with the three men who were more influential than any others in his Chicago political career and helped him along in that direction. In combination they formed a curious trio. One was the corporation lawyer—Goudy. The other was a labor leader and originally a socialist organizer—George A. Schilling. The third was a gambler, Joseph S. Martin.

Joe Martin was more or less a protégé of Michael Cassius McDonald. Under King Mike's wing he had learned the art of both gambling and politics, and their relationship. When he branched out on his own, opening a gambling establishment downtown and also others in the North Side district in which Altgeld lived, Martin became a political power in his own right and also was recognized as one of King Mike's political lieutenants. One day about 1882 a man came into Altgeld's office to complain that he lost several hundred dollars in a gambling place. He said the place was Joe Martin's, and he wanted to bring suit, for under the law such losses could be recovered. Altgeld composed a stern letter, demanded that Martin come to see him. This was no new experience to Joe Martin, who stuffed a roll of bills in his pocket and called upon "the new nuisance." Without any fuss, Martin paid over the money demanded.

"This kind of blackmail," said Martin, as he counted out the money, "is one of the outrages that men in my illegal business must submit to. Your client lost no money in my place. He won at my place, then lost the money in a lowdown gambling hell!" Martin prided himself on operating an honest house. Altgeld's response was a "searching look," so Martin recalled. A few days later the gambler received another request to see Lawyer Altgeld. "I questioned my client," Altgeld said to Martin this time. "He confessed that what you told me was true. He did not lose his money in your place. Therefore, I withheld your money, which now I return to you." He added that he had ordered his client out of his office.[6] Joe Martin was Altgeld's man from that time on and came to worship Altgeld, literally. And for Altgeld there began one of the most important associations of his life. "I love him and respect him more than any man living," Martin said once.[7] This was true, as he would demonstrate by word and deed as long as Altgeld lived, and afterward. Some years after their first meeting Martin gave up gambling as a profession simply because Altgeld suggested that he do so.[8]

4

Joe Martin's politico-gambling connections became important to Altgeld during the summer of 1884 when Altgeld tossed his hat into the ring for the Democratic nomination for Congress from the Fourth Illinois district, a strong Republican district. He had the support of Lawyer Goudy and Judge Lambert Tree, later appointed United States minister to France by Grover Cleveland, and this backing was important in so-called silk-stocking districts. But he was handicapped in the "machine wards" where the saloon vote and the patronage boys held the balance of power. And the "machine" had a candidate of its own, one C. P. Kimball. Ordinarily, Martin would have been for Kimball, but when he learned that Altgeld was seeking the nomination, he passed the word along that his "boys" should be for his friend, "the little Dutchman," so he called him. None of the "boys" had heard of young Lawyer Altgeld, but they voted for him "because Joe Martin says so."[9] When the nominating convention met in September, Altgeld was nominated "by acclamation." He appeared with a prepared acceptance speech, his first political utterance in Chicago of which there is a record. It was wholly vapid and innocuous.

He was, he said, "diffident" about accepting the nomination because there were so many others with "broader learning." But he would work hard for the whole ticket, including the election of Grover Cleveland. He "apprehended" that the nomination was not a personal tribute but recognition of the "young men of the party . . . whose only desire is to secure an honest and economical government. . . ." He had another "apprehension," too, the only significant portion of his talk. This was that he was nominated to "recognize that large element of American citizens who, though born under a foreign sky, have sought this country in order to prosper by their frugality."[10] There was shrewdness in that reference to the foreign-born citizens. His district was largely German, and anti-foreign agitation was again becoming prominent in Chicago and elsewhere. Only a month before the *Tribune* carried a long editorial on the subject, the gist of which was "the time has come when this country must protect itself from the scum and refuse of the European population."[11]

Altgeld undoubtedly was sincere in standing with the immigrants against such prejudice, but he knew, too, how valuable politically it was to appear as champion of the foreign-born.

5

Prophetically, the *Tribune* at once demonstrated antagonism. It sneered that he would be "elected to stay at home."[12] The *News* was more gracious in its news columns, but gave its readers erroneous information, such as stating that Altgeld "came here from the East about a year ago."[13] It remained for the leading Democratic organ, Wilbur F. Storey's *Times*, to come to his support. The *Times* gushed:

"In the nomination of Mr. John P. Altgeld for Congress, the Democrats of the North Side exhibited a degree of sound discretion that should assure success in the canvass. Mr. Altgeld is a prosperous lawyer, a man of large capacity and attainments, of considerable experience in public life, and highly respected among the German citizens. . . . He is energetic as well as able and ambitious and, if the party strength is harmoniously extended in his behalf, will probably draw enough votes from other than Democratic sources to overcome the usual Republican majority."[14]

Lawyer Goudy's influence explains the sudden discovery by the *Times* that Altgeld was so fine a man whereas only a handful of people in his district had heard of him before.

He campaigned solely as a "regular Democrat," made many speeches in behalf of Grover Cleveland and the entire Democratic ticket. He was active especially in the German sections, where the party made use of his ability to speak in German. He was the leading speaker at a Cleveland demonstration in Evanston on October 20, which the *Times* asserted "will long be remembered as marking a new era in the progress of society."[15] Altgeld showed then the qualities which came to make him one of the most effective platform speakers of his time, this despite certain definite handicaps, particularly that of a strained voice.

In private conversation, when talking to a friend, his voice was "musical with a caressing compassion, a deep human sonority," as would be said by Edgar Lee Masters, who knew him. But speaking in public did something to his voice which made it "harsh, sometimes shrill and sibilant," and also "somewhat forbidding."[16] The harelip may have been responsible for some of this, but self-consciousness springing out of an intense desire to make a good showing accounts for it mainly.

He told a friend that he "hoped to be an orator, and . . . worked as hard as Demosthenes to develop oratorical talent."[17] He thought he failed. But he was in error there. Newton D. Baker once heard him and forty years afterward wrote of the experience: "He spoke without interruption for two hours and twenty minutes to a crowded audience of about five thousand people. He made but one gesture and rarely raised his voice, but his audience was quite the most spellbound I have ever seen."[18]

Of Altgeld's platform performances, Clarence Darrow mentions that "he almost never told a story, yet now and then he would do that atrocious thing. . . ."[19] Some of Altgeld's stories are indicated by titles he jotted down in a notebook: "Pounding dog when dead." "The boy that God made." "Pat and Jim's dream and the chicken." "Man wrote *this side up* on both sides of box." One item in the notebook is nearly complete: "*Come-on-purpose* girl went to church to be married and when preacher asked 'do you take this man for your wedded husband,' replied 'Why I came on purpose.' "[20]

It was his practice to look constantly for such material. In 1896, he offered five dollars to anyone "who will furnish me the whole quotation beginning 'I will give my body to be flayed and my skin for a bottle.' "[21] A few years later he used that line in a letter to his friend, Judge Lambert Tree.

6

Yet, effective speaker that he was, Altgeld went down to defeat in his campaign for Congress. The vote was George Adams, 18,333; Altgeld, 15,291.[22] However, it was a party defeat and not a personal one. Even Grover Cleveland lost in Chicago and Illinois, and popular Carter Harrison was defeated for governor by Richard J. Oglesby. A Republican leader in after years testified concerning Altgeld's first Chicago campaign: "He was not elected, but our executive committee was pretty badly frightened by the strong canvass he made."[23] He had made an even better showing than Lambert Tree, veteran Democrat, made two years before in the same district. And so, in defeat, he had made real political progress.

There occurred during the next month an incident which considerably elevated Altgeld in the legal world also. In October, Wilbur F. Storey, the great Democratic editor of the Chicago *Times*, died. He left an estate worth more than a million dollars, including the *Times* property. Two wills were produced, and their existence brought litigation which became a *cause célèbre* of the period. Some of Chicago's most prominent lawyers participated, including Senator Lyman Trumbull, Wirt Dexter and Altgeld's friend, Goudy. On December 24, 1884, Altgeld appeared in the case as counsel for one of the principal litigants, Mrs. Mary Farrand, sister of the editor, who was one of the claimants to the estate. He filed a motion that produced what the newspapers called a sensation. Originally, Mrs. Farrand had asked the court to sustain her brother's first will. The case had revolved around that request. But when Altgeld appeared as her lawyer, he withdrew her request, for a highly technical reason.

"A thunderbolt fell upon the court . . . by the sudden stepping forward of Mr. Altgeld. . . . Mr. Goudy gasped for breath. . . . Judge Trumbull . . . said that he and his associates were taken completely by surprise, but he supposed it was some 'thimble-rigging.' . . . The court was filled with lawyers from contiguous courts who heard of [Altgeld's] motion and came to gain some information as to the truth."[24]

So the *Tribune* described the scene. The same lawyers who had been fighting Mrs. Farrand's original request now opposed her change of front, for Altgeld had seen a point they had overlooked. The other lawyers fought his motion bitterly, but Altgeld carried his point to the Illinois Supreme Court and was victorious over the best-known lawyers in the city.[25]

There is mystery in this somewhere.

Was it the hand of Goudy in Altgeld's career again? Obviously Altgeld's legal reputation up to this point did not warrant his selection as counsel for Mrs. Farrand in so important a case. In 1892, when Altgeld's rise in the political world was under general discussion, newspapers observed that he was boosted along the political route "by W. C. Goudy, partly as a reward for taking part in the Storey will case."[26] The inference was that Goudy, who represented Storey's brother, Anson, had private reasons for wishing Mrs. Farrand to be represented by a lawyer whom Goudy knew, although ostensibly Goudy was on the other side. If that were true, there arises suspicion that Altgeld may not have been acting entirely in accord with the highest ethics of legal practice. Yet no one on the other side, as bitterly as they fought his actions, charged any breach of ethics. Be that as it may, Altgeld was moving on.

7

Within a few months after his appearance in the Storey case there came further striking evidence of Altgeld's truly phenomenal rise as a political factor in Chicago and the state of Illinois. In January, 1885, the State Assembly met to elect a United States senator. It happened that the membership of the legislature was divided exactly even between Democrats and Republicans. From the middle of February to the middle of May the assembly was deadlocked. Scenes were enacted which, in the words of one member, were "more befitting a street mob than a deliberative body." It was the most exciting political incident of the 'eighties.

In Chicago, Altgeld had been scanning the newspaper reports of the struggle. He saw that the Democrats in the legislature were hopelessly split in their choice between Mayor Carter Harrison and Congressman William R. Morrison of Waterloo, Illinois. The Republicans were standing solidly behind General John A. Logan, but unless at least one vote could be obtained for him from the Democratic ranks they could not elect a senator either. After some weeks, there seemed a chance to cause one or two Republican legislators—men elected with Granger support—to break away from Logan if some Democrat were put up who represented the Granger idea. Neither Carter Harrison nor "Horizontal Bill" Morrison came up to that specification. A daring idea came to Altgeld. With his Granger background in Missouri, was he not exactly the man?

Without confiding his plans to anyone, he impulsively journeyed to Springfield. In doing so, he gave up an opportunity to preside at a meeting in Chicago that had been called by various labor groups to discuss labor legislation.[27] That occasion was to have been his formal introduction to the labor world, but he decided this could wait until another time. On May 14, the results of his journey became tangible. When the 109th ballot for United States senator was taken, two votes were cast for a new Democratic candidate. The new man was Altgeld, spelled "Altgeldt" in the official records.[28] That evening the Democratic legislators went into a caucus at the St. Nicholas Hotel in an effort to agree upon a compromise choice in place of either Carter Harrison or Morrison. A list of twelve possibilities was agreed upon, these to be voted on in the order of their listing until one was elected. In effect, that list was a "Who's Who" of the leading Democrats of Illinois. And Altgeld was fourth on the list,[29] coming ahead of

Governor John M. Palmer and Melville W. Fuller, who in a little while was appointed chief justice of the United States. In the end, because a Democratic legislator died and was replaced by a Republican, General Logan was elected. Though this was a defeat for the Democrats, for Altgeld it had been another personal triumph. The Chicago politician now had arrived.

BOOK THREE

THE BOMB

CHAPTER EIGHT

The Gathering Storm

1

As ALTGELD stood on the threshold of a promising public career in those early 'eighties, storm clouds of a new agitation had gathered over the nation, and more particularly over Chicago. The symptoms were similar to those of the Abolition fever that had marked his boyhood. It was the labor question now, one in which Altgeld would be tremendously involved. This question had simmered as a major problem ever since the riots of 1877. Specifically, it was concerned with wage scales, working conditions and the problem of mass displacement of manual workers by machines. But broadly it was a matter of adjusting a new economic system to American democratic ideals.

Had there then existed in America men of statesmanship in places of political power, much could probably have been done with effect to forestall or cushion later explosions in the Capital versus Labor struggle. America then was in a position to examine the problem clearly. Men and groups had not yet taken definite stands. There was opportunity for free action of the national genius for democracy and fair play. And mass opinion, insofar as it can be reconstructed today, was all for applying American democratic standards to industry. But the best in statesmanship that the country had at that crucial period was Grover Cleveland, and his qualities must be put down even by admirers as largely negative. He was outstanding, but mainly because he was not a boodler, not a spoilsman, not a self-seeking politician of the Tammany type. Aside from utterance of phrases such as "the communism of pelf," there is little in Cleveland's record to show that he recognized the emergence of a new era, or the necessity for new viewpoints if the spirit of American democracy was to be maintained in the new order. The result was national drifting on social questions, except that feudal-minded industrialists became entrenched, and, largely through propaganda, there became imbedded in the American mind the idea that governmental or other action to ameliorate certain effects of so-called natural economic laws was "un-American."

2

Meantime, labor in the 'eighties roused itself from the shell-shocked
meekness into which it had been hurled by the vigorous suppression
of the strikes and riots in '77. Strikes again became numerous, but
mainly without the foolhardy, desperate fury that marked the '77 epidemic. Fraternal organizations for workers, such as the Knights of
Labor and the Knights of St. Crispin, and also trade unions, showed
marked increase in membership. Another development was the remarkable hold that socialism had upon the workers. Never before, nor
since, has this doctrine of a New Society had so many converts among
the American laboring masses, both native and foreign-born.

In Chicago, affording Altgeld a first-hand acquaintance with this
development, the socialists achieved the strongest movement in the
country. They became real factors in city politics despite assurances
of the *Tribune* that to be a socialist is equivalent to being "a lazy
lout . . . a pestilent petrifaction, a long-haired, brawling idiot."[1] They
elected aldermen and state legislators, four of the latter in 1878 alone,
and by 1879 became a threat in the mayoralty race, with a well-to-do
physician, Dr. Ernst Schmidt, heading the ticket.

A word about these socialists. Despite the editorials in the *Tribune*,
most of them were sober-minded citizens. In the main, they believed
in "evolutionary socialism." The principal planks in their platform for
the 1879 election in Chicago were: a clean city; sanitary inspection of
food, dwellings, factories and workshops; establishment of public
baths, fixed salaries for city officials and "not a dollar of taxes to be expended until it is collected."

To be sure, there were avowed "direct actionists" in the movement.
In a little while some of them would swing from socialism to anarchism as they came to believe, because of the rôle of the national troops,
state militia and city police in the '77 strikes, that all agencies of government were against the working classes. But these direct-action revolutionists were exceedingly few.

3

However, because in time Altgeld would find his career enmeshed
in results of their activities, it is necessary despite their numerical un-
importance to give attention to the high-strung revolutionary socialists
who were present in Chicago. Intense, noisy, as zealous and indus-

trious in their propagandizing as Paul of Tarsus (and as certain of their rectitude), they were undismayed that scarcely more than fifty or seventy-five "wage-slaves" attended their "mass-meetings." The revolution was coming. They were certain of that. It was not they who would bring it. The "system" would bring it. All they were doing was to "prepare" the workers for the inevitable. So they thought. To their imaginative minds every clubbing by the police—"bloodhounds," they called them—brought the overturning a step nearer. The barking of militia rifles made it only a matter of hours or days.

Very early the agitators made a discovery. The wilder they talked, the more publicity they obtained for the "cause" in the established newspapers. Doubtless because of a general anti-labor bias, editors like Joseph Medill and Wilbur F. Storey went out of their way to play up the activities of the little band of extremists, with emphasis upon their wilder statements. Thus the names of August Spies, editor of the anarchist *Arbeiter-Zeitung*, Albert R. Parsons, editor of the anarchist *Alarm*, Samuel Fielden and a few others became household words in Chicago. They stood for blood and thunder, ruin and revolution. There is reason to believe that the attention paid these men by the press had the effect on some of turning their heads. August Spies, for one, enjoyed being pointed out as "the prominent anarchist."[2]

Some of these men developed a twisted sense of humor. Their idea of a colossal joke, cause for guffawing and self-congratulations over beer-mugs, was to scare some "capitalistic hireling" out of his wits with Bunyanish tales of preparations they claimed were laid for revolution. They spoke of "thousands of communists under arms," dilated on horror tales of the Paris Commune, and predicted the same would happen in Chicago—"only worse." Newspaper reporters were favorite butts for such comic sallies. And the jokers rejoiced when their wild tales appeared in the newspapers under blood-curdling headlines. In time the editors came to know that the brash, horrifying boasts of the revolutionaries were mainly nonsense.

"Never were men more willing to give information . . . and the stories they told as to [their] strength were truly astonishing. The younger reporters took everything down on paper, and if older and better posted hands at their respective offices did not revise their copy carefully, the people of Chicago would be treated to some astonishing revelations. . . . The information was purposely exaggerated, and when those reporters left, there was a hearty laugh at the ease with which they were filled full of chaff."[3]

So the *Tribune* reported on statements made at a gathering of radicals in March, 1879. Yet the *Tribune* and other papers never failed to give conspicuous display to the wild statements. Especially was this so when strikes occurred. As early as May, 1878, one Edward Nye, a sober-minded socialist, protested to the papers against their habit of portraying working-class movements in terms of violent deeds and even more violent talk. "If the . . . unfair way of giving reports about the doings and aims of the 'communists' has been decided on for side purposes, it should not be persisted in. . . . It is high time that the intelligent newspaper should talk about this serious matter in a more intelligent way. We have had enough of this nonsense. Let us have reasoning."[4]

But the nonsense continued, on both sides—until Haymarket.

4

It must be recognized that if some of the firebrand agitators impressed one as strutting proletarian peacocks given to exaggeration and whipped-up emotion, nevertheless they were sincere in their feelings for the working class. They suffered ten times the pangs of the actual victims over miserable working conditions and the all-too-frequent atrocities committed in the name of law and order. They brooded over skull clubbings, shootings, lockouts to enforce lower wages and the ill-concealed hatred that conspicuous industrialists and the newspapers felt for the labor movement.

And many were the incidents to give these sensitive men cause for brooding. The wholesale hangings of the "Molly Maguires" in the Pennsylvania coal district, the New York police massacre of unemployed in Tompkins Square, ruthless shooting of striking miners in the Hocking Valley and at Cripple Creek, Colorado, these were among episodes on the national scene that grated on them and ate at their hearts. Close at home, in Illinois, in and near Chicago, the period witnessed a succession of shocking episodes. Workingmen—they were called "rioters"—were shot down by militiamen with appalling frequency in the Illinois coal mines at and near La Salle, Virden, and Braidwood.

At Spring Valley, Illinois, there was enacted an incredible drama of "man's inhumanity to man," one that prompted Henry Demarest Lloyd, soon to be Altgeld's friend, to dip his pen in horror and tears to write his unanswerable *The Strike of the Millionaires against the*

Miners. It was the pitiful story of several thousand native-born workers who had been induced to come to the mining town by a corporation owned solely by eastern capitalists. When wage trouble developed, the absentee owners ruthlessly ordered all of the native-born employes locked out and imported cheap foreign labor to man the pits. Desolation of the entire community was complete—and no appeals for humanity or fair play moved the owners to recede from their policy of brutal feudalism. In time Altgeld would have something to say about Spring Valley.

At East St. Louis in 1885 occurred another incident that supplied agitators with inflaming material. When a switchmen's strike was in progress, a railroad corporation imported thugs from Kentucky, Mississippi and Texas to guard their property, i. e., to break the strike. These strikebreakers were made deputy sheriffs. Without apparent provocation, they fired upon a crowd of strikers and citizen sympathizers, killing several and wounding many. Outraged public opinion finally compelled the arrest of the thugs for murder, but the courts and grand jury of St. Clair county refused to try them.[5] That same year a counterpart of the East St. Louis incident occurred in Chicago, one involving Pinkertons hired at McCormick's on account of a strike. Hooted by a crowd, the Pinkertons answered the catcalls with bullets. Death to several bystanders resulted. "The prosecuting officers apparently took no interest in the case, and allowed it to be continued a number of times, until the witnesses were sworn out, and in the end the murderers went free." This was Altgeld's summary some years later.[6]

More maddening to the workers was the rôle played at times by certain of the city police in Chicago during strikes. During a street-car strike in 1885 not only were strikers clubbed right and left, regardless of whether they engaged in riots, but non-striking workers and even businessmen who happened to be in the strike zone were similarly treated. Police Inspector John Bonfield—of whom much more will be heard in connection with Haymarket—was the leader in that kind of police conduct. Obviously sadistic, he not only gave the orders for ruthless brutality, but cracked skulls himself on the slightest or no provocation. Unimpeachable evidence, in the form of sworn affidavits presented not by "radicals" but by businessmen, supports that characterization of Bonfield.[7] Not all the Chicago police were like Bonfield, but he was permitted to typify the department in its attitude toward labor. The workers cursed him as "Black" Bonfield. Doubtless some plotted revenge as they nursed cracked skulls.

5

Then, there was the state militia. Typical of their use in labor troubles was the incident in 1885 when quarry workers at Lemont, a Chicago suburb, staged a walkout against a pay reduction. There were the usual clashes. The militia sent by the well-meaning but con-fused Governor Richard Oglesby shot and killed two strikers before it was over.

The business element applauded, for many men of large business holdings had come to feel that state troops had no other function than to take their side in times of strikes. When the radical agitators heard of the Lemont affair they let loose a typical outburst of wild oratory. The *Tribune* quoted "Citizeness" Parsons, meaning Albert Parsons' dark-complexioned wife, Lucy, as orating:

"Let every dirty, lousy tramp arm himself with a revolver or knife and lay in wait on the steps of the palaces of the rich and stab or shoot the owners as they come out. Let us kill them without mercy, and let it be a war of extermination and without pity. Let us devastate the avenues where the wealthy live as Sheridan devastated the beautiful valley of the Shenandoah."[8]

Lucy would pay dearly for such hot oratory—if those were her words, and they very probably were. So also her husband and August Spies who spoke similarly at the same protest gathering. Only a rabid revo-lutionist could condone such extravagance as that indulged in by Lucy Parsons and her comrades.

But what was to be said for the utterances by spokesmen for the other side? As published week after week in *The Socialist*, the utter-ances of spokesmen for capital included:

"Give them [strikers] the rifle diet for a few days and see how they like that kind of bread."—Tom Scott, *Eastern Industrialist*.

"These brutal creatures can understand no other reasoning than that of force and enough of it to be remembered among them for many generations."—New York *Tribune*.

"If the workingmen had no vote they might be more amenable to the teachings of the times."—Indianapolis *News*.

And this from Storey's Chicago *Times* with reference to a strike among sailors of the Great Lakes:

"Hand-grenades should be thrown among those union sailors . . . as by such treatment they would be taught a valuable lesson, and other strikers could take warning from their fate."

And this concerning unemployed workers by a certain Mary A. Livermore, a lecturer much in demand by women's clubs:

"Owing to the lack of training for the forearm and fingers a large share of the community suffers from tramps. Tramps have no claim on human sympathy. When they invade my house and ask for bread, I bid them begone, without ceremony. The hand of society must be against these vagrants; they must die off, and the sooner they are dead and buried the better for society."[9]

Obviously neither side had a monopoly on violent expression in this battle of words. It would get hotter. In the middle 'eighties the belligerents in the labor front added to their linguistic weapons a new and fearful word: Dynamite.

"Of all the good stuff, this is the stuff! In giving dynamite to the down-trodden millions of the globe, science has done its best work. The dear stuff can be carried around in the pocket without danger, while it is a formidable weapon against any force of militia, police or detectives . . . a genuine boon for the disinherited. . . ."

So an Indianapolis agitator, one T. Lizius, wrote in an article contributed to The Alarm in Chicago.[10] With crazy journalistic indiscretion, his insanity was printed, as were other articles like it. Trouble ahead!

6

Unfortunately, some of the radicals let their sense of humor operate in the matter of dynamite too. There was, for example, August Spies' little joke on the reporter of the Daily News in January, 1886, five months before Haymarket. He gave the reporter the shell of a bomb. Take it, he said, to your boss and tell him we have nine thousand more like it—only loaded. Spies enjoyed hugely his vision of how the reporter's boss, Melville E. Stone, would react. Unfortunately for Spies, Stone had no comparable sense of the comic.[11]

Even more humorless were the Fields, the McCormicks, the Armours, the Pullmans and the Medills. They really believed, apparently, that they were the salt of the earth and that laborers, especially the immigrants, were the dregs. They appeared to see the hand of God in that, sincerely so. An Omniscient Providence had selected them to create a new ruling class—within the limits of the democratic amenities, of course. They believed, honestly, too, that patriotism was synonymous with approval of their business methods, hence criticism of their policies was un-American per se and dangerous. Joseph Medill was considered by them a modern Jeremiah, the editorials in his *Tribune* revealed truth.

In short, not all the foolish men in Chicago were named Spies, or were to be found in Neff's Saloon, Grief's Hall or other working-class rendezvous. Nor were all the agitators in the dingy offices of the miserable socialist and anarchist newspapers. A study of the files of the *Tribune*, *Times* and the other Chicago papers would reveal utterances just as inflammatory, in their way, as the radicals' insane scribblings about dynamite. Strikes were unpatriotic and revolutionary. All advocates of social and economic reform were communists intent upon destroying American institutions. Socialism, if not the labor movement as a whole, was synonymous with nihilism and anarchism. The unemployed, if they bore foreign names, were "European scum." If Americans, they were tramps, bummers and loafers. Discontented workingmen had no real grievances, but were dupes of foreign agitators or American knaves. The solution was clear. Deport the foreign scum and rabble-rousers, suppress the home-grown variety, if necessary by liberal use of Gatling guns and the gallows.

7

This constant fanning of class prejudices from both extremes made Chicago beneath its outward calm a cauldron. Both sides anticipated an "incident." The revolutionaries expected one to touch off the uprising. The reactionaries prepared for it as a signal to carry out—legally, of course—the ideas in Joseph Medill's editorials about "communistic carcasses decorating the lamp-posts of Chicago."[12] There was a sort of fatalism about it. Not many persons remained aloof.

CHAPTER NINE

"Our Penal Machinery and Its Victims"

1

YET Altgeld during that fermenting of the labor question in the early 'eighties did remain noticeably aloof insofar as his public conduct gives any clue. Certainly he was no active labor partisan. Other lawyers inserted their "cards" in the various labor and socialistic papers, but not Altgeld. Certain lawyers, some who later founded legal dynasties of the purest respectability and conservatism, were candidates for office on the tickets of the "Workingmen's Party" or the "Socialistic Labor Party," but not Altgeld. He was neither retained, nor, apparently, did he seek to be retained, as counsel in the various labor lawsuits which developed from time to time. In fact, he so conducted himself that it was possible for a political story fifteen years or so later to contain the assertion: "He has never had any affiliation, or even acquaintance, with labor leaders, and never attended any of their meetings."[1] That statement was not completely accurate but was true enough.

It would be apparent soon that he was keenly interested in police conduct toward the poor and the helpless. Yet, while officers like Bonfield overstepped the bounds of law and decency in clubbing, shooting, or rough-housing strikers and labor agitators or those simply suspected of being disturbers in industrial disputes, he remained silent. Few men were as consciously sensitive concerning a foreign heritage and name. He resented deeply the aspersions cast upon the foreign-born population. The columns of the *Tribune* and the *Times* were filled day after day with cruel and senseless attacks upon the foreign-born. A "communist" was always a "*German* communist." Strikers and labor demonstrators were always mobs composed of "*foreign scum, beer-smelling Germans, ignorant Bohemians, uncouth Poles, wild-eyed Russians.*" But during the worst period of such outbursts Altgeld said nothing.

2

If one knew nothing else about him, it might be concluded that

Altgeld kept silent because all his truly close associates sided with the class that looked down upon labor and "foreign scum." Corporation lawyers, bankers, old-line politicians who bore such "American" names as Brown, Goudy, Peckham, Shepard, Tree and Martin, these composed his circle. They considered him one of their own, and with reason.

In less than ten years' residence in Chicago, he had demonstrated a capitalistic acquisitiveness and acumen which the most ardent worshiper of "Success" could admire. His professional conduct met with exactness such standards as existed among the so-called "upper tenth." A combing of his professional career would reveal nothing "erratic" such as defending socialists or attempting to upset important legal principles. On the contrary, his practice was as conservative, if not as lucrative, as that of the attorneys for Marshall Field himself. Certainly his appearance in the Storey case stamped him as a safe and sound member of the bar.

His personal manners were also above suspicion. If his bearded face had a foreign aspect and his name sounded much like those of prominent socialists—Altpeter, a socialist candidate for alderman, for instance—his quiet way of speaking and his habit of calm discussion of current affairs, his evident devotion to the altar of private initiative and to the American exaltation of personal success, would have dispelled any doubts on that score. True, investigation would show that he specified the use of union labor for all his construction jobs, but that did not necessarily mean that he held any alarming sympathy for labor organizations. Even Jay Gould "recognized" the Knights of Labor—when he could not get away from it, as in the case of the Western Union telegraphers.

3

In politics, Altgeld inspired the same kind of confidence among the solid, practical elements. He gave the impression of being as safe and sound as Grover Cleveland, as regular as Carter Harrison, as shrewd as Lawyer Goudy or even Michael Cassius McDonald himself. In his congressional campaign he had voiced no ideas that even Democrats like Marshall Field, Potter Palmer and Cyrus McCormick could not have endorsed. He appeared as much a "Bourbon" as they, as he had been in Missouri before the Granger campaign. Probably he never mentioned bolting the party in Savannah, or his Grangerish speeches there.

As a matter of fact, labor, rather than capital, had cause to suspect him, if either side did. Had he not been a political protégé of the irascible old labor-hater, Wilbur F. Storey? Not even Joseph Medill of the *Tribune* attacked labor unions, let alone socialists, so violently as the publisher of the *Times* who called unions "strike societies" and labor unrest "strike distemper." Storey originated one of the earliest yellow-dog labor contracts, and at a public meeting Chicago workers adopted a resolution lambasting him as "not even a decent representative of the capitalistic element," a reference to his septuagenarian *affaires d'amour.* And this was the man who gave Altgeld his chief newspaper support in his congressional campaign and under whose patronage he basked more than once!

Yet his pinched beginnings, the childhood pangs, the early struggles that he endured, the gibes over his German name and appearance, these things were influencing him, perhaps more than even he realized. The first clear evidence of this came in the fall of 1884 in the form of a book over which he must have been laboring at the very time he seemed completely occupied with his ambitions of power, prominence and wealth. By peculiar timing, public announcement of his book was made on the same day he won the congressional nomination. It was entitled *Our Penal Machinery and Its Victims.*[2] In its 151 pages are to be found clear forecasts of nearly all of the later Altgeldian character.

The general thesis of the book was a plea that society get at the causes of crime rather than simply be concerned with punishing wrongdoers. Altgeld strongly felt that the penal machinery should attempt to cure and redeem instead of merely punish. He was especially interested in the plight of young people, noting that a large proportion of lawbreakers or alleged lawbreakers were young men and girls. He vigorously deplored brutal treatment of prisoners. He did not touch upon the labor question as such, except for brief references to the problem of convict labor, but underlying his composition were clear reflections of an awareness, like Henry George's, of the existence of poverty and the effects of maldistribution of wealth. But the most significant aspect of the book was its reflection of the author's profound interest in the under-dog.

4

He raised almost at the beginning the question as to the economic group with which the police and prison authorities are concerned. "Is it composed," he inquired, "of the strong, the well-raised, well-trained, well-housed and well-fed class, and must it therefore be regarded as wilfully criminal? Or is it largely made up of the poor, the unfortunate, the squalid and those who are victims of their environment?"

His answer was: "The truth is that the great multitudes annually arrested . . . are the poor, the unfortunate, the young and the neglected. . . . In short, our penal machinery seems to recruit its victims from among those that are fighting an unequal fight in the struggle for existence."[3]

Touching on the problem of vagrants—the tramps for whom the Tories and their apologists suggested doses of strychnine or lead—he commented with special concern for the young, possibly recalling his own *Wanderjahre*.

"See how tenderly we care for the homeless. If a boy who has nowhere to go, when nature is exhausted, ventures to lie down in a shed, we seize him with the strong arm of the law, as if he had committed a murder, and forthwith send him to prison. . . . Would it not be madness even to imagine that any good come of this? Experience has shown over and over that just the opposite follows: that this process produces exactly those results which society is anxious to prevent."[4]

Of surpassing later significance, he directed shafts at intemperate police methods and the treatment generally accorded persons placed under arrest for minor offenses or merely suspicion. He did this, he made clear, not because he shared the feelings of radicals who called policemen "bloodhounds," but because he wanted respect for law and order. He found that thousands of citizens "without having committed any crime, were yet condemned to undergo a regular criminal experience." And the treatment accorded these persons? "Why, it was precisely the same as if they had been criminals. They were arrested, some of them clubbed, some of them hand-cuffed, marched through the streets in charge of officers, treated gruffly, jostled around. . . ." And the effect?

"Will not every one of them feel the indignity to which he or she has been subjected, while life lasts?

"Will they all not abhor the men who perpetrated what is felt to be an outrage? Will they not look on this whole machinery as their enemy and take a secret delight in seeing it thwarted?

"Will they not almost unconsciously sympathize with those that defy this whole system, and are they not thus brought a whole length nearer crime than they were before?

"And will not those that were already weak and were having a hard struggle for existence, be further weakened, and therefore more liable soon to become actual offenders than they otherwise would have been?

"Remember, *brutal treatment brutalizes* and thus prepares for crime."[5]

In a subsequent portion of the book, he returned to that theme.

"Does clubbing a man reform? Does brutal treatment elevate his thoughts? Does handcuffing fill him with good resolves?

"Every man is sensitive about the treatment of his person, and feels that he is injured when he is rudely jostled about, or forced into humiliating surroundings. . . . Will he not wish to be avenged? Will he not wish to consider this whole machinery as his foe, and will he not be more ready than ever before to commit crime, if he can but escape detection?"[6]

There would soon come an occasion when the words just noted would take on an unforeseen significance.

5

It took courage, or recklessness, for Altgeld to permit his publishers to bring that book out on the day of his nomination for Congress. Such a book contained possibilities for twisted meanings and statements wrenched from the context, leaving him open to the cry that he sympathized with criminals and lawlessness, a charge that would be made later because of his wording. But fortunately for his political standing at the time, his first literary effort went unnoticed by his political foes. And by nearly everyone else.

The *Tribune*, which might have let loose an editorial of brimstone and fire because Altgeld's ideas were contrary to the doctrines of Joseph Medill, simply listed it as a "book also received." Only Storey's *Times* reviewed it. Even this was far from flattering, for the *Times* review betrayed certain evidence of having been written under orders. It was a patronizing piece. "The author is probably something of an enthusiast on the subject he treats. . . . The purpose is good and the author has evidently worked zealously and conscientiously. . . . It cannot be denied that he has assembled an array of facts and argu-

ments calculated to surprise most readers." But as for Altgeld's conclusions, well, they seemed visionary. For one thing, "the author does
not take sufficiently into consideration the influence of heredity . . .
that certain strains of blood constantly contribute to the criminal
classes."[7]

With this solitary review a begrudging item that deprecated his
most important ideas, Altgeld had to concede that his book was
nothing to brag about in a literary way. If he depended upon popular sales to get the book known, even at the modest price of fifty
cents, he discovered early that his effort was doomed to clutter book-
dealers' bins. But he had other plans, related to his political ambitions. Copies of *Our Penal Machinery and Its Victims* began showing up in the mails in quantities calculated to excite a book agent's
envy, unless it were known that each bore the inscription: "With
the compliments of John P. Altgeld." Of public officials, clergymen,
writers and lecturers, group leaders of one kind or another of any
prominence everywhere, there were few who did not receive a copy.
He handled most of this work himself, mulling over lists of names as in-
dustriously as a mail-order advertiser. When the first edition of 5,500
copies was exhausted, he brought out a second of 5,000. They went
like the others—to get over his ideas about penal systems. And also to
get over the name Altgeld.

6

So thoroughly did he blanket the field with the book that even an
obscure police magistrate in Ashtabula, Ohio, received a copy. The
small-town dignitary passed it on to a struggling young lawyer in the
community. Years later, the recipient of the gift testified: "*Our Penal
Code* [sic] *and Its Victims*, by Judge John P. Altgeld of Chicago . . .
was a revelation to me. This book and the author came to have a
marked influence upon me and my future."[8] One reflection of that
influence was to start the young Ohio lawyer on the way to becoming
the foremost practical criminologist and legal defender of victims of
the penal system in the nation. His name was Clarence Darrow.

When the book was received by officials of the National Prison
Reform Association, Altgeld was invited to address their convention
in Detroit on October 21, 1885. This was indeed recognition, for
Benjamin Harrison, soon to be elected President of the United
States, was head of that organization. For his Detroit talk Altgeld
selected police brutality as his theme.

"As we have been trying the brute force and the crushing policy with such unsatisfactory results, let us . . . try a system of development which, while it will protect society better than the present system, will also make it at least possible for the accused to come out with more character, moral strength and self-respect than he had when taken into custody."[9]

He made a good impression in Detroit, and other invitations to speak on the subject of penology came to him. For the first time the name of Altgeld began to have meaning outside the sphere of the Chicago law courts, the real-estate field and the Democratic organization in Chicago. Now Altgeld the intellectual was coming to the fore.

7

But of all the individual results of this systematic exploitation of his book to enhance his prestige, by far the most potent in its influence upon Altgeld's career came when he sent a copy to George A. Schilling, a cooper employed by the packing firm of Libby, McNeill and Libby in Chicago. Schilling was then one of the two or three leading labor leaders in the city and Altgeld sent him the book on noting his name in the newspapers. It was a name often in the press, usually in no complimentary fashion. In the late 'seventies Schilling had been known as a "rampant socialist." During that period Samuel Fielden, of whom much will be heard later, was a protégé of Schilling, started off by the cooper on the course that made Fielden one of the most fiery of revolutionary orators.[10] But by 1884, the little cooper had cooled off considerably and had taken to admonishing his old colleagues, especially Parsons, Spies and Fielden, against the use of intemperate language. He feared something like Haymarket.

On receiving Altgeld's book, Schilling read it carefully. Much occupied then with indignation over the conduct of the Chicago police toward strikers, Schilling naturally made Altgeld's comments on police conduct apply to the labor situation. He did the same with reference to statements in the book concerning vagrants who, to Schilling, were not loafers but willing skilled and unskilled laborers displaced by the machine. He agreed, too, with Altgeld's conclusions on the class of persons commonly found in the police courts, jails and prisons. Above all, Altgeld's analysis of the effects of police brutality coincided exactly with Schilling's own observations with relation to police tactics in labor disturbances. He knew from personal observation how certain labor men felt toward all law because blue-coated Bonfields had ill-treated them for no reason except that they were workers.

He felt that his friend Parsons was one example in point. He thought that Parsons' radicalism and implacable enmity for existing authorities had its real roots in the treatment accorded him during the labor trouble of '77. For making speeches to strikers, Parsons had been arrested and bundled off to the City Hall. In the presence of the mayor, Parsons was warned that the "Board of Trade men would as leave hang you as not." The chief of police "suggested" that he leave town, then shoved him to the street to wander about, dazed, enraged and perplexed. Some thirty or forty of the best people of Chicago were present at his interview with the police and Parsons never forgot hearing them whisper: "Hang him!" "He ought to be lynched!"

And for what? he wondered. Was it a crime to stand up for the workingman?[11] He was destined to find out.

8

Schilling wondered if Altgeld did not have just such incidents in mind when he wrote his book. He felt certain that Altgeld did and so on laying down the book he commented to his wife: "This man Altgeld seems to be a sincere man. He seems to understand our problems. I would like to make his acquaintance."[12]

For Lawyer Altgeld that resolution by the little cooper held tremendous significance.

CHAPTER TEN

The Prince and the Pauper

1

Schilling met Altgeld through the offices of one Richard Corrigan, a courthouse bailiff who knew Altgeld casually among other lawyers. He found the author of *Our Penal Machinery and Its Victims* extremely pleased to meet him. In fact, Altgeld displayed such real pleasure that there is a suggestion he sensed this new acquaintanceship was more than the usual handshaking affair. He promptly insisted that Schilling lunch with him. At their first luncheon, one of many, Altgeld wanted to treat Schilling to a bottle of wine of rare vintage, but the labor leader insisted upon beer, "because a labor leader must not accept luxuries from a representative of the upper classes." That trivial Prince-and-the-Pauper incident got them off to a good start.[1]

Altgeld's political ambitions were doubtless among the reasons that prompted him to cultivate Schilling. He knew that the cooper was a key figure in Chicago labor politics and he hoped to run again for Congress. Yet something in addition to politics is needed to explain that Altgeld warmed up to Schilling more than to any other person he had met in Chicago until then. There was a striking similarity in their backgrounds. Schilling had been born of peasant parents in Germany, not far from Nieder Selters. His family migrated to Ohio when he was an infant, about the time Altgeld's family did. On reaching his majority, he drifted westward. He worked on a railroad in the same general territory Altgeld had, and about the same time. When he reached East St. Louis in his westward trek, he had fifteen cents. After a time Schilling had an unhappy love affair. The girl's father objected to him because of his poor prospects, and the subsequent jilting caused Schilling to pull up stakes for Chicago. He arrived the same year Altgeld did. When Schilling told Altgeld his life history he noticed that his friend was "enthralled." A "strange look" came into Altgeld's eyes.

"Why," exclaimed Altgeld, "you have just told the story of *my* life!"[2]

Did there pass through Altgeld's mind the thought that this labor agitator and socialist was his *possible* self, that but for accidents their places in society might have been transposed? Certainly, after meeting Schilling and being so strongly impressed by the similarities in their backgrounds, he could never again, if he ever did, share, even to a slight degree, the antipathy that some of his associates felt toward socialists and labor agitators.

2

As for Schilling, he had a reason of his own to cultivate Altgeld. He sensed a chance to make an important convert to labor's cause, certain that this serious-minded lawyer was destined to advance politically. He was greatly pleased that Altgeld displayed a keen interest in labor matters. In fact, their conversation at luncheons was devoted almost entirely to the labor question, in particular the eight-hour day movement then developing into a major issue.

From Schilling who was a key leader in the eight-hour agitation, Altgeld learned that the eight-hour campaign, which was to come to a grand climax on May 1, 1886, was a mass movement springing from the rank and file of labor. It had gained enormous momentum despite lukewarmness or even opposition by both the extreme "right" and extreme "left" leaders of labor. The rightists, represented by Terence V. Powderly, Grand Master Workman of the Knights of Labor, feared the militancy that the eight-hour slogans generated in the mass labor mind. He abhorred strikes, and he feared he would be unable to prevent the workers from resorting to strikes to enforce the eight-hour demands.[3] As for the radicals, with their dreams of revolution and a New Society, the eight-hour day demand appeared trivial. Worse, they looked upon it in the beginning as a sop thrown to the workers to keep them satisfied.

Radicals like August Spies chided Schilling about the movement. Once these two nearly came to blows in a saloon because Spies charged that Schilling was "betraying" the workers with the "eight-hour rot."[4] But when the radicals saw how deeply the laboring men everywhere were stirred—and also the bitterness with which certain industrialists opposed the movement—they climbed on the bandwagon. In part they were prompted by loyalty to labor in a fight with the common enemy. In part, too, they hoped (or some did) that just so mild a demand might bring their beloved revolution when their stronger stuff had failed. Labor leaders of Schilling's type did not know whether to be glad or sorry that the radicals became converts to the eight-hour cause.

3

Probably as a direct reflection of his discussions with Schilling, and near the climax of the eight-hour day agitation, Altgeld came out with his first public statement on labor. This was in a long essay contributed to the Chicago *Mail* on April 26, 1886.[5] It was a strong indictment of the economic waste occasioned by strikes and lockouts and a plea for peaceful settlement of labor controversies. Altgeld entitled his contribution "Protection of Non-Combatants; or, Arbitration of Strikes."

In the main, he addressed himself to the effects upon a community of strife between employers and labor. He spotlighted and explored the rôle of government in industrial disputes, a problem that would still puzzle social scientists and statesmen fifty years later—with few discussing it any more intelligently than did Altgeld in 1886. He appears to have studiously attempted to be impartial as between labor and capital. But he was certain that it was the duty of government to take a hand in industrial disputes. He never changed his mind—and in that respect he was a "radical" for his period. His solution was compulsory arbitration, with certain safeguards against abuses.

A short time before Altgeld had come out with his essay, President Cleveland had sent a message to Congress in which he dismissed compulsory arbitration as unworkable and undemocratic. He suggested voluntary arbitration instead. In disagreeing with the President, Altgeld took the position that, while compulsory arbitration suffered from certain "natural limitations," its benefits outweighed the evils which so impressed Grover Cleveland, and that, anyway, the disadvantages were largely theoretical. This, it should be noted, would not be the last time that Altgeld and Cleveland were in disagreement.

Altgeld felt that if a law for compulsory arbitration, with certain safeguards, were in effect, the disadvantages would be even less real because such a law scarcely ever would have been invoked. There was realism in this statement:

"The consciousness that arbitration can be forced upon them would induce both employer and employe to get together and to try to adjust their own differences, and this nearly always results in a settlement, the difficulty at present being that many employers will not talk with or meet their men [with the result] the employer does not understand the men, nor the men the employer, and thus trifles frequently lead to trouble when, with better understanding, they would be unnoticed."[6]

An idea of the slant of Altgeld's thinking on labor matters then is found in the essay when he undertook to discuss the results of decisions by a hypothetical arbitration board. He first discussed a decision adverse to an employer.

"Now, if [the employer] elects not to run his mill, that is the end of the matter. But if he desires to go on, then the board can require him to do so on the terms it laid down.... If he objects that he should not be interfered with in his business, it may be replied that there was no interference until there was such a condition of affairs about his premises as was injuriously affecting the good order or well-being of society. And if he objects that he should be permitted to employ whom he pleases, it may be answered that he had interfered with the natural distribution of population . . . that if he desires to make a change it must be done gradually, so that there will be no danger of the public peace being disturbed or of the public burdens being increased."

He next discussed a decision adverse to a group of striking employes.

"Now, if they all decline to go [back to work] . . . the board can not compel them. But it is scarcely necessary to consider such a contingency, for it is not likely to happen. All experience points the other way. As a rule the employes have no alternative—they have no other means of getting bread for themselves or their children. It is true that at present they sometimes hold out to the point of starvation, but this is because they have got themselves into a situation where they can not gracefully or with self-respect back down, whereas a decision of a properly constituted tribunal would help them out of this dilemma....

"Again, in nearly all cases, many of the men who first stop work are opposed to a strike, and are only deterred from resuming by fear of being expelled from their union, in which they are interested in insurance funds, benevolent funds, etc.; and if the law were to protect them against expulsion, where no other ground existed than their compliance with the award of the board, they would go to work at once.

"Further, it is worthy of note that in nearly all labor troubles in the past, it was the laboring men who were the most willing to submit to arbitration, and I believe there is not a case of this kind on record in which an arbitration was fairly entered into that the award was not promptly accepted by the men."[7]

4

It is no exaggeration to say that Altgeld, in that article, revealed himself as one of the clearest and calmest thinkers on the labor questions in the nation at that time. His position was that of an intellectually honest, alert citizen presenting what he considered a solution to a difficult problem fair to all parties, and more particularly the innocent general public. Moreover, even his later enemies could not read "demagoguery" or partisan sympathy for the working man in his article. At a time when calm, logical thought on the labor question was conspicuously absent, his contribution looms large. Few others were thinking in terms of peace or of the "non-combatants." Nearly everyone else was contributing to a tense atmosphere in labor matters that appeared to make some calamitous occurrence inevitable.

CHAPTER ELEVEN

THE BOMB

1

Such an occurrence was at hand. This was the event in Chicago on Tuesday evening, May fourth, 1886, exactly one week after Altgeld's plea for peaceful settlement of labor controversies was published. Objective historians record the event as the Haymarket "Tragedy"; others refer to it as the Haymarket "Riots" or, even more inaccurately, "The Anarchist Uprising in Haymarket Square." By whatever designation it is known, it was the most shocking and tremendous episode of that whole period of social ferment. And Altgeld was later to be involved.

The true antecedents of the Haymarket incident are found in the misunderstandings, the passions, the prejudices, the nationalistic antipathies, the inflammatory utterances of both camps in the Capital and Labor "war" that had festered in Chicago since the 'seventies, evidences of which Altgeld was able to observe when he first arrived in Chicago in 1875. It was the natural harvest of that constant sowing of seeds of hate and violence. That it occurred at the climax of the eight-hour day movement appears merely coincidental. It might have happened anyway.

2

Since the middle of April, Chicago had nervously awaited May first, "Der Tag" of the eight-hour movement. Some fifty thousand wage-workers were on strike or locked out at McCormick's, the Pullman Palace Car Corporation, the Brunswick-Bensinger billiard firm, the packing firms, lumber yards and in dozens of other industries, large and small. Encounters between strikers and city police and Pinkertons were frequent. Generally of minor import individually, these episodes in the aggregate created a charged atmosphere. Newspaper reports of violence in Cincinnati, Milwaukee, St. Louis and other cities, and also of trouble on a wide front involving the Gould Railroad system, added to the local tension.

Conspicuous preparations by the police for strike and riot duty, while doubtless necessary, had anything but a sedative effect. "The sole idea [of the police] is that there will be a great deal of trouble" so reported newspaper correspondents.[1] The state militia prepared for action and were restive in their armories. There were rumors, not entirely unfounded, that Federal troops at near-by Fort Sheridan were in readiness to march on Chicago.

In the face of these things, responsible leaders of the eight-hour agitation, including Altgeld's friend, Schilling, labored hard to keep things on an even keel. Their task was not easy, especially since the newspapers harped on the violence motif and in other ways rubbed the workers the wrong way. For example, the *Tribune* on April 26, the day Altgeld's article appeared, emitted a Know-nothing blast at participants in a parade sponsored by the Central Labor Union. "Mostly Communists. . . . Nearly All Foreigners," the *Tribune* head-lines said. "The majority were communistic Germans, Bohemians and Poles. . . . No Americans and very few, if any, Irish, Scotch, Eng-lish or Canadians." Four days later the same paper printed a scare-story about certain unions "dominated by communists." It growled editorially: "It is time some of these communistic leaders are dealt with under the conspiracy laws."

On their part, the "communists" gave considerable cause for con-cern. "Clean your guns, complete your ammunition," said the *Ar-beiter-Zeitung* on May first. "The hired murderers of the capitalists, the police and the militia, are ready to murder. No workingman should leave his house in these days empty-handed." And *The Alarm* on April 26 printed the information that handbills were distributed in Indianapolis which said: "Workingmen, to arms, peace to the cottage, and death to luxurious idleness. . . . One pound of dynamite is better than a bushel of bullets. Make your demand for eight hours with weapons in your hands, to meet the capitalistic blood-hounds, police and militia in proper manner."[2] A matter of news only?

Yet despite all the wild talk, the martial preparations and the alarums and excursions in the press, May first arrived without incident in Chicago. The next day, Sunday, was equally calm. Monday appeared destined to pass as peacefully. Early Monday afternoon newspapers assured Chicago that it could congratulate itself because the day opened with "a quietness that was a reminder of a Sunday."[3]

But, like the poor and taxes, there was always McCormick's, scene of so many clashes. A nasty collision occurred at the reaper works between union followers and McCormick "scabs." The usual catcalling and tossing of rocks took place. To the Black Road rushed police riot squads. The crowd was belligerent; the police reinforced their nightsticks with bullets. When it was over, two rioters were shot to death, although the papers at first said six and the higher figure was widely accepted.[4] The exaggerated report helped, it turned out, to make more certain the events that followed.

3

Ordinarily, the incident at McCormick's would have had no unusual consequences. Chicago was accustomed to outbreaks there. Mayor Carter Harrison, who galloped to the scene on his white steed, felt the situation was under control. He exchanged quips with a crowd in front of a saloon near by. "Hey, Carter, buy us a drink!" they called to His Honor. "Go soak your heads!" His Honor retorted, and rode away more amused than anything.[5] What gave that "normal" Black Road incident a more than ordinary significance was the sub-surface eight-hour tension and the fact that one particular man witnessed the encounter. He was August Spies.

How the editor of the *Arbeiter-Zeitung* happened to be on the scene and what part he played was at the time subject for controversy. Cyrus McCormick, son of the founder of the reaper works, asserted that Spies incited the unionists against the strike-breakers and caused the trouble. This charge was amplified by the newspapers and accepted by most Chicagoans. It was assumed that Spies went to the Black Road that afternoon to cause exactly what happened. The *Times* thundered: "The entire affair was the legitimate result of the socialistic and incendiary doctrines that have been so loudly and persistently preached by a foreign and dangerous element of the city's population." Spies and Parsons were singled out for special denunciation.[6]

The truth? Spies was near the Black Road solely by invitation of the Lumber Shovers' Union to address a meeting that had no connection with McCormick's. He did not mention the McCormick lockout, nor did he counsel violence. It is a fact that some men in his audience did participate in the riot, but he attempted to dissuade them. "You have no business over there!" he shouted. When he finally went to the scene himself, it was in his rôle of newspaper writer.[7]

In all the years that he had been ringing the welkin against police brutality toward strikers, that afternoon August Spies probably had his first experience as an eyewitness to such incidents. The sight of policemen beating and shooting at what seemed to him to be helpless men and women sickened and enraged him. He felt "very indignant" and his "blood boiled inside" as he hastened to the *Arbeiter-Zeitung* office to write up the "outrage."[8] In that state of mind he dashed off two circulars, one in English and the other in German, and gave them to his printers. When the circulars came off the press, they bore the ominous heading: "Revenge! Workingmen, to Arms!"

The English circular said, in part:

"If you are men, if you are sons of your grandsires, who have shed their blood to free you, then you will rise in your might, Hercules, and destroy the hideous monster that seeks to destroy you. To arms, we call you, to arms!"

The German version, in part:

"Annihilation to the beasts in human form, who call themselves rulers! Uncompromising annihilation to them! This must be your motto. Think of the heroes whose blood has fertilized the road to progress, liberty and humanity, and strive to become worthy of them!"

"Your Brothers" was the signature on the circulars. "After the style," commented the *Tribune*, "of the anonymous circulars which have preceded many revolutions in Europe."[9]

4

That evening a man on horseback, never identified, was seen galloping through the West Side. He carried bundles of Spies' circulars and dropped them off near saloons and working-class halls, then disappeared "without anyone knowing from whence he had come or where he went."

Yet inflammatory in phraseology as they were, Spies' circulars failed to rouse Chicago's workers to revolution—assuming that was the purpose. While not denying the authorship, Spies himself later said that he had no clear idea why he wrote them. "I did not want them [the workers] to do anything in particular. I did not want them to do anything. That I called them to arms is a phrase, probably an extravagance. . . . I called upon them to arm themselves, not for the purpose of resisting the lawfully constituted authorities . . . but for the purpose of resisting the unlawful attacks of the police. . . ."[10]

His vagueness was not affected. Only modern psychology, perhaps, could explain his motives.

In the article he wrote immediately afterward for his newspaper, Spies was no more discreet.

"The massacre of yesterday took place in order to fill the forty-thousand workmen of this city with fear and terror—took place in order to force back into the yoke of slavery the laborers who had become dissatisfied and mutinous. Will they succeed in this? Will they not find, at last, that they miscalculated? The near future will answer this question. We will not anticipate the course of events, with surmises. . . ."

Then he really warmed up to his story.

"Wage workers, yesterday the police of this city murdered, at the McCormick factory, so far as it can now be ascertained, four of your brothers. . . . If brothers who defended themselves with stones, (a few of them had little snappers in the shape of revolvers) had been provided with good weapons and *one single dynamite bomb* [italics supplied] not one of the murderers would have escaped his well-merited fate. As it was, only four of them were disfigured. That is too bad."[11]

That reference to "one single dynamite bomb" helped as much as anything to seal the doom of Spies. It would be no excuse in the eyes of those who judged him that he was over-excited, emotionally unstrung. He calmed down considerably by the next morning, so much so that when he was shown another circular, written by Adolph Fischer, he objected to a line that read: "Workingmen, Arm Yourselves and Appear in Full Force!" [12]

But his cooling off came too late.

5

That other circular that Spies found too violent was prepared to call a mass meeting for Haymarket Square "to denounce the latest atrocious act of the police, the shooting of our fellow-workmen yesterday afternoon." Plans for the Haymarket meeting were made at a meeting of radicals in the basement of Grief's Hall on Monday night. It was a meeting that later would be referred to in the records as the "Monday night conspiracy," with what went on there painted in the darkest hues, and reasonably so. Unquestionably, there was talk Monday night of resisting the police—and talk of bombs. George Engel presented a "plan"—so testified Godfried Waller, a Swiss cabinet-maker who presided at the gathering. He told of it as a witness for the state against the Haymarket defendants, and he was not refuted.

"A committee should observe the movement in the city [related Waller] and if a conflict should occur, the committee should report and we should first storm the police stations by throwing a bomb and should shoot down everything that would come out and whatever would come in our way we should strike down. . . . We discussed about why the police stations should be attacked; several persons said we have seen how the capitalists and the police oppressed the workingmen, and we should commence to take the rights in our own hands; by attacking the stations we would prevent the police coming to aid; the plan stated by Engel was adopted by us with the understanding that every group ought to act independently according to the general plan. . . .
"If a conflict happened in the daytime, they should cause publication of the word 'Ruhe.' If at night, they should report to the members personally at their homes. . . . It [the word Ruhe] should be inserted in the paper only if a downright revolution had occurred. Fischer first mentioned the word Ruhe. . . . Engel moved that the plan be adopted; the motion was seconded, and I put it to vote."[13]

The police, prosecuting authorities and the Illinois Supreme Court professed to believe that Engel's "plan" as thus outlined actually was carried out the next evening. Certain distinct variations between the "plan" and actual happenings were dismissed as immaterial. For example, it was deemed irrelevant that the word "Ruhe" appeared in the Arbeiter-Zeitung on the afternoon of May fourth even though no conflict in the daytime took place and in violation of the resolution that it appear "only if a downright revolution occurred."
But it did appear, and the printer's copy was in August Spies' hand.[14]
There was mystery about that. Spies insisted he had been handed a sheet of paper with that word written on it, and believing it a sort of "personal advertisement," copied it in his own handwriting in his customary manner for the printers, without knowing its significance. Could an agent provocateur have entered the drama at that point? This was not beyond the realm of possibility, for the Monday night meeting was open to anyone who cared to come and it is known that agents provocateurs did attend such meetings.[15]

However, such doubt-producing possibilities would not be considered, rightly or wrongly. The reasoning was: "A plan for the perpetration of a crime . . . cannot always be executed in exact accordance with the original conception. It must suffer some change or modification in order to meet emergencies and unforeseen contingencies."[16] So the Illinois Supreme Court.

Whether or not that reasoning applied beyond reasonable doubt to Haymarket was a vital question, one never yet answered. In telling of the "plan" Waller, the state's own witness, had something to say that seemingly worked against the theory of the court.

"There was nothing said about the Haymarket. There was nothing expected that the police would get to the Haymarket. Only if strikers were attacked, we should strike down the police, however best we could, with bombs or whatever would be at our disposition."[17]

What, then, was the purpose of the Haymarket meeting in the minds of the "conspirators"? It was, stated Waller, "to cheer up the workingmen so they should be prepared, *in case a conflict would happen."*

6

The promoters of the Haymarket meeting expected at least twenty-five thousand workingmen to turn out—a gathering comparable to those during the '77 riots. They were disappointed. The highest estimate of the actual crowd at its peak was three thousand. During the meeting proper not more than one thousand were on hand, many having left because the speaking was an hour in getting started. Because of the slim turnout it was decided to change the site from Haymarket proper to the mouth of Crane's alley, a half block away. A wagon found there was used for a speaking stand.

Throughout the speaking, the demeanor of the crowd was orderly. G. P. English, a veteran *Tribune* reporter, testified under oath that such was the case. He related:

"As to the temper of the crowd, it was just an ordinary meeting. It was a peaceable and quiet meeting. . . . I didn't see any turbulence. I was there all the time. I thought the speeches they made that night were a little milder than I heard them make for years. They were all set speeches. . . . I didn't hear any of them say or advise that they were going to use force that night."[18]

Mayor Harrison was present for most of the meeting. He walked through the crowd, sized up the people, and listened to the speeches by Spies and Parsons. He concluded that "nothing had occurred yet, or looked likely to occur to require interference." He so advised Police Inspector John Bonfield at the near-by Desplaines Street station house. The Mayor suggested that the large force of police reserves concentrated there be sent home. Bonfield at first professed to agree, then ventured that he had heard of an attack to be made—not at Haymarket—but at the Chicago, St. Paul and Milwaukee Railroad depot. He thought it might be better to keep the police on hand for that last emergency. The Mayor was persuaded as to the wisdom of that and went home, unworried.[19]

By ten in the evening, after August Spies and Albert Parsons had finished speaking and while Samuel Fielden was winding up the final talk, the gathering at Crane's alley was close to breaking up because of a threatening storm. Not more than two hundred persons were now on hand.[20] And these included newspaper reporters, plainclothes city policemen, Pinkertons and the simply curious. Indeed, the word was given for adjournment. If the meeting had adjourned a minute or two earlier, or if rain clouds had carried out their threat, the gathering would have been just another of a long series of meetings to which Chicago had been accustomed to give scarcely a moment's thought, except when the red-baiting newspapers built them up.

But history was destined to be made that night. An eerie black cloud appeared over the gathering, accompanied by a cold wind that struck the faces of the people with unusual force.[21] For a mild May evening, this was a strange natural phenomenon. A sign?

7

Almost on the instant that the cloud appeared, Police Inspector John Bonfield at the Desplaines Street station gave the order for his subordinates to march on the meeting. It was a strange order in view of the Inspector's conversation with the Mayor, unless certain facts concerning Bonfield in addition to those already known about him are taken into consideration. For some days that police official obviously had been chafing under the policy of restraint and caution urged by Mayor Harrison. Bonfield's attitude was amply attested at a meeting of ranking police officers—a "council of war," the press called it—on the afternoon of May fourth. General Superintendent of Police Frederick Ebersold and nearly every other commanding officer favored a policy of watchful waiting. But "Inspector Bonfield thought that vigorous measures should be adopted, and was willing to be on hand to see that they were carried out at all times."[22] So the *Daily News* reported *before* Haymarket.

There is evidence, too, that while seeming to assent finally to the police department policy and to Mayor Harrison, Bonfield had deliberate mental reservations. On the witness stand weeks later he would maintain that he acted because he was advised that intolerable language was being used at the meeting. Yet the *Times* on May fifth quoted him as saying that when he learned of the plans for the Haymarket meeting the afternoon before, he had "resolved to disperse it." This advance determination by Bonfield appears confirmed by the official report of Police Lieutenant E. J. Steele which said: "The entire force present was informed that an *unlawful* meeting was about to be held on Desplaines Street near Randolph Street, with orders to *prohibit* same and if not complied with, to *disperse* said meeting."[23]

In short, Bonfield had pre-judged the Haymarket meeting and planned in advance the action that he took.

8

Samuel Fielden was nearly done with his speech when Bonfield did go into action. Fielden's voice was booming. "The people are trying to get information. . . ." Then suddenly the rays of a street light revealed an amazing sight. One hundred and eighty-six uniformed men were marching, military style, toward the gathering. The voice of Police Captain William Ward was heard. "I command you, in the name of the people of the state of Illinois, to immediately and peacefully disperse!"

For a split second the people around the wagon appeared transfixed. Later the authorities would make the point that the immobility of the crowd in face of the oncoming police denoted a conspiratorial frame of mind "because the usual crowd separates or runs when the police appears." The truer explanation undoubtedly was that they were amazed and bewildered at seeing the police arrive at such a time, when they were all getting ready to leave anyway.

"But we are peaceable!" Sam Fielden gasped.

It was amply proved that Fielden did not say, "Here come the bloodhounds now—you do your duty and I'll do mine!" as certain policemen later testified.[24]

At the next instant there was heard "a fiendish, defiant cry."[25] Then in mid-air there sputtered an object that everyone took for a firecracker.

The Haymarket bomb had been thrown.

CHAPTER TWELVE

November 11, 1887

1

For once pandemonium was exactly the word to describe the scene during the quarter hour after the explosion and before all the civilians had fled and the police had re-formed their shattered lines.

"Immediately after the explosion [the *Tribune* related the next morning] the police pulled their revolvers and fired on the crowd. An incessant fire was kept up for nearly two minutes, and at least 250 shots were fired. The air was filled with bullets. The crowd ran up the streets and alleys and were fired on by the now thoroughly enraged police. . . .

"When the firing had stopped, the air was filled with groans and shrieks. 'O God! I'm shot!' 'Please take me home.' 'Take me to the hospital.' And similar such entreaties were heard all over within a radius of a block of the field of battle. Men were seen limping into drug stores or saloons or crawling on their hands. . . . The open doorways and saloons in the immediate vicinity were crowded with men. Some jumped over tables and chairs, barricading themselves behind them; others crouched behind walls, counters, doorways and empty barrels. For a few minutes after the shooting nobody ventured out on the street. The big bell in the police station tower tolled out a riot alarm. . . . It was a common spectacle to see men having their wounds dressed on the sidewalk.

"Goaded to madness, the police were in that condition of mind which permitted of no resistance, and in a measure they were as dangerous as any mob of Communists, for they were blinded by passion and unable to distinguish between the peaceable citizen and the Nihilist assassin. . . ."[1]

At least on that nightmarish night the police had reason enough for their frenzied deportment. They had encountered, as the *Tribune* headlined it, "A Horrible Deed," directed at themselves. Seven of their number had been fatally wounded. One of these, Officer Mathias J. Degan, lay dead on the spot. Sixty-seven other officers had wounds.

A word about those wounds. Many of them would represent not the least mysterious aspect of the whole affair, for, while many were caused by the bomb, dozens were the result of bullets. Was it true, then, that the workers present at the meeting that night actually composed an armed mob intent upon massacring the police upon a given signal? It would be argued that this was the case, that the bullet wounds suffered by the police proved it. But did they? Probably some civilians in the crowd were armed. A few cheap firearms—little "snappers," as August Spies would call them—were found near the scene afterward. Doubtless some of them had been fired at the police, but a survey of the evidence leads to the conclusion that it was highly improbable that all of the police wounds were caused in that way. Several newspaper reporters and other competent witnesses said they saw no shooting from the crowd. Initial newspaper stories made no mention of firing by civilians.[2]

Here was a puzzle never yet solved. Could the explanation have been given in a little noticed item that appeared in the *Tribune* some six weeks later? Without comment, the *Tribune* quoted a "high police official":

"I know . . . it to be a fact that a very large number of the police were wounded by each other's revolvers. . . . There was a blunder on the part of the man who commanded the police on the night of the Haymarket murders, or this fearful slaughter would not have occurred. Bonfield made the blunder, and is held responsible for its effects by every man injured there. . . .

"The whole thing was hasty and ill-advised, arising out of Bonfield's desire to distinguish himself."[3]

In Bonfield's own report there appears the statement: "I . . . gave the order to cease firing, fearing that some of our men in the darkness might fire into each other."[4] A bullet-marked telegraph pole near the alley perhaps would have established the truth by showing from which direction the firing came. But for reasons never made public, the tell-tale pole was removed a few days after the bombing.[5]

How many civilians were wounded or killed from police bullets never was known exactly. Samuel Fielden caught a bullet in his leg and Henry Spies, brother of August, was wounded in the groin but not many others among the injured were publicly identified. The story was that many of the civilians were killed but "the anarchists stole their dead away and buried the bodies secretly." This probably was not true. One known fatality among the socialists was a German laborer known as "Big" Krueger, shot down a block away by a policeman as he attempted to escape. Later it would be said, but without evidence, that he "might have been the bomber."[6]

2

Who *did* throw the bomb, if not "Big" Krueger? Was it handsome, blond Rudolph Schnaubelt, arrested at least twice and each time released? Or the "mysterious stranger from Indianapolis?" Or the indigent shoemaker named George Schwab (no relation to Michael Schwab) mentioned for the first time in 1933? Or one Thomas Owen, a carpenter who in 1887 fell from a roof in Homestead, Pennsylvania, and "confessed" on his deathbed? Or a vague person named Klemana Schuetz, a New Yorker, whose name was introduced at the eleventh hour?

Could the bomb-thrower have been an *agent provocateur?* That possibility was seriously considered by reasonable men at the time and cannot be completely rejected.[7]

Or was it some wretched workingman who, unconnected with the anarchist movement, had been driven to the maniacal act out of personal revenge for some act of police brutality? "Remember, brutal treatment brutalizes."

For fifty years questions of that nature have gone unanswered. If the bomb-thrower were known for a certainty it is likely (although not necessarily so) that the mystery and doubts enveloping the case to this day would be dispelled. Careful and calm investigation at the time might have brought the answer. But Chicago and more particularly the police reacted with too much hysteria to permit such investigation. Actually there was little interest in discovering who threw the bomb. What difference did it make? The anarchists were to blame: such was the logic. The necessity of establishing a clear judicial case of guilt against a certain person or persons, the balancing of the moral responsibilities of the newspapers and the police against the insane incitations of the revolutionaries, the possibility of a part played by an *agent provocateur,* the legal necessity of proceeding in an atmosphere conducive to a fair trial—these things were dismissed as hair-splitting or as reflecting sympathy with elements that threatened the very fate of Chicago and America. To a community rendered suddenly mad, from indignation and terror, that attitude seemed wholly reasonable in morality and in law.

No pussyfooting now! No more coddling of vicious scum! "Public

justice demands that the European assassins, August Spies, Michael
Schwab and Samuel Fielden, shall be held, tried and hanged for murder. . . . Public justice demands that the assassin, A. R. Parsons, who is
said to disgrace this country by having been born in it, shall be seized,
tried and hanged for murder." So the Chicago *Times*. "No time for
parleying!" thus the *Daily News*, which also succumbed to hysteria
after earlier advising that "the situation calls for the widest sense of
forbearance and self-control." It continued: "These anarchists are
amenable to no reason except that taught by the club and the rifle. . . .
No mercy should be shown them." And the *Inter-Ocean*: "Even if
they had not opened their lips on Tuesday night, their very presence . . . would have been an invitation to the mob to commit acts of
lawlessness. These men are accessories before the fact to the murder . . . and to the murder of every man, woman or child who may die
within a year and a day after the date of receiving their injuries."[8]
Not inaccurately a magazine writer summed it all up:

"The intention is to hang them [the anarchists] off hand, and it is
very doubtful whether even an acquittal would save them, for that
kind of susurrus is rising in Chicago which means that if the evil cannot be stamped out otherwise, a Vigilance Committee will take the
law into their own hands, and restore social order by suspending
civilization for three days."[9]

Indeed, a Vigilante group was organized by prominent Chicagoans,
a leader in which was a young lawyer named John Barton Payne,[10]
who years later would head the world's greatest mercy organization,
the American Red Cross. Then it was the turn of the elements of
respectability, not Spies and his wretched colleagues, to voice the
cry: "Revenge!"

3

As it turned out, resort to Vigilantism was not needed. The police
and the law-enforcing authorities generally went promptly and vigorously into action. Staging "raids" in the working-class districts, the
police rounded up all the known anarchists and socialists who could be
found or who lacked the means of escaping the "dragnet." Station-
house jails bulged with members of the "red brotherhood"—also with
men and women who had no radical connections but "looked like
communists." "Make the raids first and look up the law afterward!"
publicly counseled Julius S. Grinnell, the state's attorney, when a

question was raised about search warrants.[11] In many ways, that advice established the *modus operandi* of all the events that followed.

Within eighteen hours of the explosion a coroner's jury produced a verdict that set the course for the legal proceedings ahead. It read: ". . . Mathias J. Degan [came] to his death from a bomb thrown by a person or persons unknown, but acting in conspiracy with August Spies, Albert Parsons, Samuel J. Fielden and others unknown." Later that language would be expanded copiously in refined legal terminology, but essentially it formed the basis for the Haymarket trial. Editor Melville E. Stone of the *Daily News* took credit for the phraseology and the legal point of view it expressed. Finding the county prosecutors troubled over the legal propriety of proceeding against "accessories" when the "principal" was unknown, he successfully argued that "the identity of the bomb-thrower was of no consequence . . . that inasmuch as Spies and Parsons and Fielden had advocated over and over again the use of violence against the police and had urged the manufacture and throwing of bombs, their culpability was clear."[12] As even Judge Joseph Gary, who presided at the trial, came to admit, this would be "new law." But it was made to work. Thus did August Spies' "little" joke of sending an empty bomb to the editor of the *Daily News* have a humorless sequel.

4

On May twenty-seventh, thirty-one anarchists (or socialists) were named in criminal indictments. By what process these particular ones were selected has never been made known. It is even less clear how it happened that out of the thirty-one only a certain group of eight were placed on trial—unless it was determined that those eight were the most effective labor agitators in Chicago. These were Albert R. Parsons, August Spies, Samuel Fielden, Michael Schwab, George Engel, Adolph Fischer, Louis Lingg and Oscar Neebe. Of these, only Spies and Fielden were at the scene when the bomb exploded. Parsons had left with his wife and his two small children after he made his speech. Engel was at home. So was Oscar Neebe. Fischer had been at the meeting, but had left before it was over. Lingg, although he did have bombs that night, was on the North Side, miles away.

On June twenty-first, selection of a jury was begun to place the eight on trial. (Curious procedures followed in selecting the jury will be examined later.) On July fifteenth the trial proper began. August twentieth brought the verdict: death by hanging for August

Spies, Albert Parsons, Samuel Fielden, Michael Schwab, George Engel, Adolph Fischer and Louis Lingg; fifteen years' imprisonment on a conspiracy count for Oscar W. Neebe.

The verdict was no surprise. Everything was against the defendants from the beginning. In addition to cards stacked against them by their prosecutors—and some indubitably were—others were misdealed by themselves to their own disadvantage. For example, they objected to having the case heard before Judge John G. Rogers (who later was outspoken in criticising their trial as a travesty on justice) and they got—Judge Gary.[13] A motion for separate trials, strategy which legal experts feel would have saved most or all, was bungled. Topping those errors by the defense were omissions by Prosecutor Grinnell. He had intended, so it has been said, to urge a measure of leniency for Parsons because Parsons had voluntarily taken his place with his co-defendants after making good his escape. But Grinnell "forgot" to do so.[14] He made a similar omission with regard to Neebe, against whom, as Grinnell admitted to Mayor Harrison, there was only trifling evidence of "conspiracy."[15]

As for the case constructed against the defendants, it was far from weak circumstantially. Everything they had said or done—or had not said or done—was fitted by amazing ingenuity on the part of the prosecution into a convincing pattern. Inclusion of Louis Lingg in the group was alone fatal in its consequences. Wild and impetuous, scarcely turned twenty-one, Lingg had made bombs. There was no getting around that. The evidence against that obscure organizer for the Carpenters' Union, unknown even to most of the defendants, contributed greatly toward the verdict of guilty against all eight.

The Illinois Supreme Court upheld the verdicts a year later. On November second, 1887, the United States Supreme Court spoke. It would not interfere. After that only Governor Oglesby of Illinois had the power to save any or all of the condemned men, or grant lesser sentences. There is evidence that Oglesby would have preferred to have no hangings, that he had no stomach for the way the case had gone. He had been an Abolitionist, a friend of Lincoln. It is said that he once exclaimed to State Senator Richard Burke concerning the Haymarket convictions: "If that had been the law during the anti-slavery agitation, all of us Abolitionists could have been hanged long ago."[16]

In a letter to George Schilling written a week before the executions, Colonel "Bob" Ingersoll said of Oglesby: "Governor Oglesby has as much physical courage as any man in the world. He has a good heart. His instincts are noble and all his tendencies are towards the right. . . .

The only fear I have is that he will be over-awed by the general feeling—by the demand of the 'upper classes.' " Ingersoll added, and told Schilling he would so advise Oglesby privately, that: "It will be a great mistake to hang these men. The seeds of future trouble will in this find soil. . . . It would be far better to commute the terrible sentences to imprisonment and I hope the Governor can be made to see this. As a rule power is blind. . . ."[17]

Finally, Oglesby did send word to Chicago's business leaders, during the last week, indicating that he would commute the sentences of all the prisoners if the businessmen requested it. His message was to Lyman J. Gage, president of the First National Bank, later President McKinley's secretary of the treasury. Gage called a secret meeting at his bank, to which the city's business leaders were invited. It looked at first as though a request for commutations would be made. Gage favored saving the men. But Marshall Field stood against it. After the merchant prince spoke, the meeting broke up. None cared to take issue with the great Marshall Field.[18]

As November eleventh, 1887, the day for the hangings, drew near, the eyes of the world literally were focused on the aged Illinois governor. Petitions and letters for and against mercy, swamped him. They came from everywhere, from great men and obscure persons, from sincere men and charlatans, from cranks and sober-minded citizens, people stirred as by no similar event in that century.

"There never has been a pardon application made in this country which has subjected a state executive to such an ordeal. These applications in the past have usually possessed only a local significance . . . but in the Anarchists' case the whole country has been expressing an opinion pro and con, and efforts have been made in the capitals of England, France and Germany to secure clemency. Letters urging him to hang them all, to commute them all, and to pardon them all, as well as to hang some and commute others, have poured in on him. . . .

"Petitions of every conceivable kind have poured in from all conceivable places, and many of them have been signed by good and law-abiding citizens who detest anarchy and the doctrines of force taught by these men, which in itself must have been embarrassing. Judges of courts and ministers of the Gospel have put in a plea for some of the men. . . ."

So the *Tribune* on November tenth. As that *Tribune* account indicates, there had happened a remarkable change in sentiment between the time of the bombing and execution day. Captain Michael J. Schaack, a policeman who vied with Bonfield in creating anarchist scares, would comment upon this with disgust in his probably ghost-written work, *Anarchy and Anarchists.*

"It was surprising to note how many who had hitherto clamored for blood in atonement for the Haymarket massacre now exerted themselves in an effort to secure executive clemency. With my own eyes I saw people who had made the most fuss shouting 'Hang the Anarchists!' . . . the first to weaken. They began calling the doomed Anarchists 'poor innocent men, it is too bad to hang them'. . . ."[19]

Typical was the attitude of Melville Stone. Few men had done more than he to bring about the anarchists' fate, yet before the hangings he was among the most active Chicagoans in attempting to save their lives. He was among those who persuaded Spies, Fielden and Schwab to sign a statement expressing contrition over the Haymarket episode and renouncing the doctrines of violence. He spent several feverish hours with Parsons, earnestly attempting to get him to sign a like statement, guaranteeing him a commutation if he did. But Parsons refused. "I shall die," he told Stone, "with less fear and less regret than you will feel in living, for my blood is on your head."[20]

Even the judge, Gary, and the prosecutor, Grinnell, now had a slight change of heart. The former wrote an appeal to Oglesby for Fielden and the latter for both Fielden and Schwab.[21] There was significant irony in those letters by Gary and Grinnell, not completely realized by many persons at the time. With Fielden and Schwab exculpated by judge and prosecutor, what was there left of the state's case? That question may have entered Oglesby's mind for a study of the record shows that the allegations against Fielden and Schwab in a large sense formed the keystone of the whole conspiracy theory erected against all eight men. Possibly this, as much as anything, prompted his secret message to Chicago's business leaders.

On the tenth of November, Governor Oglesby did save Fielden and Schwab from the gallows. Tears shone in his eyes during a hearing in behalf of the men.[22] In a public statement, the executive explained that he commuted their sentences to life imprisonment because they had expressed regret over their part in Haymarket. As for Spies, who had joined Fielden and Schwab and the others in their statement of contrition, Oglesby said he must abide by the decisions of the courts.

It was a hectic day when the Governor acted. A few hours before, startling news had come from the Cook County jail. Louis Lingg had acted on his own behalf to cheat the hangman. A friend had smuggled to him a percussion cap concealed in a cigar.[23] Lingg chewed it and died soon after the explosion. With his blood he wrote a farewell note: "Long live anarchy!" The impression was held by many that Lingg's act, accepted as a confession of guilt, turned the balance in Oglesby's mind against extending clemency to any of the men except Fielden and Schwab.

5

The next day, Friday, Spies, Parsons, Engel and Fischer were ushered to a specially built platform in the Cook County jail. They were stood all in a row, and the state of Illinois exacted its penalty. Until the quadruple hanging was announced as a fact, Chicago went through a period of anxiety and tension it did not soon forget. There were rumors that the jail would be bombed, and every public building. Talk of plans by "thousands of anarchists" to "invade" the city was widespread—and credited. Officials were panicky and arranged for Federal troops and national guardsmen to supplement police guards. The jail was roped off. Shopkeepers barricaded their stores. Wealthy residents found it desirable to leave town. "A cloud of apprehension lowered over the city," recalled Melville Stone. "There was a hush and men spoke in whispers. I have never experienced a like condition."[24] But nothing happened except the business of hanging four men.

Of all the citizens in Chicago only the four doomed men seemed calm. Even the *Tribune* now found words of semi-praise for them on that score. It observed of their "fortitude" that "in a righteous contest . . . they might have been heroes." Refusing stimulants offered him, Parsons a few hours before sang *Annie Laurie* in his cell. The others were equally composed, causing their jailers to comment that they would die "like John Brown."[25] Indeed, they gave the impression of somehow rising above themselves. They were more than four miserable men about to die the death of convicted criminals. They had become Symbols.

6

That they consciously felt this transcendental status was demonstrated by their last words.

Spies said:

"There will come a time when our silence will be more powerful than the voices you strangle today!"

Fischer said:

"This is the happiest moment of my life!"

Engel said:

"Hurrah for anarchy!"

Parsons said:

"Will I be allowed to speak, O men of America? Let me speak, Sheriff Matson! Let the voice of the people be heard!"

CHAPTER THIRTEEN

ALTGELD KEEPS HIS PEACE

1

EXCEPT for a few intrepid labor sheets, notably one edited by John Swinton, who had been Charles A. Dana's managing editor for the New York *Sun*, the press everywhere exulted. "Law had triumphed over Anarchy!" "Those who draw the sword against peace and law in this free country will perish by the sword!" said the Chicago *Tribune*. "An impressive moment in the history of the republic," said the New York *Herald*. In London, the *Times* thundered praise for "Chicago justice"—and took occasion to commend the hangings as a good example to be followed by the British authorities in dealing with labor troubles prevalent in London at just that time.

However, the more common reaction outside the editorial rooms was relief rather than exultation. Even those persons who had fought for a different result felt relieved, even glad. At last, they thought, the heart-breaking case was over. That was something for which all were thankful. Most people hoped they would hear no more about the Haymarket matter. Even the newspapers after a time appeared satisfied and treated memorial activities by radical groups with exceptional restraint. The strain had been terrific for every sensitive person. But was it all over? In the Illinois State penitentiary at Joliet, there were still three men, Fielden, Schwab and Neebe. And John Peter Altgeld was yet to play a part.

2

But all during that tense period, Lawyer Altgeld appeared on the stage of the Haymarket drama not at all. Nearly every other Chicagoan of liberal tendencies was moved to voice protests publicly in one way or another against the hangings, swept up by what Jane Addams, in awe, recalled as "the startling reaction to the Haymarket Riot . . . its profound influence upon the social outlook of thousands of people."[1] Henry Demarest Lloyd spoke out so strongly that his father-in-law, William Bross, part owner of the *Tribune*, changed his will, as punishment, to keep Lloyd from getting the Bross holdings in that newspaper.[2] A counterpart of Lloyd's sacrifice was the tragedy of lovely Nina Van Zandt, a girl in her teens who had attended Vassar College. She not only came to sympathize with the doomed men, but found herself in love with August Spies. Because she felt that somehow it might help save him and the others, she "married" Spies—by proxy when the authorities refused to permit a ceremony in jail. And she did it with the knowledge that an aunt, Mrs. John Arthurs of Pittsburgh, would deprive her of a $400,000 legacy.[3]

Then there was the case of Captain William Perkins Black, lawyer. He enjoyed a lucrative corporation practice as a member of a substantial law firm. When nearly every other lawyer declined to take the case of the anarchists, he became chief defense counsel in face of warnings (which proved true) that he would lose his corporation retainers.

Such instances were numerous. All over the world people were bestirred to action in behalf of the condemned. William Morris, the English poet, sent letters to his friends begging them to sign petitions for clemency. To "Dear Mr. Robert Browning," Morris wrote that he was "much troubled by this horror" and urged that Browning "sign the enclosed appeal for mercy and so do what you can to save the lives of seven men who have been condemned to death . . . after a mere mockery of a trial."[4] A young Fabian named G. Bernard Shaw was similarly agitated, walking the streets of London to obtain signatures. And in America again, even Altgeld's Civil War general, Ben Butler, was drawn into the case as a lawyer for the defense when an appeal was taken to the United States Supreme Court. Whatever else might be said about Butler, he was sincere in storming that the case was a repetition of the witch hangings in Puritan Massachusetts.[5]

3

And all the while, Altgeld was tending to his knitting, giving no sign to any except intimates like Schilling that he was even aware of the Haymarket matter. Some sixty thousand Chicagoans signed petitions for clemency. Altgeld's friends Goudy, Judge Lambert Tree and Edward Osgood Brown all signed. The name of nearly every other prominent lawyer in the city appears on one or more of the petitions, for the legal profession generally was outraged by the trial, regardless of economic position or social attitudes. Stephen S. Gregory, later president of the American Bar Association, was among them. Practically every sitting judge in Cook County joined the petitioners. And Big Business names like those of Potter Palmer, Marvin Hughitt, president of the Chicago and Northwestern Railroad, and Lyman Gage, president of the First National Bank, appeared on the petitions.[6]

But Altgeld's name was missing. His aloofness appears all the more curious in view of the prominence of his friend Schilling in the desperate efforts to save the anarchists. When a defense society was formed, to arrange for lawyers and to collect the sums needed for legal expenditures, Schilling was a key man, working closely with Dr. Ernst Schmidt, head of the defense organization. It was he who induced William P. Black to take the case and he who later engaged General Butler and Leonard Swett, Lincoln's old law associate, to make the appeals in the higher courts. Incredibly, it was only luck that kept Schilling from being made a defendant in the case. Three days after the bombing there appeared a hysterical newspaper editorial demanding that Altgeld's friend be hanged with the others. "Schilling is among the most conspicuous characters of the foreign banditti of the red flag in Chicago. . . . Fielden imbibed his anarchistic doctrines at the feet of this Gamaliel. . . . No exceptions can be made in favor of this apostle of barbarism called Schilling."[7]

Altgeld must have received a real jolt when he read that item in the Chicago *Times*, a paper that had been most favorable to himself. And still he kept his peace.

4

Yet there is no doubt that Altgeld was as profoundly moved as Henry D. Lloyd and Jane Addams, as might be expected from the man who had so short a time before published *Our Penal Machinery and Its Victims* and the essay on labor disputes in the Chicago *Mail*. On the day before the Illinois Supreme Court rendered its decision, Schilling encountered Altgeld downtown. They talked about the case and Schilling dropped the comment that he felt certain the Supreme Court would grant a retrial. "You are wrong," said Altgeld. "The Supreme Court will uphold the convictions. There is not a man on the court brave enough to go against the newspapers and the public hatred that has been stirred up." And as he spoke, Schilling recalled, "his face was the saddest I have ever seen on any man."[8]

Then why did he remain silent? As an important Democratic leader, soon to be referred to in the *Tribune* as something of a "Democratic boss,"[9] and also as a man of considerable property holdings, his views would have carried weight. Fear of public opinion? That could not have been the answer when it is realized that many of the most respected citizens in Chicago joined the movement for clemency. Fear of economic reprisals? This could not have been the reason, for he was already economically independent and secure. Moreover, at no time would he display the slightest trace of being afraid to speak his mind. Political considerations? Unquestionably this was the principal explanation. He was looking to the future and hoped to avoid making any false steps. Those anarchists, or most of them, would be hanged regardless of what he could do then. Perhaps he reasoned in that fashion. Why take chances on permitting papers like the *Tribune* and the *Times* to call him a sympathizer with anarchy before he was in a position to do something more than talk? Another conversation he had with Schilling is enlightening.

"You know," he said, "I have some of the same ideas that you have. But if I talked now as radical as I feel, I could not be where I am. I want to do something, not just make a speech. . . . I want power, to get hold of the handle that controls things. When I do, I will give it a twist!" He made a gesture with his wrist to show what he meant.[10]

And so, because he had no "handle" then, he bided his time. From a liberal viewpoint, he was, of course, much less heroic than men like Henry D. Lloyd. But Schilling at least was convinced that Altgeld was perhaps wiser. How could they tell when another Haymarket case might develop? If one did, perhaps Altgeld would be in a position to give the "handle" a "twist." However, it could not have occurred to either then that Altgeld might play any part in the present case. As they talked it appeared certain that all the sentences of hanging would be executed. Then there would have been no important part left for anyone to play. Not until months afterward did Governor Oglesby save Fielden and Schwab from the gallows, thus making possible at a later date further executive intervention with respect to the death sentences—if there should ever be elected a governor so minded.

Nobody then had any idea who such a governor might be. Least of all Altgeld. He was thinking, not of Springfield, but of the national Congress in Washington.

5

As a stepping-stone to Congress, so he considered it, Altgeld became a candidate for judge of the Superior Court of Cook County in

the month after Judge Gary pronounced sentence upon the Haymarket men and before the hangings. George Schilling was responsible
for that happening, and so was the Haymarket episode itself. Organized labor everywhere, as a result of the anti-labor hysteria that followed the bombing, felt a stronger compulsion than ever to enter the
political arena in self-protection. In New York City a labor party
that year entered Henry George in the mayoralty race. He ran ahead
of a young "scholar in politics" named Theodore Roosevelt, the Republican candidate, but lost to the Tammany entry, Abram S. Hew-
itt—counted out, according to opinion which persists to this day. A
full labor ticket swept the field in Milwaukee. And in Chicago there
developed one of the strongest such movements yet known there,
with Schilling a powerful leader.

When that happened, Altgeld sounded Schilling out on the possibility of being nominated for Congress by the United Labor party.
Personally, Schilling was agreeable, but felt forced to shake his head.
Every bricklayer and carpenter feels qualified to go to Congress, he
said. Hence the labor movement would not accept nomination of anyone for that office who was not a laborer. "But we will nominate
judges," Schilling suggested. "And you could qualify there." At
first Altgeld scorned the suggestion.

"All a judge is supposed to do," he said, "even in important cases,
is to blow dust off volumes which you are led to believe fit the particular case in hand."[11] He wanted to be no dust blower.

"As soon as a man is elected to the office of judge, all growth seems
to cease. . . . He literally and figuratively *sits down.* . . . A large portion of his thought is taken up with the consideration of little things—
drawing learned distinctions between tweedle-dee and tweedle-
dum. . . ."[12]

So he would later express his disdain for the judicial life. But finally
he determined that a term as judge would be good background for
something more in line with his ambitions. And when the United
Labor party convention met in September, five candidates for judicial
office were nominated—Altgeld among them, thanks to Schilling's
influence. Earlier, Altgeld himself had managed to get the Democratic nomination for the same office, convincing the party leaders
that because he could get the labor nomination he was even better
material than former United States Senator Lyman Trumbull.[13] Thus
he ran on both tickets.

6

Once again the *Tribune* displayed hostility toward him. Lawyer Altgeld, said the *Tribune*, is a "foreigner by birth." And later it called him a "hack candidate . . . stamped all over with popular rejection,"[14] a reference to his defeat for Congress in 1884. But that was mild in contrast with what the leading Democratic organ, the *Herald*, shortly would be shouting.

The Labor party was composed mainly of persons who defended the condemned anarchists, hence anyone endorsed by the party was an anarchist sympathizer. So the *Herald* reasoned. Thus, ironically, despite all his caution with regard to the Haymarket matter, the charge of sympathizing with the anarchists was raised against him in his judicial campaign, and it was the *Herald* that did so. "Shall the Reds Win?" it demanded, with reference to the Labor party judicial candidates. The newspaper called for the defeat of Altgeld (and his colleagues) as a means by which Chicago would "repudiate emphatically the sentiments which animate assassination" and show its opposition "to the Reds, to dynamite, to the murder of policemen. . . ."[15] Soon the *Tribune* took up the same cry.

But Altgeld used the strategy that proved so successful for him in his Savannah, Missouri, campaign. He ignored the charges against him. Instead, he called the other judicial candidates on the Labor ticket to his office and suggested that they jointly meet the anarchist cry by raising a special campaign fund to be used for hiring extra ticket peddlers. At first the other candidates objected to putting up any money. They had been assured that endorsement by Labor would not cost them anything.

"Hell!" said Altgeld. "Wait until the wolves of our regular parties get to us for campaign assessments. These labor people have no money and we ought to give them as much as possible."

Contributions of five hundred dollars each were then suggested. "Make it a thousand dollars," Altgeld insisted.[16] He carried his point, and election night showed that the only victorious judicial candidates on the Democratic ticket were those endorsed by the Labor party.

"Glory Halleluja!" cried *The Knights of Labor*. "The Power of the Lord is Coming Down!"[17]

7

On December first, 1886, Lawyer Altgeld turned over his private legal practice to John W. Lanehart and mounted the bench of the

Superior Court of Cook County. He was then a colleague of Judge Gary, a member of the judicial system of Illinois when Parsons, Spies, Fischer and Engel were put to their death the following November, by what many called "judicial murder." Still he said nothing in public. But, when the men were hanged, a new friend of George Schilling's, a young man recently come to Chicago from Ohio, made an observation that struck the little group who heard it as well-intended, but wishful, thinking. "What ought to be done now," said young Clarence Darrow, "is to take a man like Judge Altgeld, first elect him mayor of Chicago, then governor of Illinois."[18]

The remark sounded fantastic—then.

BOOK FOUR

THE JUDGE

CHAPTER FOURTEEN

THE LIBERAL JURIST

1

JUDGE Altgeld found the judicial office more to his liking than he had anticipated. "There was much of the autocrat in his nature," a shrewd political associate observed.[1]

That observation explained that he insisted upon the utmost deference when he was on the bench and that he ruled his courtroom with an iron hand. That no one could interrupt when he spoke, that people had to stand when he entered the courtroom and that he could impose a fine or a jail sentence if anyone refused to obey an order—all this gave him a certain special pleasure, as was noted particularly on one occasion by Mrs. Adolph Heile.

She had called at the Altgeld residence to ask Judge Altgeld to sign a petition for granting to women the right to vote in educational matters. He was heartily in accord with that movement. Yet he insisted that his friend and neighbor come to his courtroom the next day before he would sign. When Mrs. Heile arrived, he escorted her with great dignity to the bench and had her sit beside him as he heard a case. She thought he was especially dignified and severe with the litigants—for her benefit. After the case was over, he turned to Mrs. Heile with a smile. "How do you think I did?"

He beamed when she showered him with praise for his "fine judicial manner."[2]

2

Lawyers quickly discovered that Judge Altgeld intended to run his court in *his* way, not theirs. Frequently he would order a lawyer to step aside and would take a hand questioning witnesses himself. More than one case was appealed from his court to the Supreme Court on the charge that he had exceeded his judicial prerogatives. In a few cases the Supreme Court appeared to agree, finding him "unnecessarily arbitrary," but it usually ruled that Judge Altgeld had committed no such excess as would permit a reversal on that ground alone.[3]

Curiously, Lawyer Goudy was among those who complained most often of his "arbitrary rulings and conduct." Out of a half-dozen

cases that Goudy, representing the Chicago and Northwestern Railroad, tried before his young friend, he found Altgeld ruling against
him in nearly every one.[4] After a while there will be noted a cooling
in the friendship between Goudy and Altgeld, and in time a complete
break. Unquestionably, Goudy expected his political protégés to favor
him when they could. Yet here was this young man, whose path to
wealth and political place had been greatly eased by Goudy, showing
not only complete independence but something smacking of antagonism when Goudy appeared in his court. Probably Altgeld was leaning
the other way when Goudy had a case before him, to avoid the slightest suspicion that he could be influenced. For he was keenly zealous
of his reputation for integrity. At least that was true where public
matters were concerned. When Goudy began taking an interest in
Altgeld he may not have suspected the strength of that Altgeldian
trait.

3

But if Goudy felt let down, no one ever had any *legitimate* complaint
against Judge Altgeld's conduct on the bench. It is certain that he
gave no cause for criticism that he consciously permitted his personal
views on law and social justice to color improperly his judicial acts.
Lawyers like Elbert H. Gary, later president of the United States Steel
Corporation, practiced before him—and found no reason to consider
Judge Altgeld a "radical."[5] Altgeld was prejudiced against utility
operators of the type exemplified by Charles T. Yerkes, yet Yerkes
was an admirer of Judge Altgeld's brand of justice. This financial buc-
caneer had good reason. In 1889, Yerkes brought suit against a broker
for recovery of five hundred dollars which he claimed was due on an
investment transaction. Judge Altgeld heard the case. When Yerkes
took the stand, the opposing counsel asked the question: "Have you
ever been convicted of a crime?" Yerkes was forced to admit that he
had been convicted of a felony in Philadelphia. He sought to explain
the circumstances, but the opposing counsel attempted to shut him
off. However, Altgeld insisted that Yerkes be permitted to explain.[6]
It was a favor Yerkes never forgot, when there would be later contact
between those two.

4

Judge Altgeld despised much of the law, but on the bench he took
it and applied it as he found it. Clarence Darrow would write that "as

a judge . . . he was always in sympathy with the under-dog,"[7] and another friend, Judge Charles A. Williams, would declare that "this sympathy was so strong as to keep him from being a really good judge."[8] But these comments are misleading. There are cases which show that he went out of his way to help some poor litigant to obtain a judgment against a corporation for injuries sustained in the course of employment.[9] But in just as many cases he is found ruling for a corporation. In fact, one lawyer felt justified in sarcastically commenting, for political reasons, that "Judge Altgeld could not be accused of prejudice in favor of the poor man against the corporations."[10] Somewhere between those opposing judgments lies the truth.

5

At times Altgeld presided in the Criminal Court of Cook County. If he had chosen, there was an opportunity to convert his court into a sounding board for his advanced ideas on criminology. Yet he restrained himself, carefully following the law there also. In a few cases he did express ideas from the bench reminiscent of his book *Our Penal Machinery and Its Victims*. When a petition for a writ of *habeas corpus* was presented to him in behalf of one "Clabby" Burns, described as a notorious police character, Altgeld delivered a lecture against arresting a man for no reason except his bad reputation. "It is bad practice," he said, "to lock up men without any pretense of making a charge against them. There is no law for it, and it is against justice. It is calculated to make desperate men of ordinary criminals, for when you commence to persecute a man all the venom of his nature is fired and he becomes a fearless, fearful lawbreaker."[11] He granted the writ.

In another case, he delivered a stinging lecture to the county prosecutor for calling a police officer to testify on the number of times a defendant in a pickpocket case had been arrested. "I won't let a policeman make evidence against prisoners by telling how often they have been arrested," Altgeld declared. "If they have been convicted in a court of record, that's another matter. But an arrest is no evidence against a man!"[12]

But for every such incident there is found in his record a matching one wherein he was as stern with criminal defendants as any admirer of Judge Gary could have wished. Where the evidence was ample, he displayed neither sympathy for the accused nor patience with technicalities offered to get them freed.[13]

6

What had happened, then, to the author of *Our Penal Machinery and Its Victims?* He was there. But he made a distinction, consciously so, between Judge Altgeld on the bench and John P. Altgeld personally. At the very time he was impressing the legal world with his relative conservatism as a judge, Altgeld began making himself heard as a dissenter, with more directness than ever, upon the "great questions, both economic and social, that are calling for attention."

One of his first opportunities for public expression of his liberal social views after his election as a judge came when Father Edward McGlynn, the New York priest who was excommunicated for his political activity in behalf of Henry George, delivered an address on New Year's Day, 1888, before the Anti-Poverty League in New York City. In that speech the social-minded clergyman quoted Cardinal Manning of England: "Necessity has no law, and a starving man has a right to his neighbor's bread." An outburst of hysteria swept the press of the nation. Was not this priest encouraging the poor to take to thievery? In Chicago, prominent citizens were interviewed, and nearly all reported themselves horrified over the priest's "inciting utterances." Many who denounced the priest were preachers. Judge Altgeld was among the Chicagoans asked to comment by the *Chicago Times.* The result was his first definitely pro-labor utterance in public—one considerably more definite than his essay on labor disputes written two years earlier.

First he insisted that Cardinal Manning's statement was "neither radical nor revolutionary." It simply announced "a principle which society has long recognized, viz., that it is the duty of society to take care of its indigent, by lawful means of course." Then he pointed a finger of scorn at the preachers who were attacking Father McGlynn. Certainly these clerics knew that "both Christ and His apostles satisfied their hunger—and they were not yet starving—by eating another man's corn, without his consent. . . . When one thinks of this and then reads some of the letters of the clergy . . . holding that a starving man should die rather than touch his neighbor's bread, one cannot doubt that it is a long time since Christ was on earth. . . ."

Next he directed a blast at those who ascribed unemployment and poverty to faults of the workers themselves.

"There was a time [he wrote] when the adage, 'He who will not work neither shall he eat,' seemed to cover almost the whole question, because there was, especially in this country, plenty of work to be had at living wages. . . . But times have changed, so that now there are tens of thousands of men in our large cities and a good sprinkling all over the country who are ready and willing to work, but can get nothing to do. . . .

"Now it is an insult to talk . . . about laziness or shiftlessness—expressions which are constantly on the tongues of people who started in life with good brains, good training and excellent advantages, and who are now well-housed, well-clothed and well-fed, who know nothing about the actual conditions or wants of the poor; who never entered a really poor man's hovel, where there was little fire, or saw him sit down with a large family to a table upon which there was nothing but a little black bread."[14]

7

Those were strong words to come from the man referred to about that time in the press as "the richest judge on the bench in Cook County." Labor folk pricked up their ears. That fall, he followed up with another public statement on the labor question, equally strong. The sweatshop problem had been brought to the fore in Chicago, and at just about that time Altgeld had been reading a great deal about social legislation in Europe. He had digested Professor Thorold Rogers' monumental work, *History of Labor in England* (1884). He had read, too, the current sensational utopian work, *Looking Backward*, by Edward Bellamy. Moreover, his favorite author was Victor Hugo, "with Dickens and Thackeray next."[15] Not surprisingly, when the *Times* asked him to comment on the sweatshop problem his response reflected his reading.

Social legislation like that already in force in Europe was needed in America, he said. And at once, to meet the sweatshop issue. Specifically, he declared laws were needed to prevent child labor and also to compel employers to provide decent working conditions. Of course, such legislation will be opposed by "so-called statesmen, political economists, philosophers and many of the clergy" who will argue that economic wrongs should be permitted to work themselves out by "natural laws" or through the influence of religion. So it had been argued abroad, he said. This, he continued, was sophistry.

"Moral suasion and the benign influence of religion are beautiful, but unfortunately in all ages there have been men who went straight from the sanctuary into the world and plundered and trampled upon the weak, and what is more, they lost neither their seats nor their in-fluence in the temple."

He conceded that legislation could not be a cure-all. But he in-sisted that "legislation can prevent children of tender years from being stunted in factories when they should be at school" and that "legisla-tion can secure to every shop-girl good ventilation, good light, reason-ably comfortable quarters while at work, healthy sanitary conditions, such as sufficient wash-bowls (not dirty sinks), ample closet-rooms, etc. . . ." He linked the sweatshop evil to the dominant American idea on high tariff for industry. Supposedly, he observed, the tariff was designed to protect the standards of American wage-earners from the effects of competition with low European wages. But, he ob-served, the same manufacturers who demand tariff "protection" were importing cheap European labor into America, and paying these men low wages, so that in effect the American laborer was forced to com-pete with the cheapest kind of labor despite the tariff. In short, "everybody was protected but the laborer." "The proprietors have been protected but the laborers have had to move on . . . and that, too, in many cases by the assistance of policeman's clubs and Pinker-ton rifles."[16] His first reference to violent police conduct in labor matters.

8

By this time, in the closing days of 1889, he was becoming recog-nized as a liberal spokesman in Chicago, perhaps second only to Henry D. Lloyd. He did not yet know Lloyd, but in November, 1889, a mu-tual friend wrote to the latter: "He [Altgeld] is very much interested in your views. . . . You ought to know Altgeld intimately. He is one of the most genuinely brainy and sympathetic men I have met." Six months later, Altgeld went out of his way to drop Lloyd a note to compliment him on his pamphlet The New Conscience. "I would rather be the author of one such article than to hold any office in the gift of the American people," he wrote. Soon they were seeing each other socially after Altgeld suggested to Lloyd that they "get better acquainted." There began, then, one of his most important friend-ships, one that strengthened his liberal outlook.[17]

Thanks in large part to missionary work by George Schilling, the economic views of Chicago's "richest judge" became so well known to the labor movement that Altgeld was invited to be the principal speaker at a labor meeting in Chicago on February 22, 1890, his first appearance before a labor group. The meeting marked a revival of the eight-hour movement, and he announced himself as wholly in accord with the demand for eight hours. He dealt scornfully with the argument that shortened hours are "bad for the workers."

"One set of men have no right to set themselves up as judges of their fellows and deprive the latter of the rights they enjoy. . . . Take the rich and the sons of the rich. They enjoy privileges and advantages which were never enjoyed before. All art, all science are open to them, and a field for doing good such as never before was seen. Yet nobody will say that they are making a fair use of their privileges. Will it therefore be claimed that they should be deprived of them?"[18]

The speech was well received by labor, especially since it was known that the speaker was an employer of a large number of workingmen on his various building projects, a fact stressed when he was presented.

A few weeks after that address there occurred in Chicago a city-wide strike by the Carpenters Union for union recognition and shorter hours. The Chicago *Morning News* asked Altgeld to comment, and featured his statement as coming from one who "has made a deep study of the labor question [and whose] views on the question appear to have been arrived at regardless of his personal or private interests." It was only right and a matter of common sense, he asserted, that the employers recognize the right of their workers to form unions, since the employers themselves were well organized. Counter-organization is needed, he declared, to prevent abuses.

But what about the argument that unionism destroys "individual freedom"? he was asked. "A noticeable thing," said Judge Altgeld, "is that this argument is made almost exclusively by the class who, either by instinct or interest, are antagonistic to the laboring man."[19]

9

He had made it clear by then that he did not belong to that class. Yet he was careful, too, to make certain that he did not appear antagonistic to productive capital either. In his speech at the eight-hour meeting he was at pains to observe that most employers are "men of brains . . . and generally, too, they have hearts." The worst enemies of labor are not employers as a class at all, he asserted, "but a class of men who can be designated as hangers-on, men who want to bask in the smiles of the rich . . . men who will resort to methods and measures to hinder reforms and abuses which would make employers blush." He made clear, also, in that address that he abhorred violence in labor disputes. "I do not believe that violence can accomplish any substantial results. On the contrary it has repeatedly injured, if not defeated, the movement. . . . Violence has in nearly all cases come from the rabble and those outside the labor organizations."[20]

His first public reference to Haymarket?

Through such qualifications of his position on labor, he succeeded remarkably well in establishing a reputation for relative conservatism—even in the conservative press—despite his now outspoken championship of labor unions and the labor union program. As an example there is his appearance before the Economic Conference Forum in March, 1889, to discuss prison reforms. In his audience were Lucy Parsons and other "anarchists, socialists, Single Taxers and land reformers." They "peppered Judge Altgeld with questions in attempting to draw him into a discussion of topics which were near to their hearts." But he satisfied the *Herald* that he was no friend of such "misguided" persons, even though he was courteous to them.[21] And the Chicago *Journal* devoted a long editorial to the point that "one gratifying result of the meeting" was that Judge Altgeld "met the heckling of his anarchistic listeners so skillfully that they were called back for a moment from Utopia."[22]

Such was the one and only occasion that Altgeld had any connection, even indirectly, with the anarchistic element in Chicago.

10

Nonetheless, in that period Altgeld did not escape an attempt to pin the label of "radical" upon him. Joseph Medill of the *Tribune* had been watching him. Curiously enough, when this editor did let loose a blast at Altgeld for "radicalism" it was not a labor matter at all that provoked the outburst. In the December, 1889, issue of *The Forum Magazine*, Altgeld read an article entitled "Immigration and Crime," by William M. F. Round. It annoyed him. Its gist was the argument that foreign-born citizens were responsible for most of the crime in America, a theme upon which the Chicago papers had been harping for years, and more than ever after the Haymarket case. For example, the *Tribune* had observed that the bomb resulted because "Chicago has become the rendezvous of the worst elements of the socialistic, atheistic, alcoholic European classes." And the *Times*: "The enemy forces are not American [but] Hussite desperadoes with

such names as Wazinski, Hitt and other Cossack and Teutonic appel-
lations . . . rag-tag and bob-tail cutthroats of Beelzebub from the
Rhine, the Danube, the Vistula and the Elbe."[23]

Scarcely anyone of importance attempted to defend the foreign-
born. But in *The Forum* for February, 1890, there appeared "The
Immigrant's Answer," by John P. Altgeld.[24] He indignantly denied
that foreign-born citizens more frequently engaged in riots and social
disorder than native-born Americans. "Nationality," he said, "has
nothing to do with the case." When riots had occurred in America,
just as many Americans were involved as naturalized citizens.

"But even if this were not so [he continued] it does not lie in the
mouth of an American to make this charge, for the most disgraceful
acts of riot and mob violence that stain our annals were committed,
not by the foreign-born in their rags, but by Americans dressed in
broadcloth, and that not in a Dutch or an Irish settlement, but in the
streets of Boston."

He referred there to the Abolition days of his boyhood, in particular to the incident in Boston when a "broadcloth mob" sought to
"tear William Lloyd Garrison to pieces." And for what? Was it
"over a question of starvation wages?" Or "to avenge an act of injustice and oppression?" No, said Altgeld, Garrison was attacked
"simply because he dared to proclaim that no man can have a right
of property in another human being."

"If there have been mobs and riots among the foreign-born in our
country, they were nothing but impotent protests by ignorant, though
honest people, against that rapacious greed which took the bread they
toiled for away from their children's mouths, while the broadcloth
American Boston mob shrieked for the life of the man who dared to
advocate human freedom."

Haymarket was in his mind there, too.

11

But what got under the skin of Joseph Medill was not this distinction that Altgeld drew between mobs, but the analysis of the political
affiliations of the scorned foreign-born. He insisted (giving figures)
that "but for the assistance of the immigrant, the election of Abraham
Lincoln as president would have been an impossibility." The Re-

publican party, he asserted, was strongest in those states that had the largest proportion of foreign-born citizens. If not for the foreign-born, he declared, the Civil War might have ended differently. The foreign-born were Unionists, whereas "the men who sought to destroy our institutions, who proclaimed the principle of inequality . . . and who finally fired upon the flag of the Republic, were not only Americans but sons of Americans." Yet, see what has happened: the "party of Lincoln" is the one from whose ranks there "comes with increasing frequency the cry 'America for the Americans.' "

In the *Tribune* there appeared a long and bitter editorial: "Judge Altgeld's Malignant Mistakes." Judge Altgeld's assertions, said the newspaper, were "untruthful. . . . He produces no evidence—for he has none." And what is this about the Republican party favoring restrictions upon immigration? What about the Democratic party? Did not Thomas Jefferson advocate strict limitations on immigration? "And," the editorial concluded scornfully, "Judge Altgeld is a follower of Jefferson—and Karl Marx!"[25]

For the first time, then, in 1890, Altgeld was referred to by the Chicago *Tribune*, inferentially, as a "communist." From then on it was war between Joseph Medill of the *Tribune* and John Peter Altgeld.

CHAPTER FIFTEEN

The Lawsuit

1

No MORE amusing moment for cracking down upon Judge Altgeld for "radicalism" could have been chosen. For the "follower of Jefferson and Karl Marx" was never so deeply engaged in capitalistic enterprise as at that particular time. His judicial duties at last had begun to pall upon him. One reflection of his fretting spirit was his relatively vast literary product at this time, the writing of articles for a half-dozen magazines and newspapers on subjects ranging from "Justice to Deaf Soldiers" to "Anonymous Journalism and Its Effects." An even clearer reflection was an intensification of his real-estate venturing. And one of these ventures led to the most peculiar, and in many respects most important, incident of his career in this period, one that was anything but Marxian in its implications.

In September, 1887, Altgeld had purchased an eight-story building located on the Chicago River, fronting Market Street between Adams and Jackson Streets. His plan was to convert the warehouse property, for which he paid $200,000 to the the Union Warehouse Corporation, into an office building. A few months before, an ordinance providing for construction of a bridge over the river at Jackson Street was passed by the city council. In June, 1888, Judge Altgeld appeared at the City Hall, in consequence of the bridge project, with a complaint. His Market Street property, he said, had been damaged by the city and he desired satisfaction. At the office of the City Corporation Counsel he was directed to take the matter up with the official designated as city attorney, then Hempstead Washburne, who later was to become mayor of Chicago.

To Mr. Washburne, Judge Altgeld told his story. After the Jackson Street bridge was built, the city had changed the grade of Market Street to accommodate the approach to the new bridge. He would have to make alterations in his building, and he calculated that he was damaged $60,000. He wanted an immediate settlement. Mr. Washburne observed that so large amount could not be settled. It would have to be handled through a lawsuit.

"But," said Judge Altgeld, "it is a matter of great importance to me to get this claim adjusted as soon as possible, so that I can proceed with my alterations." When the City Attorney again insisted that the matter could be handled only through court action, Altgeld made a proposition. If the city would agree to try the case immediately, out of turn, he would agree to accept as damages any amount fixed by appraisal experts of the city, and call no witnesses himself.[1] The City Attorney agreed. At the trial on June eighteenth, experts for the city testified that Judge Altgeld's property had been damaged $26,494.60. Judge Altgeld accepted that figure. The case then was ready for the jury, when suddenly the City Corporation Counsel, John W. Green, accompanied by his first assistant, Clarence A. Knight, hurried into the courtroom. The Corporation Counsel demanded that the proceedings be halted forthwith. He was the head of the city's law department, he declared. The City Attorney had no right to make an agreement with Judge Altgeld, he insisted. Moreover, the Mayor, John A. Roche, had ordered that the agreement be repudiated.

2

When this interruption occurred, Judge Altgeld was sitting at a table with his cousin, John W. Lanehart. He "seemed tense" while Mr. Green was addressing the court. But he remained silent until Mr. Green stated that Altgeld had been given prior notice by the Corporation Counsel that the city desired to delay the case, implying a breach of legal ethics on Altgeld's part. The Corporation Counsel also let drop a remark that Altgeld was using his judicial influence improperly. At this, Altgeld, the judge who had leaned over backward in cases like those of Goudy's to maintain a reputation for integrity unsullied, "lost control."[2] He leaped to his feet. "His face turned very white," related the *Times*. "He clenched his fists and waved one hand in the Corporation Counsel's face as if he intended to strike him." "It's a lie! A lie! An infamous lie!" he shouted. "And you," he snapped at Corporation Counsel Green, "are a damned liar!"[3]

Sensation! So the newspapers called the scene. Judge Arba N. Waterman, who was presiding, was flabbergasted at the conduct of his brother jurist. Of all men, certainly Judge Altgeld should have known how to respect the dignity of a court. Judge Waterman ordered Judge Altgeld to apologize. He did but "his face was still very white and his anger unabated." Nor was his mood helped any when he heard First Assistant Corporation Counsel Knight refer to him as "pig-headed."

"He should see that he is standing in his own light and ruining himself in the eyes of the people," lectured Mr. Knight.

Probably Altgeld felt like mercilessly tearing into the city lawyer for those remarks, but now he contented himself with some acid retorts. The Corporation Counsel seemingly had "some reason not apparent," for trying to make it appear that he was "trying to rob the city," he asserted. Of course, that was not true, no more than the charge that he was employing "judicial influence to prevent the city from making a proper defense," he said. He denied that he had been given notice beforehand of Mr. Green's desire for delay. To which, however, he could not resist adding: "But even if I had been given notice, I probably would not have paid any attention to it, because I consider the City Attorney authorized to make an agreement!"

Judge Waterman agreed with Altgeld. He ruled that there was nothing unusual in having the case tried out of turn, and that the City Attorney was empowered to make the agreement that was made. He saw no moral or legal reason to permit the Corporation Counsel to intervene, and ordered the case to the jury. A verdict for Judge Altgeld resulted for the amount agreed.

3

Then Mayor Roche entered the case. Through public statements, mainly in the *Tribune*, the Mayor declared that Judge Altgeld's claim would be fought to the highest court, if necessary. Judge Altgeld, he declared, had no right to damages, for he had purchased his Market Street property *after* the Jackson Street bridge was under construction. Hence not Altgeld, but the original owner, was injured, said the Mayor. The City Attorney took up the debate with the Mayor. "All politics!" said Mr. Washburne. "This is an old fight against me, not Judge Altgeld, that is breaking out in a new manner. The Mayor has always been against me."[4] Significantly, the *Daily News* agreed editorially that a political feud, in which Altgeld played no part, was at the bottom of the business. "Mr. Green's intervention was a clear piece of . . . presumption," said the *News*.[5] The *Tribune*, however, took the Mayor's part. "Judge Altgeld," it said, "owes it to his reputation, to the dignity of his position and to the honor of the judiciary not to interpose any obstacles in the way of a re-trial."[6]

Nobody could say that the *Tribune* was wrong there, regardless of the legal aspects of the case. But on June twenty-second, when the motion for a re-trial was heard by Judge Waterman, Judge Altgeld again was victorious. Not, however, without being subjected to some judicial disciplining. His outburst was "too grave an offense to be condoned by mere apology," announced Judge Waterman. Therefore he felt impelled to hold Judge Altgeld guilty of contempt and fine him $100. Altgeld declined to appear in court to be fined, but did come around later. He seemed calm.

"Judge Waterman did exactly right," he told newspaper reporters. "I would not have blamed him had he sent me to jail. My display of temper was both wrong and unwise."[7] He expressed himself similarly when Edward Osgood Brown and some other lawyer friends visited him in his own chambers to express their indignation over an "unjust act by a fellow judge." "Nonsense," he said. "It was exactly right. I was angry, acted foolishly and was treated according to the judge's duty and my own deserts."[8]

4

Yet he seethed inwardly, if not over the contempt action, certainly with rage against the Mayor and the Corporation Counsel. A brief that was filed in his behalf in the Appellate Court the following November, after the city appealed, revealed his smoldering resentment. Ostensibly, it was prepared by John W. Lanehart, as his attorney, but nobody but Altgeld could have written that document. It read not so much like a legal paper as a polemic.

"Consider the record a moment [his brief said]. The plaintiff [Altgeld] had put the whole case into the city's hands. He wanted simply to get the matter adjusted and be done with it. To accomplish that purpose, he made a proposition that is without parallel in the entire history of the city. He offered to have his damages fixed by experts to be retained by the city alone. Surely any city official who was willing to deal honestly with a citizen would accept such a proposition. [But] the plaintiff is put to the expense and delay of litigating this case through the Appellate Court and Supreme Court. He is to be harassed for years as a matter of petty spite. . . .

"We submit that this is an outrage. . . . Men temporarily holding public position under the city, and being paid out of the city treasury, public servants, should not be allowed to thus trifle and sport with the property and rights of a citizen."[9]

Whether right or wrong, the man who placed words like that in a legal brief was not a man to be crossed, without causing some fur to fly. The City Corporation Counsel sensed this trait in Altgeld and so, when arguments were heard before the Appellate Court, the Corporation Counsel was at pains to state that he had no desire to reflect upon Judge Altgeld's character. Only a legal question was involved. Judge Altgeld had done nothing "immoral" in bringing his case, the city lawyers assured the Appellate Court.

5

Before examining the effect of that effort by the city lawyers to soothe Altgeld, it is necessary to ask: Was he in the clear in that case where "moral" aspects are concerned? He was always among the first to assail improper conduct on the part of a judge. When, about that time, the newspapers made an issue of the propriety of judges accepting railroad passes, he announced emphatically that when passes were sent to him he "always sent them back. I do not think that a judge should accept favors from parties who either are or may become litigants in this court. . . . Even if it did not influence him, it tends to make the public and even the bar feel a little distrustful, and to that extent weakens his usefulness," he said.[10]

Yet in his own case he not only accepted a favor from City Attorney Washburne, but actually courted it. His conduct, indeed, was all the more indefensible because basis existed for a reasonable difference of opinion as to the validity of his claim.

His case was not open and shut. Mayor Roche spoke the truth when he declared that Altgeld had purchased the property after the bridge was under construction. Altgeld conceded that. But he contended that the change in the grade on Market Street constituted a separate act by the city, and since the grade change occurred after he acquired the property, he was entitled to damages as the owner. His point was one of those phases of law against which he frequently preached—legal technicalities. Not that his was a frivolous technicality. Judge Waterman, a jurist of unimpeachable integrity, upheld its validity, and so did still another judge later. Nevertheless, his claim for money from a public treasury was based upon a technical point, and so his conduct, for one who preached the gospel of civic rectitude, did not reflect credit upon him.

He seems to have realized this after having started in the case. But he was too stubborn to admit his error. Instead, he reacted as if he was under some irresistible compulsion to defend himself all the more vigorously. Hence, the intemperance of his brief. Hence, too, his violent reaction when the Appellate Court rendered its decision in his case on April 17, 1889.

That Appellate Court decision in the case of *John P. Altgeld v. City of Chicago* was an evasive affair, one calculated to irritate a man of Altgeld's legal views even if he were not personally involved. Two months earlier, a General Assembly committee considering judicial legislation had asked Judge Altgeld to give his views on the operation of the courts. With some feeling, he expressed the idea that one of the principal faults of the judicial system was the frequency with which higher courts reverse decisions of the lower courts "not because an actual injustice has been done . . . [but] on some point which neither side thought of or urged in the court below."[11] He mentioned the Appellate Court specifically. And now, here was a decision in his own case which seemed to him a glaring example of his general complaint. It patently dodged every point at issue. No decision was given on the validity of Altgeld's agreement with City Attorney Washburne. And Altgeld's main contention—his legal technicality—was scarcely mentioned. Yet, somehow, the court reached the conclusion that the judgment of the lower court be reversed and another trial held.[12]

But that was the least objectionable feature of the decision to Judge Altgeld, for the court had done an unusual thing. It had appended a statement which read:

"Considerable feeling has been manifested in the case, and the counsel for the city on oral argument having expressed the hope that decision might be made which would not reflect upon the appellee [Altgeld] and, as, under such circumstances our silence on the subject may be misconstrued, we think it right to say that, from the facts disclosed by the record, it appears that the course pursued by the appellee was fair, open and free from any just grounds of censure."[13]

6

When Altgeld read that statement, he once more "lost control." The court had presumed to give him, Judge John Peter Altgeld, a bill of good character! Waiting not an instant for a sober second thought, he summoned a stenographer and dictated a letter to "the judges holding the Appellate Court at Chicago." He got to his point immediately.

The judges, he told them, had stepped outside the question submitted to them by attempting to give him a "certificate of character." Now, he declared, he did not complain of its decision in the case itself and he had "nothing to say against [the judges] as individuals." But he "declined" to accept their "certificate of good character." And his reason? "I have long thought that your court simply picked at the bark with its fingernails, and seemed almost incapable of deciding a case on its merits." In fact, he considered the court "a kind of obstruction to the administration of justice by it so frequently reversing meritorious cases on grounds that nobody cared about or thought of when the cases were being tried." It had been so in his own case, he said. Not that he was complaining, however, for "better men than I am, with equally honest claims, have had to submit to like treatment."

"But [he concluded] when you render a decision which some people would regard as a moral outrage, and you in the same opinion undertake to patronize me, then I protest and say to you that this was not submitted to you, and even if it is no more foreign than the point on which you reverse the case, still the statute does not authorize you to force this on me, and as I do not want your praise I ask you to strike it out.

JOHN P. ALTGELD."[14]

Probably nothing more contemptuous had ever been experienced by the judges of the Appellate Court than that letter dispatched to them so impulsively by a fellow judge. Nothing was done or said about it in public, but the letter was not forgotten. Not at least by one of the three to whom it was addressed, Judge Gary, who three years before had presided over the Haymarket trial.

7

In his little book *The Cost of Something for Nothing*, Altgeld would observe that "taking something for nothing, or wronging a fellow being in any other way, will recoil on the actor with deadly results."[15] If that really were the "law of the world," his general conduct in his case against the city probably ought to have resulted then in some sort of setback for him. Actually, it had just the opposite result in his political career.

Ten days before the Appellate Court gave its decision, the 1889 mayoralty election in Chicago had been held. Mayor Roche stood for re-election. During the campaign, it had appeared that Roche would win easily. He had the so-called "good government" elements behind him. Likewise, a majority of the labor leaders were for him, for one particular reason. Roche had discharged both Inspector John Bon-

field and Captain Michael Schaack from the police force, something
even Mayor Carter Harrison declined to do.[16] Moreover, the
Democratic organization was badly split when a former superintendent
for the streetcar company, De Witt C. Cregier, defeated Carter Harrison for the nomination.

Yet election night revealed that Roche was beaten by some 12,000
votes. Hunting for the cause, the political editors and the politicians
discovered that voters numbering almost exactly 12,000 had voted
their choice for mayor by using a new—and mysterious—ballot that
was labeled "The Anti-Machine Ticket." And that ticket, while containing the names of some Republicans to give it a non-partisan aspect, was marked for Cregier. It was plain that the "Anti-Machine
Ticket" had swung the balance for Cregier and caused Mayor Roche's
defeat. So Roche's managers conceded. Who was responsible for that
bit of Machiavellian strategy?

Politicians and newspapers alike wanted to know. Fuming against
the perpetrator of the Anti-Machine Ticket "scheme," the Tribune
guessed that it was either one Frank Collier or Judge Richard Prendergast, whom it called the shrewdest politicians in Chicago. On second
thought, however, the Tribune said, the scheme must have been engineered by both. "It was far too clever to have come from any one
man's brain."[17]

But while the Tribune guessed, the Times knew who had executed
the coup.

"It originated [said the Times] with a calm, resourceful, silent man
of indomitable industry and of acute perceptions, who believes in the
maxim that what you would have well done do yourself. He is a man
of strong originality, a democrat, who had no personal end to serve. . . .

"This gentleman knew that if the sentiment against the Republican
machine was given concrete expression, the Mayor would be beaten.
A keen observer of events, an intelligent interpreter of public opinion,
he confirmed his own view by personal inquiry made among electors.
. . . He knew also the great potency of party habit and the unwillingness of electors publicly to scratch a ticket. He proposed to meet
that situation by placing the so-called Anti-Machine ticket in the hands
of electors on the day before election. The point of attack was
Roche. . . ."

The editorial went on to describe the enormity of the task which the
"calm . . . silent" man undertook.

"All this work was done hurriedly but thoroughly and without a serious break of any kind. Its cost was about $5,000. The whole expense was discharged without a murmur by the projector of the plan. A check for $100 was tendered and declined."

Then the *Times* took issue with the charge of the *Tribune* that the scheme was "unscrupulous." It was shrewd, but legitimate, said the *Times*. The paper had nothing but admiration for the technique, although it had supported Roche. "It was a swift, noiseless weapon . . . fatally effective if well employed and silent upon the identity of the hand that wielded it." To which the *Times* added: "Its author is entirely satisfied with the results."[18]

8

Every statement in that revealing editorial was true except one. The "author" of the Anti-Machine Ticket (not named by the *Times*) was not wholly lacking in a "personal end to serve." For it was Altgeld who had carried through that scheme—and he did it to get his personal revenge upon Mayor Roche.[19]

CHAPTER SIXTEEN

THE BUILDER

1

WHEN word of what Judge Altgeld had done to Mayor Roche percolated through the political world, even master manipulators like King Mike McDonald doffed their hats. A man who could defeat mayors single-handedly deserved some respect, even if he espoused ideas that appeared "queer," like those in his second book, *Live Questions*, published in April, 1890.[1] What impressed the McDonalds most of all was Judge Altgeld's willingness to spend his money for political purposes. They never forgot that "important" political fact.

In 1891, when talk of a successor to Mayor Cregier was heard, Altgeld was mentioned frequently. "Judge Altgeld," observed the *Daily News*, "is regarded as one of the strongest men that could be named by either party." However, it added, "he doesn't want to be mayor."[2] That was true. But he did want to be in Congress—specifically, to be a United States senator. Probably first stirred in Missouri by the prominence of Carl Schurz and later by his nearness to election as a senator in 1885, that ambition had become "one of his consuming passions."[3]

In January, 1891, the Illinois General Assembly convened to elect another United States senator. In that assembly the Democrats had 101 members, the Republicans, 100, and once more there was a deadlock. Three so-called Independents, Grange men in reality, held the balance of power, for it took 103 votes to elect. Through January, February and into March, the three groups stood pat—the Democrats for former Governor John M. Palmer, the Republicans for John V. Farwell, the Independents for Allanson J. Streeter. It was 1885 repeated, except that the chances now favored a Democrat. Although supposedly bound by party allegiance to support Palmer, Altgeld set up his senatorial lightning rod again. Party loyalty? It had not troubled him much in Savannah, nor did it this time.

144

2

Later, when it would have been bad politics to admit anything, Judge Altgeld vehemently denied that he had attempted to steal the 1891 senatorial election from John M. Palmer.[4] But he did, a forgotten aspect of that chapter in Illinois political history usually referred to as the "Story of the Immortal 101." Secretly, he used practically all of the tricks known to political art in an effort to make himself a United States senator that year at the expense of the aging Palmer— something Palmer never forgot. In telling of Altgeld's part in that senatorial election, the Chicago Tribune a year afterward spoke of "the unbounded treachery, to call it by no harsher name, practised by John P. Altgeld toward John M. Palmer, who was the regular nominee of the Democratic organization."

"His work [said The Tribune] was done with a 'fine Italian hand.' He showed himself in Springfield during the contest as a friend and supporter of the regular nominee, Palmer. He was in the Palmer councils, and pretended a zeal for the success of the party not at all consistent with the treacherous work he was in fact doing through his agents, and which had for its object the undermining of Palmer and the substitution of Altgeld as the Democratic nominee."[5]

Discounting the righteousness of the Tribune's indignation over "treachery" to Senator Palmer (the Tribune itself was then engaged in heroic efforts to "undermine" Palmer), there is no doubt that the truth was told there.

One of Altgeld's "agents" in that episode was none other than Clarence Darrow. Ostensibly, Darrow had gone to Springfield about February first on business for the city of Chicago, for Altgeld had had Mayor Cregier appoint him assistant corporation counsel. But Darrow's true motive was to interview State Representative James Cockerell, one of the three Independents, in an effort to swing his vote to Altgeld. His argument was that Judge Altgeld, because of his views on labor, would represent the independent voters, both rural and urban, better than any other man.[6] A Chicago newspaper got wind of Darrow's meeting with Cockerell and blasted it on its front page. There were quick denials by everyone, including Altgeld.[7] But soon afterward—according to Cockerell—Altgeld himself was in secret conference with the Independent assemblyman. And later State Senator Richard Burke, close friend of Schilling and a labor leader in Chicago,

also called on Cockerell in Altgeld's behalf, to assure Cockerell that
one of the other three Independents, a Dr. Moore, already had been
won over to Altgeld.[8]

3

That reference to Dr. Moore ties in neatly with a letter that Altgeld
hurriedly dispatched from Chicago to Springfield in March. It was
to R. A. D. Wilbanks, well known as an under-cover political manip-
ulator.

"Chicago, March 9, 1891.
"Dear Wilbanks: I think you are mistaken. I have later advises
[sic]. —Show or give enclosed to R and have him read it to Moore—
and assure him that it is all right—
"Then have paper returned to you—for if it gets out it may cause
change of programme—*it is vital to have Moore seen at once—Make
arrangement as definite as possible.*

ALTGELD."[9]

That letter was written by Altgeld at a crucial moment in the Palmer
contest. For at that very time it appeared that the 101 Democrats
who had been standing by Palmer since January might at last break
away for another candidate, one who could get the votes of the Independents. Was that what was referred to in the enclosed "paper"
that Altgeld sent to Wilbanks? If not, it was at least plain that Altgeld's "Dear Wilbanks" letter boded no good for Palmer, despite a
statement by Altgeld later that it was written to help Palmer rather
than to undermine him,[10] for Altgeld's statement explained nothing.
And Wilbanks made an affidavit swearing that his presence in Springfield was as the paid agent of Altgeld. He spent Altgeld money, Wilbanks swore, in an effort to get the senatorial nomination for him.[11]
On the night when the deadlock finally broke to give Palmer the
senatorship—a poker game in which considerable money changed
hands supposedly had much to do with the break—Altgeld was in
Springfield. A great celebration was held there by the Democrats.
But Altgeld, noticeably, took no part. Instead, he departed immediately for Chicago and from there sent Palmer a telegram. "I congratulate you on the splendid generalship shown in this fight. JOHN
P. ALTGELD."[12] It was a message far from remarkable for its
enthusiasm, a fact that gives some color to the observation by the

Tribune that after Palmer's victory "Altgeld stole out of Springfield like a thief in the night, defeated and disgusted."[13]

4

He did not sulk for long. "If all the efforts I have made which produced no results were collected and piled on top of me, they would bury me so deep that Gabriel's horn could never awaken me."[14] So he joked in addressing the University of Illinois graduates, and that doubtless was his attitude on the Palmer matter. Moreover, he had something else to occupy him—achievement of what he himself called his greatest ambition, construction of "the finest and best office building on earth."[15] For some time he had confided to his intimates his plan for building a skyscraper in Chicago. A number of his friends sought to dissuade him.

When he told Adolf Kraus, who was corporation counsel under Mayor Carter Harrison, of his plan to sink $400,000 of his personal fortune into the scheme, and borrow even more, Kraus was aghast. "Four hundred thousand dollars at six per cent will bring you a yearly income of twenty-four thousand dollars. The way you live you cannot possibly spend it. If the venture should prove a failure, as I fear it will, you would probably never again be in as good financial position as you are now. Why should you take the risk?"

"Because I have no children," Altgeld said. "I have to create something, and so I am creating buildings."[16]

Thus he went ahead, driven by that desire to "create something," a drive that psychiatrists would translate as coming from a tremendous urge for Power. So far, the political world had failed to give him much power. Hence, he fell back upon his own resources.

5

In January, 1890, he purchased a ninety-nine-year leasehold on an eighty-foot lot (now 127 North Dearborn Street) practically the most expensive part of downtown Chicago, agreeing to pay an annual rental of $18,000. Then, in the month of the Palmer election, he organized the Unity Company, a million-dollar corporation for the erection and management of what was to be known as the Unity Block. Lanehart was designated as president and there were four other directors: Charles J. Ford, Elmer Kimball, Isaac M. Kuebler—and Altgeld. But the corporation was all Altgeld. Kimball was a law clerk, Ford was

Mrs. Altgeld's brother, and Kuebler was Altgeld's court bailiff, whose only business experience was running a small grocery in a suburb.

"No one else acted for the Unity Company," Altgeld once declared.[17] Apparently he insisted upon that. He interviewed the architects and contractors, went over all of the plans, selected the materials, and handled all of the financing details. His private bank account was consolidated with that of the corporation. He issued checks against his private account and the corporation funds without discrimination. This was the first of a number of disastrous errors. For, while he had a genius for business affairs that required imagination and boldness, he was careless in details. Illuminating is the testimony that he had a habit of dashing off checks wherever he happened to be, with "many coming through written on brown wrapping paper."[18]

Another error was his impatience to see the sixteen-story structure take form. In August, 1891, he let it be announced with considerable pride that "the Unity Block is being put up in less time than has been consumed in the erection of any other building in Chicago. . . . Everything is systematized and each man knows his duty without being told."[19] This haste proved costly, for after the framework was nearly complete, Altgeld received dismaying news. The framework had been placed too close to the wall of the adjoining McCormick Building, and because mortar and brick had fallen between the two walls, the Unity Block superstructure was thrown dangerously out of plumb. It cost Altgeld in the neighborhood of an extra $100,000 to fix it.

6

He made an even more serious mistake in the financing. His scheme called for issuance of bonds for $400,000 to raise a total of $800,-000. He interested a number of bankers in the bond plan, several of whom bid for his business, among them John R. Walsh, president of the Jennings Trust Company and of the Chicago National Bank. Now Walsh was the last banker with whom Altgeld should have done business voluntarily. His reputation then was that of a "fast operator." Moreover, he was the publisher of the *Herald*, which had been so antagonistic toward Altgeld in his judicial election. And Walsh habitually mixed politics with banking. Probably it was this fact that caused Altgeld to look favorably upon a business deal with Walsh. Doubtless he believed that an alliance with Walsh would prove advantageous politically. As for Walsh, he appears to have gone out of his way to get Altgeld's business for the same reason. It would not hurt to get this Altgeld, then being mentioned for mayor, in his financial web!

They made a deal, Walsh agreeing to underwrite the $400,000 bond issue. Among the terms insisted upon by Walsh were two provisions that seemed unimportant at that time. The bonds were to be redeemable in gold, and (to protect Walsh) the tenants' leases of the Unity Block had to provide that rent payments were payable, on demand, in gold. There was embarrassment ahead for Altgeld in that gold clause, but he did not see the point at the time.[20] More serious immediately was another provision: Altgeld was required to go ahead with the construction as far as his own money would carry it. Only afterward would Walsh advance additional sums as the money was required.[21]

In May, 1891, payments by Walsh suddenly were held up after only a small amount had been paid.

"I went to see Mr. Walsh [Altgeld testified in court later] and he seemed quite excited and said money was too scarce, that he could not raise it, and couldn't advance any more. I had several interviews with him on the subject, and he gave practically the same answer.

"I finally told him that it left us in a position where we would be ruined if we could not get any more money. We had already advanced all we could raise, and could not go on, and that we must get more money."[22]

Altgeld was indeed desperate. He had sold or mortgaged nearly all the property that he owned, including a streetcar line in Newark, Ohio, near Mansfield, that he had acquired for $100,000 in 1890. And he had made a number of short-term personal loans. From John M. Oliver, a lawyer with whom he had become acquainted while in the Reaper Block, he had borrowed a total of $70,000 at eight per cent.[23] Banker Walsh knew that he had Altgeld in a tight spot, for the building was half up. Walsh insisted that the former contract be torn up and a new one made providing for a bond issue of $300,000 instead of $400,000. Later, in a legal brief, that act of Banker Walsh's would be referred to flatly as "treachery,"[24] and from that time on bad blood existed between Altgeld and Walsh. But Altgeld affixed his signature to the new contract on June 27, 1891. He was $100,000 short—on top of the extra expense occasioned by the sag in the superstructure.

"I was obliged to raise that $100,000 myself . . . mostly on short-term paper, and do it as I could. I carried it along for several years that way. It embarrassed me very much." To which he added:

"But we finished the building!"[25]

7

Yes, he finished the building, a truly magnificent structure for the period, one so well built that more than forty years later it remained one of Chicago's best. And he had no regrets, even though he possibly sensed then that in this venture he had gone too far. In 1893, when he lunched, as a guest of Jane Addams, with Sidney and Beatrice Webb of England, the British sociologists asked him to sketch the story of his life. After he did so, they asked what achievement had given him the greatest personal satisfaction. "The Unity Building," he said.[26]

He would stand for hours on the sidewalk across from the building as it was going up, his short, stocky legs spread apart, his hands stuffed in his pockets, and gaze at the superstructure. It gave him a peculiar pleasure. Once Judge Theodore Brentano, later United States minister to Austria-Hungary, encountering him thus, noticed that he had a "dreamy look."

"You know," Altgeld said to Brentano when the acquaintance interrupted him, "I have put all my money in that building!"

He impressed Brentano as having been deliciously proud of his recklessness.[27]

8

But because Walsh reneged on the original bond deal, Altgeld felt he had to devote all his energies to seeing the Unity Building project through. And, anyway, by then he was completely fed up with the judgeship. On July first, 1891, four days after he was forced to accept the new contract with Walsh, he sent a crisp message to the Governor of Illinois resigning as judge. On July thirty-first, he spent a half hour on the bench, disposing of an unimportant motion submitted by a lawyer's clerk. Then, in the words of a newspaper reporter, "the well-known jurist and able lawyer was ready to lay aside the honors and duties of the judgeship."[28] The next day he replaced Lanehart as president of the Unity Company—a "private individual" once more.

CHAPTER SEVENTEEN

THE CANDIDATE

1

HE THOUGHT that his beloved Unity Block would serve to keep him a "private individual" for some time, at least until another chance at the United States Senate developed. But the Unity Block had exactly the opposite effect—almost immediately.

His resignation "caused a great deal of surprise."[1] There was skepticism in political circles about the reasons he gave. Knowing his past performances for springing political surprises, and still impressed by what he had done to Mayor Roche, the politicians wondered what Altgeld was up to now. A governor was to be elected in 1892. It looked like a Democratic year, although no Democrat had been elected governor in Illinois since 1856. Was Altgeld preparing for that?

He wasn't, for he was sincere in wanting to be a "private individual," except for the senatorship. But nobody believed him.

"Have you then no future policy in regard to political life?" a reporter asked him on his last day in court.

"Absolutely none."

"Is there any truth in the statement that you are a candidate for the office of governor?"

"No. I am not a candidate for any office."

"Suppose you were tendered the nomination? Would you accept it?"

"There is going to be a scramble next year for the nomination of governor," he said. "I do not want to be governor, and naturally I do not wish to enter a scramble for something I do not want." To which he added: "Understand me, I am not declining something that has not been offered and that is not within reach."[2]

But suppose it were within his "reach"? The politicians buzzed. The buzzing fed upon itself, and within a few weeks an incipient Altgeld-for-Governor boom had developed without his so much as lifting a finger. It grew stronger as the Unity Block grew higher. For the politicians looked at the Unity Block and saw a "million dollars."

151

They recalled the money Altgeld had spent to defeat Mayor Roche. What better timber for a governorship campaign could possibly exist than a candidate with a million dollars? Altgeld, a "man with a barrel," could pay for his own campaign! That seemed an irresistible qualification to the politicos.

2

Some of Altgeld's friends began feeding the boom—Joe Martin, Schilling, Darrow and Lambert Tree. Soon, too, Lanehart took a hand. Already he was something of a boss on the North Side. Altgeld did not help; he did not hinder either. He watched. The press began taking notice. "Mr. Clayton E. Crafts wishes to be Governor, but the Democrats of Chicago say they think Judge Altgeld ought to be Governor. . . ." So one newspaper as early as August, 1891.[3] In October, 1891, the *Daily News* reported a groundswell of Altgeld sentiment in southern Illinois. There was a good reason, for copies of *Live Questions* began going into the mails to politicians after the manner used by Altgeld for distributing *Our Penal Machinery and Its Victims*. "Reports from the southern counties are very encouraging to Judge Altgeld. . . . Mr. Crafts does not feel at all comfortable," related the *News*.[4]

Also uncomfortable was General John C. Black of Danville and Chicago, brother of Captain William P. Black of the Haymarket trial. As a close political ally of Grover Cleveland, General Black felt that the gubernatorial nomination was coming to him for "loyal party service." Moreover, he closely represented the aristocracy of the Democracy in Illinois, the "Old Guards," symbolized by Senator Palmer, "Horizontal Bill" Morrison, Carter Harrison and William C. Goudy, the men who had been controlling things (along with King Mike McDonald) for a generation. But the Altgeld boom began overshadowing Black's, too.

3

On December thirtieth, the *News* confided that "the really grave question" is not whether Altgeld can get the nomination "but whether he will accept."

"A gentleman who is intimate with Judge Altgeld is authority for the statement that Mr. Altgeld is not exactly desirous of being elected governor. He is not unwilling to make the race and *pay the bills,* but he really doesn't want to be governor. . . . He is willing to run for governor, provided, if elected, he is not thereby debarred from becoming a candidate for United States Senator to succeed Senator Shelby M. Cullom in 1894. . . . But Altgeld, it is believed by those who are intimate with him, will make the fight if the nomination comes to him in any fashion that looks like a demand upon his party fealty. . . ."[5]

Altgeld himself probably gave out that interview, as a trial balloon.

Among those who saw the balloon was King Mike McDonald. Joe Martin had been talking to him about Altgeld. That helped. But Mike appears to have had a reason of his own to favor the judge. He had some scores to even with the "Old Guard" of the Democracy, the Palmers and Harrisons who were getting rather touchy about being associated with the gambling boss. Did King Mike see a way of getting subtle revenge upon the blue-bloods by supporting this Judge Altgeld who, while a "good government" man, probably impressed McDonald as one who would seek to destroy the aristocrats like Palmer?

"Judge Altgeld is O.K.," said King Mike.

4

On March 4, 1892, the Cook County Democratic convention met at the North Side Turner Hall to select delegates to the state nomination convention to be held at Springfield the following month. Altgeld men, directed by Lanehart and State Senator John P. Mahoney, planned for a resolution instructing the full Cook County delegation to vote for the nomination of Altgeld. All that the "Stop Altgeld" movement, in which Goudy was secretly a leader, hoped for was not to endorse someone else but to keep the delegates unpledged. The Altgeld resolution was introduced with a whoop by an Irish state senator, John F. O'Malley, as King Mike "stood looking on under his plug hat.[6] . . . Whereas, the Democratic party of Illinois wants a candidate . . . who can win. . . . Whereas, we have in our midst that fearless, able and efficient jurist. . . . Whereas, Judge Altgeld's association with the masses. . . . Whereas. . . . Whereas. . . ."

One or two voices of protest were raised. A Crafts man demanded to know "what great services Mr. Altgeld had rendered the party to entitle him to the high honor of an endorsement above all the other candidates." He was hooted down and then, as was said by the *Herald,* "the little man who puts up high buildings was named as Cook

County's choice for Joseph Fifer's seat."[7] Only downstate Illinois remained to be won.

5

All through the development of the Altgeld boom, the leading Democratic newspaper in Chicago had remained noticeably non-committal. Apparently Banker Walsh, who had come to hate Altgeld because of the Unity Company deal, was biding his time. But when he saw that Altgeld, after the Cook County triumph, was heading for the nomination at Springfield, Walsh's *Herald* rallied to the "Stop Altgeld" forces. At first it gave the impression of being concerned only with the best interests of the party. Judge Altgeld was an estimable character, but was he "the strongest man"? However, when Altgeld's strength increased downstate, Walsh gave the signal for his editors to go after him without restraint.

"No Boss Gambler Bossism!" shouted Walsh's *Herald* on March twenty-eighth as its opening gun. "It becomes more and more evident that the Democrats of Illinois . . . are not going to nominate a man for governor of this state simply because the boss gambler of Chicago says they must. It is the misfortune of John P. Altgeld that his candidacy represents nothing else so much as the impudence and greed of a man who has brought discredit upon Democracy upon many occasions." The reference was to King Mike. Old Guard Democratic journals downstate reprinted that editorial. "The plan," observed the *Daily News*, "is to create the impression that Altgeld is Mike McDonald's tool and ally . . . because it is known that connection with Mike McDonald will blight any man's prospects in the rural counties."[8]

Soon the *Herald* let loose another charge, one based upon Altgeld's book *Live Questions*. "A serious objection to Judge Altgeld . . . is the absence of evidence showing he is a Democrat. Nothing can be quoted from his public writings to establish his Democracy, while quotations *ad libidum* can be made from that source which will be used by the enemy to prove that Judge Altgeld is a socialist." Of course, the *Herald* said, it did not "claim that Judge Altgeld has any sympathy for anarchy or anarchists." But, it observed, "his writings are popular with socialists and anarchists."

The *Daily News* was amused. "The slight incompatibility of being Mike McDonald's man and being a red and an anarchist is not allowed to interfere with trotting out the stories in double harness," it observed.[9]

Altgeld said nothing, but gave the order for printing 17,000 more copies of *Live Questions*. "If Walsh wants a fight over that book of mine, we will make it worth while for him," he said.[10]

6

But Walsh had other ammunition. On April twenty-second, the *Herald* retold the story of Altgeld's case against the city. "What do the Democratic voters of Illinois think of a candidate for governor who, while occupying a judicial seat in Cook County, appeared in the court of another judge . . . and so conducted himself that he was rebuked by the court and compelled to apologize . . . and was fined for contempt?" The "scandalous condemnation suit . . . [was] evidence of his unfitness for high office," the paper declared. Next the *Herald* dished up the story of the "Anti-Machine Ticket" in the Roche campaign. True, Altgeld had helped the Democrat Cregier. But had he not placed the name of the Republican candidate for city attorney, George Sugg, a German, on some ballots, instead of the Democratic candidate, Michael J. Bransfield, an Irishman? "This," declared the *Herald*, "represented not only party disloyalty, but German Know-nothingism!" Finally, the *Herald* told part of the story of Altgeld's "duplicity" in the Palmer senatorial election. This, it said, was "despicable . . . stamping him as a man unworthy of the confidence of Illinois Democrats. . . ."[11]

Publicly, Altgeld answered none of the *Herald* editorials. But when he went to Springfield for the convention, Michael J. Bransfield was with him, and Altgeld let it be known that he favored a resolution commending Senator Palmer as a candidate for president at the Democratic national convention that same year. Thus he met what he considered the most damaging charges, that he was "against the Irish" and "treacherous" to Palmer. The state convention turned out to be a duplicate of the Cook County gathering. It was Altgeld on the first ballot.

Probably a few delegates favored him because of his ideas on social problems. But most were impressed by what they had heard of his Unity Building and the million-dollar fortune that structure supposedly denoted.

7

Until his nomination was announced, Altgeld had stayed in the background, remaining at his hotel, where he shook hands with visitors

and passed out so many cigars that "Altgeld smokes" became a standing joke. Now, however, he stepped into the open to acknowledge the
cheering and make a speech, one that had been prepared by him in
advance. It was a good political talk, but worthless as revealing anything about him except his political shrewdness. Most loudly cheered
of his remarks was a not-too-subtle reference to jobs. The Republicans
must go, to be replaced by deserving Democrats.

He scarcely touched upon the labor question and, when he did,
linked it up with the tariff. By indirection he rebutted the charges
that he was a "radical." "Why," he said, "your candidate has spent
his whole life in the enforcement of the laws." (Applause.) If he is
elected, there will be "prompt and thorough enforcement of the law
because a state that hesitates in the enforcement of the laws soon becomes pusillanimous." (Cheers.) His sympathy for labor? It is simply
that " he does not believe that because he may have been a little more
successful than some of the men who toiled with him, therefore he
should now put his heel upon their necks." And: "He believes that
the man who toils with his hands to support his family . . . must have
justice done him; must have what the laws give him, but neither more
nor less." (Cheers and cries of "Good! Good!")[12]

8

One aspect of his speech was noteworthy for its treatment of his erstwhile opponents. The attacks upon him from the "Old Guard" had
been vicious, especially the references to the city case. Ordinarily he
could have been expected to strike back. Instead, he showered the
men who had opposed him with praise. He purred with good will and
charity. This was not Altgeld the lawyer and judge, but it was Altgeld
the candidate. For the duration of the campaign, the proud, seemingly frigid Judge Altgeld impressed all who met him as an ingratiat-
ing, warm and even humble "good fellow."

When with rural folks, he sat around "contemplatively picking his
teeth."[13] Newspapermen were struck by his modesty. Willis J. Abbott, then helping Carter Harrison edit the Times, recalled how Altgeld walked into the office, hat in hand, to introduce himself. "My
name is Altgeld and I am a candidate for governor."[14] Brand Whitlock, then political reporter for Walsh's Herald, had a similar experience. During an interview, Altgeld suddenly interrupted to ask Whitlock where he could get "a cravat like the one you have on." Flattered,
Whitlock offered to give Altgeld the necktie. "His face changed, the

mask fell, and he shook his head and said, 'No, it would not look like that on me!' "[15] So Whitlock wrote about it, believing that incident revealed something wistful in Altgeld's character. It was a pose, Altgeld the candidate again.

His whole campaign was largely based on that pose of being "just folks." That, and an industriousness such as never had been witnessed in Illinois politics before. Ordinarily, candidates for governor, although nominated in the spring, waited until fall to begin active campaigning. His Republican opponent, Joseph W. Fifer, standing for reelection, announced in May that "there is no haste about opening the campaign." Fifer would wait "until the harvest, when the farmers will have leisure to talk and listen to politics."[16] When Joe Fifer made that statement, Altgeld had been in the field nearly a month. Disregarding even the grand opening of the Unity Block, he gave himself scarcely more than a week end after the nomination before "he stuffed some things into a little brown valise and tramped out into the prairies of Illinois."[17] He was started on what the Republicans sneered at (in the beginning) as "Altgeld's political handshake." Before fall, it took him all over the state.

9

Meantime, the Republican press opened up—the *Tribune* in the lead. The Republican candidate, as even supporters admitted privately, had been a fair governor, but not a great one. And except for his Civil War record, "Private Joe" Fifer was colorless. He had offended no one as governor, but he had not pleased many groups either. And so, instead of defending or praising Fifer, the Republican press concentrated upon attacking Altgeld. The Democratic *Herald* had supplied most of the material, and it was used. The first line was to picture Altgeld as a dangerous radical, a socialist if not an anarchist. It was the *Tribune* that led off.

"The anarchists and socialists will rally around this man who professes to be an anti-capitalist, the 'workers' and 'strikers' will be enthusiastic for the rich man who will bleed at every pore. . . .

". . . The criminal classes will take kindly to a man who thinks that they are the victims of society rather than its enemies, sufferers from an arrested development for which they are not responsible and who should be tenderly cared for. . . ."[18]

He would be an easy man to beat, opined the *Tribune*, for which it gave thanks that Altgeld had published his book *Live Questions*. It would "furnish the best ammunition to be used against him," the paper believed.

The *Daily News* disagreed, feeling that Judge Altgeld, "while a man of means," would win many labor votes because of his "consistent record of sympathy for the working classes." It felt, too, that he would be strong "with a large proportion of the foreign-born." Moreover, the *News* called him a "clean candidate" with "an admirable record for probity in public and private status."[19] But few of the other Republican papers felt the same way.

"Anarchist!" "Demagogue!" was the cry heard through the state. Later Altgeld would be termed "scoundrel" as well, and labeled (by the *Tribune*) "a shameless falsifier," a "bloody blackguard."[20] It was denied that he had ever served in the Civil War, with "documentary proof" submitted. "Altgeld's war record," volunteered one journal, "is like the man who lost his nose—he simply hasn't any!"[21] When such tactics appeared not sufficient, the anarchist charge was dropped and he was pictured as a "machine monster . . . a tool of Mike McDonald." And finally, the cry was that he was not even a socialist, but only pretended to be. He didn't like the working people at all. He was a "millionaire fraud." To alienate a growing body of silver and bimetallist Democrats, the *Tribune* dug up the gold clauses in the Unity Building leases. "Altgeld is just a gold-bug after all!"[22]

And all the while, Altgeld simply kept on shaking hands and making, for the most part, only informal little speeches in village halls or stores. He had learned how to meet abuse in a political campaign. Ignore it. Almost the only charge he answered was the socialist accusation, because it was influencing the farm vote. But he did this in an interview, not deigning to dignify the matter in any set speech.

"Pshaw! Statements about my socialistic tendencies excite only a smile. Such stories are intended for country consumption exclusively. But the country people are not fooled. . . . The country people will know that it is absurd to talk about a man being a socialist or anarchist who has spent his whole life enforcing the majesty of the law and who has built some of the finest business blocks in Chicago!"[23]

But while downstate he was careful to visit the town bankers and the leading businessmen as well as talk to the workers and the farmers. He talked of business conditions, mentioned his Unity Block, and left the impression that he was as sound a man as ever ran for office. Yet it was the workingmen who were impressed most of all, especially the coal miners. "He met the miners as they were coming up out of the ground and shook their grimy hands and looked into their faces before they had a chance to dig coal dust out of their eyes." So Brand Whitlock stated in the *Herald* in a story that he persuaded Banker Walsh to let him write.

And Altgeld tramped into the cornfields to talk with the farmers in the same way. The hostile Chicago *Inter-Ocean* sneered that "Judge Altgeld has visited more families, kissed more babies, inspected more dairies and helped set more hens than any man before who wanted to be Governor."[24] Probably that was true. He was indefatigable. Temperature of ninety-six degrees in the shade found him driving in a horse and buggy over dusty roads to make a meeting in some hamlet of less than a thousand in population. The *Herald* noted of him during the dead heat of August: "Judge Altgeld, after a fifty-two-mile drive, reached [Carthage] at ten o'clock last night. . . . He was up holding a public levee at 6 this morning, and at 9 started for Duquoin and Pinckneyville."[25] He made a point especially of spending considerable time in communities where Germans predominated, and talked German to the men and their *Frauen*. "This remarkable feature of his campaign cannot be commented upon at too great a length," said Reporter Whitlock. "To the Germans, the privilege of talking in their native tongue to a man who is the candidate for the highest office in the state is so rare that they never tire of talking about it and marveling at it."[26]

The *Tribune* wisecracked once that "the Illinois Democrats want Altgeld to quit shaking hands and shake his barrel,"[27] but he kept on. When results of his handshake became noticeable, attracting even the favorable attention of Grover Cleveland, who believed it would help him win the presidential election that year,[28] the *Tribune* and others of the opposition took to snarling again. In contrast, Altgeld showed himself always good-humored, never more so than when he came to the state capital, Springfield. Instead of dodging a meeting there with his opponent, he went directly to the Executive Mansion to call upon Governor Fifer. He had come, he said, "to make a few converts." Newspaper reporters howled with delight. When Governor Fifer responded by offering to let Altgeld sit in his chair to "see how it fits," there was more laughter at Altgeld's answer. "Not just now, Governor. I will take it next winter and keep it four years. You don't want this place any longer anyway. You have sucked that orange dry and got all there is in it!"[29]

10

Yet when the formal speaking campaign opened in the fall, he was merciless in denouncing Fifer. Answering no charges against himself, he made many against his opponent. Fifer was violating state laws in perpetuating convict labor. Fifer was responsible for "criminal" maladministration of the state institutions. Fifer, he said, was a tool of the Know-nothing elements, a charge that apparently had no, or little, basis. And Fifer made the mistake of answering his charges, so that the campaign seemed to be all about Altgeld and no one else.

Shrewdest of all, Altgeld blamed Fifer for a school bill passed by the General Assembly of 1889 that had the Catholics and the German Lutherans up in arms. This bill, known as the Edwards Act, provided generally for compulsory education of children up to the age of twelve. Two provisions excited the religious groups. One was that reading, writing, arithmetic, history and geography must be taught in English (which the Lutherans resented) and the other that state truant officers should inspect both public and parochial schools (resented by the Catholics).[30] Early in the campaign, Altgeld recommended that this issue of "the little red schoolhouse" be made the principal basis for the Democratic attack on Fifer,[31] and he hammered upon it to the last day.

It was a deadly issue—and one unfairly trotted out against Fifer. It was unfair for two reasons. First, the Edwards Act had been a nonpartisan measure, with nearly as many Democrats voting for it as Republicans. Second, impressive evidence indicates that Altgeld himself had as much to do with getting the Edwards Act passed as Fifer. He had served at times as a voluntary lawyer for the Chicago Woman's Club, the organization that originally sponsored the measure, and there is creditable evidence that he sat in on conferences when the bill was prepared, probably helped draft it.[32] Moreover, before he became a candidate for governor, he had discussed the Edwards Act with Schilling and told his friend that he approved the act in principle. "It is right that foreign-born children should be taught in the English language. It is necessary if they are to become good American citizens," he said.[33]

And yet there he was in the campaign bitterly strafing Fifer because of that act which he had favored! Too late did the *Tribune* learn of his earlier position, and shout that the school act was the "child of Altgeld's brain!" By that time Lutheran and Catholic sentiment throughout the state had been crystallized. And so, as one observer commented later, Judge Altgeld had managed to group behind him some "unnatural alliances and incongruous combinations. . . . Roman Catholics for the first time [finding] themselves in accord and voting with their ancient Protestant foes, the German Lutherans . . . the champions of law and order in church and state in fellowship with communists and anarchists and workingmen. . . ."[34]

11

More legitimately, but no less shrewdly, Altgeld worded his speeches in that campaign so carefully that while he appealed to labor and took advantage of a growing labor unrest, he appeared to say nothing that could be labeled "radical." For he dealt with the labor question in the most general terms, and this even in a Labor Day speech at Elgin, Illinois, when he might have been expected to "open up." He was against a high tariff. He was against monopoly. Big corporations were profiting by the tariff and not passing on enough of their profits to the workers. Something should be done to prevent exploitation of the workers. Thus far did he go, and no farther. He was even mild when there occurred that summer the bloody Homestead, Pennsylvania, steel trouble. "It is unfortunate . . . pitiable," he said about the Homestead massacres. "The policy of the government in the hands of the Republicans is to take care of the rich on the pretense that the rich will take care of the poor. The Homestead affair shows how misleading and pernicious is this doctrine."[35] Even old Senator Palmer commented more "radically" on Homestead than Candidate Altgeld.

Yet the liberals, including Henry D. Lloyd, and the principal labor leaders believed they had a friend in Altgeld nonetheless, and worked like beavers for his election. Schilling formed an "Altgeld Labor Legion" that covered the state with propaganda on the labor views of the Democratic candidate. Altgeld paid most of the cost of that activity personally. His personal outlay, in fact, was placed at $100,000, meaning the relinquishment of nearly the last of his property holdings that had not been pledged on Unity Company loans.

12

On November seventh, the *Illinois State-Register* at Springfield told the result of the campaign. "Shout The Glad Tidings, Our Country Is Free! Everything Democratic and The Majorities Increasing!"

Grover Cleveland was re-elected president, and a new "Little Giant in Illinois" had been elected governor, the first foreign-born, the first Chicago resident in the history of the state.[36] The governor-elect received the returns in the study of his Frederick Street home, Mrs. Altgeld with him. Mrs. Altgeld was proud of what her "little Dutchman from over the hills" had achieved. And yet she had a flicker of regret, too. He had promised to take a trip with her abroad if he were defeated.[37] And she knew how very much he needed such a trip. Perhaps, too, she had a perception, womanlike, of what lay ahead, of what that nervous energy of his, his many-sided character and his drive for power, might lead him to do as governor.

BOOK FIVE

The Pardon

CHAPTER EIGHTEEN

The Governor

1

He began his term in misery. Was he suffering because unemployment once more stalked the land, Wall Street pressed a cross of gold upon the mortgage-laden farmers, Grover Cleveland planned betrayal of the Democracy, and three men brooded in Joliet prison over a conviction for a bombing which everybody admitted they did not perpetrate? The Altgeld Legend, as constructed by his admirers, would have it so.

However, from his story up to now, one that shows that he was not always one hundred per cent "ethical" in his private capacity, not above a certain amount of political chicanery where his personal interest was concerned, nearly always motivated as much by his desire for wealth and personal aggrandizement as by his liberal instincts, enough is known to suggest the necessity for sprinkling the Legend with a quantity of salt. Altgeld was a humanitarian whose heart ached over injustice. But he was also a human being—and a politician loving the perquisites of political success, the sensation of being in the public eye, the acclaim, the prestige, and all the rest of it.

And he began his term in suffering because that was so. When he should have been resting after the strain and excitement of the campaign (enough to have broken a truly robust person) he yielded to indulgence in a round of parties, banquets and receptions to honor the Governor-elect. Nor were they working-class affairs; far from it. They called for the starched shirt and swallowtails. Night after night immediately after the election, he decked himself out in such plutocratic garb to spend the evening shaking hands, consuming banquet food, making and listening to fatuous speeches, and in dancing. And he did those things because he enjoyed them, not from a sense of duty.

The fashionable North Shore Club of Chicago, for example, gave a dinner and dance in his honor. He was quite the life of the party with no one whirling handsomely bedecked partners about the ballroom more frequently or with greater zest than he. So many of the elegantly

165

dressed ladies now wished to dance with John Peter Altgeld! And he
loved it. To one partner, he gaily remarked: "I would rather dance the
Oxford, and dance it well, than be governor!"[1] Thus, instead of con-
serving his energy, he burned it up on the ballrooms. The Ohio Society of Chicago suddenly discovered that Altgeld was a credit to the
Buckeye State and tendered him a banquet. No one sang the glories
of being born or reared in Ohio more eloquently than he that night, or
laughed louder at the toastmaster's joke about the Negro who did not
vote for Altgeld for governor "because he stands for 'arnica.'"[2] Or,
possibly, ate more freely of the banquet food. Two dozen oysters were
a mere appetizer for him when in good form.

In addition to such social affairs he gave himself over to endless conferences with the politicians who came to express their congratula-
tions—and also to ask for that Railroad and Warehouse Commission
membership or this or that prison or state hospital job. At first they
came in two's and three's. Then they filled to overflowing the spacious
reception room of his fourteenth-floor offices in the Unity Block.
Finally, it was like a mob. Later, this parceling out of spoils would
mainly be a source of bitterness. The time was to come when he would
relate:

"At first they come with their hats in their hands and are very
grateful when you do something for them. The next time they come
with their hats on their heads and when you give them something they
scrutinize your gift. When they come again and you are forced to refuse them, they roundly abuse you."[3]

But as governor-elect he took sheer delight in it all. Here was
Power indeed! Especially was it pleasing to him to be in a position to
repay some old debts of gratitude. He gave to his first friend in Chicago, Edward Osgood Brown, the position of attorney for the Lincoln
Park Board in Chicago. He appointed faithful George Schilling, then
eking out a living as business manager for the revived (and much less
violent) Arbeiter-Zeitung, secretary of the State Board of Labor Statistics. Nor did he forget other men who had helped him along.
Even Josiah Kent, the school trustee in Missouri whose potatoes Altgeld had dug to get the job of teacher, was remembered. He showed
up with a position in the Governor's office, and nobody except Altgeld
knew why this Missouri farmer was able to get on the Illinois payroll.
All that gave him real pleasure, but it finally caused a complete
physical breakdown before his inauguration. His ailment appeared to

be nervous exhaustion, plus a return of the old fever that he had picked up from the James River marshland in '64, plus the first signs of another and crueler affliction to be noted later. So serious was his collapse that he himself expected to die without ever becoming more than governor-elect.[4] Bundled off to Hot Springs about the first of December, he rallied there somewhat, but suffered a relapse when he returned to Chicago after a month.

2

His inauguration was set for January 10, 1893. While on his sickbed, feverish, he had pieced together his inaugural address. But his doctors shook their heads in warning. They were not interested that thousands of faithful Democrats, who were already crowding Springfield to cheer Altgeld (and later drop around to see him about a job), would be disappointed. Did he want the signing of his oath of office to mean also the signing of his death warrant? Yet because he could not resist the appeal of a scene of triumph, he defied the doctors. A "slow-way" train which left Chicago for Springfield on January eighth found him aboard, doped with medicine, uncomfortable, but resolute to go through with the rôle of conquering hero—if it killed him, as it very nearly did. For once, even the *Tribune* was sympathetic. Of his trip, it noted that "all the while, the hero of the Illinois Democracy lay in the rear stateroom of the parlor car, curled up on one of the seats, with his face drawn and pallid."[5]

On the morning of the tenth, Governor Fifer waited in the Executive Mansion to escort Altgeld to the inaugural ceremonies in the chamber of the state House of Representatives. Unquestionably, "Private Joe" was bitter toward his successor, because of the charges Altgeld had made against him during the campaign. But when he saw Altgeld that day, Fifer had not the heart to be other than sympathetic. It is not known what coldly polite greeting Fifer had planned for his successor, but what he said was: "Mr. Altgeld, you are looking bilious." Then, with the tenderness of a nurse, the retiring Governor offered Altgeld his arm to lean upon as they walked slowly to the inauguration.

Altgeld needed the support. He was "very pallid" all through the wild cheering. The atmosphere was so stifling that other men collapsed from the heat, but he kept on his overcoat, for he was chilled. When the time finally came for him to make his speech, after a long valedictory by Governor Fifer, he made a supreme effort to go through with it. But he had to quit after two or three minutes. He tried to make a joke of this necessity saying, "I will now have the reading clerk, who has a pleasant voice, finish the reading of the address."[6] But he looked so ill, even from a distance, that it was freely predicted by many in the hall that he would not live out his term. And at a reception that night he again defied his doctors to take his place with other state officials in the receiving line. Supposedly an affair of dignity, the reception was a riot. Not even Vice-President-elect Adlai E. Stevenson could get through the crowd. But there was Altgeld, white as paper, in the center of it. Only when he came near fainting did he give in and go to bed.

Ten days later Dr. Charles Pague advised Mrs. Altgeld that her husband had to go south for a complete rest. "His life depends upon it," the doctor said. On January twenty-fourth, so weak that it was considered remarkable that he could walk from the Mansion to a carriage, he was placed aboard a train for Asheville, N. C. As he reclined in his sleeper he remarked, "I feel so well, I think I will change my mind about going."[7] But this time he followed orders.

He returned in February, but even after the spring thaw set in he was an invalid. Over at the Capitol, the Legislature was in session, with Speaker Clayton E. Crafts running things, sometimes in accord with the Governor's views as expressed in his inaugural, sometimes not. It would be late in the term before Altgeld paid much attention to the lawmakers. On sunny days, as his strength gradually but slowly returned, he would take walks around the Mansion grounds. Mrs. Altgeld was often with him, carrying a book to read aloud as they sat on a bench. Sometimes he would be accompanied by his secretary, William F. Dose, who brought papers along for him to sign.

3

He was seen on these occasions by a boy, one not yet in his teens, who lived in a house across from the Mansion grounds. Nicholas Vachel Lindsay had seen Oglesby and Fifer, but this new governor, with his emaciated face and shoulders stooped from illness, fascinated him as no other man before or after. Even from afar, the boy felt the quality of Altgeld's deep blue eyes and somehow sensed the strength and deep feeling mirrored in them. It was then that Lindsay began forming his poet's impression of Altgeld. A new Lincoln had come to Springfield, so the watching boy felt![8]

In later years Vachel Lindsay would find those first impressions of

Altgeld superbly corroborated. But at the time scarcely anyone else thought of Altgeld in that admiring way. The more general idea was in accord with the view expressed by William H. ("Buck") Hinrichsen, who was elected secretary of state with Altgeld. Hinrichsen wrote: "Had Altgeld died during the illness with which he was seized immediately after his inauguration, he would have had a place in the history of the state as no more than a lucky politician. . . ."[9]

If the boy Vachel Lindsay had known the subject matter of the papers he saw Altgeld perusing and signing in that period, he might have shared the politicians' opinion of Altgeld. For in those papers there was no glory or drama, nothing to inspire a poet's devotion— such as found fruit in The Eagle That Is Forgotten. They dealt mainly with the shabby business of "vicing" Republican hold-overs in state positions in order to make way for "deserving Democrats." In this respect, Altgeld was no reformer, only rarely an idealist. If he was Jeffersonian in his political philosophy, more so than any other public figure of that time, he also was definitely Jacksonian (as the term has come to be understood). He had made up his mind to clean house of the Republicans, and he carried through his plan without much discrimination or many twinges of conscience.

Good men went with the bad. There was, for example, the case of Dr. Richard Dewey, later one of the nation's most honored psychiatrists. He had been head of the state insane asylum at Kankakee, Illinois, since 1879, and was thoroughly competent. He had even pioneered in methods which Altgeld himself admired and wanted introduced generally. Yet Dr. Dewey was ousted with the others. Even some of Altgeld's friends protested at this, pointing out that it was inconsistent with his authorship of Our Penal Machinery and Its Victims, but Altgeld declared: "I am determined to have some new blood at the heads of these institutions, and no amount of whimpering will prevent it."[10]

Worse still, in addition to failing to discriminate in removals, he did not always discriminate in exercising his appointive power as between "good" Democrats and "bad" Democrats, even when it was politically possible for him to do so. It happened that he replaced Dr. Dewey with a man equally good, Dr. Shoval Vail Clevenger. He did not even know what Dr. Clevenger's politics were. Yet when Dr. Clevenger suffered a nervous breakdown within a few months from worrying over the venality of certain other officials appointed by Altgeld, he obtained little sympathy from the Governor. Dr. Clevenger, according to his own story, went to Altgeld to ask his help to "defeat the big thieves of the hospital." Altgeld, he said, paced up and down in his office, thought a while, and then said: "Doctor, the machine is not satisfied with your administration and calls for your resignation."[11]

Perhaps Dr. Clevenger was too zealous in his efforts to balk the politicians. He admits having been a chronic "reformer" and having looked for trouble. However, Altgeld personally had nothing but contempt for the same trustees who had made Dr. Clevenger's life miserable. He gave one of them a verbal lacing at a dinner party that caused the victim to "hang his head like a hurt spaniel and nearly swallow his knife."[12] The man was a brewer, who apparently believed he was appointed trustee of the state hospital so that he could sell beer to the visitors. Yet Altgeld stood by the brewer against the conscientious doctor.

Not all of his appointments were like those of the trustees at Kankakee. But too many were. As a result, there were scandals, shortages in accounts, fires due to carelessness, even incidents of brutal treatment of patients in state institutions. The explanation is that he was still thinking of attaining his ambition to sit in the United States Senate. If he wanted to be senator, he could not offend the "boys," especially not legislators when they came around for jobs for wives, brothers, cousins, sisters, in-laws—and mistresses. Editor Henry W. Clendenin, of the Democratic Springfield *State Register*, always friendly to Altgeld, recalled that he tried to prevent the appointment of men unfit in character, "but Altgeld was obdurate." "You must give me specifications," the Governor would say when told that so-and-so's reputation was not good.[13]

4

Still, on the credit side, it should be stated that in the matter of cleaning house of Republicans so ruthlessly, he was motivated also by views not of a spoils character. He honestly believed that a "complete change of management at reasonable intervals [was] absolute necessity for good public service," he wrote to a South Carolinian.[14] Moreover, in certain major appointments he did ignore politics entirely. Appointment of Maj. R. W. McLaughry as warden at Pontiac Reformatory was an instance. McLaughry, later warden of the Federal prison at Leavenworth, always had been a Republican. But Altgeld had met him while gathering data for *Our Penal Machinery and Its Victims*, liked his progressive ideas and defied the organization in appointing him. An outstanding instance was his appointment of Florence Kelley, associate of Jane Addams at Hull House, as chief state factory inspector. Perhaps that one selection made up for a hundred, even a thousand, mediocre-to-bad appointments. Both the politicians and the business interests howled over the Kelley nomination, but Altgeld proved as obdurate then as in the other cases, and for once Illinois obtained real factory inspections.

He did his level best, too, to get his appointees to perform properly once they were in the jobs. More than any other governor of his state before or since, he visited the various state institutions to see for himself what was going on. He snooped in the kitchens and sleeping quarters of inmates.[15] He lectured, cajoled and scolded. He laid down definite rules, relating even to the menus. If followed, his rules would have produced the finest possible type of administration. Even though the law did not require it then, he insisted that bids be requested from "every business house that is at all within reach" when supplies were to be purchased, and the lowest bid accepted in every case.[16] "This," he told a conference of trustees, "is a subject upon which we can tolerate neither evasion nor trifling."[17] He abolished the offices of purchasing agent because, he felt, those agents were nearly always corrupt or subject to corruption.

More than any of his predecessors, he encouraged a spirit of inquiry for improved methods, particularly with regard to prison management. He ordered a study of prison methods used in other states and also in Europe and personally encouraged laboratory experimentation to seek cures for the insane and the crippled. On his initiative, the practice of forcing convicts to wear striped uniforms was abolished, because he felt it was unnecessary and degrading. Also on his initiative, young offenders were segregated from hardened criminals, and he pushed through a law providing, in effect, for parole of prisoners on good behavior. It was the first such law in the Middle West.

Because he took so great an interest in the affairs of the state, the results of his bending to the "exigencies" of politics were not so disastrous as they might have been, and the complete picture at the end was more on the credit than the debit side. But this was so only because he exerted himself at the cost of further inroads upon his already weakened physique.

5

Probably it would have been just as well had he taken things in the field of administration a little easier.

He only *thought* he was greatly interested in keeping down expenditures, and causing the politicians to take their feet off the desks. Had these things really mattered to him, it is certain he would have shown a different character to the politicians despite his senatorial ambitions. For a man soon to be found defying almost every newspaper and magazine in the nation, even his own strong ambitions, in order to be right with his conscience—such a man could not have been taken in by petty politicians against his will. Had he devoted himself to being a so-called "good government" reformer and nothing more, perhaps he might even have gone to the Senate. For then the Tory newspapers might have sung his praises, as long as his reform did not get much beyond a matter of bookkeeping.

But Altgeld's destiny was not to be a bookkeeper. His destiny was to be—a Voice, one "crying in the wilderness for the maimed, the beaten, the sightless and the voiceless."[18]

CHAPTER NINETEEN

THE CONSERVATIVE LIBERAL

1

HE WAS not a very strong voice in the beginning of his governorship. Nor was this to any large extent because of his illness. Always there was in his mind the idea of the senatorship. Always then, too, there was his idea of caution until he attained the proper forum for expressing the views that he had assured George Schilling he possessed. He thought that forum had to be a national one to mean anything. When had a governor, as governor, caused any stir outside his own state, especially with regard to the issues in which Altgeld was interested? On his last day as judge, in 1891, he had raised that point when interviewed by the press.

"We have in this country [he said] now forty odd governors, and it would be difficult for any man to point out wherein the whole forty had, for ten years, done anything of an enduring character for their country or for the progress of civilization . . . anything that can be regarded as raising the standard of public morals, creating a healthy public sentiment, or solving in a proper manner any of the great questions, both economic and social, that are calling for solution."[1]

He had hoped to be different, although he was not especially optimistic. But the senatorship—that would be his opportunity, he thought.

His attitude of caution was reflected in his inaugural message. Except as it is examined closely in the light of what is known of him before his gubernatorial campaign, and also in the light of his later actions as governor, this first utterance of his after he became governor gave scarcely any promise, either in tone or content, of what was ahead. The address showed him cognizant of the labor problem, of industrial exploitation of women and children, of improper use of troops in strikes, of injustices in the judicial system and of need for more enlightened policies in the care of the wards of the state. But it did

173

not reveal, superficially, much more than mere cognizance. There were no fiery phrases and only suggestions of standing for definite progressive policies.

2

When the Tories read his inaugural with their coffee next morning they ought to have felt that Governor Altgeld represented no greater threat to their economic interests or prejudices than his predecessors. True, the *Tribune* muttered about certain "semi-socialistic" passages,[2] but it was plain that this was little more than partisanship. Obviously, Altgeld was in no wise to be classed with "radical" governors then holding forth in other states, Hogg of Texas, Pennoyer of Oregon, Lewelling of Kansas or "Bloody Bridles" Waite of Colorado. Those were wild men! Populists! But Altgeld? He would be safe enough, judging from his inaugural.

Only two passages in the speech could have been at all disturbing to the "interests." One was a reference to municipal ownership of utilities. Yet this was only a reference. "A number of large cities, both in this country and in Europe, have made the experiment of supplying their inhabitants with water, gas, electric light, and even operating the street railways, with very satisfactory results. I commend this subject to your careful consideration."[3] The other was an indirect recommendation, the first ever made in Illinois, for an inheritance tax. But this was free from any ranting against huge unearned fortunes. His recommendation amounted only to a calm observation that "some of the states have tried the experiment of a heavy graduated succession tax on the estates of deceased persons [and] I commend this fact to your consideration."[4]

Probably the Tories felt that the new Governor devoted an uncomfortable amount of space in his speech to labor matters. But they could not complain that his remarks were in the least inflammatory. He spoke of the sweating system and of growth-stunting child labor, upon which some of the best families in Chicago based much of their big incomes. But what, after all, did he say? Simply that such conditions "call for more thorough legislation."[5] As a matter of fact, some of his statements had a rather capitalistic ring. For example, he went out of his way to mention that in Chicago "hundreds of millions of capital" were invested in industry. And while he asserted that "the State [in strikes] must not pursue such a policy as to convince the masses of the laboring people that the authority of the State is simply a convenient club for the use of the employer," he prefaced that observation with a warning that law and order would be rigidly maintained while he was governor.

"The State must do justice to both employer and employe; it must see to it that law and order are maintained, and that life and property are thoroughly protected. Any weakness in this regard would be pusillanimous and invite incalculable evils."[6]

He discussed the effects of strikes and lockouts, but mainly from the point of view of the public, "the non-combatants," (as in his first pronouncement on labor in 1886). He mentioned the idea of arbitration. But now he was not nearly so strong on this as he had been while a private citizen. He talked about "the practicability of arbitration" and was found admitting that "the State cannot compel an unwilling employer to run his shop, nor can it compel unwilling employes to go to work."[7]

At first blush he may have sounded disquieting when he gave his views on the use of state troops and Pinkertons in labor disputes.

"We must not forget that the law contemplates that the civil officer shall protect life and property, and for this purpose may order out the *posse comitatus* when necessary, and that a too hasty ordering out of the military creates irritation and bitterness which frequently results in unnecessary bloodshed.

"Many civil officers have shown a disposition to shirk their duty during a strike, and this has been followed by the introduction of an irresponsible force controlled by private individuals. The presence of these armed strangers always acts as an irritation and tends to provoke riot and disorder, and we should take warning by the experience of some of our sister states and absolutely prohibit the use of these armed mercenaries by private corporations or individuals. *At the same time, we should see to it that the civil officers do their duty.*"[8]

But what did he say there, in so many words at least, with which even young Cyrus McCormick could find fault? Was he not telling the local police to do their duty in strikes?

Actually, labor leaders had more reason than employers to be critical of that section in Altgeld's talk. Not many of them would have agreed with the thesis that "armed mercenaries" were used, say, at McCormick's in the 'eighties, only because the local police did not perform. Probably Altgeld himself did not truly believe that. But

he was in earnest about local officials doing their full duty before
troops, state or Federal, are ordered into action in strikes and lockouts. It will be seen how consistent he was in that view, especially
with regard to trouble brewing even then in George M. Pullman's so-
called "modern industrial community." Few portions of his speech
held more vital future significance than that section, unless it was one
in which he discussed justice: "If we are to prosper, we must make
all of our people feel that the flag which floats over them is an em-
blem of justice."

Did he have in mind justice—even for anarchists?

3

So much for Altgeld's inaugural. Yet, mild and cautious as it was,
it contained the basis—in its emphasis upon the problems of labor, its
views on the use of troops, its plea for justice to the defenseless poor,
its references to municipal ownership of utilities and to inheritance
taxation—for nearly everything he would do to make astigmatic conservatives decry him as a radical and to make grateful workingmen
and liberals hail the staunchest friend they had in any position of
prominence. For one thing, his message contained more promise of
liberal action than appeared on the surface because of a fact which
only a few men saw at the time, or later. This was that in large part
his message was reiteration, at times phrase for phrase, of his utterances
on social questions made when he was much less of a politician than
now—especially the ideas in Our Penal Machinery and Its Victims, in
the Chicago Mail essay on labor disputes of 1886 and in his discussion
of the evils of sweated and child labor contributed to the Chicago
Times in 1888. They were toned down now, yet the knowing eye
could see reflected in that message Altgeld's earlier not-so-cautious
ideas on economic conditions. In short, the seeds of his liberalism
still remained, despite the surface soil of practical politics and personal
ambition.

Not, however, for six months—a long time to wait in a four-year
term of office—would the first real harvest of those seeds show itself.
In the meantime, as the snows of January gave way to the spring rains
and summer was at hand, Altgeld was still conducting himself, so far
as could be seen, in no extraordinary way at all. He let the legislature
at that session do about as it pleased. For a man with so strong a
will to dominate as he possessed, he was singularly modest with respect to guiding or prodding the assemblymen. The legislature did

pass a fairly strong bill, called the Factory Inspection Act, designed to eliminate sweatshops, restrict employment of children in factories (though not in mines and mills) and also to prevent employment of women for more than eight hours. It also passed a bill—one of the first in America—a forerunner of the Wagner Labor Act of 1936, making it a misdemeanor punishable by a fine for an employer to discharge a worker because he was a member of a union. Yet Altgeld himself would say when the first measure was emasculated by the State Supreme Court (the second was killed entirely) that he "was not instrumental in securing the passage of the bill." "It was," he said, "a result of a legislative investigation made into the 'sweatshop' system in Chicago which came to me simply as chief executive of the state."[9]

As for his ideas about establishing boards of arbitration for labor disputes, for improving the quality of justice in the Chicago police courts, for establishing the system of indeterminate sentences, for imposing high fees upon corporations, for an inheritance tax and for overhauling the taxing system in general to make the wealthy pay a fairer share of the cost of government—these matters in which he was so deeply interested personally were ignored entirely by that first legislature, although he did jam most of his recommendations through the second legislature. The legislators' only concession to his views on police treatment of the poor was a bill "to prevent the use of uncovered patrol wagons for the conveyance of prisoners."[10]

He sent two messages of rebuke to the Statehouse for its lethargy, but these were mild in subject and tone. One "respectfully" called attention to the fact that the assemblymen had not acted on his recommendation for abolition of certain "useless boards and commissions." The other, also "respectfully," reminded the assembly that it likewise had ignored his views about the wretched judicial system in Chicago. In addition, he made only one notable veto, that of a bill for enlarging two existing insane asylums whereas he felt it was sounder to build additional institutions that individually would house fewer inmates.

Thus, when the assembly adjourned on June 16, 1893, the legislative phase of the "Altgeld revolution" was over, with affairs of state in Illinois running not much differently from before. "Is there not one Democrat in the General Assembly who thinks enough of the Governor to draw up bills to carry out his recommendations?" the *Tribune* jeered.[11]

In fact, if anybody had reason to be disappointed in Altgeld, it was not the disciples of the *status quo*, but the apostles of progress; not the capitalists, but the liberals and laboring folk; not his enemies, but his friends. His friends were thinking: Where is the Altgeld whose writings have given promise of so much achievement? Whose character has given to those who know him so much hope that he will prove an exceptional governor?

Except for the Factory Inspection Law, the women's eight-hour law, and the law prohibiting discrimination against union men, his legislature had been rather disappointing. Perhaps this could be excused on the ground that, after all, he was only the governor. Yet there were certain things that he could do as governor. Specifically, there was the matter of the imprisoned anarchists. Was he going to be another Governor Fifer in that regard? That question especially agitated liberals as adjournment of the legislature reminded them that half of Altgeld's first year as governor already was over.

True, during the very last days of this period, he demonstrated a few flashes somewhat suggestive of the conception they had formed of him—of what Vachel Lindsay in later years called "the Altgeld Temperament." When he learned of the lynching of a negro at Decatur, Illinois, on June 3, 1893, he let loose a blast from the capital that was heard over the nation. Nor did he issue a mere "statement," but a formal, signed and sealed proclamation to remain forever in the records of the state. It bristled with indignation.

"Being authoritatively advised that at two o'clock this morning a mob broke down the doors of the jail at Decatur, overpowered the officers of the law, took from his cell a negro confined there, dragged him out and killed him by hanging him to a post nearby, I hereby denounce this cowardly and diabolical act as not only murder under our laws, but as a disgrace to our civilization and a blot upon the fair name of our State. . . . No matter with what crime he was charged and no matter whether he was guilty or innocent, he was entitled to a trial—a fair trial according to law. It must never be said that the laws of our great and proud state do not afford protection to all without regard to color or condition."[12]

As a footnote to this episode it may be mentioned that no complaints were registered in the press then that the new Governor "sympathized with anarchy and lawlessness." Neither did much praise, if any, come to him from self-styled "law and order" champions. Could it be that they were not overly-much concerned about "law and order" when only the life of a hapless colored wretch was concerned?

A second proclamation reflecting "the Altgeld Temperament"

thundered from the Governor's office ten days later after he learned that some stunt promoters planned a seven-hundred-mile horse race from Chadron, Nebraska, to Chicago. Fond of horses, Altgeld was outraged. In tone quite as indignant as his other proclamation he called upon "all officers upon whom devolves the execution of the laws, as well as upon all good citizens" to see that the race was not held in Illinois.

"We will welcome the so-called 'cowboys' into glory and have a thoroughly enjoyable time while with us, but we cannot permit the laws of Illinois to be trampled under foot simply as a matter of sport."[13]

Much more significant in that period was his conduct on the occurrence that June of the first outbreak of labor trouble to mark his administration. The trouble occurred at Lemont. It was there, eight years previously, that state militia under Governor Oglesby fired on the striking quarry workers and killed two men. That had been one of the incidents so maddening to the anarchistic orators before Haymarket—the very one, indeed, that provoked Lucy Parsons to her outburst about "every dirty, lousy tramp" doing to the rich what Sheridan did "to the beautiful valley of the Shenandoah." And now the picket lines had formed in the Lemont sector again.

On June ninth, there occurred the inevitable clash. As with nearly every such case, it was never known definitely exactly what produced the final tragedy; what part was played by passions of desperation and hatred; what by *agents provocateurs*; whether the employers sought to prevent trouble or encouraged it in order—as often has been the case before and since—to bring state troops as a means of cowing the strikers into submission. But it was known that armed "scabs" fired upon a group of strikers. Two men were killed and many others wounded. The usual public excitement ensued, with much talk about the need for militia intervention. If the militia did come, Altgeld would have to send them.

Holding to the policy that he had enunciated in his inaugural message to the effect that the local authorities must do their utmost in labor disorders before the state stepped in, he declined to order out the troops until advised that such action was necessary. Late that night, however, there came to the Executive Mansion a telegraphic appeal for troops. The telegram, signed by the sheriffs of three counties, Will, Dupage and Cook, stated that "there was rioting, that a number of men had been killed, that the sheriffs' deputies were not able to maintain peace and order and protect life and property, and that a mob of about 5,000 strikers was threatening violence."[14]

Altgeld dispatched an acknowledging telegram asking the sheriffs to advise him how many deputies they had sworn in for strike duty—also "whether anyone had been hurt other than the strikers." That night the lights in the Executive Mansion blazed long after Springfield was asleep as Altgeld waited for an answer. Only the sheriff of Will County responded. But when that official reported that he had one hundred and twenty deputies on hand and still was not able to control the situation, Altgeld acted at once. "Believing the telegram signed by the three sheriffs stated the facts correctly," he gave the order at midnight for five hundred and fifty militia to proceed at once to Lemont.[15]

Except for the inquiry to the sheriffs raising the question of how they were performing their own duties, Altgeld, up to this point, had acted no differently from Oglesby or Fifer in similar circumstances. He had been asked for troops to control a "mob," i. e., strikers, and he had sent them. But his later actions did reveal a difference. Instead of remaining at the capital, he dashed to the scene himself, taking young Brand Whitlock with him.

4

His purpose in going to Lemont was mainly to make certain that the militia did not make matters worse. But he wanted also to learn for himself if the local authorities actually were justified in appealing for troops. What he learned concerning that second objective, as much as anything, gives meaning to Brand Whitlock's recollection of the "expression that clouded his face that afternoon."[16] For he discovered that the three sheriffs had for patrolling a fourteen-mile trouble zone only eight deputies when the trouble occurred, and that the Will County sheriff actually had only twenty-two deputies on duty, instead of a hundred and twenty, after the shooting.[17] In short, as he had suspected, the local authorities had passed the buck to him—or wanted state troops for special reasons. Altgeld was indignant, and showed it, then and later.

However, his first concern was to assure the laboring community that the militia was not there to shoot down strikers, for he found the Lemont workingmen sullen over the presence of the militia. They, too, recalled 1885. But the atmosphere of suspicion soon changed as Altgeld showed the workers by word and action that the militia would confine itself strictly to maintaining order impartially. Glares of the strikers turned to smiles as they witnessed a rare spectacle, that of a governor going among the workingmen to get information on a strike. He walked the legs off his companions, talked to everyone around, climbed railroad embankments, went into the stone pits. In order to get the full story, he traveled a distance perched on a train crew's handcar, his legs dangling in the breeze, while amazed workers cheered "a new kind of governor."[18]

And labor's sympathizers were pleased to note that as a result of his visit to the strike zone Altgeld discovered and published facts considerably at variance with statements broadcast in the Tory newspapers. The *Tribune*, for example, had asserted that the shooting followed an effort of a "mob" of unionists to "march" upon a group of non-striking workers. The strikers, said the *Tribune*, were engaged in a "lawless expedition." The "scabs" had a right to work. Hence, they were justified in shooting.[19] However, Altgeld announced that his investigation showed there was no intention upon the part of the strikers to use violence. The company gunmen had wantonly opened fire "upon some strikers who were walking along a towpath . . . and who were not making any demonstration and were not going in the direction in which the . . . work was being done." He felt it significant that when the first shots were fired "the men on the towpath began to run . . . and were followed by these men with rifles for a distance of about a mile, and they kept shooting the entire distance." That did not sound much like self-defense tactics, and Altgeld plainly indicated his feelings. "The only men who seem to have violated the law yesterday, and that in cold blood, were the men who had been armed by this contractor and who did the shooting," he declared.[20] In short, he sided with the strikers, the *Tribune* with the gunmen, with regard to the incident itself.

5

Yet when Altgeld sent a special report on the Lemont trouble to the legislature, the gist of his message was practically identical with the views of the *Tribune* as to the larger responsibility for the fatalities. After the shooting, the *Tribune* had declared that there would have been no killings if the local authorities had done their duty in the first place. Essentially, this was exactly Altgeld's statement to the legislature.

"It was very apparent to me [he said] that had the sheriffs made
even moderate efforts to enforce the law and protect life and property
by putting on special deputies they would have had no trouble at all;
that instead of there being at one time 5,000 people there, rioters and
all, it was doubtful whether there had been at any time as many as a
thousand people seen there. . . .

"If the law does not already make the sheriffs and his deputies liable
for failing to make a proper effort to swear in special deputies when it
is necessary to protect life and property, then the law should be at
once so amended as to hold them responsible."[21]

And so, even in that incident, while having no reason to complain
about Altgeld, the labor sympathizers and liberals still had no reason
for much satisfaction either. Officially speaking, his "liberalism" in
the Lemont matter appeared to be not much different from the "liberalism" of the *Tribune*. What special satisfaction could be found in
that?

CHAPTER TWENTY

SOME VISITS ABOUT HAYMARKET

1

HE WAS well aware of the disappointment felt by his liberal friends. Early in March, young Clarence Darrow, then thirty-six when Altgeld was forty-five, had been in Springfield to tell the Governor that Altgeld's friends were especially chagrined over his failure to act in the one matter which to many was more important than anything else associated with his elevation to the governorship. This was the case of the Haymarket prisoners.

Darrow had believed, and so told Altgeld immediately after his election, that a pardon for Fielden, Schwab and Neebe would be Altgeld's "first act" as governor. But Altgeld had shaken his head. There were many "affairs of state" that would come ahead of even consideration of that case. "When he could spare the time, he would go over the case and do what he thought was right, but he must take his own time in this matter." Well, three months were enough time, Darrow believed. And so "impatient and worried" and also apparently bewildered by the thought that possibly he "could have been deceived in Altgeld," the young lawyer had journeyed to the capital to talk it over with the Governor.[1]

Altgeld listened with strained patience. He heard Darrow relate that his liberal supporters and friends "were growing doubtful and restless and disappointed." Altgeld was expected to pardon the anarchists, and "at once." "Why, everyone expected it! It had been generally asked for by all the people." This, of course, was exaggeration, if not downright misstatement. Voicing an even greater misstatement, Darrow said, "It will not even create hostility toward you." Finally, rather challengingly, he flatly declared: "I and the others see no excuse for waiting!"

2

Altgeld's feelings at being thus lectured on his duty may readily be surmised. On matters involving his duty he was even less tolerant of criticism than on anything else. There was the fact, too, that he had the right, or must have thought so, to expect something better from this young man who was now in effect rebuking him for infidelity to his principles. Why, Darrow's own liberalism was in large part owing to Altgeld! So Darrow himself would say in the twilight of his life. "Altgeld made my life what it is."[2]

Not only that. Altgeld practically had "made" Darrow professionally by getting him his legal position with the city of Chicago in the Cregier administration and also recommending him to William C. Goudy for the well-paid job he was then holding in the law department of the Northwestern Railroad. In addition, Darrow ought to have recognized that Altgeld was governor. Less than ever now could he be any soap-box orator on such matters, even if he felt so inclined. And what sort of nonsense was Darrow uttering about the political effect of a pardon? Did Darrow and the others take him for a fool?

Moreover, Altgeld knew he was not shirking this matter. Within ten days or so after he took over at Springfield, while still quite bed-ridden, he had quietly asked former Sheriff Kern in Chicago to send him the files on the anarchist case.[3] At about the same time he had obtained the complete transcript of the court records from the State Supreme Court at Ottawa, Illinois. True, he had not yet gone over the papers. They were then in his study at the Mansion, stacks and stacks of them on the tables. However, the matter was never far removed from his mind, even when he was dealing with the politicians.

And he had every intention of acting. But it was no easy thing, aside from the political implications. After all, the highest court in the state had wholeheartedly approved the convictions. The Supreme Court of the United States in effect had also given its approval. Moreover, he knew from his talks with Schilling that certain of the defendants were not so lily-white in their conduct as the liberals now professed to believe, wishfully. No, it was not an easy matter, but the kind of responsibility that would haunt a conscientious man day and night. Darrow's remarks were not much help.

"Go tell your friends," Altgeld told his young admirer, "that when I am ready I will act. I do not know how I will act, but I will do what I think is right."

He spoke "deliberately and calmly," recalling the time another friend, Charles Booher of Savannah, had rebuked him for "forsaking" the Democratic party in the Granger days and how he had "assumed a forced calm demeanor." Probably only his real affection for Darrow prevented a rancorous outburst.

"We have been friends for a long time," Altgeld finally said in addressing himself to Darrow personally. "You seem impatient . . . I know how you feel. I don't want to offend you or lose your friendship. But this responsibility is mine, and I shall shoulder it." And then: "I have not yet examined the record. I have no opinion about it. It is a big job. When I do examine it, I will do what I believe to be right, no matter what that is."

Darrow was convinced of the truth of that last statement. He was "sure that [Altgeld] would have told me his intention if he would have told it to any man. . . . Certain that [Altgeld] did not know then what he would do."

"But don't deceive yourself," Altgeld continued. "If I conclude to pardon those men, it will not meet with the approval that you expect. Let me tell you . . . from that day, I will be a dead man!"[4]

3

On his return to Chicago, Darrow told the other pardon advocates that "it was useless to bother Altgeld again." All they could do was to wait. But a few days after Darrow's visit, another earnest amnesty advocate, also a friend of Altgeld's, appeared in Springfield on a similar mission. He was Judge Samuel P. McConnell, who had been almost as indefatigable as George Schilling in efforts to prevent the hanging of the anarchists, not from any special partisanship for labor but rather from a sense of outraged legal justice. He was the son-in-law of Chief Justice John G. Rogers of the Cook County Criminal Court, who had charged the grand jury that voted the anarchist indictment and later was rejected by the defendants as the trial judge—fatal error!—because of supposed prejudice. After the executions, Judge McConnell was especially active in agitation for release of Oscar Neebe.

Against Neebe the strongest evidence for complicity in the "conspiracy" consisted of two facts: he had owned two dollars' worth of stock in the *Arbeiter-Zeitung* and he had helped distribute a few of the circulars for the Haymarket meeting. Friends felt his chances for release would be better if his case were disassociated from that of Fielden and Schwab, and so they conducted an independent agitation. In accord with that strategy, McConnell called on Altgeld to make a plea for Neebe alone.

But when Altgeld responded that he had "the whole record of the anarchist case in his library and was going carefully over it," McConnell was electrified. He found himself pleading for all of the prisoners. "Altgeld, I believe when you go over that record you will find that Fielden and Schwab were wrongfully convicted and ought to be pardoned the same time Neebe is! I am afraid that it will end your political career, but still I cannot help but urge you to pardon all three of the men, and I hope you will do so."

To McConnell's amazement, the reaction of the Governor was one of "resentment and annoyance."

"By God! If I decide that they are innocent, I will pardon them if I never hold office another day!"

Years later, Judge McConnell conjectured that Altgeld so reacted because he resented a suggestion that he might be swayed by political considerations.[5] In this, McConnell was more correct than he knew. For Altgeld had considered the political consequences of a pardon. Moreover, he had toyed with the idea of permitting such considerations to influence him. This is learned from a reminiscence of George Schilling. In a letter intended for publication in The Public, but suppressed at the time and never made known until now, Schilling had written that shortly after his election Altgeld had discussed with Schilling the possibility of pardoning Neebe at once but reducing the life sentences of Fielden and Schwab to a fixed term. "But he doubted whether any man could continue to live in Illinois and pardon all three."[6]

In short, McConnell's innocent remark had riled Altgeld because it had hit home, in a way which psychologists will understand. His discussion with Schilling betrayed him wavering between the "polestar of duty"—a favorite expression—and his political ambitions. And, clearly, he felt that wavering to be a sign of weakness of which he was ashamed. Unquestionably, at the time McConnell visited him Altgeld was a man tormented by a tremendous struggle because of the Haymarket case. It can be guessed if Judge McConnell's remark helped resolve it for him.

4

McConnell left Springfield that day feeling there was nothing for the liberals to do but wait. In the meantime, the Amnesty Association was active. It quietly continued soliciting signatures for a petition to be presented to Altgeld in behalf of all three of the prisoners. Before the petition was ready the Trade and Labor Assembly of Chicago determined to give Altgeld—and also the public—advance warning. On Sunday, March 19, 1893, the labor body authorized the sending of an "open letter" to the Governor.

"To John P. Altgeld, Governor of Illinos, Dear Sir: In the near future a committee of the Amnesty Association of Illinois, of which the Trade and Labor Assembly of Chicago is a part, will appear before you and ask that Oscar Neebe, Samuel Fielden and Michael Schwab be restored to society and their families as free men. In considering this subject we express the hope that your excellency will be governed by a broader principle than that usually followed in reviewing petitions of persons found guilty of violating the law. . . ."

So the letter began. There followed a plea for clemency, based, not on the premise of unfair conviction, but on mercy. "Their mistakes have been freely confessed. . . . The years of 1885 and 1886 were years of great turmoil in the labor world. No doubt many mistakes were made by both employers and employees. If the bomb which exploded on the Haymarket 'shook the world out of its dream of safety' we must also remember that the balls fired from the rifles in the hands of Pinkertons sent many a worker to his doom without redress, thereby engendering feelings of bitterness that were impossible to avoid."

The closing of the "open letter" placed the matter wholly on the basis of mercy.

"If England can forgive the political conspirator Michael Davitt . . . if Germany can open its hospitable arms and welcome back the revolutionists of 1848, if France can extend, without stint, amnesty to the communards of 1871, then surely the people of the State of Illinois can afford to forgive these men who have suffered so long for their fanaticism and excessive zeal."[7]

Obviously, that presentation of the case afforded an easy "out" for Altgeld. Pushed aside were the controversial questions over the jury, Judge Gary's alleged prejudice, the unfair tactics of Prosecutor (now Judge) Grinnell—and, above all, of the true guilt or innocence of the men executed and the men imprisoned. Mercy alone was requested. Who but the most craven red-baiters could object to such mercy, especially since it was plain that society was now (if it had ever been otherwise) wholly secure from overthrow by anarchists?

In line with that letter, all Altgeld had to do was compose a message of a few lines. "Because the ends of justice have been served. . . . The men are repentant. . . . Society can afford to be generous . . . I, therefore, grant pardons to Samuel Fielden, Michael Schwab and Oscar Neebe." Perhaps he would have been praised more than criticized. Certainly clemency so granted would have proved scarcely more than a one-day newspaper sensation. The act would have been no more than a footnote, rather anticlimactic even, to the Haymarket tragedy.

There is reason to believe that once he had made up his mind what he would do in the case, Altgeld intended not much more than just such a pardon of mercy. Why stir up dead bones, needlessly? It could only serve to prove his remark about being a "dead man." Such were the thoughts that ran through Altgeld's head when, on March twenty-first or so, he read the Trade and Labor Assembly "open letter." As a result of that reading he sent a cryptic message to a Chicago labor leader: "Come down to Springfield on a certain matter."

5

When State Senator Richard Burke, the labor leader, received that message he was puzzled as to its meaning. Burke expressed his perplexity to the one man to whom Altgeld ought to have sent the message but, probably because of the watchfulness of the newspaper reporters, did not. This was George Schilling. He thought that he knew "instantly" what the "certain matter" concerned. He felt excited. "I'll go to Springfield with you!"

It turned out that Schilling had correctly guessed the meaning of the telegram. In that private meeting with Schilling and Burke, Altgeld did not say *how* he would act in the Haymarket matter, but he did then indicate for the first time that he *would* act. He did it with a characteristically impulsive and egoistical comment. He asked that the leaders of the Amnesty Association and of the Trade and Labor Assembly be told that it was not necessary to present any petition to him. In fact, he preferred not to have a petition presented at all.[8] Such devices might have been necessary for governors like Oglesby and Fifer, but not for Altgeld. He would do his duty without thousands of persons, whether of high or low station, conservatives, liberals or radicals, telling him what it should be.

Thus it happened that no petition actually was presented to Altgeld in the Haymarket matter, except the "open letter" of the Chicago labor body—this despite many published statements to the contrary. A petition was ready. It had already had the names of many promi-

nent persons, such as Lyman J. Gage, president of the First National
Bank of Chicago. But Altgeld spurned it, foolishly. Alone with Schilling that day, Altgeld discussed the Trade and Labor Assembly letter
in detail.

"You say here," he pointed out, "that the years 1885 and 1886
were years of great turmoil in the labor world. You mention the activities of the Pinkertons. You speak of the public being wrought up.
You suggest that wrongs were committed against the workers by employers and the police. . . ."

"That is right," said Schilling. "As you know. . . ."

"Yes, but it is one thing to make assertions, and another thing to
back them up with evidence. For example, here is a newspaper article
which appears to have a vital bearing upon this matter."

He produced a clipping from the Chicago *Daily News* of May 10,
1889. It was an interview with Frederick Ebersold, chief of police of
Chicago at the time of the Haymarket bomb. In that interview, Ebersold had attacked Captain Michael Schaack, by way of getting back
at him for uncomplimentary remarks in Schaack's book *Anarchy and
Anarchists.*

Ebersold had declared:

"It was my policy [as Chief of Police] to quiet matters down as
soon as possible after the 4th of May. . . . On the other hand, Capt.
Schaack wanted to keep things stirring. He wanted bombs to be
found here, there, all around, everywhere. . . . Now here is something
the public does not know. *After we got the anarchist societies broken
up, Schaack wanted to send out men to organize new societies right
away. You see what this would do. He wanted to keep the thing
boiling—keep himself prominent before the public. . . .*

"After I heard all that, I began to think there was perhaps, not so
much to all this anarchist business as they claimed, and I believe I
was right."

Altgeld did not have to explain to Schilling the significance of the
Ebersold statement. "But," he said, "this is only a newspaper story.
Ebersold might deny having made it. Before it could be used, I would
have to have an affidavit, or a letter signed by Capt. Ebersold, on its
authenticity. That is what I mean by 'evidence.' Can you get me that
kind of evidence to back up your statements?"

"Altgeld, I can get you a stack of affidavits this high!"[9]

Then they talked of how Schilling would proceed. It would not
do to have word leak out as to what Schilling was up to. Could Schil-

ling work alone? Well, his handwriting was "rotten," Schilling said. He was thinking of asking a friend, Charles Seib, a cigarmaker, to help. Altgeld did not like that, for he did not know Seib. He suggested a name that made Schilling jump out of his seat. The name was that of Edward Furthmann, one of Prosecutor Grinnell's chief assistants in the Haymarket case. Altgeld had known Furthmann for many years. They had made the rounds of political meetings together when Altgeld was a candidate for Congress,[10] and it was for that service, presumably, that Furthmann was named an assistant to Grinnell when that gentleman won the election as state's attorney as a running mate of Altgeld's on the Democratic ticket in 1884.

"All I want that Furthmann to do is to keep his hands off! I want no part of him in this work!" So Schilling blazed at Altgeld's suggestion. He had two reasons. One was Furthmann's general participation in the Haymarket case. It was he who had charge of the detective work for Grinnell. He had worked closely with Captain Schaack in gathering—it would also be termed "framing"—the evidence against the anarchists. The other reason related to a specific instance that had concerned Albert Parsons.

6

Parsons had fled to Wisconsin after the bombing, for he remembered the threats made to him by the Chief of Police of Chicago in 1877. By refraining from indulging his little conceit of dyeing his famous mustachios and by dressing as a farmer, he was safe from detection in Wisconsin. Unquestionably he could have remained in hiding until after the trial of the others. But on the day the trial proper began, Parsons voluntarily walked into Judge Gary's court to take his place with the other defendants. Mainly, Parsons' surrender was sheer heroism.

But it also was in accord with a daring (and tragic) bit of strategy conceived by Captain William P. Black, his lawyer. Convinced of the innocence of Parsons, Captain Black felt that a voluntary surrender, if arranged with the proper dramatic effect, would convince court and jury that Parsons was guiltless. Black, said one of his lawyer colleagues, possessed "a sense of the dramatic."[11] And so Black advised Parsons to come out of hiding. In the meantime he prepared a speech for delivery in open court. He felt that speech in itself would serve to win acquittal for his client.

But Captain Black's speech never was delivered. Before he could open his mouth, Prosecutor Grinnell leaped to his feet, called for Parsons' "immediate arrest." A great chill engulfed the heart of Lucy Parsons as she saw the lawyer's plan fail and Judge Gary order Parsons placed in the prisoner's box without the jury knowing of her husband's voluntary return.[12] It was Furthmann who caused that disastrous denouement, for he alone had recognized Parsons on his entrance into the court and his whisper to Grinnell brought the call for Parsons' arrest. And now, Altgeld was offering Furthmann's services to help in a project that Schilling hoped (he did not yet know) would go toward avenging the wrong he felt was done Parsons and the others!

7

In objecting to Furthmann's help Schilling fell below his usual shrewdness. Obviously, it would have been a powerful point to support the wisdom of clemency for Fielden, Schwab and Neebe, if it could have been revealed that one of the men vitally responsible for their fate had helped gather material for their pardon. Altgeld saw that point. But he, too, fell below his usual foresight, for he indulged Schilling's contempt for Furthmann's services. Thus, after rashly spurning the Amnesty Association petition, Altgeld let slip a second potent means of fending off criticism of a pardon for the trio in Joliet Prison.

CHAPTER TWENTY-ONE

The Re-entry of Judge Gary

1

With George Schilling busy running down affidavits while Altgeld then scrutinized in earnest the voluminous record of the anarchists' trial, the scene in the final act of the Haymarket tragedy suddenly changed to reveal the unexpected reappearance of a leading character long since inactive and silent. This was Joseph Eaton Gary, the trial judge who, up to Altgeld's action, was alternately the most hated and most praised of any participant in the case.

Seemingly urged on by the same hidden currents of human passions that made the bombing and its aftermath assume so strong an aspect of inevitability, Judge Gary returned to the stage to give Altgeld far greater and more vital impetus toward his ultimate determination in the case than the importunities of his friends or his own discoveries in going over the record. This is not to say that Judge Gary prompted Altgeld to make up his mind *what* to do, but it is to say that the trial judge did become a major factor in determining how Altgeld came to act, more important in many respects than the act itself.

Judge Gary did this by conduct as uncharacteristic on his part as it was unexpected—authorship of an extended magazine article about the trial. It appeared in the April, 1893, issue of *The Century Magazine* about ten days after Altgeld's interview with Schilling and was entitled: "The Chicago Anarchists of 1886. The Crime, The Trial, and The Punishment. By The Judge Who Presided at The Trial. And The Law is Common Sense."[1]

The judge probably composed his article about the time Altgeld first began thinking of the case as governor. Gary never had written anything of that kind before. During all the years of the stormy controversy over his conduct in the Haymarket case, he had held himself discreetly aloof. Only once was he discovered giving a newspaper interview on the subject. Just before the executions, when he saw that nearly all of his colleagues on the bench had signed petitions against the executions or issued public statements criticizing the verdict, he complained that his colleagues were acting "unfairly," that in a time of "crisis" when (so he thought) the forces of anarchy and revolution were arrayed against law and order, it was up to all the judges to stand together. He frankly feared assassination.

But afterward, the nearest he came to showing publicly that he was at all responsive to the furore over his conduct, both favorable and disapproving, was his reaction to a verbal bouquet tossed to him at a dinner of the Chicago Bar Association six weeks after the hangings. Lawyer Wirt Dexter, recognized spokesman for Chicago's wealthy class, was discussing the importance of the legal profession, and had said:

"We offer the bulwark of a conservative element. . . . How needful is this bulwark at the present time I need not say, with the deep unrest that exists about us. When men armed with destructive theories seek their enforcement, which would speedily make for us an earthly hell, other professions will expostulate, but the law—and I say it with Judge Gary sitting in our midst—will hang!

"I mention his name in obedience to an impulse of the heart too strong to resist, for I don't believe he will ever know how we feel towards him and how we love him!"[2]

There was much applause, and Judge Gary enjoyed it. When it came his turn to make a speech at that dinner, his own remarks were wholly in line with Lawyer Dexter's enthusiasm for crushing the labor agitators. However, he did not then mention the anarchists' trial himself. But now, for the purposes of *The Century* article, Judge Gary doffed his sphinxlike attitude at a fateful time.

2

Before examining Judge Gary's article, together with its effect upon Altgeld, it is important to set down some observations concerning Gary. From the trial of the anarchists in 1886 until the present, Gary has been pictured in speeches and writings by radicals and also liberals as wholly vicious. This, however, is a mistake, just as it would be a mistake to view Altgeld as wholly saintlike. Unquestionably, he was a prejudiced judge. He practically admits it in so many words in his article.[3] Moreover, in its general tone the article itself would constitute impressive evidence of prejudice if no other facts existed, for, as even the *Tribune* admitted, he is found writing "feelingly" against the anarchists six years later.[4] Since that was true, how much more actively prejudiced must he have been during the heat of the trial itself?

Unquestionably, the anarchists were not given a fair trial by Judge Gary, this aside from the question of their guilt or innocence. Depending upon the point of view, the trial might have resulted in a strictly just determination. Certainly the men hanged and imprisoned had urged resistance to law officers. They *had* spoken and written of dynamite and bombs. However, all the supreme courts in the world could not make of the Haymarket trial a fair proceeding, if only because of the manner in which Judge Gary permitted the prospective jurors to be chosen, and the actual jurors selected. More effectively than any who saw this point, Altgeld would bring it out to the world.

Yet it would be wrong to believe that Gary acted, even in regard to the manner of selecting the jury, from vicious or corrupt motives. He was simply a glaring example of the thesis which Altgeld in his mellower years expressed concerning judges in general. "The judge too often, unintentionally and unconsciously, becomes merely the expression of what is for the time the dominant influence in the land. . . . It requires tremendous strength of character to rise above it."[5] At the time of the Haymarket trial, the "dominant influence" was for hanging the accused anarchists, and that as quickly as possible.

A bit of doggerel which the *Tribune* saw fit to place on its editorial page when the defense was sweating in its effort to get a fair jury illustrates the temper of the community.

> "Proper jury they're trying to get
> At least that is what they say—
> And they make a great pother, and yet
> They's adopting a curious way.
>
> "It's challenge, demur and object
> As the measured days go by;
> It's question, and jeer and regret
> and quibble and falsify.
>
> "It may be the conventional thing
> This labor of counsellor's jaw
> But better a vigorous ring
> of Justice in all this law. . . ."[6]

Rather macabre, those lines, in view of the kind of jury that finally was forced upon the defense. They were hardly in keeping with supposed American ideas concerning trial by jury. But most Chicagoans enjoyed the verse and approved the sentiment.

Understandably, that demand for "speeding justice" flowed quite as much from bias against Labor as it did from the craving for revenge for a terrible act. Now, Judge Gary frankly hated organized labor. His dislike for labor unions was active and strong—of that there can be no doubt. He showed this plainly in the address he made at the bar association dinner after Lawyer Dexter had complimented him. In that address, Gary spoke of "the arrogant assumption of the labor organizations to control the acts of every man who lives by manual labor." He contrasted the "evil" caused by trade unions with the results of monopolies of capital and of political corruption. His conclusion was:

"The monopolies of capital are a mischief which calls for a remedy, but the burden from them upon the individual is so light as to be scarcely felt. Corruption in office adds temporary burden to taxes, and frauds at elections put the wrong men in office. But none of these evils, unless in very rare instances, deprives anybody of the necessities of life. The tyranny under which labor groans [meaning labor unions] stops industry and takes bread from the mouths of hungry women and children. *What can we do to break it down?*"[7]

So much for Judge Gary's clearly defined prejudices against organized labor, let alone socialists or anarchists. He was, in short, as strongly anti-labor as Altgeld was pro-labor but, we must believe, also as honestly and sincerely. And so, it is not to be wondered that he fell in step with the "dominant influence" when the anarchists were before him for their lives.

3

His purpose in writing *The Century* article was twofold, Judge Gary said. His principal motive was to answer the charge that the anarchists were convicted for their political beliefs. This was not so, he said. "The anarchists were rightly punished, not for opinions, but for horrible deeds."[8] His other motive—and here as much as anywhere else he revealed his underlying prejudice against the men tried before him—was to "show that the real passions at the bottom of the heart of the anarchists were envy and hatred of all people whose condition in life was better than their own, who were more prosperous than themselves," that their claims of concern for the welfare of the workingmen "was a sham and a pretense."[9]

Now, in voicing his second motive, Gary was guilty of needlessly heaping abuse upon the anarchists, five of whom had been dead nearly six years. Only a starkly prejudiced man would have done so in a case of that kind, in a political rather than an ordinary crime. But more serious, he was also guilty of uttering an untruth, as any objective person familiar with the facts should have known, unless blinded by hatred.

Fools the anarchists were. Undoubtedly also they were viciously irresponsible in many of their speeches, writings and acts. Doubtless at times they violated the law with reference to inciting (although to this day it remains doubtful if they did so at the Haymarket). They were muddle-headed and addle-brained in the belief, if they really believed it, that they could defy the police, the militia and the army, even with dynamite. They hated capitalists fiercely and it is probably true, as Judge Gary would say, that they would have "praised my assassination as a virtuous act."[10]

Men of the type of Louis Lingg probably should have been institutionalized long before Haymarket. Those things, yes. But to say that the men of Haymarket were insincere in their sufferings because of wrongs done the workers, that they were motivated merely by "envy," this was at variance with every fact known then and since about the anarchists punished for the bombing. Insincere men could not have died as they did, could not have spoken in open court as they spoke. A man prompted only by "envy and hatred" would not have voluntarily surrendered to the hangman as Albert Parsons did—or written so fervently of the wrongs done labor, not in public dispatches, but in private letters, day after day to his wife, Lucy.

And there was August Spies, whom Judge Gary held up, along with Parsons, as an illustration of his point. Show-off that he was, a peacock revolutionary, enjoying the sensation of being pointed out as "the great anarchist"—it is incredible that he could have written Governor Oglesby, when there seemed a chance of his offer being accepted, that his life alone be forfeited, had he not been sincere. And Sam Fielden. As noted earlier, Gary himself had written to Governor Oglesby in Fielden's behalf:

"There is in the nature and private character of the man a love of justice, and impatience of undeserved sufferings. . . . In his own private life he was the honest, industrious, and peaceful laboring man. . . . In short, he was more a misguided enthusiast than a criminal conscious of the horrible nature and effect of his teachings and of his responsibility therefor."[11]

Yet, in his magazine article, Gary did not exclude Fielden in his blanket slur against all eight of the defendants. More convincing evidence of Gary's prejudice than this could hardly be asked.

4

And yet, there *was* more convincing evidence in the article. It is found in the fact that, while undoubtedly honest in his intention to carry out his "principal motive" of showing by his article that the anarchists were convicted "not for opinions, but for horrible deeds," actually the article does nothing of the kind. The greater portion of it is devoted to excerpts from the speeches and writings of the anarchists—principally those of Parsons and Spies—the most horrendous, and presumably, in Gary's mind, the most incriminating. In short, his emphasis was on opinions, not deeds, despite his disavowal of that idea. The next largest portion of the article is devoted to quoting law relating to conspiracy, together with liberal quotations from his own interpretation of that law to the jury at the trial.

He had the candor, incidentally, to quote himself as having said in overruling the motion for a new trial:

"The conviction has not gone on the ground that they did have actually any personal participation. . . . The conviction proceeds upon the ground that they had generally, by speech and print, advised large classes of the people, not particular individuals, but large classes, to commit murder, and had left the commission, the time and the place and when, to the individual will and whim or caprice, or whatever it may be, of each individual man who listened to their advice, and that in consequence of that advice, in pursuance of that advice, and influenced by that advice, somebody not known did throw the bomb that caused Degan's death. . . ."

Moreover, while insisting, in one breath, that the verdict was wholly in line with established law, Gary, at the trial and in his magazine article, admitted that it was on the basis of new law that Parsons, Spies, Engel and Fischer were hanged. For he added, significantly: "This case is without precedent; there is no example in the law books of a case of this sort. No such occurrence has ever happened before in the history of the world. . . ."

He also admitted emphatically that the actual bomber was not known, hence there was no pretense of being able to state definitely that the bomber did act upon the advice of the men convicted. This

was the nub of the case. And it was this that Judge Gary in his magazine article failed to support any more strongly than it had been supported before.

He ignored entirely the point that impressed many at the time,
including Governor Oglesby, that there was a similarity between the
Haymarket affair and the Abolition activity which culminated in John
Brown's raid at Harper's Ferry, that Judge Gary's theory of the law
logically would have made all the Abolition leaders equally guilty
with John Brown and his men. Leonard Swett, Lincoln's associate,
was among those who saw this. In his brief filed with the Illinois
Supreme Court, Swett wrote:

"I know of no more appropriate illustration of the legal status and
liability of the defendants in relation to their intemperate utterances...
than to recall the history of the formation of the Republican party.
It was a party which had for its object the reformation of the civil
society and the civil institutions in this country. The most radical of its leaders characterized the constitution of the United States
as 'a league with hell.' Underground railways were everywhere established . . . and people conspired to do the act, contrary to the constitution and the laws of the United States, of aiding and abetting the
slave in his escape. . . . The storm finally culminated, and by and by
old John Brown, caught by the inspiration of the occasion, committed
an offense against the laws of Virginia. . . ."

Applying the reasoning of Judge Gary to the John Brown incident,
you would get, said Swett, this:

"If there had been no Republican party, there would have been no
John Brown's raid, and, therefore, all Republicans who made speeches
and believed in the utopian idea of a change in society for the benefit
of a class were like the Anarchists and were *particeps criminis* with old
John Brown and ought to be hung."[12]

But that argument found no response in Judge Gary.

5

Curiously enough, while supposedly intent upon demonstrating
that it was deeds for which the anarchists were punished, Judge Gary
glossed over what factual circumstances existed to support that thesis.
He did not mention the "Monday night conspiracy," except by a
passing reference. He barely mentioned Louis Lingg, except to sneer

at his self-destruction. He did not tell that George Engel, somehow, had at his home a contraption that could have been used for making bombs. He did not mention a correspondence between Spies and Herr Johann Most, letters presumably dealing with the subject matter of explosives. In short, he touched only lightly or ignored entirely facts, or supposed facts, that could have been used to make a strong case of circumstantial evidence. Nor was it lack of space that explains this peculiarity.

He found space, large amounts, to interpolate personal comments, some slightly irrelevant. He found space for a dissertation that might be entitled "Judge Gary on Labor Unions and Pinkertons."

"There seems [he wrote] to be prevailing . . . a vague, unexpressed feeling or sentiment which no demagogue dares run counter to, that in all disputes between employers and employees, regardless of the 'why and wherefore'—especially if the latter class are very numerous,— they, if not justifiable, are excusable in taking control of the property of the employers, so far at least as may be necessary to prevent the aid of other employees in making such property of use or profit; that to that end force may be used, and that if, in the exercise of force (if it be only such as the moment may show to be necessary to make the prevention effectual), the employees kill anybody,—much more if the slain had been called in by the employers to keep the control of their property from the employees, and to resist their anticipated attacks,— such killing is, on the whole, rather a useful lesson to somebody, and should be a warning for the future."[13]

Thus did he indicate his attitude on the labor question.

It is noteworthy, too, that when he did turn his attention to factual matters, he made palpable errors and also was guilty of significant omissions of fact. Moreover, he managed to give to the facts an emphasis clearly prejudiced, putting in nothing that was at all in favor of the defendants; or, if so, in a deprecating manner. For example, after relating that Spies had declared that it was at his insistence that the line, "Workingmen, arm yourselves and appear in full force!" was removed from the circulars calling the Haymarket meeting, Judge Gary commented: "I am not concerned with the truth of that explanation."[14] He quoted Parsons as saying: "To arms! To arms! To arms!" and also Fielden as saying, with regard to the law: "Throttle it! Kill it! Stab it!" but failed to indicate anything at all about the inflection of the voices of the speakers, or to suggest even the remotest possibility of mitigating circumstances concerning the full text or the reaction of the crowd—despite ample, and convincing, evidence to that effect in the court record.

Of the temper of the crowd that night and of the effect of the speeches, he is found writing:

"A crowd of people, variously estimated by different witnesses at from eight hundred to two thousand, filled a public street of the city after ten o'clock at night. They were listening to, and shouting their approval of, speeches urging them, in language the most exciting and arguments the most persuasive that the speakers knew how to use, to violence and bloodshed."[15]

There is no mention in the article that Mayor Harrison had attended the meeting and testified to a different description of the effect of the speeches and the attitude of the crowd. Nothing in the article indicates that there had been testimony, in addition to that of the Mayor, from persons fully as antipathetic toward the defendants as Gary himself, that the meeting was mild. The *Tribune* reporter, for example, had testified, "as to the temper of the crowd, it was just an ordinary meeting . . . peaceable and quiet," that "the speeches . . . that night were . . . milder than I heard them make for years," that none was heard to "say or advise that they were going to use force that night."[16] Gary ignored such testimony. He praised Captain Bonfield, but neglected entirely to bring out that the meeting was about to break up because of the threatened storm before Bonfield went into action, that it would have been adjourned completely had Bonfield delayed his "Fall in!" order another minute or two.

And as an instance of plain misstatement of fact, there is Gary's account of the episode at McCormick's.

"On the third day of May a very serious riot, in which Spies, by his own account, participated, took place at the McCormick Harvesting Machine Workers, where the police protected the men at work. Some of the rioters were hurt, but *probably none killed.*"[17]

Now, it was stretching things to declare that Spies "by his own account" participated in that riot. Spies had testified that he *witnessed* the riot—something very different. As for the statement that no workers were killed by the police that afternoon, this remark by Judge Gary was palpably false. The records show now, as they did then, that two men were killed. And it was indignation over those actual deaths that caused the call for the meeting at Haymarket. Hence this was no unimportant detail.

6

However, most gratuitous of all was a slur that Judge Gary saw fit to direct in his article not at the dead or living anarchists, but at the unquestionably gallant defense lawyer, Captain Black, and also Captain Black's wife. Perhaps Gary did not mean personal malice. He was making the point that the anarchists "were men who fascinated those with whom they came in contact," that "men and women of a high order of intelligence, of pure lives, amiable in their own dispositions, seemed under a spell to them."[18] To illustrate his point, he first cited—not Judge Tuley, nor Leonard Swett, nor Senator Lyman Trumbull, nor even Altgeld's old Civil War general, Ben Butler; nor did he cite William Dean Howells, Henry Demarest Lloyd, Colonel "Bob" Ingersoll, William Morris or Annie Besant of England, all of whom had written eloquently and suffered emotionally in behalf of the condemned men. Instead, he cited the wife of Captain Black.

Mrs. Black was a woman of active social consciousness and also of deep feeling. When her husband, on the plea of George Schilling,[19] consented, as a matter of professional duty, to help defend the anarchists, Mrs. Black followed the case with intense personal interest. She attended nearly all the sessions of the long trial and at times spoke to the prisoners. Perhaps it was "fascination" that moved her so greatly in their behalf, although others might call it profound human sympathy. When the verdict of death for all but Neebe was pronounced, she was stunned. A few days before Judge Gary was to hear a motion for a new trial, she could not resist the impulse to express herself. She did so in a long letter to the Chicago Daily News. In that letter she poured her heart out.

"I have never known an anarchist, did not know what the term meant, until my husband became counsel for the defense. . . . Like every one I knew, I felt horror for the tragic events of that eventful night. . . . But one day one came to speak for that side which so long had been unheard,—the accused—and I found out that, as to everything, there were two sides to this.

"When I learned the facts, I became assured in my own mind that the wrong men had been arrested, and thrown into cells and subjected to horrible treatment. . . . During all that long trial a kind of soul crucifixion was imposed upon me. Often, as I took up one or the other of the daily papers, I would recall reverently those words of my Divine Master: 'For which of my good works do you stone me?' . . .

"Anarchy is simply a human effort to bring about the millennium. Why do we want to hang men for that, when every pulpit has thundered that the time is near at hand? . . ."[20]

For anyone to have considered Mrs. Black's emotional letter an item to be held up for public scorn appears rather cold-blooded. Yet, quoting parts of Mrs. Black's heart-pouring, this was exactly what Judge Gary did in his Century article. Moreover, after so treating Mrs. Black, he concluded his article with an even stronger arraignment of Captain Black for remarks the lawyer made at burial services for Parsons, Engel, Fischer, Spies and Lingg in Waldheim Cemetery. Captain Black had said:

" . . . I loved these men. I knew them not until I came to know them in the time of their sore travail and anguish. As months went by and I found in the lives of those with whom I talked the witness of their love for the people, of their patience, gentleness and courage, my heart was taken captive in their cause. . . . I saw that whatever fault may have been in them, these, the people whom they loved and in whose cause they died, may well close the volume, and seal up the record, and give our lips to the praise of their heroic deeds, and their sublime self-sacrifice."

Those sentiments by Captain Black at the grave struck Judge Gary at the time as especially outrageous. He was still outraged when he came to write his article. They were, he wrote, another horrible example of maudlin sympathy for anarchists.

"If," Judge Gary wrote, "these words [of Captain Black's] have any meaning, they refer to the acts of the anarchists of which I have in part told." That is, they refer to murder. He then proceeded to interpret Captain Black's meaning, as he saw it. "The people whom they loved"—why, Black should have said that these people were those whom the anarchists "deceived, deluded and endeavored to convert into murderers." "The cause they died in"—Captain Black should have said that the cause "was rebellion, to prosecute which they taught and instigated murder." Heroic deeds? "Causeless, wanton murder done," so interpolated the Judge. Gary sneered at Captain Black's use of the expression "sublime self-sacrifice": "The only one to whom the words can apply was a suicide, to escape the impending penalty of the law incurred by murder," wrote the Judge. Such was the note upon which Judge Gary closed his article, designed, he said, to set at rest misgivings about a case which, even six years afterward, still was stirring the world.

CHAPTER TWENTY-TWO

The Decision

1

WHEN Judge Gary's article appeared, an editorial in the Chicago *Tribune* said: "It is timely."[1] However, the reference was not to its probable effect on Governor Altgeld, but rather the effect on a Chicago mayoralty election campaign just then drawing to a close. The slouch hat of Carter Harrison, who was four times mayor before this, was in the ring again, this time for the honor of being World's Fair Mayor. As always, the *Tribune* opposed Harrison and one of its arguments against him was that he had been responsible for the Haymarket "massacre," presumably because he was so earnest in upholding the right of free speech. As it turned out, the *Tribune* was disappointed in the "timeliness" of the article, for Harrison was elected by a handsome majority.

But there were others, those who despised the *Tribune* equally as much as they despised Judge Gary, and for identical reasons, who viewed the Judge's literary effort as a good thing. Perhaps, they felt, the dilatory Governor at Springfield would now fulfill their hopes. Perhaps he would accept Judge Gary's composition as a challenge, consider it a bit of *lese majeste*, and at last decide to act on the case of Fielden, Schwab and Neebe. So hoped sympathizers with the prisoners. But they, too, were disappointed.

No sign came from Springfield that Altgeld had even read the article. The old controversy over the trial, the suspicions of a packed jury, the alleged prejudice of the trial judge and unfairness of the prosecutor—all flamed suddenly anew. And yet, there was Altgeld, the one man who now could do something besides talk, conducting himself, as far as the public knew, without so much as a thought for the case. Was his liberalism all a pose? Was the *Tribune* right after all in sneering at him as the "millionaire friend of labor"? Did he not realize that he was made governor in part at least by the votes of men who hoped he would "do right" in this matter? And, if he intended to act, why was he stalling now, when the Bourbons once more were heaping joyous praise upon Judge Gary?

Questions like that were fired at his friends in Chicago and voiced in the labor halls, the turner *Bunds* and in the working-class saloons. Altgeld's friends, themselves mystified, could answer only, "Wait." Especially was George Schilling on the spot. His active support of Altgeld had been accepted by not a few as a sign that Altgeld would act in the Haymarket matter. But Schilling, breathing not a word of the assignment that Altgeld had given him before Gary's article appeared, uttered only noncommittal responses that were more annoying than reassuring. Even he was in the dark as to Altgeld's reaction to Gary's review of the case. He recognized that Gary's article, in raising old questions about the trial, had the effect of wrenching the case away from the mild zone of mercy into which the Amnesty Association had carefully steered it. Yet, so far as Schilling knew, if Altgeld contemplated anything, it was a mercy pardon. Such, indeed, was Schilling's idea even after Altgeld gave him another secret mission in the case.

2

High drama is found in this second mission that Altgeld gave to George Schilling. After going over the record and by other ways refreshing his memory on the events of 1886, his mind was made up as to how he should act, if he were to act in accord with his conscience and his understanding of the case. Yet forboding assailed him.

Cautiously, with seeming casualness, he had sounded out various Democratic leaders as to the possible effects of a pardon. They were aghast at even the thought. It would hurt the party. It would be especially bad because the Democracy had only just returned to power. As for Altgeld himself, well, if he still had any ideas about the United States Senate, he had better forget them if he were so rash as to free those anarchists! To some of these men, he replied in effect: "The party could take care of itself. . . . As to the Senatorship, no man's ambitions had a right to stand in the way of performing a simple act of justice."[2]

Yet, in his private thinking, he was not quite so brave at this time. If only he had not been so impulsive and egoistical in spurning that petition of thousands of names! Foolish, indeed, that conceit. Well, he could not bring himself to backtrack. But to do this thing alone, with no support at all! Dare he risk the consequences? On the one side, would be the glory of it, the strength of character that such an act would reveal. All good. But on the other side—the inevitable abuse. And on that other side, too, were his ambitions, the senatorship, the desire for national power, and all that. These would be endangered anyway, even with strong support. But should he not have some protection, some little cushion? He wavered.

His wavering is revealed in the new mission he gave Schilling. It was to call on the great former United States Senator, Lyman Trumbull, and request that Trumbull make a personal appeal for pardoning the imprisoned anarchists.

"Say to him that the Governor of Illinois wishes him to appear before him and ask for the pardon of the anarchists. Tell him that the Governor doesn't care what reasons he may assign for making the request—whether on grounds of justice or mercy, but that I will deem it a great favor if he will come and ask for the liberty of these men."[3]

To Schilling, the import of Altgeld's request was a source of marvelous joy. At least, then, it was definite that Altgeld would pardon Fielden, Schwab and Neebe! It only remained for Lyman Trumbull to grant Altgeld's wish. Then Schilling's dream of six years' standing, also his original confidence in Altgeld, would be fulfilled.

Schilling was certain that Lyman Trumbull would grant the Governor's request, for the great Senator had been one of the first to sign the petitions circulated in 1887, and at that time had issued a strong statement criticizing the trial and urging executive clemency on that ground. How strongly Trumbull felt was told to Schilling by Judge McConnell, who obtained his signature to the petition sent Oglesby. "Almost the first signature that I obtained," recalled McConnell, "was that of Lyman Trumbull. . . . He read the petition, then buried his face in his hands, and said: 'I will sign. Those men did not have a fair trial!' "[4]

Knowing that incident, neither Altgeld nor Schilling had the slightest doubt about Trumbull's response to the Governor's request. There was no need, either, to emphasize to Schilling the Altgeldian shrewdness of the selection of Trumbull for the Governor's purpose. Why, this one name was as good as sixty thousand on a petition! His whole career, extending back before the Civil War, had been the very epitome of respectability. He had been an early member of the Illinois Supreme Court. When Abraham Lincoln made his try for the United States senatorship in 1855, and saw he could not get enough votes for himself, it was to Trumbull that he threw his support finally. As a senator, Trumbull, as much as Lincoln, smoked out Stephen A. Douglas on the slavery issue in the beginning, and at the time of the Lincoln-Douglas debates he was considered "an even bigger man than Lincoln."[5]

Originally a Democrat, Trumbull was one of the founders of the Republican party and nearly its candidate for president in 1860, instead of Lincoln. It was Trumbull, too, who wrote the Fourteenth Amendment to the Federal Constitution, and, in the turbulent reconstruction period after Lincoln's assassination, was recognized as one of the few really statesmanlike leaders left among the Republicans, a fact emphasized by his return to the Democracy when he could no longer stomach the ring around Ulysses S. Grant. At the time Schilling was on his way to him, Trumbull was in his declining years, but practicing law. He was then beginning to line up more with labor than with capital, but was still honored and revered by the dominant classes.

3

Trumbull displayed great cordiality when Schilling arrived at his office. But, to Schilling's amazement, instead of agreeing with alacrity to Altgeld's request, Trumbull "thought it over a moment, shook his head and declined." Schilling pressed him. Finally Trumbull took Schilling to a back room for greater privacy. He talked freely about the Haymarket case. He had not changed his mind about the verdict in Judge Gary's court. "The time will come," he told Schilling earnestly, "when mankind will look back upon the execution of the anarchists as we of this day look back upon the burning of the witches in New England."

At this statement Schilling's spirits rose. Again he repeated his request that Trumbull appear before Altgeld. How could Trumbull refuse after saying what he had just said? But again Trumbull "shook his head and declined."

"Why do you decline?"

Trumbull's response now was a look that was "both pained and nettled."

"I knew then," recalled Schilling, "that whatever his reasons he would not tell." There was no further use in pressing him.

Heartsick and bewildered, Schilling could not resist talking to someone about what had happened, even though pledged to secrecy by Altgeld. So he went to see Clarence Darrow at the offices of the Northwestern Railroad. Darrow, too, was disappointed and amazed. Goudy happened in, and was told what had happened. For all his corporation interests, he, too, genuinely hoped for the pardon of the anarchists. Goudy said with some feeling: "As a lawyer, it was his duty to take the case—for that is what it would amount to. It was his professional duty to accept."[6]

Those were very nearly Goudy's last recorded words, for it was his fate not to know how his protégé, the young lawyer whom he had helped to wealth and place, would acquit himself in the Haymarket matter. On April 27, 1893, Goudy fell dead of a heart attack.

4

Back to Springfield went Schilling. He was more than disappointed. He was fearful over the effect his report might have on Altgeld's determination to go through with a pardon. He found Altgeld at his desk in the Capitol. At once, "with great particularity," Schilling told the result of his mission. Through the recital, Altgeld was silent, his face mask-like. At the end of the story, recalled Schilling, "there was a long pause. . . ." The two men simply looked at each other. Schilling, at least, was thinking: "And now what? Was this the end?" Finally, Altgeld broke the silence.

"How do you explain Trumbull's action?"

"I can't explain it. I can only surmise."

"Surmise then," said Altgeld.

"Listen," said Schilling, "here is a man who has spent many years in the public service with clean hands, and therefore has no wealth. He is past eighty, without a competency and is still obliged to work for his daily bread. He has perhaps a few clients. Among them are large corporations, who now and then give him a fee for an important opinion. . . . Perhaps he fears that if he mixed up in this matter, these corporations would withdraw even this opportunity for him to earn his bread."[7]

At this point, Schilling "drew himself up," and "with a sterner voice," continued:

"Governor, if my surmises are true, the corporations have even this great man hamstrung, so that out of fear he does not do what he would like to do. In like manner they have their iron heel on the neck of every man of prominence in this country. If you expect any aid in this matter from prominent citizens you will be disappointed!"

Excited now, Schilling found himself saying:

"Governor, unless you are willing to do this all alone—without regard to consequences, and thereby serve notice that there is at least one man in public life that the corporations have not cowed—the situation is hopeless. Then we might as well drop it!"

Altgeld remained silent, the mask still in place. Then he gave a sigh and got up from his chair. He paced the floor, to and fro, as Schilling now watched, now bowed his head.

"Finally," recalled Schilling, "he stood still, and gazed at a picture on the wall." The picture was of another bearded man who had made history in Springfield, Illinois—a portrait of Abraham Lincoln. In a few minutes, Altgeld returned to his desk and sat down. He leaned toward Schilling.

"Schilling, we don't need them! We don't need them!"[8]

5

And so, it was settled that day. Yet April passed, and May, and June arrived, long weeks for those concerned with a pardon for the Haymarket prisoners. Still no positive public move in the case was made by the Governor. It had been given out in the press, and not denied, that a public hearing might be held on the matter,[9] but no steps whatsoever were taken in that direction. Even George Schilling appeared to show signs of misgivings as the weeks passed. He had handsomely acquitted himself on the assignment of the affidavits, delivering to Altgeld toward the end of April a stack literally "this high."

He had written to and interviewed scores of persons, men who had been clubbed or shot by the police and militia, or who had witnessed such incidents as far back as 1877. He tracked down workingmen who had been tossed into jail cells in the "red hunt" after the bombing. For example, he found Vaclav Djmek, who related how he had been beaten, kicked, clubbed and threatened with hanging; how, too, when abuse failed, he was "promised his freedom . . . and considerable money if he would turn state's evidence."[10]

Going back to the troubles of 1877, Schilling hunted for S. Philip Van Patten, then the fiery secretary of the first socialist group in Chicago. He traced Van Patten to Hot Springs, Arkansas, and obtained from him an affidavit on the breaking up of labor meetings in July, 1877.[11] He rounded up affidavits on Inspector Bonfield, notably in connection with the 1885 streetcar strike. He made trips to East St. Louis and other trouble zones for additional documentary evidence of outrageous incidents. These, and others, he transmitted to Altgeld toward the end of April.

Years later, among Schilling's papers, there was found, written out in Cigarmaker Charles Seib's bold hand, the original tabulation of the documents collected for the Governor by Schilling. This list is interesting in itself, a tabloid chronicle of much of the turbulent history of labor strife in Illinois from the 'seventies, through Haymarket, and into the 'nineties. As given to Altgeld, it read:

*Pinkerton Circular, to Corporations and other large employers of labor, 1885.

Invasion of Public Meeting, "Market Square," Chicago, by police, July 25th, 1877. Affidavits of Simon Philip Van Patten and Frederick Korth.

*Invasion of Furniture Workers meeting, 12th St. Turner Hall, by police, July 26th, 1877. Opinion by Judge McAllister.

Election frauds, 14th Ward, Chicago, April 6, 1880. Affidavits of Frank A. Stauber. Opinion by Judge Gardner. Verification of same by Judge Rich. Prendergast.

*McCormick Strike, shooting of Geo. Roth, by Pinkerton police, April 10th, 1885. Affidavits of Miles E. McPadden and Marie Roth.

*Quarrymen's Strike, Lemont, Illinois, shooting of Andrew Stelter and others, by the State Militia, May 4, 1885. Transcript of Coroners Inquisition.

*Conductors and Drivers Strike, W.D.R.W.Co., (street car), July 1st, 1885. Petitions and statements of citizens filed for the removal of Captain John Bonfield.

Invasion of the saloon of Mathias Spies, by police, March 1st, 1886. Affidavit of Henry Miners.

*Coal Miners Strike, St. Clair County, Illinois. Shooting of William Henderson, by the State Militia, May 28th, 1883. Transcript of Coroners Inquisition.

*Rail Road Strike, East St. Louis, Illinois. Shooting of Major Richard Rykman, Patrick Driscoll, John Boner, Mrs. L. Pfeufer, Oscar Washington, Mike Boener, S. W. Thompson and Jane Scollard, by Deputy Sheriffs, April 9th, 1886. Transcript of coroner's inquisition. Resolutions by Senator Richard M. Burke.

*Unlawful arrests. (Haymarket raids.) Affidavits of Jacob Milolanda and Vaclav Djmek. Opinion by Judge McAllister in the case of Mrs. M. C. McDonald.

*Interview of Chief of Police Ebersold. Daily News, May 10th, 1889.

Letter of Benj. F. Butler to Captain William P. Black.

Chart of Haymarket prepared by the Police Department. List of officers.[12]

6

But when Altgeld continued delaying action after receiving those documents, Schilling followed up with more. On May 12, 1893, he sent the Governor a telegram reminding him of the meeting of Chicago businessmen that Governor Oglesby had asked Lyman J. Gage to call in 1887 in behalf of the condemned men.[13] Also in May, he sent an amazing letter which he contrived to get Police Captain Michael J. Schaack to write to G. E. Detwiler, editor of *The Rights of Labor*. In that letter Schaack, self-styled nemesis of the anarchists, the man whom Chief Ebersold exposed for organizing fake anarchist organizations, is found in turn denouncing Inspector Bonfield for his brutal conduct in the 1885 streetcar men's strike.[14] Thus, in Schilling's view, it was proved that when police officials fall out, the result is the same as when thieves fall out.

Important as those supplementary documents were, it appears that Schilling sent them as much to prod Altgeld along as to bolster up the case for pardoning. For he observed, along with others, how active the Governor was in everything except the Haymarket matter—even after the interview that followed his failure with Lyman Trumbull. For a sick man, the Governor at the end of April and through May and June was unusually prominent at banquets, dedications, receptions and other public affairs, most of them in connection with the Columbian Exposition.

On May first, he participated with Cleveland in a tremendous dedication ceremony at the fair grounds. The next evening he was at an elaborate dinner given by Chicago's society folk in honor of the Duke of Veragua. It was noted by the *Herald* that at this society affair, when the Governor was introduced for a speech, "the air was filled with cries of 'Altgeld!' . . . and the applause was tremendous."

No comfort there for the people who were watching his every move for a sign on the anarchists' fate.

Nor did there seem much comfort as they watched him perform at similar events through the month of May and into June. He was making speeches here and there, nearly all to stuffed-shirt affairs. A notable exception was his famous address on June 7, 1893, to the graduating class of the University of Illinois. It was a talk so outstanding that men have committed it to memory, and forty-three years later Professor James Weber Linn, of the University of Chicago Department of English, read it at a public meeting and challenged his audience to guess if it were a composition by Emerson or some other well-known philosopher. Yet, at first blush, that address appeared to be more of a glorification of capitalistic enterprise than anything else.

Here is Altgeld—shortly now to be assailed from coast to coast as an anarchist, a socialist, an enemy of American ideals—speaking, and in dead earnest, at the state university that day:

"This is an age of individual achievement. . . . The men of this age, whom history will deign to notice, are the men who have spanned our rivers, built and operated our railroads, built our cities, reared our mighty temples of learning and of industry; the men who have harnessed the lightnings and made them beasts of burden for man; the men who are covering the earth with intelligence. . . . They will be the kings and princes of this century."[15]

And:

"Let me tell you something, confidentially, here. If you are sent to bring something, bring it, and not an explanation. If you agree to do something, do it; don't come back with an explanation. Explanations as to how you came to fail are not worth two cents a ton. Nobody wants them or cares for them. The fact that you met with an accident and got your legs broken, your neck twisted and your head smashed is not equal to a delivery of the goods."[16]

No wonder the Tribune on that occasion found words of praise for Altgeld, observing that he gave the students at the university some sound advice.[17]

7

Yet, the Tribune would not have been so pleased, nor the liberals so impatient, had they bothered to examine closely the full text of the seemingly innocuous and "sound" talks made by Altgeld during that period. Thus, in his speech at the banquet for the Duke of Veragua, he managed to squeeze in—and make the bluebloods at least pretend to like it—this concerning Columbus:

"Reflect a moment! The wealthy people were against him; the scientific men were against him; the men in office were against him; the elements were against him, and it seemed as if the fates were against him; but he was immovable . . . the most magnificent example of cool nerve, of inflexible purpose, ever witnessed upon earth."[18]

A basis for liberals' hope could easily be read into that statement.

Likewise, in a statement tucked into another World Fair speech delivered at the opening of the Illinois Building on May eighteenth in which he glorified the fact that:

"It was on the continent discovered by Columbus that there was the first successful experiment among men of absolute freedom of religion, freedom of conscience, freedom of thought, freedom of speech, freedom of action, and the highest form of a free man's government."[19]

However, it was in his address at the University of Illinois, praised as it was by the *Tribune*, that Altgeld gave clear clues to his final action in the Haymarket case. Here is one clue from that address on the seventh of June:

"You turn to the courts of justice; you think of a goddess, blindfolded, holding the scales; you recall eloquent things about eternal justice, etc., and you say, here I will find exact right, here wrongs are corrected, the strong are curbed and the weak protected.

"You will be disappointed. The administration of justice, or rather of the laws, is better than it ever has been, but it is only a struggling toward the right; only a blind groping in the darkness toward light. The men who administer the laws are human, with all the failings of humanity. They take their biases, their prejudices with them on to the bench. Upon the whole, they try to do the best they can; but the wrongs done in the courts of justice themselves are so great that they cry to heaven. . . ."[20]

He included even a thinly-veiled reference to the doctrine of anarchy in that address. Thus, speaking of the shortcomings of government agencies in general, he said:

". . . the wrongs done by government are so great that they can be measured only by the eye of omniscience. Some shortsighted people, seeing this fact, conclude it ought to be abolished. *This is a fatal mistake.* Defective as government is, it is yet the best that man has been able to devise and until the level of morality and intelligence is elevated, no better can be devised.

"People who talk about the abolition of government fail to consider the one great, all-important factor, and that is human selfishness. The same selfishness which has disfigured the governments of the present will shape the new ones and make them worse than the present, because it is only after centuries of effort that they could be made as good as they are. . . ."[21]

What was Altgeld uttering there if not an anticipatory defense against charges that he sympathized with anarchy or socialism?

This much is clear. His address at the University of Illinois was a public, though obscured, declaration of his intentions in the Haymarket case.

No one saw this at the time, or even later; neither the conservatives nor the liberals. And so the former praised him and the latter continued to grumble. Yet it is clear that when Altgeld made that address on June seventh he had completed a statement prepared by him in connection with the Haymarket matter.

He was then only awaiting the proper time for its release.

8

The proper time turned out to be Monday, June 26, 1893. It is not exactly plain why Altgeld selected that date. Doubtless an occurrence the day before had much to do with the selection. For on that Sunday, several thousand Chicagoans had gathered at Waldheim Cemetery for the unveiling of a monument on the graves of Parsons, Spies, Engel, Fischer and Lingg. The ceremony had the effect of placing the dramatic incidents of the Haymarket case once more in the headlines, where Altgeld could read them in the Monday morning newspaper.

From a dramatic standpoint, a pardon at that time was exceedingly timely—as perfect in that respect as it was politically inexpedient. But, for this action, Altgeld had by then pushed politics aside completely. Impulse once more had the upper hand, and the Governor set the machinery for a pardon in motion at once by sending for one of the few men in Springfield whom he trusted implicitly—young Brand Whitlock.

Whitlock tells about it in his memoirs, *Forty Years of It*. "Very early," he recalled, "I was called to the Governor's office, and told to make out pardons for Fielden, Neebe and Schwab." That was not in line with his regular duties on the staff of the Secretary of State, but the reason of his selection became clear when Private Secretary Dose said to him: "And do it yourself, and don't say anything to anybody!"[22]

In the meantime, Altgeld had summoned Whitlock's superior, the

Secretary of State, "Buck" Hinrichsen. Hinrichsen was taken completely by surprise. He thought Altgeld broke the startling news to him "rather carelessly," considering his status as chairman of the Democratic State Committee.

"I am going to pardon Fielden, Schwab and Neebe this morning," Altgeld said. "I thought you might like to sign the papers in person rather than have your signature affixed by your chief clerk." He looked at Hinrichsen "rather curiously."

"Do you think it good policy to pardon them?" asked Hinrichsen. Before Altgeld could answer, Hinrichsen quickly added that he did not think it was.

Altgeld struck his desk with his fist.

"It is right!"[23]

9

When Brand Whitlock arrived with the papers, he found Altgeld sitting at his desk, one other man in the room. This was E. S. Dreyer, a private Chicago banker.

"Dreyer . . . who had never wearied, it seems, in his efforts to have those men pardoned . . . was standing, and was very nervous; the moment evidently meant much to him. The Governor took the big sheets of imitation parchment, glanced over them, signed his name to each, laid down the pen, and handed the papers across the table to Dreyer.

"The banker took them, and began to say something. But he only got as far as—'Governor, I hardly'—when he broke down and wept.

"Altgeld made an impatient gesture; he was gazing out of the window in silence, on the elm-trees in the yard. He took out his watch, told Dreyer he would miss his train—Dreyer was to take the Alton to Joliet, deliver the pardons to the men in person, and go into Chicago with them that night—and Dreyer nervously rolled up the pardons, took up a little valise, shook hands, and was gone."[24]

So Whitlock described the scene, but he overlooked a point in the drama. E. S. Dreyer had been foreman of the grand jury that voted the murder indictments against the accused anarchists. He had been vociferous in the demand that the men should be hanged. Undoubtedly he was sincere then, although August Spies charged that Dreyer had a personal grudge against him because Spies had "exposed" a certain supposedly improper real-estate deal. Spies felt this was a factor in Dreyer's insistence upon murder indictments.[25] Be that as it may, by the 'nineties Dreyer showed a complete change of heart—so complete that he made the earnest request to Altgeld that, when and if the anarchists were pardoned, he be permitted to atone for his earlier stand by taking the pardons to the prisoners.

10

The story broke to the world the following morning. About the time that the eyes of people all over America were popping as they read the news in their morning papers, Altgeld was calmly taking a morning constitutional about the Capitol grounds astride a militia horse. He saw Brand Whitlock near by and drew up for a word of greeting. He "bowed and smiled that faint, wan smile of his."

"Well," said Whitlock, "the storm will break now."

"Oh, yes, I was prepared for that. It was merely doing right."

Whitlock voiced some words meant to convey his admiration for Altgeld's act, then the Governor continued his ride. As Altgeld rode away Whitlock remembered that he had on his face that same "wan, persistent smile."[26]

CHAPTER TWENTY-THREE

THE REASONS

1

ALTGELD could not have said that his "Reasons for Pardoning" were not provocative of just such a storm as resulted. Considered as a piece of literature and of logic, his was the calmest, clearest, most incisive and most factual dissertation of all the hundreds of tracts, legal discussions, magazine articles and books ever composed on that stirring case. Yet, with all that, it was also the most devastating and the most explosive in character, second only to the bomb itself for the concussion that it produced upon those who read it.

He began the eighteen-thousand-word document by reciting swiftly the events of the night of May fourth, 1886. He emphasized in this opening section the important fact overlooked by Judge Gary, that "the meeting was orderly and . . . attended by the mayor, who remained until the crowd began to disperse." He emphasized at once, also, the fact that "the prosecution could not discover who had thrown the bomb and could not bring the really guilty man to justice. . . ." Likewise, he touched in the beginning on the part played by Inspector Bonfield. "As soon as Captain Bonfield learned that the Mayor had gone, he . . . hurried to the meeting for the purpose of dispersing the few that remained." Then he mentioned that "several thousand merchants, bankers, judges, lawyers and other prominent citizens" had urged clemency, "mostly base[ing] their appeal on the ground that, assuming the prisoners to be guilty, they have been punished enough."

On this matter of mercy, Altgeld made clear promptly his own position with regard to anarchy, also that not mercy, but justice alone, would sway him. Not even Judge Gary took a stronger position on the side of law and order than Altgeld.

"Upon the question of having been punished enough, I will simply say that if the defendants had a fair trial, and nothing has developed since to show that they are not guilty of the crime charged in the indictment, then there ought to be no executive interference, for no punishment under our laws could then be too severe.

216

"Government must defend itself; life and property must be protected, and law and order must be maintained; murder must be punished, and if the defendants are guilty of murder, either committed by their own hands or by some one else acting on their advice, then, if they have had a fair trial, there should be in this case no executive interference. The soil of America is not adapted to the growth of anarchy. While our institutions are not free from injustice, they are still the best that have yet been devised, and therefore must be maintained."

But, he said, "there were a number of men who have examined the case . . . carefully and are . . . familiar with the record and with the facts disclosed by the papers on file." These base their appeal for a pardon "on entirely different grounds." Without naming anyone, he observed that these persons have asserted:

"First—That the jury which tried the case was a packed jury selected to convict.

"Second—That according to the law as laid down by the Supreme Court, both prior to and again since the trial of this case, the jurors, according to their own answers, were not competent jurors, and the trial was, therefore, not a legal trial.

"Third—That the defendants were not proven to be guilty of the crime charged in the indictment.

"Fourth—That as to the defendant Neebe, the State's Attorney had declared at the close of the evidence that there was no case against him, and yet he has been kept in prison all these years.

"Fifth—That the trial judge was either so prejudiced against the defendants, or else so determined to win the applause of a certain class in the community, that he could not and did not grant a fair trial."

Actually, that summation represented not so much the "assertions of a number of men" as Altgeld's own views. Hence there was some justification for the remark of Edgar Lee Masters, with regard to this section and a later portion, that "there was something slightly disingenuous . . . in characterizing Judge Gary out of the mouths of petitioners, instead of doing it by words of his own."[1] However, there was nothing "disingenuous" in the balance of the document. It was devoted to substantiating the five points listed.

2

First he took up the question, "Was the jury packed?" "The jury in this case was not drawn in the manner that juries usually are drawn," he asserted. The record of the trial shows this. "Instead of having a number of names drawn out of a box that contained many hundred names, as the law contemplates shall be done in order to insure a fair jury and give neither side the advantage, the trial judge appointed Henry L. Ryce as a special bailiff to go out and summon such men as he [Ryce] might select to act as jurors." And how did Ryce proceed?

"It is shown that he boasted while selecting jurors that he was managing this case; that these fellows would hang as certain as death; that he was calling such men as the defendants would have to challenge peremptorily and waste their challenges on, and that when their challenges were exhausted they would have to take such men as the prosecution wanted."

As proof, Altgeld presented an amazing affidavit by Otis S. Favor, a businessman who had been an intimate friend of Special Bailiff Ryce's. Favor himself had been summoned by Ryce as a juror, but was excused for prejudice, not in behalf of the defendants, but *against* them. His sworn story, never seriously challenged, exactly corroborated Altgeld's statement concerning the special bailiff.

Most devastating of all, Favor's affidavit brings out the following facts: first, when he offered to testify as to Ryce's conduct, if subpoenaed, he was summoned to the prosecutor's office by State's Attorney Grinnell; second, when he told his story to Grinnell in the presence of Ryce, it was not challenged; third, when he said he would feel compelled to testify in court *if subpoenaed*, but would refuse at that time to make an affidavit [because he did not wish to be pictured as a friend of anarchists], he was "then and there asked and urged to persist in his refusal and make no affidavit."[2]

It should be explained that Favor took that curious position because he did not wish to be publicized as voluntarily doing anything to assist the anarchists. If he were subpoenaed, he could then defend himself on the ground of compulsion. It was only after the Supreme Court failed to save the prisoners from hanging that he finally did make an affidavit. Plainly, however, it was Prosecutor Grinnell's duty to bring out the facts related to him by Favor. In short, Prosecutor Grinnell (later rewarded with a judgeship for his part in the case) is by this evidence found guilty of suppressing a vital point.

Nor was Judge Gary in the clear in respect to this aspect of the case, for Altgeld revealed:

"On page 133, of Volume I, of the record, it appears that when the panel was about two-thirds full, counsel for the defendants called attention of the Court to the fact that Ryce was summoning only prejudiced men, as shown by their examinations. Further: That he was confining himself to particular classes, i. e., clerks, merchants, manufacturers, etc. Counsel for defendants then moved the court to stop this and direct Ryce to summon the jurors from the body of the people; that is, from the community at large, and not from particular classes; but the Court refused to take any notice of the matter."

Altgeld commented:

"While no collusion is proven between the judge and State's Attorney, it is clearly shown that after the verdict and while a motion for a new trial was pending, a charge was filed in court that Ryce had packed the jury and that the attorney for the State got Mr. Favor to refuse to make an affidavit bearing on this point, which the defendants could use, and then the court refused to take any notice of it unless the affidavit was obtained, although informed that Mr. Favor would not make an affidavit, but stood ready to come into court and make a full statement if the court desired him to do so. These facts alone would call for executive interference, especially as Mr. Favor's affidavit was not before the Supreme Court at the time it considered the case."[3]

3

Did Special Bailiff Ryce in fact carry out the plan he voiced to Otis S. Favor?

That he did was amply proved, Altgeld felt, from the court record relating to the examination of prospective and actual jurors. He cited the cases of eighteen men called by Ryce, four of whom actually sat on the jury, to show, first, that by their own words the men called by Ryce were prejudiced against the defendants and, second, that the conduct of Judge Gary, reflected in his own words, resulted in forcing a packed jury upon the trial.

It is important to note in this connection some law concerning selection of juries. The law permits the defense in murder cases an unlimited number of challenges against prospective jurors when the challenges are based upon cause, i. e., prejudice, but only a limited number of so-called peremptory challenges. The trial judge has the power to determine if cause for a challenge exists. When the allotted number of peremptory challenges is exhausted, the defense must then accept any jurors called unless cause for a challenge can be demon-

strated. It was this legal provision that Special Bailiff Ryce had in mind when he said to Favor:

"Those fellows are going to be hanged as certain as death. I am calling such men as the defendants will have to challenge peremptorily and waste their time and challenges. Then they will have to take such men as the prosecution wants."[4]

And it is in the light of the foregoing that the typical examples cited by Altgeld take on grim meaning.

He first directed attention to fourteen men whom the defense challenged for cause, only to have Judge Gary in each case overrule the challenges. First of the fourteen was William Neil, manufacturer.

4

Neil had testified that "he had heard and read about the Haymarket trouble, and believed enough of what he had so heard and read to form an opinion as to the guilt of the defendants, which he *still* entertained." He stated, further, that he had *expressed* his opinion that the defendants were guilty.

He added:

"It would take pretty strong evidence to remove the impression that I now have. I could not dismiss it from my mind; could not lay it altogether aside during the trial. I believe my present opinion, based upon what I have heard and read, would accompany me through the trial, and would influence me in determining and getting at a verdict."[5]

He was, of course, challenged by the defense for cause. But Judge Gary took a hand personally in examining the prospective juror. Question after question was fired by the judge at the manufacturer, some confusing, most leading. Finally the judge extracted from Neil the assertion that, after all, he "believed he could give a fair verdict on whatever evidence he should hear."

Why, then, declared Judge Gary, he was a fit juror.

Then there was the case of George N. Porter, a grocer. He had admitted that "his mind was certainly biased now, and that it would take a great deal of evidence to change it." He was challenged, but Judge Gary overruled the defense when Porter finally guessed, on prompting by the judge, that he could render a verdict in accord with the evidence and "would try to do so." But the defense asked more questions, and Porter now stated:

"I believe what I have read in the papers; believe that the parties are guilty. I would try to go by the evidence, but in this case it would be awful hard work for me to do it."[6]

He was challenged the second time. But again Judge Gary intervened. He wormed from the grocer another statement to the effect that he "believed" he could hear the case fairly, notwithstanding his feeling that the prisoners were guilty.

"Challenge overruled," said Judge Gary.

Judge Gary's reasoning in these and dozens of similar instances was revealed by a remark he made in the instance of James H. Walker, dry goods merchant. Walker also had frankly admitted prejudice. He stated flatly that he felt his prejudice would "handicap" him.

Q. (By counsel.) Considering all prejudice and all opinions you have, if the testimony was equally balanced, would you decide one way or another in accordance with that opinion or your prejudice?

A. If the testimony were equally balanced I should hold my present opinion, sir.

Q. Assuming that your present opinion is that you believe the defendants guilty, would you believe your present opinion would warrant you in convicting them?

A. I presume it would.

Q. Well, you believe it would; that is your present belief, is it?

A. Yes, sir.

He was challenged by the defense, only to have Judge Gary take him in hand. The judge examined him at length, yet obtained responses scarcely different from those just noted, until the following:

Q. (By Judge Gary.) Do you believe that you can sit here and fairly and impartially make up your mind, from the evidence, whether that evidence proves that they are guilty beyond a reasonable doubt or not?

A. (By well-worn witness.) *I think I could, but I should believe that I was a little handicapped in my judgment, sir.*"

Whereupon there came from Judge Gary what probably deserves to be placed among the most astounding observations in judicial history.

"Well, that is a sufficient qualification for a juror in the case; of course, *the more a man feels that he is handicapped the more he will be guarded against it.*"[7]

No wonder, as Altgeld's reading of the court record revealed, Judge Gary not only approved men who admitted violent prejudice on general grounds, but also men who confessed that certain of the wounded policemen were personal friends, as in the case of H. N. Smith, hardware merchant,[8] and in one case at least, that of M. D. Flavin, a venireman actually related to one of the policemen killed at Haymarket![9]

5

So much for Judge Gary's conduct toward prospective jurors challenged for cause by the defense. More vital even was the manner in which the actual jurors were selected. These, Altgeld pointed out, "were of the same general character as the others, and a number of them stated candidly that they were so prejudiced that they could not try the case fairly, but each, when examined by the court, was finally induced to say that he believed he could try the case fairly upon the evidence that was produced in court alone."

He cited the instances of the following actual jurors:

JUROR THEODORE DENKER, shipping clerk for Henry W. King and Co., who testified:

"I have read and talked about the Haymarket tragedy, and have formed and expressed an opinion as to the guilt or innocence of the defendants of the crime charged in the indictment. I believe what I read and heard, and still entertain that opinion.

"Q. Is that opinion such as to prevent you from rendering an impartial verdict in the case sitting as a juror, under the testimony and the law?

"A. I think it is."

Judge Gary called him a fit juror.

JUROR JOHN B. GREINER, clerk for the Northwestern Railroad, who testified:

"I have heard and read about the killing of Degan . . . and have formed an opinion as to the guilt or innocence of the defendants now on trial for that crime. *It is evident that the defendants are connected with that affair from their being here.*

"Q. You regard that as evidence?

"A. Well, I don't know exactly. Of course, I would expect that it connected them or they would not be here.

"Q. So, then, the opinion that you now have has reference to the guilt or innocence of some of these men, or all of them?

"A. Certainly.

"Q. Now, is that opinion one that would influence your verdict if you should be selected as a juror to try the case?

"A. I certainly think it would affect it to some extent; I don't see how it could be otherwise."

Judge Gary, over protests, ordered him to sit in the jury box.

JUROR G. W. ADAMS, salesman and former painting contractor, who testified:

"I read and talked about the Haymarket trouble and formed an opinion as to the nature and character of the crime committed there. I conversed freely with my friends about the matter.

"Q. Did you form an opinion at the time that the defendants were connected with or responsible for the commission of that crime?

"A. I thought some of them were interested in it; yes.

"Q. And you still think so?

"A. Yes.

"Q. Nothing has transpired in the interval to change your mind at all, I suppose.

"A. No, sir.

"Q. You say some of them; that is, in the newspaper accounts that you read, the names of some of the defendants were referred to?

"A. Yes, sir."

He, too, was approved for jury service by Judge Gary.

JUROR H. T. SANFORD, clerk for the Northwestern Railroad.

"Q. Have you an opinion as to the guilt or innocence of the defendants of the murder of Mathias J. Degan?

"A. I have.

"Q. From all that you have heard and that you have read, have you an opinion as to the guilt or innocence of the defendants of throwing the bomb?

"A. Yes, sir; I have.

"Q. Have you a prejudice against socialists and communists?

"A. Yes, sir; a decided prejudice.

"Q. Do you believe that that prejudice would influence your verdict in this case?

"A. Well, as I know so little about it, it is a pretty hard question to answer. *I have an opinion in my own mind that the defendants encouraged the throwing of that bomb.*"

Judge Gary passed him, too, after extracting a statement that, after all, he believed he could try the case fairly.[10]

6

It should be stated that Judge Gary's rulings were called to the attention of the Illinois Supreme Court. That court, in its opinion of two hundred and sixty-seven printed pages, dismissed criticism of the judge's conduct as immaterial.

". . . . We have carefully considered the examinations of the several jurors challenged by the defendants peremptorily, and while we cannot approve all that was said by the trial judge in respect to some of them, we find no such error in the rulings of the court in overruling the challenges for cause as to any of them as would justify a reversal. . . ."[11]

The high court professed to believe, too, that the defense had no valid complaint even if Judge Gary had erred, because the defense had forty-three peremptory challenges left after the eleventh juror was in the box, and, said the court, "many of the forty-three challenges were exercised arbitrarily and without any apparent cause."[12] In short, the court fell back upon a technical point to sustain Judge Gary.

Perhaps exceedingly revealing is this excerpt from the Supreme Court decision with reference to the prejudices of the Juror Sanford:

"The juror Sanford further stated [said the court] that he had a prejudice against socialists, communists, and anarchists. This did not disqualify him from sitting as a juror. If the theories of anarchists should be carried into practical effect, they would involve the destruction of all law and government. Law and government cannot be abolished without revolution, bloodshed and murder. The socialist or communist, if he attempted to put into practical operation his doctrine of a community of property, would destroy individual rights in property. Practically considered the idea of taking a man's property from him without his consent for the purpose of putting it into a common fund for the benefit of the community at large, involves the commission of theft and robbery. Therefore, the prejudice, which the ordinary citizen, who looks at things from a practical standpoint, would have against anarchism and communism, would be nothing more than a prejudice against crime."[13]

With regard to undeniable evidence that prospective and actual jurors had formed and expressed opinions and admitted to prejudice, the court denied that this violated the Bill of Rights provision in the Illinois Constitution guaranteeing trial by "an impartial jury." It observed that an Illinois statute provided that if such prospective jurors state under oath that they believe they can impartially hear a case upon the evidence "and the court shall be satisfied of the truth of such statement," they may serve.[14] This was true, except that in the statute quoted by the court there was also a provision that the prospective juror *must NOT have expressed an opinion* as to the truth of statements read or heard about the guilt of defendants.

Well, said the court, referring to the case of Juror Sanford alone, it is true he expressed opinions. But they were not "strong and deep impressions,"[15] and so not to be considered as disqualifying him.

And, anyway, the court went on, its interpretation of the law in this way does not lead to approval of "partial jurors. On the contrary it tends to secure intelligence in the jury-box, and to exclude from it that dense ignorance which has often subjected the jury system to just criticism."[16]

7

Now Altgeld was, of course, familiar with that Illinois Supreme Court decision. But—and here he introduced one of the most telling points of all—he was also familiar with a later Illinois Supreme Court decision rendered on January 19, 1893, nine days after his inauguration as governor. This was in connection with the celebrated Dr. Cronin murder case, which occurred three years after Haymarket. There were certain points about the Cronin case that recalled the Haymarket matter. One such point was that great public excitement was produced by the murder in Chicago. Another that members of the police department were involved—but this time not as victims, but as the accused murderers, among them a detective named "Big Dan" Coughlin. It happened, too, that the trial judge in the Cronin case was Altgeld's friend, Judge McConnell.

In hearing the case Judge McConnell found that, because of political intrigue and public excitement, the same kind of prospective jurors were showing up in the trial of Detective Coughlin, *et. al.,* as were called in the Haymarket case. Nearly all admitted to prejudice and to expressions of opinions. Finally, McConnell determined to rely upon the Supreme Court ruling in the Haymarket case. Therefore, he approved jurors who, despite their prejudice, stated that they believed they could hear the case fairly.

And, lo! In a decision of January 19, 1893, in the Cronin case, the Illinois Supreme Court reversed the conviction on the ground that Judge McConnell had permitted prejudiced jurors to hear the case. Although the court made an effort to distinguish the Cronin case from the Haymarket case, it was plain that it had in fact overruled itself on the vital point as to what constitutes an impartial juror. Indeed, Chief Justice Benjamin D. Magruder, who wrote the Haymarket opinion, dissented in the Cronin case because he recognized that the court now was expressing views counter to those set down when it upheld Judge Gary's conduct.[17]

An apocryphal story, widely circulated in legal circles at the time, has it that Justice Magruder, a man of brooding, melancholy reserve, but lion-like when aroused, had bitter words over the Cronin decision with his colleagues. He is supposed to have accused his fellow justices of "catering to the Irish vote," compared them to "railroad lobbyists" and finally exclaimed: "If this is the view of the court, it is a pity that those anarchists were hanged!"[18]

Altgeld did not refer to Justice Magruder's rage, but he did quote at length from the Cronin case decision, also from Justice Magruder's dissenting opinion, and this with devastating effect. For example, he pointed out that the court now declared:

"The holding of this and other courts is substantially uniform, that where it is once clearly shown that there exists in the mind of the juror, at the time he is called to the jury box, a fixed and positive opinion as to the merits of the case, or as to the guilt or innocence of the defendant he is called to try, his statement that, notwithstanding such opinion, he can render a fair and impartial verdict according to the law and evidence, has little, if any tendency to establish his impartiality. This is so because the juror who has sworn to have in his mind a fixed and positive opinion as to the guilt or innocence of the accused, is not impartial as a matter of fact. . . . It is difficult to see how, after a juror has avowed a fixed and settled opinion, as to the prisoner's guilt, a court can be legally satisfied of the truth of his answer that he can render a fair and impartial verdict. . . ."[19]

Altgeld also brought out a statement by the court in the Cronin decision that appears almost a direct answer to Judge Gary in his surprising remark after interrogating Walker, the dry goods merchant.

"Under such circumstances [now said the Supreme Court] it is idle to inquire of the jurors whether they can return just and impartial verdicts. *The more clear and positive were their impressions of guilt, the more certain they may be that they can act impartially in con-demning the guilty party.*" [20]

Likewise, Altgeld spot-lighted the following observations: "To try a cause by such a jury is to authorize men . . . unjustly to determine the rights of others, and it would be no difficult task to predict, even before the evidence was heard, the verdict. . . . The theory [Judge Gary's, as later followed by Judge McConnell] seemed to be that if a juror could in any way be brought to answer that he could sit as an impartial juror, that declaration of itself rendered him competent. Such a view, if it was entertained, was a total misconception of the law. . . ."[21] "To compel a person accused of a crime to be tried by a juror who has prejudged his case is not a fair trial. . . ."[22]

Thus, Altgeld accurately stated, with reference to the Haymarket trial, that "the very things which the Supreme Court held to be fatal errors in the Cronin case, constituted the entire fabric of this case, so far as relates to the competency of the jury." If anything, the prejudice admitted by the Haymarket jurors was stronger than the facts which caused the Supreme Court to upset the Cronin verdict.

Altgeld summarized in his own way:

"No matter what the defendants were charged with, they were entitled to a fair trial, and no greater danger could possibly threaten our institutions than to have the courts of justice run wild or give way to public clamour; and when the trial judge in this case ruled that a relative of one of the men who was killed was a competent juror . . . and when, in scores of instances, he ruled that men who candidly declared that they believed the defendants to be guilty, that this was a deep conviction . . . and . . . when in all these instances the trial judge ruled that these men were competent jurors, simply because they had, under his adroit manipulation, been led to say that they *believed* they could try the case fairly on the evidence, then the proceedings lost all semblance of a fair trial."[23]

8

Obviously, Altgeld could have stopped there—probably should have, unless determined to throw to the winds all consideration of expediency. He had made a case showing the prisoners had been tried unfairly. Moreover, he had done this almost entirely by quotations from the record and from the Illinois Supreme Court. There was little up to this point of what Judge McConnell called "too much Altgeld."[24] But Altgeld did not quit.

He went on to discuss the evidence of the case, the peculiar tactics of Prosecutor Grinnell, the rôle of the police. He followed, too, with additional discussion of the conduct of Judge Gary. He did this, it is clear, not only because of impulses related to his profound personal indignation over what he discovered in the record of the trial itself but, more significantly, because of Judge Gary's article in *The Century*. For the balance of his statement, as much as anything else, proves upon close examination to be direct and indirèct answer to Judge Gary.

Gary had been heard from as to the guilt of the anarchists. "They were hanged, not for opinions but for horrible deeds." Now the world would hear about this from Altgeld!

9

"The State has never discovered who it was that threw the bomb that killed the policeman, and the evidence does not show any connection whatever between the defendants and the man who did throw it."

Thus flatly did Altgeld take issue with Judge Gary at the very beginning of the section of his statement entitled "Does the Proof Show Guilt?" That he meant to cross swords with Gary is made plain by a reference immediately. following Gary's contribution to *The Century*. Thus, in quoting the trial judge's explanation as to the basis for the conviction, that the bomb was thrown in consequence of the defendants' "advice," Altgeld prefaced the quotation with the remark that it was voiced by the Judge "*recently in a magazine article.*"[25] There was ill-concealed contempt for Judge Gary's interpretation of the law in Altgeld's comment.

"The judge certainly told the truth when he stated that this case was without a precedent, and that no example could be found in the law books to sustain the law as above laid down. For, in all the centuries during which government has been maintained among men, and crime has been punished, no judge in a civilized country has ever laid down such a rule before."[26]

He added that "the petitioners claim" that Gary's rule was laid down "to appease the fury of the public, and that the judgment was allowed to stand for the same reason. I will not discuss this," he wrote. However, granting for the moment the logic of Gary's reasoning, he observed:

"It was necessary under it to prove, and that beyond a reasonable doubt, that the person committing the violent deed had at least heard or read the advice given to the masses, for until he either heard or read it, he did not receive it, and if he did not receive it, he did not commit the violent act in pursuance of that advice."[27]

There, said Altgeld, is where the case fails. He went on, more outraged than before over Gary's magazine article.

"With all his apparent eagerness to force conviction in court, and his efforts in defending his course since the trial, the judge, speaking on this point in his magazine article, makes this statement: 'It is probably true that Rudolph Schnaubelt threw the bomb,' which statement is merely a surmise and is all that is known about it, and is certainly not enough to convict eight men on."[28]

Next Altgeld directed his attention to Judge Gary's liberal use of quotations from the writings and speeches of the anarchists.

". . . The mass of matter contained in the record and quoted at length in the judge's magazine article, showing the use of seditious and incendiary language amounts to but little when its source is considered. The two papers in which articles appeared . . . were obscure little sheets, having scarcely any circulation, and the articles themselves were written at times of great public excitement, when an element in the community claimed to have been outraged; and the same is true of the speeches made by the defendants and others; the apparently seditious utterances were such as are always heard when men imagine that they have been wronged, or are excited or partially intoxicated; and the talk of a gigantic anarchistic conspiracy is not believed by the then Chief of Police, as will be shown hereafter, and it is not entitled to serious notice, in view of the fact that, while Chicago had nearly a million inhabitants, the meetings held on the lake front on Sundays during the summer, by these agitators, rarely had fifty people present, and most of these went from mere curiosity, while the meetings held in-doors during the winter, were still smaller."[29]

At this point, Altgeld introduced his own theory as to the motive of the bomb-thrower. It was, he felt, an action of personal revenge.

He would amplify this view with a statement so strongly reminiscent of his book *Our Penal Machinery and Its Victims* as to show clearly the link in his thinking between his first liberal writing of 1884 and his pardon message of 1893. He now wrote in his "Reasons":

"While some men may tamely submit to being clubbed, and seeing their brothers shot down, there are some who will resent it, and will nurture a spirit of hatred and seek revenge for themselves, and the occurrences that preceded the Haymarket tragedy, indicate that the bomb was thrown by someone who, instead of acting on the advice of anybody, was simply seeking personal revenge for having been clubbed, and that Captain Bonfield is the man who is really responsible for the death of the police officers."[30]

To substantiate that view, Altgeld here used a good many of the affidavits and other documents supplied him by George Schilling. He introduced these with the observation that "a course had been pursued by the authorities which would naturally" produce an act of personal revenge, to which he added:

". . . for a number of years prior to the Haymarket affair there had been labor troubles, and in several cases a number of laboring people, guilty of no offense, had been shot down in cold blood by Pinkerton men, and none of the murderers were brought to justice.

"The evidence taken at coroner's inquests, and presented here shows that in at least two cases men were fired on and killed when they were running away, and there was consequently no occasion to shoot, yet nobody was punished; that in Chicago there had been a number of strikes in which some of the police not only took sides against the men, but without any authority of law invaded and broke up peaceable meetings, and in scores of cases brutally clubbed people who were guilty of no offense whatever. . . ."

Then he quoted from the decision of Judge McAllister in the Turner Hall case of 1877, in which, as already noted,[31] the judge condemned police attacks upon labor meetings as illegal.

"Now," commented Altgeld, "it is shown that no attention was paid to the Judge's decision; that peaceable meetings were invaded and broken up, and inoffensive people were clubbed." He told of the streetcar men's strike of 1885, with emphasis upon the brutality of Captain Bonfield. He presented here the affidavits of businessmen concerning Bonfield's wanton clubbings of workingmen, strikers and non-strikers.[32] Here, too, he presented Captain Schaack's letter in which that policeman denounced Bonfield's activities in the 1885 strike, citing further instances of skull-clubbings, and calling Bonfield's conduct "brutal and uncalled-for." He observed that during labor troubles of 1886, according to evidence presented, the police so conducted themselves that "under the leadership of Captain Bonfield, the brutalities of the previous year were even exceeded." He mentioned specifically a clash at McCormick's that spring, in which, he said, at least four workingmen were fired upon while running away from the police and "that this was wanton and unprovoked murder, but there was not even so much as an investigation."[33]

As for the Haymarket meeting, its character, he said, sustains the view that the bombing was an act unconnected with a conspiracy, for the meeting was peaceable and orderly.

"Had the police remained away for twenty minutes more there would have been nobody left there, but as soon as Bonfield had learned that the mayor had left, he could not resist the temptation to have some more people clubbed, and went up with a detachment of police to disperse the meeting; and that on the appearance of the police the bomb was thrown by some unknown person, and several innocent and faithful officers, who were simply obeying an uncalled for order of their superior, were killed.

"All of these facts tend to show the improbability of the theory of the prosecution that the bomb was thrown as a result of a conspiracy . . . if the theory of the prosecution were correct, there would have been many more bombs thrown; and the fact that only one was thrown shows that it was an act of personal revenge."[34]

Next Altgeld branded "much of the evidence given at the trial . . . a pure fabrication." To back up this, he presented Chief of Police Ebersold's interview exposing Captain Schaack's activities in organizing fake anarchistic groups and also the affidavits of Jacob Mikolanda and Vaclav Djmek, which relate how they were thrown into cells, subjected to the third degree and offered money in efforts to cause them to testify that a conspiracy existed. He strongly implied that what evidence was given of a conspiracy, such as the testimony of Godfried Waller concerning the "Monday night conspiracy," was elicited by such means. He concluded this section with another thrust at Gary.

"There was no case against them, even under the law as laid down by Judge Gary."[35]

10

Next the specific cases of Fielden, Schwab and Neebe claimed Altgeld's attention. It should be noted here, although Altgeld did not emphasize this, that the strategy of the prosecution during the trial centered largely on what Fielden supposedly did or said at the Haymarket meeting. His conduct was put forth as the link between the "Monday night conspiracy" (although he was not present at that basement meeting) and the bomb. The jury was made to believe: That Fielden's reference to "throttling the law" was directly in line with the conspiracy, that it was not mere oratory, but a planned incitement to violence on that night; That when Fielden said, "We are peaceable," he was in fact giving the signal for the bomb, a reference to the word "Ruhe" which means "peace" in German; That Fielden, when Bonfield's men approached, exclaimed: "Here come the bloodhounds now. You do your duty and I will do mine!"; That Fielden drew a revolver and was the first to open fire on the police.

Concerning these charges, Altgeld accurately observed:

"On the other hand, it was proven by a number of witnesses, and by facts and circumstances, that this evidence must be absolutely untrue. A number of newspaper reporters, who testified on the part of the State, said that they were standing near Fielden—much nearer than the police were—and heard all that was said and saw what was done; that they had been sent there for that purpose, and that Fielden did not make any such threats as the police swore to, and that he did not use a revolver."[36]

Independent study of the Haymarket trial record thoroughly substantiates that statement by Altgeld.

"But [continued Altgeld] if there were any doubt about the fact that the evidence charging Fielden with having used a revolver is unworthy of credit, it is removed by Judge Gary and State's Attorney Grinnell."

He referred to the letters that Judge Gary and Grinnell wrote to Governor Oglesby urging clemency for Fielden and Schwab, letters which, as noted, Gary "forgot" to mention in his magazine article.

"If," said Altgeld, "either Judge Gary or State's Attorney Grinnell had placed any reliance on the evidence of the police on this point, they would have written a different kind of letter to the then executive."

He then referred to the meeting in Lyman J. Gage's office.

"Mr. Grinnell was present and made a speech, in which, in referring to this evidence, he said that he had serious doubts whether Fielden had a revolver on that occasion, or whether indeed Fielden ever had one."

Yet, Altgeld commented, in arguing the case before the Supreme Court the previous spring, Grinnell placed "much stress" upon the evidence relating to Fielden and "that court was misled into attaching great importance to it."[37]

11

Neebe's case was taken up last. Altgeld began by referring to a letter to Governor Fifer in 1889, written by Mayor Harrison, and concurred in by Frederick S. Winston, then corporation counsel of Chicago, also for many years a noted lawyer for large corporations. In that letter, Mayor Harrison related that he and Mr. Winston were in court "in earnest conversation" with Prosecutor Grinnell when a motion was up by the defense to dismiss the case against Neebe for lack of evidence.

"Mr. Grinnell stated to us that he did not think there was sufficient testimony to convict Neebe.

"I thereupon earnestly advised him, as the representative of the State, to dismiss the case as to Neebe, and, if I remember rightly, he was seriously thinking of doing so, but, on consultation, with his assistants, and on their advice, he determined not to do so, lest it would have an injurious effect on the case as against the other prisoners. . . ."

Mr. Winston added:

"March 21, 1889.
"I concur in the statement of Mr. Harrison: I never believed there was sufficient evidence to convict Mr. Neebe, and so stated during the trial.

F. S. WINSTON."[38]

Altgeld conceded that Grinnell uttered a denial of the Harrison-Winston letter in a communication sent Governor Fifer in January, 1890. (Grinnell could not very well have admitted the facts as stated without convicting himself of a horrible act.) Grinnell's version of the incident was:

"I said to Mr. Harrison at that time, substantially, that I was afraid that the jury might not think the testimony presented in the case sufficient to convict Neebe, but that it was in their province to pass upon it."

To which Altgeld commented:

"Now, if the statement of Messrs. Harrison and Winston is true, then Grinnell should not have allowed Neebe to be sent to the penitentiary, and even if we assume that both Mr. Harrison and Mr. Winston are mistaken, and that Mr. Grinnell simply used the language he now says he used, then the case must have seemed very weak to him.

"If, with a jury prejudiced to start with, a judge pressing for conviction, and amid the almost irresistible fury with which the trial was conducted, he still was afraid the jury might not think the testimony in the case was sufficient to convict Neebe then the testimony must have seemed very weak to him, no matter what he now may protest about it."[39]

Altgeld's own conclusion concerning Neebe, against whom, as noted, the only real evidence concerned his ownership of two dollars' worth of stock in Spies' paper, was sweeping.

"I have examined all the evidence against Neebe with care, and it utterly fails to prove even the shadow of a case against him. Some of the other defendants were guilty of using seditious language, but even this cannot be said of Neebe."[40]

12

Here, again, was a place for Altgeld to stop. But apparently he could not, with Judge Gary's magazine article rankling him, especially the references to Captain and Mrs. Black. And so, he continued with another section under the heading "Prejudice or Subservience of Judge."

"It is further charged with much bitterness, by those who speak for the prisoners," Altgeld started off this section, "that the record of this case shows that the judge conducted the trial with malicious ferocity. . . ." He cited these "charges":

That the judge forced eight men to be tried together.

That the defense counsel, in cross-examining witnesses, were confined to points touched upon specifically by the state, whereas the

State's Attorney was permitted "to go into all manner of subjects entirely foreign to the matters on which the witnesses had been examined in chief.

That "page after page of the record contains insinuating remarks of the judge, made in the hearing of the jury, and with the evident intent of bringing the jury to his way of thinking."

That Judge Gary's "speeches" were "much more damaging than any speeches by the State's Attorney could have been."

That the State's Attorney often took his cue from the judge's remarks.

Then Altgeld turned his attention again to Judge Gary's *Century* article, relating that "it is further charged" that:

"The judge's magazine article recently published, although written nearly six years after the trial, is yet full of venom; that, pretending to simply review the case, he had to drag into his article a letter written by an excited woman to a newspaper after the trial was over, and which therefore had nothing to do with the case and was put into the article simply to create a prejudice against the woman, as well as against the dead and the living."

He continued:

"And that, not content with this, he, in the same article, makes an insinuating attack on one of the lawyers for the defense, not for anything done at the trial, but because more than a year after the trial, when some of the defendants had been hung, he ventured to express a few kind, if erroneous, sentiments over the graves of his dead clients, whom he at least believed to be innocent.

"It is urged that such ferocity of subservience is without a parallel in all history; that even Jeffries in England contented himself with hanging his victims, and did not stoop to berate them after death.

"These charges are of a personal character, and while they seem to be sustained by the record of the trial and the papers before me, and tend to show the trial was not fair, I do not care to discuss this feature of the case any farther, because it is not necessary."

And now his conclusion:

"I am convinced that it is clearly my duty to act in this case for the reasons already given, and I, therefore, grant an absolute pardon to Samuel Fielden, Oscar Neebe and Michael Schwab, this 26th day of June, 1893.

JOHN P. ALTGELD,
Governor of Illinois."

CHAPTER TWENTY-FOUR

The Storm

1

As a surprise move, the pardon was an overwhelming success, for none outside the little group in the Governor's office that morning was prepared for it. Even George Schilling was taken off guard. "It was like a bolt out of the sky," he recalled afterward. Most amazed of all were the three beneficiaries.

When Banker Dreyer arrived at the prison, the prisoners were at their regular convict jobs. Studious, bespectacled Michael Schwab was binding books in the library. Brawny Sam Fielden was sweating under a hot sun in the stone yard—working, incidentally, on a prison contract let to the firm that had employed him in Chicago up to 1886. Mild-mannered Oscar Neebe was at a commissary job "holding a dish of prunes." In less than thirty minutes, the bewildered trio found themselves in new civilian clothes and on a train bound for Chicago—free men. Banker Dreyer hovered about them like a mother hen. In their excitement and astonishment, they did not even resent his patronizing lectures on the theme "go and sin no more."[1]

What amazed them most of all was the text of Altgeld's message. A year previously Schwab had warned the Amnesty Association against presenting their case to Governor Fifer on the basis of an unfair trial. No hope lay in that direction, he said. He wrote from prison on June third, 1892:

"We have, of course, to deal with facts. No governor, whatever may be his political complexion, will openly antagonize the decisions of the courts. This stumbling block in our path cannot be removed."[2]

Yet that "stumbling block" was the very basis of the message that had restored freedom and citizenship without qualification! It was breath-taking, immediately incomprehensible and, to them at least, proof that the "system" which they had once railed at so fervently could do justice to the workingman after all. Despite rather stilted

236

phrases, the intensity of their emotion may be gathered from a letter to Altgeld which they composed a week later. Written out in Schwab's hand, their expression of gratitude to the Governor ran:

"Your Excellency have given us back wife and children home and liberty. You did this after having carefully considered the facts which could be known. Having weighed evidence against evidence you pursued the course dictated by your conscience, regardless of the torrent of abuse which you knew would be the consequence of your courage. This was the deed of a brave heart, and it will live as such in history.

"The dark and heavy mists of prejudice, of hate, and of narrow-minded party-spirit will pass away and vanish, and truth will shine in bright and brilliant splendor. Even today there are thousands of men of all conditions of life which approve your act, unqualifiedly. It is true most of them belong to the poorer classes, but in our country the sentiment of the poorest should not weigh less than the sentiment of those who revel in wealth. This is at least the sense of our political ambitions. And those men who did not approve of your action, did not dare to deny the facts on which your Excellency based your decision. Facts once established cannot retreat and force even unwilling minds to conclusions in harmony with them.

"*Some people prophesy all kinds of disaster which they say will follow in the wake of our liberation. To disprove their baseless assertions shall be one of the aims of our life.*

"As a reward for your noble deed, take, in addition to the approval of your conscience, the blessings of our wives, of our children, and of thousands of good men whose sense of justice you gave new strength, and the feelings of admiration and gratitude of the undersigned."[3]

2

It may be noted here, as a farewell to the anarchists, that Fielden, Schwab and Neebe faithfully kept their unsolicited pledge to Altgeld that he would have no occasion from any act of theirs to regret the pardon. From the moment of their release, they conducted themselves with complete circumspection, politically and otherwise. To avoid a scene on their arrival that first day in Chicago, they alighted from their train in the freight yards outside the city and made their way on foot, through a maze of box cars, to the homes of family and friends. "We want to be obscure," were their first words to reporters who sought interviews.

That answer epitomized their existence for the rest of their lives— much to the annoyance of certain radicals who felt the liberated men ought to have rejoined the ranks of radical agitators. An erstwhile "comrade" complained of this in a letter to Schilling.

"Altgeld released them as innocent men; he didn't pardon them as criminals. . . . He enabled them to hold their heads up like men, yet they are lagging far behind and hanging their heads like guilty hounds. . . . They are lost to us forever! How different their spirit from that of the martyrs of the eleventh of November!"

But such criticism from the extreme left did not dissuade them. They had had enough. And then, there was their pledge to Altgeld. . . . "To disprove their baseless assertions shall be one of the aims of our life."

Fielden got back his old stone teamster yard. The nearest he came to his old life was one afternoon when his job took him to the scene of the bombing. He dropped into the saloon on the corner, ordered a glass of beer, wiped his massive brow, and confided to the bartender: "You know, I'm Sam Fielden." He smiled, rather sheepishly, at the astonishment his remark caused, gulped his beer, and was seen there no more. Another last glimpse of Fielden shows him walking with George Schilling down the Midway of the Columbian Exposition, passing the concession where Little Egypt was cavorting and where Floradora girls were dancing, singing *Ta-ra-ra Boom-de-ay!* It was all very thrilling to Fielden.

"Sam," asked Schilling, suddenly, "do you know who threw that bomb?"

"No, I don't," said Fielden. "If I did, I would certainly tell you."[4]

A short time after that, Fielden received wonderful news from his native land. A relative in England had left him a legacy of something like $18,000. With that money, he moved his family to Colorado, purchased a ranch at La Veta, and lived there until his death in 1922, a successful, respected rancher. He was never again heard from in political news.[5]

Oscar Neebe, whose wife died while he was in prison, married a widow named Hepp, who owned a saloon near the Chicago stock yards,[6] and for a time operated the widow's saloon. His only political activity, and that slight, was participation in the Populist movement, at a time when even Lyman Trumbull was a Populist.[7] He lived until 1916. Interest in the Populist movement likewise was Schwab's only political activity.[8] He scribbled again for the *Arbeiter-Zeitung*, but his stuff was mild now, and by 1897 he was dead, his family moved to California.[9]

And so, the men freed by Altgeld faded from the public view almost at once. Because they so conducted themselves, the newspapers after the first few days of their release even ceased sending reporters around. Probably they would not have been hounded much even had they returned to agitation. It was not their scalps the press wanted after the twenty-sixth of June, 1893, but that of Altgeld.

3

Pitifully few were those who approved Altgeld's act. The sixty thousand persons who had signed petitions during the terms of Oglesby and Fifer? For the most part, they were inarticulate—the majority of "the poorer classes," as the liberated trio had written to the Governor. The judges, the bankers and the prominent lawyers who had felt the trial was unfair? Almost without exception these men, while approving liberation of the imprisoned anarchists, violently disapproved of Altgeld's reasons. It was to them a shocking thing to have errors of the courts exposed publicly, even if nothing but the truth was told. It offended "good manners," too, to have Judge Gary treated as Altgeld treated him—even if the truth was told there also. And so, among the respectable people who had urged amnesty for the anarchists, those who wholeheartedly approved Altgeld's action, could have been counted on the fingers of two hands.

One who did defend the pardon was Altgeld's first Chicago friend, Edward Osgood Brown, who was so overjoyed that he asked Schilling to arrange for a meeting with Schwab, Fielden, and Neebe to shake their hands so as to "make my part of the apologies society owes to them." He exclaimed: "What a good fellow Altgeld is!"[10] Another was Henry Demarest Lloyd. He wrote to the Chicago Record that "the governor did a much greater thing than an act of justice or mercy to individuals. . . . As far as in him lay, he broke the wheels of a judge-made revolution which would deprive the people of trial by jury of their peers."[11] Some isolated newspapers, like the Grand Forks, North Dakota, Evening News, praised the action, but these were so rare as to be negligible. The labor press, what there was of it, was generally laudatory. The Boston Labor Advocate carried a poem "To John P. Altgeld."

> "Altgeld the brave—so men to come shall say—
> Fit compeer, thou, of Lincoln's honored name. . . ."

In New York, John Swinton was overjoyed. He declared that Altgeld's pardon message should be sent, for its salutary effect, "to the Pope, the German and Austrian Kaisers, the President of the French . . . and sundry other kings, princes and high cockalorums."[12] And *John Swinton's Paper* made a brave effort to place the pardon in a favorable light.

But not many other approving voices were raised. Ironically, not even Clarence Darrow was wholly pleased with the action, nor Jane Addams, and both for the same reason. They felt Altgeld had erred in attacking Judge Gary personally. "I feel that Governor Altgeld was wrong in laying all the blame to Judge Gary. . . . If only [he] had consulted some one . . . ,"[13] Darrow wrote. And Miss Addams later observed regretfully in *Twenty Years at Hull House* that "a magnanimous action was marred by personal rancor, betraying for the moment the infirmity of a noble mind."[14] McConnell shared that view also. Only a few felt as did Schilling that Altgeld's bold, even bitter, arraignment of the court "was the bravest aspect of his action, for it took real courage to defy the aura of sanctity placed around the courts."[15]

Thus the uproar that resulted was all one-sided. Never in American history, certainly never since the Abolition days, had any man been so assailed in the press, so fiercely or so irrationally. So intense and sustained was the outburst that Altgeld later once observed to his friend Brown that it seemed somehow "sublime, like a fearful storm."[16]

4

The Chicago *Tribune* led the onslaught. Then and henceforth it reserved for Altgeld its supply of invective which heretofore had been used against communists and tramps. Its opening editorial comment, on the first day, was:

"The anarchists unveiled their monument to Spies and Parsons a few days too soon. Had they waited, Fielden, Schwab and Neebe could have been with them. . . . It was generally understood that they were to be let go in the event of Altgeld's election [sic]. The anarchists believed that he was not merely an alien by birth, but an alien by temperament and sympathies, and they were right. He has apparently not a drop of true American blood in his veins. He does not reason like an American, not feel like one, and consequently does not behave like one. . . ."[17]

But that was mild in contrast to what was to come. The next day the *Tribune* reiterated the charge of alienism against Altgeld, but this time it added the idea that Altgeld himself was an anarchist!

"Governor Altgeld has shown himself the apt and willing pupil of Fielden. . . . Fielden's simple creed of 'Kill the law; stab the law; throttle the law' is expanded by the Governor. . . . Altgeld could have kept his bargain with his anarchist supporters without producing the ideas of Fielden from the state house. The simple pardon of Fielden, Schwab and Neebe would have paid that debt . . . but his un-American feelings got the better of him. Poorly concealed for years, they broke forth at last in this hysterical denunciation of American principles, law, judges, executive and judicial officers and of people who deliberately and conscientiously approved of them."[18]

Day after day, with growing intensity, similar attacks upon the Governor and his pardon roared from the pages of Joseph Medill's paper in cartoons and editorials. "Anarchist!" "Demagogue!" "Un-American!" "Foreigner!" "Socialist!" "Apologist for Murder!" "Fomenter of Lawlessness!" Such were the epithets rushed into type against him. The news columns, so-called, were as blistering as the editorial pages. Any and every person, prominent or not, was able to get his name in the paper by making a statement denouncing Altgeld. Typical was the case of the obscure mayor of Racine, Wisconsin, one M. M. Secor, who sent an insulting telegram to Altgeld that read:

"You are a disgrace to our American republic, to the State of Illinois, to the Democratic party and to the nationality you belong to. . . . Resign your office and join the brothers you have pardoned. . . ."[19]

It was not long before the whole tribe of publicity-seeking small-fry politicians discovered this certain means of getting their names publicized. The *Tribune* accommodated them all. True, it printed some statements in praise of Altgeld's action. But these were nearly all from notorious anarchists, thus the effect was all one. Especially did it feature statements by Herr Johann Most, then editing his anarchist paper in New York, but lately released from a prison sentence for sedition in that city. Gleefully did the *Tribune* announce that "Most hails Altgeld." It quoted the editor as saying:

"This brave action of Governor Altgeld will do our cause more good than thousands of speeches and pamphlets, and our people will not forget to reward him."[20]

5

On June twenty-ninth, the *Tribune* scored what Publisher Medill doubtless considered a ten-strike. This was a story concerning the Governor and Judge Gary. The trial judge had kept publicly taciturn with regard to Altgeld's message. "It is not becoming either to my years, my position, or my long service to go into any defense of my judicial acts on any occasion,"[21] he said. But Judge Gary, or associates, rushed into Medill's hands a letter that struck Medill as peculiarly a godsend for a final blow against the "anarchist in Springfield." It was the letter that Altgeld had dispatched to the judges of the Appellate Court four years previously when enraged over the "certificate of good character" given him in his damage suit against the city of Chicago. Thanks to Judge Gary's careful preservation of the letter, including even the envelope addressed in Altgeld's scrawl, the *Tribune* was able to splash a photographic reproduction of it down the full length of its front page. The caption read: "ALTGELD DISPLAYS HIS VENOM."

For that time at least, the *Tribune* dropped its stock argument that Altgeld was motivated in the pardon by "alien temperament." Pushed aside also, for the time being, was the idea that Altgeld was, as the *Tribune* later called him, "a slimy demagogue, and . . . everybody knows it."[22] Discarded temporarily, too, was the charge that the pardon was fulfillment of a "bargain for votes with the anarchists." The real motive, the *Tribune* now exclaimed, was something infinitely worse. Its scare-lines told what it had in mind:

ALTGELD'S GRUDGE
When He First Began to Hate Judge Gary

———

A FOUR-YEAR GRIEVANCE
Indecent Letter Written to the Appellate Judges

———

JUST DECISION ANGERS HIM
His Effort to Stick the City for $26,000 Defeated

———

CAN'T FORGIVE ONE WHO BEAT HIM

———

There followed a two-column "story"—actually an adroitly worded, only thinly disguised, editorial—that rehashed in detail Altgeld's litigation with the city.

Omitted were all facts showing that Altgeld had some basis for the suit: for example, that two indisputably honest judges of the Circuit Court, one acting before the Appellate Court decision and one after, had sustained his claims; that even the Appellate Court did not deny a possible claim existed, but merely required a rehearing. All that could be gathered from the *Tribune* account was that Altgeld, with no justification at all, did in fact attempt to "stick" the city. Glossed over and finally ignored were the facts that not Judge Gary, but Judge Garnett, had written the decision to which Altgeld had taken offense, and that the letter was written to three judges *en banc*.

The *Tribune* flatly informed its readers:

"He [Altgeld] blamed Judge Gary for the decision which prevented his getting the $26,494. . . . Altgeld has sought to get even with him. His animus against Judge Gary has grown in intensity since the judgment was filed in 1889."[23]

With Altgeld's bold signature on the letter, none could doubt the authenticity of the *Tribune's* revelation. Moreover, the facts as recited appeared convincing. Even persons not unfriendly to Altgeld were convinced. Surprisingly, the Chicago *Daily News*, which in 1889 had defended Altgeld in his suit against the city, and was much less hysterical than the other papers over the pardon, accepted the *Tribune's* version as to Altgeld's true motives.

"It [the letter] makes it plain that in pardoning the anarchists and in assailing the court . . . he was not acting solely from motives of justice or mercy. . . . His vindictiveness has reacted upon himself. Judge Gary stands unscathed before the world, while Governor Altgeld— Well, the less said of him now the better."[24]

So the *News* editorialized, and thus did Altgeld's temperamental error in 1889 come home to roost in 1893 at the most unpropitious moment possible.

6

The press outside of Illinois, if anything, was even more ferocious and hysterical. Especially venomous, both in "news" and editorials, was the New York *Times*. Solemnly, the *Times* advised its readers on the first day in a "news" story:

"The American portion of [Chicago] feels outraged. . . . Irishmen are indignant because most of the policemen are Irishmen. The only people who are pleased are those who are tinctured with Anarchistic sentiments."

New Yorkers were further informed by the *Times* story that the pardon very probably was a result of a campaign pledge by Altgeld. True, Altgeld "never said in any speech that he would do this," but, the *Times* added, "nor did he deny that he would. . . . His course was regarded as equivalent to a promise of a pardon."

"Altgeld's position on socialism was well known. He had made many friends among the socialists by his pamphlets and by an article in 'The North American Review' [sic] in which he said that foreigners did more for America than natives, and that whenever a traitor was found, he proved to be a native-born American[sic!]."

Following the lead of the *Tribune* in Chicago, the New York *Times* kept up the bombardment for days. On one day there was featured a dispatch strongly suggesting that Altgeld was mentally unbalanced. He "laughed immoderately" when a *Times* correspondent called upon him, said this tale. He was quoted as saying: "Let them pitch in and give me the devil if they want to. They could not cut through my hide in three weeks with an axe!"[25] Another day the *Times* devoted front page space to a fantastic yarn—lifted from the Chicago *Journal*—to the effect that Altgeld, besides being an anarchist, a demagogue and possibly unbalanced, was not even a citizen of the United States. "They Call Altgeld an Alien—His Right to the Governorship of Illinois Questioned," the *Times* headlines ran. "When did the Governor's father take out his citizenship papers?" it wanted to know. But even if he were a citizen, Altgeld was still an "alien temperamentally," and not fit to be governor, the story continued.

"He cannot forget that he is of foreign birth and foreign ideas are at all times dominant in his mind. He looks upon America as a place in which to make money, not as a place in which to make a home and surround it with such precautions as will insure peace and happiness. It is probable that the Governor would have developed into an out-and-out Anarchist if his lucky real estate speculations had not turned the course of his natural tendencies."

Yet the *Times* was not so certain about Altgeld's radicalism after all. Perhaps it was simply a pose to get votes. "He is too selfish to be

a Socialist in fact," the newspaper reasoned now. "His own real estate
holdings are too large to admit of his wishing to divide with those
who work hard for a living." And how did he grow rich? "By hoard-
ing his money. He has never been known as a generous man. His
interest in his fellow men is very great, but he has confined it to seeking their votes." His political rise? "Treachery!" said the *Times*,
mentioning what had been whispered of Altgeld's connection with
the Palmer senatorial election of 1891.[26]

And a typical *Times* editorial:

". . . Governor Altgeld has done everything in his power . . . to en-
courage again the spirit of lawless resistance and of wanton assault
upon the agents of authority, . . . exactly in tone with the wildest Anarchist leaders. . . ."[27]

As for the New York *Sun*, its outrage could be adequately expressed
only by poetry:

TO ANARCHY

"Go fling the dark and bloody rag
Of Anarchy on high,
Go move it over land and sea
And with it sweep the sky.

"Stand up in line of proud array
The Red Caps everywhere
And shout the praises far and near
O' those who do not care.

"The Governor of Illinois
Has set the dreadful pace
And fleet must be the going foot
That beats him in the case.

"He overturns the courts decree,
He puts the laws to shame,
He sings the Anarch's fame.

.   .   .   .

"O, Wild Chicago, When the Time
Is Ripe for Ruin's deeds,
When constitutions, courts and laws

Go down midst crashing creeds,
Lift up your weak and guilty hands
From out the wreck of states,
And as the crumbling towers fall down
Write ALTGELD on your gates!"

In fairness to the editors of the *Sun*, it should be added that they apparently did not mean all that poem suggested, for there was appended an "epilogue."

"So runs the poem. We are safe
From Anarchy's misrule,
And Altgeld stands before the world
As either knave or fool!"

7

From coast to coast and border to border, the story was the same. The Washington *Post*, referring to Altgeld as "a mysterious fragment of jetsam from the Lord knows where," declared that he had "aspersed a Judge the latchet of whose shoes he is unfit to unloose." "Pernicious politics!" said the Boston *Herald*, while the Pittsburgh *Commercial-Advertiser* raged at Altgeld as a "wild-haired demagogue." The New Orleans *Times-Democrat* declared that Altgeld "complimented and commended the bomb-throwers of the Haymarket." The Atlanta *Journal* assured its readers that another outbreak of anarchy might be expected momentarily for "Governor Altgeld has fired the hearts of the demons with fresh courage and fresh hatred of all that we consider sacred." In Milwaukee, the *Journal* called for Altgeld's impeachment. "Governor Altgeld has encouraged anarchy, rapine, and the overthrow of civilization," said the Toledo *Blade*. The contribution of the Los Angeles *Times* was: "Altgeld's picture makes him look like an anarchist himself!" To which the St. Louis *Star* agreed, adding: "If he would let his hair and beard grow, he would pass muster in any gang of reds in the country."

Murat Halstead who composed a column syndicated to newspapers all over the nation, pontificated:

"There are three current themes of world-wide importance and the highest interest: The World's Fair, the action of India on silver money and the activities of the Governor of Illinois as an anarchist. . . .

"Touching the pardon of the anarchists by the Governor of Illinois, the greater offense is not in the act of clemency, for there is always charity found near the surface for errors of that kind (and it is possible it was reasonable to turn loose one of the parties pardoned) but the disgrace and the danger is the most unseemly, scandalous and incendiary reasons given by the governor for his action.

"His assault upon the officers of the law who did their duty in a most trying situation is inconceivably base. The mistaken demagoguery of it must be clear to the country."[28]

So much for the press of America. The Chicago *Tribune* told the truth when it announced that "for once at least, the newspapers of the United States are of the same mind. Republican or Democratic, North or South, they unite in denouncing . . . Governor Altgeld."[29]

8

To join the newspapers in the chorus soon came the magazines, like *Harpers Weekly*, *Leslie's* and *The Nation*. The comment of *The Nation*, typical of the contribution of the magazine editors, was: "The document reads almost as if the Governor himself were an anarchist!"[30] Pulpit and platform thundered in the same way. The Reverend Mr. H. A. Delano of the First Baptist Church of Evanston, Illinois, devoted his sermon on the Sabbath following the pardon to a diatribe entitled "The Shame of Our Governor."

"A Nero in Rome, a Paul of Russia, a Napoleon in France showed more care for the people than has this man by this deed. . . . Thank God, ours is the very form of government which makes possible a change!"[31]

On the day the preacher was speaking, Altgeld received sad news that caused him to journey from Springfield to the hills of Ohio near Mansfield. His mother had died on July second, following a stroke of paralysis. But even there he did not escape the torrent, for he was confronted by such headlines in the Ohio papers as: "The Reds Are His Friends Anyway, Though Gov. Altgeld Seems to Have Lost Others."[32] Of some comfort, however small, was the fact that the old folks of the Little Washington community had reserved opinions on the matter. They listened respectfully when, after the funeral, he gave his side of the story to a small group, including the Pollocks, who gathered around him. "Those fellows did not have a fair trial, and I did only what I thought was right," he said.[33]

He returned to Illinois, after making arrangements to buy a farm for one of his sisters, to learn that in the town of Naperville, near Chicago, some one-hundred-per-cent patriots had burned his effigy in the town square. The newspapers applauded. He discovered, too, that for that Fourth of July his "anarchism" had provided the orators from coast to coast with a new theme. One such orator was a justice of the United States Supreme Court, David J. Brewer, who in a year was to write the decision sending Eugene V. Debs to jail. "Is Governor Altgeld waiting to be another Jefferson Davis?"[34] said Mr. Justice Brewer in his Fourth of July speech.

At the annual alumni dinner of Harvard University at Cambridge that year Altgeld was the theme of the principal speaker.

"This act of a demagogic governor with a little temporary power, this slander upon justice, I must denounce. . . . If I did not I would consider myself an apostate to my own State of Illinois. It is for you Harvard men to stand firm in the midst of such dangers in the republic."

The speaker at this banquet was Robert Todd Lincoln.[35] There is a certain irony in that, until it is recognized that Abraham Lincoln's son stood not so much for the common people, even though "God made so many of them," as for the large corporations, whom he served as lawyer.

9

In addition to the Naperville effigy-burning affair, Altgeld was subjected to other public insults. When his friend, Philip Henrici, the famous Chicago restaurateur, presented a portrait of Altgeld to the Germania Club, a number of directors raised public protest.[36] In May, 1894, G. A. R. leaders in Chicago announced that the tradition of having the governor of Illinois review the annual Memorial Day parade would be ignored in Altgeld's case. "The boys like some Democrats, but they don't like Altgeld and won't have him review their parade!" said the grand marshal.[37] Several weeks later, certain trustees of Northwestern University advised the press that they objected "strenuously" to the issuance of an invitation to Governor Altgeld to attend the commencement exercises of the institution. They felt he "would be a bad example for the students." The *Tribune* told of that under the headlines: "Class Him As An Evil—Altgeld Put on a

Level with Cigarets and Yellow Backs."[38] The following September, when Altgeld and his wife stayed at a hotel in the East, the press gleefully heralded the news that other guests moved out, refusing to stay under the same roof with "that anarchist."[39] And so in this period at least, it was true that "it was the crowd on one side and John Peter Altgeld on the other."

CHAPTER TWENTY-FIVE

The Counter-Charges

1

How much truth, if any, was there in the various accusations, expressed and implied, hurled against Altgeld in connection with the pardon? Disregarding such inanities as "Altgeld looks like an anarchist" or "he hates policemen, especially Irish policemen," the most serious charges were these: First, that he was an anarchist himself or a sympathizer with the philosophy of anarchy; second, that the pardon was a demagogic action calculated to further his ambition to be elected to the United States Senate; third, that it was done in fulfillment of a "deal," actual or "understood," in connection with his gubernatorial campaign of 1892; and fourth, that he was motivated chiefly by a personal grudge against Judge Gary.

While the first charge was the most widely believed, and its echoes are found today in standard histories, it deserves scarcely any serious attention at all. The fact that otherwise intelligent newspaper and magazine editors sincerely for a time believed that Altgeld was an anarchist, and that these editors, with few exceptions, made not the slightest effort to ascertain the facts, remains an amazing commentary upon the profession of journalism in America of that day. For it must be conceded that while many of the editors raised that cry and continued it for political reasons, the majority indicated that they were sincere.

The truth, of course, is that Altgeld was no more an anarchist in either spirit or deed than Joseph Medill of the Chicago *Tribune*. His whole career, up to now, and later, placed him at the opposite pole from the philosophy labeled anarchy. Nor was there anything in either his action or his writings which smacked of socialism—Marxian, Christian or "scientific"—unless belief in municipal ownership of certain public utilities could be so conceived. As for the remarks that his ideas came from his "alien background," it is clear, of course, that the only thing "foreign" about him was the accident of his birth. If from anything, his "radicalism" stemmed, not from German socialism, but from so indigenous an American product as Missouri Grangerism.

Justice, yes. Freedom of speech, yes. A square deal for labor and advocacy of trade unions, yes. Likewise, sympathy for the weak who have fallen into crime and also for the under-dog in nearly every situation. Likewise, opposition to monopoly and the "trusts," and an open mind for measures designed to regulate (but definitely not to destroy) capitalistic enterprise. Such was Altgeld's "anarchism" and "socialism," and not more than that. In view of what is known of him from his birth through his rise as a lawyer, his climb to wealth, his association with the Vanderbilt lawyer, Goudy, his passion for material achievements, and for the game of practical politics, his devotion to "American" individualism, we may dismiss the anarchy charge once and for all at this point. It was buncombe, pure and simple.

The second charge, that his pardon was conceived to further his ambition for the senatorship, may be dismissed as emphatically as the first, which it so glaringly contradicts. The politics charge makes no sense whatever, even if none of the facts were known about Altgeld's tremendous inner struggle over the pardon for the very reason that he felt it would ruin him politically. As far as could be foreseen by any politician, including one so shrewd as Altgeld, the pardon, if not ruinous, could prove nothing but a drag upon any man's career in public life.

Only a fool could have reasoned differently—and Altgeld was anything but that politically. "On the one side, there was nothing—the anarchists were a lot of friendless devils without sympathy from the vast majority. Every man's hand was against them. On the other hand I knew that in every civilized land, and especially in the United States, the press would ring out loud and bitter against me for what I did." So Altgeld declared in September, 1894, and he spoke the truth.[1]

2

In an objective study, the other two charges may not be handled so easily.

To the accusation of enemies that there was a "deal" in the 1892 election color is lent by statements of Altgeld's friends. There is the statement by Clarence Darrow in his *Story of My Life*: "It was commonly believed, and often stated, that if he were elected, he would pardon the anarchists."[2] That statement does not necessarily mean a definite deal was made. It could mean simply that there was an accepted "understanding." Yet the implication might be otherwise. There is the testimony also of "Private Joe" Fifer.

"It was always my understanding that Governor Altgeld entered the race for Governor fully pledged to pardon the anarchists. I do not know that this was true, but, as I say, it was my understanding, and I think the people very generally expected him to do what he did do, whatever their opinions of its justice or policy may have been."[3]

Now, that statement of Fifer's is not to be dismissed as the utterance of a disgruntled, defeated rival, nor as an utterance by one who believed the pardon of the anarchists was wrong. True, Fifer had declined to act upon the case while governor. Yet, after having been assailed for nearly a half century by liberals and radicals for his supposed reactionary views in the anarchist case, he expressed his true sentiments to James O'Donnell Bennett, Chicago *Tribune* reporter, in 1935, when he said:

"I think there were pretty just grounds for Altgeld's pardon of the anarchists. I had begun study of the case during my administration, and I don't think Altgeld can fairly be blamed for that pardon."[4]

There is the fact, too, (which the partisan press carefully concealed at the time) that Altgeld and Fifer became warm personal friends. Politically, Fifer always opposed the man who defeated him, but he developed real affection for Altgeld personally and came to refer to him as "a lovable man . . . sturdy and fearless."[5] Thus, Fifer's testimony concerning a "deal" deserves consideration. But was there a "deal"?

Unquestionably, agitation over the Haymarket case was a political factor after the trial in 1886. It appears to have been a fact that negotiations toward a "deal" were attempted in the gubernatorial campaign of 1888 when John M. Palmer was the Democratic candidate against Fifer. In his memoirs, Palmer relates that he rejected an offer from an unnamed "agent" to "deliver fifty thousand votes" if he would agree beforehand to pardon the anarchists.[6] Palmer told the truth, but there is reason for doubting the validity of the offer. It was made by Albert Parsons' brother, General William H. Parsons.[7] But General Parsons, who had no political influence in Illinois, was acting for himself alone. In professing to consider the proposed arrangement seriously, Palmer was naïve.

As for the 1892 campaign, it is certain that not even that kind of offer was suggested to Altgeld or to anyone else associated with his campaign. The avowed anarchist groups were so negligible as to make laughable a "deal" from that source. The Amnesty Association of Illinois was the only group in any sense numerically important enough for such an arrangement. Careful investigation of the activities of that group has shown that it had no election "understanding" with Altgeld.

Two facts alone are convincing. One is that leaders of the Amnesty Association debated at length, privately and publicly, the question of injecting the clemency issue into the 1892 campaign. A split in the organization very nearly resulted, with the final decision being to keep the amnesty movement entirely out of the election.[8] This policy was adhered to strictly.

More significant was the other fact—that the chairman of the Amnesty Association was William Penn Nixon. He was a staunch Republican, and editor of the Chicago Inter-Ocean. And the Inter-Ocean, under Nixon's direction, not only was considered as the official Republican organ in Chicago, but hotly opposed Altgeld. It was even more vigorous in its anti-Altgeld campaign in 1892 than the Tribune. Obviously, no offer of an election "deal" could have come from that source.

Indeed, because William Penn Nixon was chairman of the Amnesty group, the only important reference to the anarchist case during the 1892 campaign was an editorial in the Democratic Chicago Herald (which firmly opposed a pardon for the anarchists) suggesting that the Republicans had made a deal with the anarchists to support Governor Fifer. Under the bold heading "Is It a Deal?" the Herald on August 10, 1892, declared:

"In view of the sudden appearance at this time of the chief Republican journalist of Chicago at the head of a society for the release of anarchists who were convicted on exactly the same testimony as that which sent four other anarchists to the gallows, the Herald is bound to say that the matter has a very surprising look. . . . If the Republican party has not made a deal with the anarchists and socialists, why should its leading editor be put forward to head the organization that represents those elements? . . .

The Herald editorial was, of course, nonsense. Yet it is significant that the Republican press failed to answer it. The Tribune at that time thought so little of the "deal" idea with reference to Altgeld that it mentioned only casually during the campaign that Altgeld was asked by a reporter how he "stood" as to a pardon for the three anarchists, and that he replied: "I have never signed a petition or paper of any kind for the release of those men."[9] There was evasion in Altgeld's answer. But the *Tribune* made nothing of it. Its only reference was a smirking editorial paragraph on August tenth, 1892.

"The attitude of Candidate Altgeld on the pardoning of the anarchists will disturb no one, since he will have no occasion to take a hand in the game."

And so, the "deal" accusation was not taken seriously during the campaign itself when, if there were any indications of such an arrangement at all, the *Tribune* most certainly would have made the most of it.

3

Superficially, the fact that Altgeld was supported enthusiastically by men who were constantly active in behalf of a pardon may have been a suspicious factor. But it is known that men like Henry Demarest Lloyd and George Schilling supported Altgeld for reasons unrelated to the anarchist case. It is indubitably true that they *expected* Altgeld to pardon the anarchists, because of his generally liberal views. For example, they probably knew of the letter he had written on November 14, 1891, to Chief of Police McLaughry, of Chicago, in which are to be found the most direct references to the Haymarket case that he ever made prior to the pardon—statements, in fact, which are to be found later in his pardon message. That letter, never made public until Altgeld included it in his second volume of *Live Questions*, published in March, 1894, was a protest against a repetition in 1891 of the Turner Hall incident of 1877. In that same hall, on November 10, 1891, police invaded a labor meeting and commanded the gathering to disperse unless the American flag was displayed. The next evening another police squad stormed into Grief's Hall, where a meeting in memory of the hanged anarchists was in progress. Without warrants, in the pretense of "looking for anarchists," the police smashed doors and ordered everyone present to hold up his hands. Persons who protested were clubbed.

Many prominent citizens—even Bonfield, then off the police force—protested publicly against those incidents. Altgeld—still cautious—did not join the public protest, but he did write privately to Chief McLaughry.

"I do not know any of the men who were at those meetings on Wednesday and Thursday nights, or who were clubbed and arrested; never saw any of them, never spoke to any of them; nobody ever spoke to me concerning any of them, and I have no interest in them. But I will ask you, can you think of anything more calculated to create a thirst for revenge in the minds of ignorant men; can you think of anything more calculated to plant the seeds of hatred and even of murder in the hearts of men; can you think of anything more calculated to make them hate the flag that floats above them and pray for the destruction of the government that thus bullies them . . . ?

"In the Spring of 1886 we had some extensive strikes and labor troubles on the West Side. At that time there were meetings of labor people and the Police Department then pursued the course which your officers have just been pursuing; when there was no trouble meetings were broken up, men were clubbed without any provocation, and this was kept up for weeks, until finally some wretch, whose name, if they knew it, the police have never been willing to make public, threw a bomb at a squad of police who were in the act of dispersing another peaceable meeting—a meeting which the Mayor had attended and pronounced peaceable—and the result was the killing and maiming of a large number of policemen, most of them officers who were simply obeying orders of their superiors, and were not responsible for the brutal bullying done by other officers. . . .

"As a citizen and a tax-payer, as a man who loves our country and believes our government to be the best on earth; as a lover of liberty, of law and of order; as a man who is proud of our great city and who does not want its fair fame beclouded by this dramatic and farcical police demonstration, I protest against these unlawful acts, and I will say to you that it will be an evil day for our country when the poor and the ignorant, misguided though they may be, shall feel that a bullet is the only minister of justice which can right their wrongs, and the conduct of your officers now, *like the conduct of certain officers in the spring of '86*, will certainly tend to create that feeling, and to accelerate its growth, and thus tend to endanger the lives and property of our people."[10]

Knowing that Altgeld entertained such ideas as expressed in that letter, Lloyd and Schilling could have felt no need for an understanding with Altgeld before his election with regard to the Haymarket matter. Schilling, in fact, deliberately blocked an effort to get Altgeld on record before election. During the campaign he had learned that a group of young German socialists planned to interview Altgeld on the Haymarket case. Schilling hastened to Altgeld to warn him of the plan. While Altgeld could see no harm in talking with the group,

Schilling insisted that he "show them the door immediately." Schilling said:

"Altgeld, I could not be for you for Governor or any other office, despite our friendship, if I thought you could stoop to bargain for votes by agreeing beforehand to pardon those men. God knows that I want them freed, but whoever does it must act upon the facts and because of justice alone!"[11]

Schilling was sincere. Moreover, he was not disappointed. There was no "deal."

4

And the charge of prejudice against Judge Gary? Altgeld, in his pardon message, did, of course, treat Judge Gary in a manner indicating prejudice. There can be no question about that. But did his manner denote prejudice for personal reasons, or was it prejudice against "Garyism"? Altgeld himself would suggest the latter, saying, "I denounced, not Gary, the man, but Garyism."[12] If he told the truth there, then the criticism on this score collapses for lack of meaning. Bitterness toward Judge Gary, if based solely or even almost solely upon his conduct of the trial or upon his authorship of The Century article, may have been inexpedient, "injudicious" or unkind. But it could be called nothing more. This matter is worth consideration only if Altgeld was influenced chiefly by personal animosity toward Gary unrelated to the Haymarket case itself.

The case against Altgeld in this regard rests upon four "counts":

First, the letter denouncing the Appellate Court for its decision in his case against the city.

Second, that Altgeld may have resented a comment made by Judge Gary in an Appellate Court decision overruling the result of a civil trial heard by Altgeld as a judge. Gary's comment was: "The rules of law cannot be departed from to administer fireside equity in hard cases."[13]

Third, Altgeld, it would be charged, could not distinguish a man from his views; he naturally would be antipathetic toward Gary because of their essentially opposite attitudes on social and economic questions.

Fourth, Altgeld seemed to have been the spearhead of an effort to defeat Judge Gary for re-election in November, 1893.

On its face, the first count appears convincing. The letter Altgeld sent to the Appellate Court after it set aside his judgment against the city did display what the *Tribune* called "venom." There was no answering that, and Altgeld wisely never attempted a direct answer. It would have been useless for him to try to explain the legal merits of his case as he saw them. Probably it would have been just as useless to point out that his castigation of the higher court "as a kind of obstruction to the administration of justice" was in accord with views expressed by him before his own case was decided.

Assume, however, that his sense of personal grievance was all-motivating in his attack upon the Appellate Court. Was that attack directed at Judge Gary? Judge Gary was only one of three judges on the court at that time. There is nothing to show that he participated any more actively in the Altgeld case than Judges Garnett and Moran, if he participated at all except perfunctorily. Judge Moran was, and remained, on friendly terms with Altgeld. He was one of the judges who agreed with Altgeld that Judge Gary's conduct was abhorrent to principles of justice. More pertinent is the fact that not Judge Gary, but Judge Garnett, wrote the decision which so offended Altgeld. And so, despite the *Tribune*, these facts, together with other evidence, appear convincing enough to acquit Altgeld completely of the charge that any connection existed between his letter to the Appellate Court and his pardon of the anarchists.

When examined, "counts" two and three are likewise found of no or little validity. The case in which Judge Gary referred to Judge Altgeld's "fireside equity" was of no importance to Altgeld one way or another. It had been one of many prosaic real-estate cases that came before him as a judge. When Gary rendered his decision, Altgeld had been off the bench for months. He had pushed aside his judicial career completely. He may not even have seen Gary's decision until it was trotted out after the pardon.

As for the charge that Altgeld "hated" Gary because of their antipathetic economic views, it is true that Altgeld in some cases manifested personal dislike for men whose views on public questions he despised. But it also was true that some of his closest friends, including those of longest standing, were men who violently disagreed with his principles. Goudy, Lambert Tree, Adolf Kraus, are examples, and the list could be extended.

There remains, then, the fourth "count." It is true that an effort was made in the election of November, 1893, to defeat Gary for reelection to the Superior Court and that this was in face of a near-tradition that Gary be accorded endorsement by both major parties.

It is true, too, that Altgeld played some part in the campaign. In so doing, he used bad judgment. Participation by a governor in a judicial election was accepted as presumptuous, if not counter to the theory of separation of the powers of government, and Altgeld's interest in Gary's candidacy was resented by the general public without regard to its views on Judge Gary. Gary was re-elected.

But while Altgeld blundered in that episode, investigation does not bear out the thesis of the *Tribune*, and nearly every other newspaper in Chicago at the time, that Altgeld directed the movement to unseat Gary. The initiative was taken by the Chicago labor movement, represented by the Trade and Labor Assembly. George Schilling, Thomas J. Morgan, Henry Demarest Lloyd and the "whole motley crew of malcontents serving under Captain Altgeld," as the *Tribune* called them, were aggressively active in the fight on Gary. This was the "proof" that Altgeld engineered a "plot" against Judge Gary. But it was proof only for political purposes. Actually, after the campaign was over— one in which the people of Chicago were assured that "10,000 anarchists" were waiting only for the defeat of Gary as a signal to rise up against law and order—even the *Tribune* admitted that Altgeld displayed not the slightest concern that Judge Gary squeezed through.[14] He was more disappointed that his friend, Edward Osgood Brown, was defeated for the bench in that election mainly through the efforts of the *Tribune*, which went after him hammer and tongs because "he favors the pardon of anarchist law-breakers . . . is a single-taxer and a friend of Altgeld."[15]

5

So much, then, for the charges of impropriety and personal malice brought against Altgeld for the pardon of the anarchists. But while he is magnificently acquitted of those charges—actually the transcendental nature of the pardon message itself is the most convincing refutation of base motives—it would be a mistake nevertheless to assume that he was not influenced by some personal considerations aside from his profound sense of justice. Unquestionably, he approached the Haymarket case in accord with views slanted as definitely in the one way as Judge Gary's were slanted the other. It appears certain, too, that he was influenced by deep prejudices. However, those were not against men, but against certain institutions, for example, the courts and the police, as he felt them to be unjust or brutal. It is clear, too, that his tendency toward quick resentment and even vindictiveness played a part in the pardon message—bigger than those who have praised the act have been willing to recognize. For, had he not resented Judge Gary's article in *The Century*, the pardon would not have been what it was. Potent, too, was another personal factor. In Altgeld, there existed a strong desire for a certain kind of immortality. As Edgar Lee Masters remarked, he was always, or at least frequently, saying, "Let us build for the ages!" He expressed this idea in a letter to Lloyd. Desiring to compliment him for his book *The New Conscience*, the superlative thought that came to him was: "The future will know you and coming generations of suffering humanity will rise up and bless you."[16]

Such fame and remembrance from future generations was desired by him, too. One reflection of that desire was his beloved Unity Building. His action in the Haymarket case must be put down as another. Unquestionably, against the political ruin that he expected, he weighed the probability of obtaining a permanent place in history. Unquestionably, too, he was motivated by his desire to show the world his strength of character.

And so, if explanation is needed for the pardon—the complete explanation—it is to be found in the complete Altgeldian character that began forming back in the days when he was a boy in Ohio.

CHAPTER TWENTY-SIX

RIDING THE STORM

1

AND Altgeld during the storm? At first he was defiant. However, when the uproar exceeded anything he had anticipated, when he saw the press of his own party deserting him, when even close friends indicated dissatisfaction, his defiance at times gave way to an attitude of defense, even bewilderment. But not for long.

In the main, he was resigned and philosophical about the abuse. To a friend who inquired years later how he stood up under the abuse resulting from the pardon, he remarked: "I looked up at the sun, and smiled."[1] But sometimes there was little sun. This does not mean that he ever took the vituperation lying down, or was silent. He did give up hope of causing his most virulent critics to cease what he deemed was unconscionable misrepresentation of his act and his own beliefs. There were periods, too, when he despaired of ever making his voice heard above the shouts of his enemies. Yet, withal, he gave back, on every possible occasion, blow for blow. He winced more than once, but the full picture shows him standing strong and firm. If anything, he came out of the storm a stronger character and more of a fighter, more determined to chart his course in accord with his honest convictions, than before.

Admittedly, this picture of Altgeld's reactions is at variance with the impression given by nearly all that has been written of him heretofore. From the writings of Whitlock, Darrow, Edward Osgood Brown, Edgar Lee Masters and Waldo R. Browne, the impression is conveyed that Altgeld's heart was broken, perhaps his spirit, too, by the intensity of the criticism. Thus, in *Forty Years of It*, Whitlock recorded: "And the storm did break, and the abuse it rained upon him broke his heart. . . . I never again heard him mention the anarchist case."[2] And Edgar Lee Masters: "From now on Altgeld's life was . . . strife, misunderstanding and tragedy to the end."[3] And Waldo R. Browne: "The attack upon him . . . was powerful enough to wreck his fortunes, to crush all his hopes, to break his heart."[4]

260

Even Darrow, while stating that Altgeld "did not wince and never complained," suggests that his heart was "torn and bleeding."[5]

True, Edgar Lee Masters recognized that Altgeld "never asked for quarter" and that afterward he "dealt with the most powerful coteries and influences and newspapers as if he had nothing to fear." Likewise, Waldo Browne would amend his doleful comment with the observation that "through it all, his courage never faltered . . . to the last day of his life he went on fighting with unbroken will." Yet the sharper picture etched by those commentators shows Altgeld as a broken man. That picture fits the Altgeld Legend. But it does not fit the Altgeld that might be expected from the career and character seen up to now.

It was not the true Altgeld.

2

He was, as stated, despondent at times. Mrs. Altgeld reflected his mood in writing to Mrs. Henry D. Lloyd some three weeks after the pardon, confiding that her husband had dropped the remark that "it might not be long before Altgelds took up their abode by the wayside."[6] Another reflection of his mood is a remark he made to Schilling on one occasion: "The press has got me down."[7] And no wonder!

There was hardly ever a let-up by the *Tribune* and other papers in their raging against him, with his every act, except on rare occasions, misrepresented or misinterpreted. On the slightest pretense the cry of anarchy was raised against him. When Mayor Carter Harrison was assassinated in October, 1893, by a lunatic who conceived the idea that he should have been appointed Corporation Counsel, the press contrived to blame Altgeld for that tragic crime. Typical was an editorial in the Brooklyn *Union*.

"The Governor of Illinois is very much shocked at the murder of Mayor Harrison. The Governor cheapened human life in his state by his free pardon of Anarchists and the abuse of the stern and just judge who tried them. Such a performance as that of Altgeld is a direct incentive to bloodshed by cranks."[8]

More distressing was a horrible incident at Danville, Illinois, in May, 1895. Two men charged with rape had been lodged in the county jail there, and a lynching mob gathered. A local judge stood upon the jail steps and pleaded with the mob to let the courts take their course. He assured them that the prisoners would be dealt with severely. His words seemed to have an effect, until the leader of the mob shouted:

"Yes, we know the jury will convict and give a good sentence. But that anarchist governor of ours will pardon them out! If any other man than Altgeld was governor, we would not lynch those men, but we are determined that he will never have a chance to turn them loose!"

And so the crowd, composed of men who obviously had been whipped up against Altgeld by the newspaper attacks, stormed the jail and carried through the plan for the double lynching.[9] Once more the press of the nation raved—not at the lynchers, but at Altgeld. The *Tribune* in Chicago called the Danville lynching "the evil fruit" of Altgeld's pardon of the anarchists. The St. Louis *Globe-Dispatch* predicted that worse would happen as long as Altgeld remained governor. The Minneapolis *Tribune* took the occasion to exclaim: "Altgeld may properly be classed as the Nero of the last decade of the nineteenth century!"[10] Throughout the nation the press presented the same story. And he was truly shaken by that Danville incident. He showed it when George Schilling shortly afterward saw him about a pardon for a man in whom he happened to be interested.

"Schilling, I can't do it!"

"Haven't I given sufficient reasons?" Schilling asked, startled.

"Yes," said Altgeld.

"Then why do you refuse?"

"Because," said Altgeld, "the newspapers have poisoned the minds of the people. To grant any more pardons would be to jeopardize the lawful rights of persons accused of crime because of the prejudice existing against me personally."[11]

Earlier, a few weeks in fact after the pardon of the anarchists, Brand Whitlock had found Altgeld in a similar mood. George Brennan, later "boss" of the Illinois Democracy, then a clerk in the Statehouse, had asked Whitlock to see Altgeld about a young prisoner who was dying of tuberculosis and whose mother hoped he would be permitted to die at home.

"No! No!" Altgeld said. "I will not pardon any more. The people are opposed to it. They do not believe in mercy. They love revenge. They want the prisoners punished to the bitterest extremity."[12]

But those moods were the exception with him. In fact, in the case brought to his attention by Whitlock he changed his mind within a few days—only to learn that it was too late, for the prisoner already had died.

And that change of mind gives the truer picture of him in face of the raging of the press.

3

He was far from silent about the criticism, despite the contrary impression conveyed by his friends. He deliberately walked into the journalistic lion's den three days after the pardon by going to Chicago and inviting the press to interview him at the Unity Building. In that interview, with the reporters crowding around, he was noticeably composed, also somewhat disdainful of his critics. "He sat with his elbows squarely fixed on the table before him and he spoke in a deliberate judicial tone. He showed no resentment in his manner, and even when he condemned his critics most severely, there was not a single trace of animosity in his words. He might have been talking about the last expedition to the North Pole, so apparently disinterested was he in expressing opinions." So related the *Daily News*.[13]

"What have you to say to the criticism of the eastern papers concerning the pardon?" the reporters asked him on that occasion.

"Like their western contemporaries, they have confined themselves simply to abuse."

"Why abuse?"

"Well, they leave the merits of the case entirely alone. Generalities are thought to be sufficient. Nothing like a careful, unprejudiced review of my facts and arguments is anywhere attempted. In most cases, too, my critics have no knowledge of the facts. Probably none of them had studied the case sufficiently to make this opinion of great importance."

Then he asked some questions.

"How many have referred to what Chief Ebersold said about there being nothing in this anarchist business? How many of them referred to his statement about Schaack being desirous of forming new societies and stimulating public excitement? Then, again, my critics have avoided all reference to the manner in which the jury . . . was impanelled. Nothing is said of the declaration of these jurors that they were prejudiced.

"It appears to be taken for granted that it is a principle of American jurisprudence that men who are victims of a popular outcry are not entitled to a fair trial. . . . My unfriendly critics lay no stress on the fact that the State never found out who threw the bomb nor, in fact, anything about it. The State was never able to prove that the fellow who did throw the bomb had ever heard any of these men talk or had ever read anything they had written. . . . Not a single scintilla of evidence was brought out and no connection was made between the bomb-thrower and the men who were pardoned."

He shot this at his critics:

"Those who have been so full of angry and hostile criticism ignore rational considerations entirely. . . . They shut their eyes to the truth. . . . Instead of discussing the case calmly, logically and reasonably, and in the spirit of intelligent fairness, the critics grow wild, fierce and frenzied and in that mood say things that they will probably be sorry for when cool, good sense reasserts its reign."

On finishing that statement, he "lifted his eyebrows and a shadow of a smile flitted across his face."[14] He had had his say, he indicated. Then a reporter brought up the charge of prejudice against Judge Gary.

"That I am prejudiced against Judge Gary is all nonsense," he said. "The reasons I gave for signing the pardon have been published and they must stand or fall by themselves. To those persons who ascribe mean motives in an act of public character, I have nothing to say. They sufficiently answer themselves. My reasons have been given to the public. If they are good they will stand. If they are not good, they will fall. . . ."[15]

4

Other interviews that he gave, and he gave many, were of the same tenor. The following August, the *Tribune* and other Republican papers blossomed out (as a prelude to the fall election of that year), with stories about the "revival of anarchy in Chicago," all with pointed references to Altgeld. He flatly charged such stories were inspired by politics and from even worse motives. For example, he asserted—and there are facts to support him—that certain persons had a financial interest in anarchist scares. They collected vast sums of money from frightened businessmen "for the ostensible purpose of watching the maneuvers of a class of people who in reality had no existence." Talk of anarchist activity in Chicago, he called a "malicious libel" on Chicago.

He added that he had "examined the whole subject carefully," and was convinced that "there are not and there never have been more than fifty anarchists in the whole State of Illinois." That, incidentally, was the conclusion even in 1886 by the grand jury that indicted the Haymarket defendants. [16] Of course, there are discontented people, he said, and also "all manner of theorists, but they are law-abiding." When strikes occur, there is "more or less irresponsible and wild talk, all of which subsides and is forgotten the moment the labor trouble is over," he observed. He predicted that "we may have an occasional bread riot," in view of hard times because "nobody likes to starve." But "it will be by people nearly every man of whom would fight for the Stars and Stripes."[17]

In July of the following year, Nellie Bly came to Springfield to interview him. He took the occasion to defend the pardon again.

"The evidence failed absolutely to show that they had committed any crime whatever. The police had never shown nor found out who threw that bomb, and, of course, could not connect anybody with it. In addition to that, the record of the trial showed that they had been tried by a packed jury, and convicted on public clamor. Third, the Supreme Court of the state had laid down a rule of law in relation to the competency of jurors that was just the opposite of that laid down in the so-called Anarchist case. There were, therefore, these grounds, any one of which made it imperative to interfere. So I found that I either had to take the step I did, or shirk a duty, and, while I have been badly whipped at different times in my life for holding my ground, I never ran away from anything, and I could see no reason for running away from my duty in this case. . . ."[18]

In September, 1894, while in New York, he defended his action again when interviewed by newspapermen there.

"Have you ever regretted pardoning those anarchists?" He thumped the back of a chair with his fist. "Never! If I had the matter to act upon again tomorrow, I would do it over again."[19]

As late as 1899 or so, Altgeld wrote about the case in a letter to Henry Demarest Lloyd, who had asked him for help in preparing an article on "Anarchism in America" for the *Encyclopedia Britannica*.

"If the prosecution did know who threw the bomb, it was unwilling to reveal the identity—which is a suspicious circumstance. At all events until they did show some connection between him and the defendants there was a failure of proof. To my mind the police brutality preceding the Haymarket meeting is most important as it furnishes an explanation and a motive. Prejudice of Gary is important because it accounts for the result of the trial. You will also see that the Supreme Court subsequently reversed the rule in regard to the qualification of jurors. The public fury which was worked up by the newspapers is also important. . . ."[20]

So much, then, for the impression that Altgeld remained silent about the Haymarket case.

5

Nor did he remain silent on the absurd charge that he was an anarchist, this despite the flat statement by Waldo Browne that "certainly in no single instance did he ever stoop to answer by even so much as a word the charge of being himself an anarchist."[21]

In October, 1893, when Republican campaign orators made an issue of Altgeld's "anarchism," a reporter ventured: "Governor, if you will not be offended by this question, what connection or association have you ever had with any organization or people of this class that you should be called an anarchist?"

"Oh, pshaw!" Altgeld answered. "None whatever. The idea is ridiculous. From the time that I was sixteen years old I have spent my life, first as a soldier, trying to uphold the flag of my country, then as a teacher in the cause of education; then as a lawyer at the bar, in the enforcement and upholding of the law, having acted in the capacity of both city attorney and state's attorney, and for five years judge on the bench; having besides at different times with my pen assisted in promoting reform and placing our institutions upon a higher plane. Besides that, I have in Chicago designed and built six of the finest business blocks of their kind in this city, one of them being among the finest on earth. Did you ever hear of an anarchist *building* a city?"

"If this is the case, why not answer these gentlemen who accuse you of having anarchistic tendencies?"

"In view of the facts," he said, "the talk of a few idle hangers-on around clubs, who spend other people's money, and of some gentlemen who have never done anything in their lives except suck blood from the public—who, if they own property usually manage to shirk paying the taxes on it—the talk of this kind of individuals is not worthy of notice."

He addressed himself to that same charge in the Nellie Bly interview, which the New York *World* prominently displayed under the headings:

ARE YOU AN ANARCHIST?
——————

Nellie Bly Asked Gov. Altgeld that
Question and He Said, "Pshaw!"
——————

FINALLY A SMILE WON AN ANSWER
——————

His answer satisfied Nellie that Altgeld was no anarchist. She admitted that she had approached him "in fear and trembling," for she had expected to find something of an ogre. She left him after the interview completely captivated by his personality. Nellie Bly wrote:

"We shook hands and parted and I am glad to say that I have met and talked with Gov. Altgeld, who is going to do as he thinks right every time, if the whole world stands still. I shouldn't be surprised if he were nominated for President of the United States some day...."[22]

6

There remains to be considered another misapprehension concerning the effect on Altgeld of the pardon, one that became more firmly imbedded in the public mind than the mistaken belief that his heart was broken. This is that the pardon act ruined him completely as a public man, that he was driven from the political scene, discredited, dishonored and silenced forever in the forums of public affairs. In 1931, Henry F. Pringle expressed that idea, writing: "Altgeld ... paid the penalty of courage. He vanished from public life."[23]

Altgeld himself, as noted, believed such would be the case. But he was mistaken, for ahead lay his most powerful years.

BOOK SIX

The Strike

CHAPTER TWENTY-SEVEN

Depression

1

On the very day Altgeld pardoned the anarchists the cables from London brought news that found its way into most American newspapers only as filler, if at all. The British government had closed the mints in India to the free coinage of silver. In that same month of June, 1893, there was announced in Chicago the formation of a new kind of labor union. It was the American Railway Union, organized for railroad workers along industrial instead of craft lines. Chief creator and its president was a tall, baldish labor organizer named Eugene Victor Debs.

In the excitement over the Haymarket matter, Altgeld probably paid little attention either to the London cable or the formation of the nation's first important "one big union." Certainly he could not have guessed their intimate and fateful relationship to each other or their importance to himself. Yet, those two seemingly unrelated and minor developments in the same month as the Haymarket pardon formed the basis for nearly all of his career ahead. The general background was a new business depression.

It was called the "panic of 1893." Actually it had begun at least two years earlier. The Democratic sweep in the elections of 1891 and, more definitely, that of 1892, bringing Grover Cleveland back to the White House, were reflections of general dissatisfaction with economic conditions. The Democratic landslide of '92 had been hailed as a certain means for stemming the tide of the depression. But within a few months after the Democrats took hold at Washington in March, 1893, it was apparent to everyone that the political switch had not helped the economic situation. Conditions, in fact, became worse.

There would be explanations for that development, with Altgeld giving some of the most vigorous, and these far from complimentary to Grover Cleveland. But whatever the cause, whether Cleveland was out of step with his party or the party was out of step with Cleveland, or the depression was inevitable, the fact that his policies did not restore prosperity was undeniable.

271

The nation reeled under an economic crisis reminiscent of the fiercely hard times of the 'seventies. But there was a difference. Except for an isolated instance or two, there was no repetition of wild labor riots and no real fear of "revolution." For that difference, the propertied classes and their spokesman had to thank (though only a few did) new factors which they had vigorously opposed. One was the ever-growing strength of the labor unions, bringing a measure of discipline for the workers that was lacking before. And there was the fact that the masses had confidence in their newly-elected officials. In the beginning, the masses felt certain that even President Cleveland was on their side. As for Altgeld in Illinois, a state always a trouble zone in times of economic distress, it is certain that his presence in the Executive Mansion at Springfield was worth a hundred regiments of militia for preserving order in Chicago and the rest of the state, a fact that may be set down as one of the minor ironies related to the outcry that his pardon of the anarchists would produce disorder and lawlessness. Even firebrand workers had implicit confidence in his acts and his counsel after the pardon.

2

He recognized the unique position he occupied in that respect, and used his influence to prevent violence in labor disputes. That summer the Chicago labor movement asked him to be the principal speaker at a Labor Day mass meeting. But he declined, in accord with a studied policy of avoiding too open contacts with labor as such. However, as the depression deepened and some minor bread "riots" occurred in Chicago he rescinded his refusal. "I felt that possibly it was my duty as Governor to be present and candidly discuss the situation with these people."[1] And so, that Labor Day of 1893, Altgeld stood before the distressed laboring men of Chicago and frankly discussed their troubles.

"There seems to be a long dark day ahead of you," he said. "It will be a day of suffering and distress, and I must say to you that there seems to be no way of escaping it." But labor, he added, should keep in mind that employers in the present situation also were suffering from what he termed "mistaken policies" adopted by "men here and in Europe who call themselves statesmen." Therefore, he said he was forced to counsel that labor face its condition "squarely and bear it with that heroism and fortitude with which an American citizen should face and bear calamity."

He did not mean, he made clear, that the state government under his direction would leave the unemployed to shift for themselves completely. It would do all that could be done in the way of public works to provide jobs. However, he cautioned labor not to expect too much from its government in that direction because "the powers of government are so hedged about with constitutional provisions that much cannot be done." But he made one flat statement startlingly new from a chief executive of that day, one that expressed a philosophy of government forty years ahead of its time. This was:

"Let me say that it will be the duty of all public officials to see to it that no man is permitted to starve on the soil of Illinois, and provision will be made to that end."[2]

He made clear, too, that he did not mean that labor, by any means, should be supine. Labor, he said, should strengthen itself in order to get its just returns from industry, and the only way it could do so was through organization. Unless labor was organized it would be "annihilated," he warned, "for the world gives only when it is obliged to, and respects only those who compel its respect. The earth is covered with the graves of justice and equity that failed to receive recognition, because there was no influence or force to compel it, and it will be so until the millennium."[3] Yet, he emphasized, and this was his main purpose in attending the gathering, that labor must move along "lawful lines." Otherwise, all its plans for betterment "must fail."

"Let me caution you that every act of violence is a hindrance to your progress. There will be men among you ready to commit it. They are your enemies. There will be sneaks and Judas Iscariots in your ranks, who will for a mere pittance act as spies and try to incite some of the more hot-headed of your number to deeds of violence, in order that these reptiles may get the credit of exposing you. They are your enemies. Cast them out of your ranks. . . ."[4]

3

In addressing regiments of the state militia assembled at the Columbian Exposition for Illinois Day two weeks before that Labor Day, Altgeld had made another "law and order" contribution when he expressed his views, as commander-in-chief of the state militia, on the conduct of troops in cases of labor trouble. Amazingly enough, he succeeded in outlining a policy pleasing to reasonable men of both capital and labor.

"Your duties [he told the militia] are almost opposite from those required of the soldier in time of war. Then the object is to annihilate the enemy, but in the service you will be called upon frequently to perform, he is the best soldier who can maintain law and order and protect life and property *without killing anybody*, and it frequently requires more judgment and nerve to do this than to rush upon an armed enemy. . . .

"It may happen at times that the men whom you are called upon to subdue, while ignorant and for the time riotous, are industrious and law-abiding and may have justice and equity on their side, yet there is but one course for you to pursue, and that is to do your duty.

"*A soldier cannot right wrongs between individuals, but he becomes a murderer if he needlessly kills.*"[5]

A short time later, he implemented that policy in an official order emphasizing that, in his state administration, troops could be used only for impartial enforcement of law and order. Yet, then and later, by word and deed, he demonstrated that, regardless of his personal views on labor matters, he would do his full duty in accord with the law if unlawful labor demonstrations occurred.

This should be kept in mind in view of the imminence of an event, growing out of Eugene Debs's new union, in which Altgeld would be misrepresented even more than he had been for pardoning the men of Haymarket.

4

Altgeld proved a competent prophet in his warning to the laboring man of Chicago on Labor Day, 1893, that times for them would become worse. Factories by the scores shut down completely or nearly so that fall and winter. Banks crumpled. Wages nose-dived. In December, 1893, the Chicago City Hall presented a startling spectacle. Night after night, men by the hundreds had taken to sleeping in the corridors and on the staircases. It was the same in every police station and other municipal buildings. Significantly, in that same month, the manager of the Pullman Corporation found it necessary to issue a public statement denying existence of extreme distress among the Pullman workers.[6]

No improvement came with spring, 1894. And there were heard rumblings of protest from labor all over the nation against repeated wage cuts and mass unemployment. As in the 'seventies, the rumblings arose from stark desperation. No "agitators" could have been responsible, although the Chicago *Tribune* editorialized about the "Hun and Slav Rebellion," and attributed discontent solely to "barbarians, anarchists . . . aliens."[7] An eruption appeared inevitable, for the lessons of Haymarket had not yet been taken to heart.

Yet the first eruption did not, strictly speaking, come from a labor group at all. Nor was the force of this eruption directed at the employing class. It was directed, for the first time in American history, at the national government itself. This fact, that the Federal government was, for the first time, called upon to assume responsibility for unemployment and mass starvation and to take official steps for relief, was the significance, hardly recognized heretofore, of the strange American phenomenon of 1894 known as "Coxey's Army." Its spearhead was a mild-mannered, religion-steeped little businessman of Massillon, Ohio, named Jacob S. Coxey.

5

It has been the fashion for even earnest historians to laugh a little at Coxey's Army, which started moving across Ohio toward Washington, D. C. on March 26, 1894. Certainly, Jacob Coxey, described as "reformer, theosophist, horse-breeder and seller of silica,"[8] was a man of enormous naïveté to imagine that he could get the statesmen of Washington and the leaders of business to pay any attention to demands of nonentities like himself or to the raggedy-baggedy band of unemployed who followed his banner of "The Army of the Commonwealers of Christ."

Coxey's Army did seem to be a laughing matter when it was all over, especially after the little group of two hundred and fifty men who finally marched into Washington were tossed into jail for walking on the Capitol lawns. Yet there were some persons who viewed the Army of the Commonweal of Christ as a serious matter. One who did watch Coxey and his followers in a serious way was Richard Olney, attorney general of the United States by appointment of President Grover Cleveland. Especially had Olney been concerned over the means adopted by some of the Coxeyites in the Far West for getting to Washington. When the railroads refused to permit the men to ride on freight cars, some of the men stole trains, literally. Mr. Olney was proud of how he checkmated the Coxeyites who made off with whole trains that spring.[9]

His method was to use against the Coxeyites the legal process known as the injunction, issued by the Federal courts, and—major fact—to have the injunctions enforced by Federal troops. Olney was impressed tremendously by his own astuteness in that regard, and it was uppermost in his mind when summer brought the Pullman strike. Because this was so, the supposedly comical episode of Coxey's Army in fact was a serious prelude to the great railroad strike which came in the month after Coxey's ignominious arrest in Washington, D. C. It was a prelude that vitally concerned Altgeld.

But before the Pullman strike occurred, the nation was confronted by a miners' strike of tremendous fury. It was called by the United Mine Workers of America on April 21, 1894, while the Coxeyites still were marching. Unlike the episode of the Commonwealers, the coal strike was no comedy. The tie-up of mines in every coal state was practically complete, especially in Illinois.[10] In the beginning, while the miners waited for coal supplies to be exhausted and while the mine owners marked time in hope of starving the strikers into submission, there was little violence in Illinois or elsewhere. Later, as scabs were brought in to operate the mines the story would be different, notably in Illinois, and this development came to concern Altgeld in connection with the Pullman episode.

6

During the first ten days of the coal strike, Altgeld eyed events from afar, under doctor's orders. With Mrs. Altgeld he was lolling in the sun of the South, at New Orleans and later at Hot Springs. The complications that had nearly kept him from his inauguration returned, although fortunately in milder form. But added to these was a nervous strain that arose partly from the reaction to the pardon and partly because he, too, was a victim of the general business depression. For one thing, matters were not going too well at the Unity Building. Rents were hard to collect and tenants were moving out. And so, as he told Nellie Bly, he was "nerve-exhausted and nerve-wearied."[11] He went south in February.

After three weeks in the sun, he felt recovered and returned to his desk at Springfield on March 7th. Immediately he involved himself in a political tempest in Chicago by summarily calling for the resignations of half the members of the Lincoln Park Board. It had been one of his ambitions to extend Chicago's Lincoln Park from its then northern limit at Diversey Avenue all along the Lake Michigan shore to Evanston. By that means, he felt, Chicago's north shore would be preserved for the people, even if the south shore lake front had been given over to the railroads. But for one reason or another—there were valuable riparian property rights involved—certain board members failed to fall in with his plan. Most of them were his own appointees, but, disregarding party lines, he sent out a batch of resignation demands. "I have for some time been dissatisfied with the management of the affairs of Lincoln Park. . . . I will therefore ask for your resignation at once. . . . No further correspondence or interview will avail anything."[12] There was much gnashing of teeth and some permanent enemies in his own party were made by him because of that move, but he was firm—and, in the end, Lincoln Park was extended, to form "an enduring monument of Governor Altgeld's administration."[13]

In the midst of that Lincoln Park tempest, he suffered another relapse, and was forced to go back to Hot Springs. He was there when Coxey's Army began moving and when the coal strike was called. However, on the day Coxey reached Washington, Altgeld hastened back to Springfield. He was not completely recovered from his illness, but alarming reports on the coal situation had come to him. Some of the large coal operators had imported armies of "scabs" to break the strike. Violence was certain to result, Altgeld was advised. In fact, five days before, on April twenty-sixth, the sheriff at Toluca, Illinois, had requested troops from Acting Governor Joseph Gill because of a report that "5,000 men from Spring Valley and LaSalle were marching against the mines at Toluca to close them." Adhering to the policies laid down by Altgeld in his inaugural message and as followed in the Lemont quarry episode in June, 1893, Acting Governor Gill refused to send troops until assured that there was real danger and that the local officials had done their utmost to maintain order. Going to the scene, Gill found the report a false alarm.[14] Yet there was great tenseness throughout the Illinois coal districts.

In the weeks following, Altgeld was confronted with several such false alarms. However, in the cases of each of a half-dozen or more requests for troops from sheriffs in various parts of the state, Altgeld sent troops when there seemed the slightest basis for anticipating trouble. In at least two cases in the month of May he found that he had been imposed upon. When he sent troops to LaSalle and later to Pana, the militia in both instances discovered no disturbance had occurred and that there was little likelihood of any happening. Actually, as the Mayor of LaSalle admitted inferentially, the troops had been wanted for purposes of guarding the mines while imported scabs worked in them.[15] Altgeld's response to that was to issue publicly his General Order No. 7 to the Militia of Illinois.

"May 25, 1894

"To Adjt.-Gen. Orendorff:

"It is not the business of the soldiers to act as custodians or guards of private property. The law authorizes them simply to assist the civil authorities in preserving the peace, quelling riots and executing the laws wherever troops have been or may hereafter be ordered; and when an owner of property feels it necessary to have it guarded, he must do so at his own expense. In such cases troops can be used only for the purpose of properly quelling disturbance or of suppressing a riot or in some other way enforcing the laws.

JOHN P. ALTGELD,
Governor and Commander-in-Chief
U. S. Campbell,
Adjutant and Aide-de-Camp."

Certain employers did not like the idea that the state troops could not be used as private guards, but there was little serious criticism of Altgeld on that point. As a matter of fact, the only real criticism directed at him for his use of the militia during the coal strike was that he had been too quick in getting troops to the scene of reported disorder. For example, the Chicago *Tribune* criticized him because he had dispatched a regiment to Pana, Illinois, on May twenty-seventh, only to discover no need for them. The *Tribune* declared that he had acted "on the strength of a wild, unfounded rumor, and committed a grievous blunder."[16] This fact should be kept in mind when the *Tribune* leads the pack in misrepresenting Altgeld for his conduct in the Pullman strike.

7

One other incident should be remembered. At Mount Olive, Illinois, striking coal miners interfered with the movement of trains to prevent shipment of non-union coal. Trains carrying United States mail were among those held up. When that happened, the Federal Court for the Southern District of Illinois, at Springfield, issued injunctions against the strikers. The injunctions forbade interference with railroads in Federal receiverships or any trains that carried United States mail. The United States marshal at the scene felt his force was inadequate to enforce the injunction and the Federal judge asked Attorney General Olney in Washington for advice. Back from Olney came this message:

"Washington, June 16, 1894.
"Allen, U. S. Judge, Springfield, Ill.:
"Understand State of Illinois is willing to protect property against lawless violence with military force if necessary. Please advise receivers to take proper steps to procure protection by civil authorities of the State. *If such protection proves inadequate, the governor should be applied to for military assistance.*
OLNEY, Attorney-General."[17]

In accord with that procedure outlined by Olney, the Federal authorities appealed to Altgeld for state troops to keep the mail trains moving. On June seventeenth, state militia were on the ground. They succeeded in moving the mail and other trains—a fact which the *Tribune* prominently displayed in its issue for June eighteenth. Other instances of the same nature occurred in southern Illinois and in each case Altgeld came to the assistance of the Federal government. He acted swiftly, willingly, and effectively.[18]

True, he did not permit state troops to re-enact the bloody scenes of 1877 or of 1884-86. True, the militia under Altgeld were not permitted to serve as strike-breakers, but conducted themselves so that a labor-sympathizing Catholic priest at Spring Valley would write to Henry Demarest Lloyd that "the Governor deserves great credit for not permitting the militia [at Spring Valley] to be used beyond what absolute necessity requires."[19]

Yet, as noted, he met fully his duty to use the militia for maintaining law and order in Illinois, to the extent even of suffering criticism for being too zealous and of assisting the Federal government itself. He did not change his attitude when the Pullman strike occurred. But another public official did undergo a change concerning the proper procedure to follow in the case of strikes involving movement of trains. This was Attorney General Olney. The result was an amazing chapter in United States labor history, one with momentous effects upon the Democratic party nationally—and upon Altgeld. It was a chapter known as the Pullman strike.

CHAPTER TWENTY-EIGHT

THE PULLMAN STRIKE

1

THE great Pullman strike had its immediate beginning when 2,000 employes of the Pullman Corporation engaged in manufacturing sleeping cars and equipment failed to show up at the shops on May 11, 1894, following a strike vote over wage cuts. With business slack anyway, George M. Pullman simply shrugged his shoulders and closed down all of the shops. To the newspapers, he professed pained surprise that any of his men were discontented. "Why," he said, "the average wage being earned is $1.87 a day!"[1]

Not until late in June did many persons except the Pullman employes themselves give more than passing attention to that strike. It was the least important labor episode in the country at the time. And nobody doubted that the fabulously wealthy Pullman Company would soon bring its workers to terms. It had done so in the past, notably in the strike period just before the Haymarket bombing.

Of course, a few persons who had hearsay knowledge of the "model industrial town" that George M. Pullman had laid out for his workers in the early 'eighties were amazed to learn that industrial trouble could flare there. It was such a pretty town! In pamphlets distributed at the Columbian Exposition, the company had proclaimed that "at an early date the beautiful town of Pullman will be as a bright and radiant little island in the midst of the great tumultuous sea of Chicago's population; a restful oasis in the wearying brick-and-mortar waste of an enormous city."[2] Such, indeed, had been Pullman's dream when the town was conceived. His town was to be an antidote for industrial unrest, a prophylaxis against the virus of trade unionism and socialism, "a town from which all that is ugly, discordant and demoralizing is eliminated . . . a solution of the industrial problem. . . ."[3] All of the land was owned by the Pullman Corporation, likewise all of the homes. The stores, schools, the churches, and the public utilities were all Pullman-dominated. Nobody but the corporation could control anything. The workers rented their homes from the company. Their rent was deducted from their pay-checks. And it was a pretty town, with all the latest architectural improvements, recreation devices, gardens, lawns and parks for the workers and their families to enjoy. Yet all this somehow even in good times failed to have the desired effect upon the workers. As early as 1885, young Professor Richard T. Ely saw what was wrong when he wrote about the town of Pullman in *Harpers' Magazine*. He conceded that Pullman's motives were probably enlightened, but summarized:

"The conclusion was unavoidable that the idea of Pullman was un-American. It is not the American ideal. It is benevolent, well-wishing feudalism, which desires the happiness of the people but in such a way as shall please the authorities."[4]

In less academic language, a Pullman worker told the whole story in one sentence: "We are born in a Pullman house, fed from a Pullman shop, taught in the Pullman school, catechized in the Pullman church, and when we die we shall be buried in the Pullman cemetery and go to a Pullman hell!"[5] And George Pullman himself gave the whole thing away about a year before the strike in an unexpectedly frank comment to a young social worker, Graham Taylor. The social worker inquired of Mr. Pullman how the company managed to ally its employes and other residents of the town with its policies. He responded quickly: "A clause in every lease enables us on short notice to be rid of undesirable tenants!"[6]

2

It was this feudal spirit that brought on the strike, after hundreds of employes were laid off while others received in their pay envelopes scarcely anything except their rent receipts. Most maddening of all, there were no reductions in rents or other items, such as gas—items all priced higher than others in Chicago were forced to pay. Altgeld revealed, and was not challenged, that the Pullman Corporation was getting $15 a month for flats which would bring no more than $4 other places.

When a committee of Pullman workers asked an interview with the management to discuss their wages and the laying-off policy of the company, they were peremptorily refused a conference. Immediately thereafter the members of the committee were fired from their jobs.[7] The strike vote followed.

Because many of the strikers, and afterward all of them, were members of the American Railway Union, Eugene Debs personally visited Pullman several days later. He was convinced that a strike was justified, especially after learning from the pastor of the Pullman Methodist church, the Reverend William H. Carwardine, of the desperate condition of all the corporation's wage employes. Yet Debs did not then have in mind a general strike by his union.

On June twelfth, the American Railway Union national convention met in Chicago. It was a jubilant, cocksure gathering, for the union had just staged—and won—a strike against wage cuts on the Great Northern Railroad System. James J. Hill, "the empire builder," had said he would not deal with Debs's union, ordered the discharge of all its members and sympathizers throughout the Great Northern System. But the great Hill was forced to eat crow. It was a magnificent labor victory for the new union, and unquestionably made the membership overconfident when the Pullman matter was brought up on the floor of the convention. A motion was made to boycott all Pullman cars until Pullman came to terms with his workers. As chairman, Debs refused to entertain the motion. It was too serious a matter, he said. On his suggestion a committee was appointed to seek arbitration.[8]

"There is nothing to arbitrate," said the Pullman Corporation.[9]

That attitude of the company was reported to the convention on June sixteenth. While the matter was being considered—Debs still counseling caution and the exhaustion of every avenue for settlement without a strike—the Reverend Mr. Carwardine addressed the convention. He made an eloquent appeal for the boycott. "Act quickly in the name of God and humanity!" Stirred to the depths, the delegates overruled Debs. They voted a boycott against handling Pullman cars, to take effect at noon on June twenty-sixth (by coincidence the first anniversary of Altgeld's pardon of the anarchists) unless Pullman agreed to meet another committee for arbitration.

It was more than cocksureness that prompted that action by the delegates to the American Railway Union. It was sheer idealism, too. The railroad men had nothing to gain for themselves by risking their jobs to help the workers of Pullman, who were not, strictly speaking, railroad men at all. It was not the fight of the members of the Debs union. But they were swept away by sympathy for their class.

"There was more of human sympathy, of the essence of brotherhood, of the spirit of real Christianity in this act than in all the hollow pretenses and heartless prayers of those disciples of mammon who cried out against it, and this act will shine forth in increasing splendor long after the dollar worshipers have mingled with the dust of oblivion."[10]

So ten years later Debs wrote of the action of that convention and the men who followed its decision—and there has been no evidence since to refute him, except evidence that the act, while inspired, probably was wildly foolish, as Debs himself knew.

3

After the ultimatum of the American Railway Union, strong pressure was brought upon George Pullman to meet with his employes. Even the Tory papers urged arbitration. Years later, it would be revealed that Marcus A. Hanna, of Ohio, fearful of the effect of Pullman's attitude on his ambition to elect Governor William McKinley of Ohio as President of the United States in 1896, attempted to get Pullman to arbitrate. Hanna sent McKinley's brother, Abner, to Chicago to plead with the sleeping-car manufacturer.[11] He exploded when he learned that Pullman continued to refuse. "The damned idiot ought to arbitrate, arbitrate, arbitrate! What for God's sake does he think he is doing! . . . A man who won't meet his men half-way is a God-damned fool!" When someone pointed out that Pullman was not so bad, citing the model houses for his workers, Hanna's comment was:

"Oh, hell! Model—!"[12]

In 1899, mellowed after realizing his ambition with regard to McKinley, Hanna gave a newspaper reporter in France a surprising new sidelight on Pullman's stubbornness. "Everybody blamed Mr. Pullman for refusing to arbitrate that strike," Hanna was quoted as confiding. "I blamed him myself. But it was one of his big stockholders who caused the trouble."[13]

Whether indeed Marshall Field, the biggest Pullman stockholder, was to blame, or if it was Pullman himself, the corporation did persist in spurning arbitration. The day before the time limit set by the union another agency—an illegal agency, it would be revealed later—entered the picture. This was the General Managers Association, representing all of the western railroads. Formed in the year of the Haymarket tragedy to fight labor unions, this body formally resolved that the railroads, concerned only indirectly in the Pullman controversy, would unitedly resist the proposed boycott "in the interest of their existing contracts [with Pullman] and for the benefit of the traveling public."[14]

On the following morning telegrams went from the Chicago head-quarters of the American Railway Union to railroad points through the West.

"Boycott against Pullman cars in effect at noon today. By order of convention.

E. V. DEBS."

Next day that crisp order by Debs was amplified by other messages, which read:

"Boycott against Pullman Company is in full force and effect and no Pullman cars are to be handled and hauled. Convention ordered boycott of Pullman cars and this means they shall be cut out and de-tracked.

E. V. DEBS."

Contrary to his own views, Debs, magnificent leader, was proving that he could follow, too. The Pullman strike—boycott, to be accu-rate—was on.

4

Considering that the standard railroad brotherhoods for the most part held aloof, as did the American Federation of Labor officially, and considering, too, that the railroad corporations ganged up behind the Pullman Company in accord with the resolution of the General Managers Association, the boycott was amazingly and swiftly effective. It was exaggeration to say, as was said, that all railroad operations from Chicago to the Pacific Coast were paralyzed. For mail trains did go through in most cases, even in Chicago—and many lines, with the help of local authorities, non-striking railroad union men and also scabs, were functioning almost normally. Certainly this was true of most freight trains and even passenger trains which did not include sleeping cars.

But Debs's men proved so loyal to the union—in not a few cases strikers flung themselves on the tracks in front of locomotives to stop the train with their bodies if necessary—that the boycott was a practi-cal success. In fact, it is clear that the strike was won, "clear and com-plete," as Debs would say,[15] for the railroads were against the wall. For selfish motives alone, the railroads could have been expected to bring pressure upon the Pullman Corporation to agree to arbitration. It was "won," moreover, against all of the combined western railroads, for it became apparent on the first day that the boycott against Pullman was in fact a strike against the railroads.

It was a strike against the railroads because the railroads began hauling Pullman cars on all their trains, even on mail trains that customarily did not include Pullman cars. There was reason for that strategy. Simply stated, the reason was to force the union into the position of blocking mail trains, despite definite orders given by Debs that there was to be "no forcible interference with mail trains."[16]

In the beginning and throughout the episode, Debs also had warned his followers against violence. "A man who will destroy property or violate the law is an enemy and not a friend to the cause of labor!"[17]

The public, final arbiter of such disputes, liked that attitude, and the railroads knew it. It was plain to the railroads, wrote Harry Thurston Peck in Twenty Years of the Republic, impartial in this episode, that "if the strike remained a peaceful one, the railways would be defeated. If, however, violence and crime were associated with it, public sympathy would no longer sustain the strikers, and the power of the law would be invoked against them."

To which Peck added, "singularly enough . . . just when this situation became plain," some slight violence, although nothing that the regular law forces could not handle, did occur on June thirtieth.[18]

And it was just at that time that the true fate of the strike was sealed, by Attorney General Richard Olney, in whom Grover Cleveland "reposed greater faith than any other member of his cabinet."[19] Ever since the boycott had occurred, busy-bodyish, impulsive Richard Olney had been itching to step into thè picture on the side of the railroads. So his own writings later reveal unmistakably. And now his hour had come.

It was the hour, too, or soon would be, when Altgeld, who was watching events closely, alert always to his duty as governor and commander-in-chief of the militia, but alert too that his militia not take sides except as the law was violated, would find himself involved in historic fashion. For Olney had selected Illinois—Chicago specifically—as the theater for his curious activities.

5

Olney's conduct is explicable only too clearly by his background. Nobody knew at the time how Cleveland happened to make him head of the Department of Justice, a cabinet post second only to secretary of state, unless it was on the suggestion of certain of Cleveland's many "corporation" friends. For Olney was scarcely known in the Democratic party and Altgeld told the truth, if pungently, when he later declared that "Mr. Olney has never come any nearer to the Democratic fold than to play hide-and-seek in a mugwump alley."[20] Even Olney's laudatory biographer candidly admitted that "he seems to have become a Democrat, not in the least from doctrinaire sympathy with Jeffersonian principles but because he somehow got started that way."[21] But if Cleveland's Attorney General was not known as a Democrat, he was sufficiently known in financial circles as a railroad lawyer—in fact, one of the biggest in the nation.

Not only were numerous New England railroads his clients, but he had been retained by a number of the largest western railroads also— several of whom were members of the General Managers Association fighting the American Railway Union. And he had been a director of railroads, also.[22] In short, he was railroad and corporation-minded if any man ever was, and he so approached the Pullman boycott in his capacity as chief law-enforcing official of the United States government. For Olney's purpose, frankly, was, not to enforce the laws, but to *smash* the strike, his own word.[23]

How to break the strike was suggested to Olney by means he adopted when the Coxeyites in the Northwest began making off with railroad trains. First slap upon the offenders a Federal Court injunction, then enforce the injunction with the Federal army. He was convinced that this procedure in the preceding spring had saved the nation from something not far from revolution.[24]

In professing to believe that the Pullman strike and the train-thievery by the Coxeyites presented identical situations justifying the use of Federal troops, and only Federal troops, Olney conveniently overlooked a pertinent fact. This was that the trains were stolen in states which did not have militia organizations, hence, if the United States marshals were unable to enforce injunctions, it was almost necessary to fall back upon the national army.[25] Otherwise, the procedure of appealing to the governors of the states in which the offenses were committed could and doubtless would have been followed—as in the case of the incident at Mount Olive, Illinois, during the coal strike when Altgeld was asked for state troops and sent them promptly.

But neither Olney nor the railroad operators, as it turned out, had any intention of appealing to Altgeld where Chicago was concerned. They wanted troops to break the strike, not simply for enforcing law and order. And they wanted, not state, but Federal troops. All Olney's actions made this perfectly clear. It is just as clear that the Attorney General, with or without Cleveland's prior approval, literally turned over the resources and prestige of the Federal government to the railroads themselves, and that in the case of the Pullman strike the United States government became in fact a strike-breaking agency.

6

Olney's first step for putting the government into the strike-breaking business was taken on June thirtieth, when he appointed Edwin Walker of Chicago as special assistant attorney general at Chicago. Walker superseded the regular United States attorney there and was given full charge of the government's activities in connection with the strike. Probably no more amazing appointment ever was made, for Attorney Walker since 1870 had been counsel for the Milwaukee Railroad, one of the major railroads involved in the strike. More astonishing, he was suggested to Olney by the General Managers Association itself![26]

Olney revealed his plans for breaking the strike in a telegram of instructions that he sent to Walker as soon as the Chicago railroad lawyer was placed in charge of the Federal machinery.

"It has seemed to me [Olney advised Walker] that if the rights of the United States were vigorously asserted in Chicago, the origin and center of the demonstration, the result would be to make it a failure everywhere else and to prevent its spread over the entire country. With yourself directing matters for the government, I am sure all legal remedies will be resorted to that the facts will warrant.

"In this connection it has seemed to me advisable not merely to rely on warrants against persons actually guilty of the offense of obstructing United States mails, but to go into a court of equity and secure restraining orders which shall have the effect of preventing any attempt to commit the offense. . . .

"The Marshal and the District Attorney have wired me about the employment of fifty deputies. I authorized it, of course. *But I feel that the true way of dealing with the matter is by a force which is overwhelming and prevents any attempt at resistance.* In that particular, however, I must defer to the better judgment of one who is on the spot and familiar with all the facts of the situation."[27]

Such was Olney's none too subtle way of indicating that the government was desirous of breaking the strike, and for that purpose Federal Court injunctions were to be procured, these to be enforced by "a force which is overwhelming," i. e., the army.

Walker caught the injunction suggestion at once. And on July second, the United States District Attorney at Chicago presented to the Federal Courts of Judges Peter Grosscup and William A. Woods a petition for the most sweeping injunction ever issued in a labor dispute. It was directed at the American Railway Union, its officers and "all persons combining or conspiring with them and all other persons whomsoever."[28] That all-inclusiveness was amazing enough, but the acts forbidden were more astonishing. Under the injunction, not only was obstruction of trains forbidden, but so was the act of striking or even suggesting to any railroad worker that he go on strike—in the words of the injunction, from "ordering, directing, aiding, assisting or abetting any person in the commission of the acts forbidden."[29] In short, a street-corner conversation with a railroad worker could have been a crime.

Judges Grosscup and Woods granted the injunction instanter, without blinking an eye. And no wonder. The judges had, Allan Nevins has revealed, "by what seems an indefensible procedure," assisted the attorney in revising his own draft of the injunction beforehand, then mounted the bench to consider a motion which in effect was their own.[30] The General Managers Association joyously proclaimed the government's action "a gatling gun on paper," to which Professor Nevins aptly adds, "it was rather an entire battery."

So it was—for that injunction, copies of which soon were plastered all over Chicago, was the stroke that broke the strike. So conceded Debs.

But in Olney's mind, the injunction itself was not an end, but a means—to get the army into Chicago. Through the War Department, he had arranged for a troop train "with the steam up" to be ready at Fort Sheridan, near Chicago, on the day the injunction was requested.[31] He had, it transpires, urged Grover Cleveland to send troops before there was any court action, on general principles. But Cleveland rejected such crude advice.[32] However, Olney knew his man. He was certain that Cleveland would act if the occasion were a matter of enforcing judicial orders.[33]

Olney did not wait long for such an occasion to arise. On the day the injunction was granted, the United States Marshal at Chicago, J. W. Arnold, selected a trouble spot, seemingly by design, to read the injunction personally to a group of strikers. A large crowd gathered. The Marshal and his deputies were hooted at. Supposedly there were cries of "To hell with the government! . . . We are the government!" Some cars were overturned by the crowd to show their contempt for the injunction. Finally in a clash, a deputy was stabbed and Marshal Arnold himself "in all his dignity was rolled in the dirt." Thus ruffled, the Marshal immediately sent a telegram to Olney.

"I am here at Blue Island. Have read the order of the court to the rioters here and they simply hoot at it. . . . We had a desperate time here all day and our force is inadequate. *In my judgment it is impossible to move trains without having the Fifteenth Infantry from Fort Sheridan moved here at once. . . .*

ARNOLD, Marshal."[34]

7

Was that the request for which Olney was hoping? Olney finally decided that it wasn't, that the word of a marshal alone was not enough to set the army moving. He wanted something stronger and so he sent to District Attorney Milchrist at Chicago the following:

"Congratulate you upon the legal situation, which is all that could be desired. Trust use of United States troops will not be necessary. If it becomes necessary, they will be used promptly and decisively upon the justifying facts certified to me. In such case, if practicable, let Walker and Marshal and United States Judge join in statement as to the exigency.

OLNEY."[35]

There was not too much subtlety in that message—and the government men in Chicago understood. Back came the following, dated Chicago:

"When the injunction was granted yesterday a mob of from two to three thousand held possession of a point *in the city* near the crossing of the Rock Island by other roads, where they had already ditched a mail train, and prevented the passing of any trains, whether mail or otherwise. I read the injunction writ to this mob and commanded them to disperse. The reading of the writ met with no response except jeers and hoots. Shortly after, the mob threw a number of baggage cars across the track, since when no mail trains have been able to move. I am unable to disperse the mob, clear the tracks or arrest the men who were engaged in the acts named, and *believe that no force less than the regular troops of the United States can procure the pas-*

sage of the mail trains or enforce the orders of the court. I believe people engaged in trades are quitting employment today, and in my opinion will be joining the mob tonight, and especially tomorrow, and it is my judgment that the troops should be here at the earliest possible moment. An emergency has arisen for their presence in this city.

J. W. ARNOLD,
United States Marshal."

To which was added the following "endorsement":

"We have read the foregoing, and from that information and other information that has come to us, believe that an emergency exists for the immediate presence of the United States troops.

P. S. GROSSCUP, Judge
EDWIN WALKER
THOMAS E. GILCHRIST, Attorneys.[36]

On receipt of that message, Olney paid no attention to some rather obvious misstatements that it contained. The dispatch "bristled with misleading points," as Allan Nevins has pointed out. First, the disturbance mentioned took place not in "this city" (Chicago), but in Blue Island. Second, the mob had been dispersed, with all competent testimony showing that by July third the trouble had subsided even in Blue Island. Third, the Marshal and his endorsers failed to mention the availability of local police or the state militia while asserting the belief that Federal troops alone would serve—Olney's idea, of course. Finally, talk of larger mobs was simply hearsay.

But Olney had what he wanted. He rushed to the White House.

8

Now return to Altgeld. At that moment he was busy doing his duty, distasteful as it may have been, dispatching state troops here, there and seemingly everywhere, to maintain order and keep trains moving. Moreover, he was succeeding—better even than in nearly every other state of the Union. Bear in mind, however, that Altgeld's troops were giving assistance in that portion of the state outside of Chicago—for no call for help came from the Chicago district. Henry Demarest Lloyd happened to be an overnight guest of Altgeld at the time. He found the Governor devoting all his energy to the strike situation, constantly in communication with militia officers, frequently studying "a huge map . . . on which was marked, with tacks and pins, the position of every company of militia" and also a "great sheet . . . showing exactly what companies were under arms and what railroads would be most efficient in taking them." Moreover, at that very time, he was making plans for the most expeditious way of getting troops to Chicago—if a call came.[37]

Once, when a telegraphic appeal for troops came in while Lloyd was there, Altgeld turned to Lloyd and said: "I have reason to fear that these troops were wanted at that place only to help the railroad defeat the demand of their men for higher wages, but I cannot refuse to send them, in the face of allegations of public danger." In short, Altgeld was even willing then to bend a little from his usual policy of caution. Lloyd remembered "particularly" a remark made by Altgeld concerning the Chicago situation. "If it becomes necessary," he said, "I could and would put 100,000 men into the city of Chicago inside of five days. The whole state would answer to the call as one man."

He even went outside his strict realm to tell the railroads how to operate their own trains. "As an instance, while I was there," related Lloyd, "it was reported to him that a train bearing a detachment of soldiers was stalled on the outskirts of Springfield because some sympathizer with the strike had put soap into the boiler of the locomotive. Governor Altgeld at once suggested that one of the fire engines of the city and a watering cart go there to pump out the locomotive, so that it could proceed at once."[38]

Henry Demarest Lloyd's version of Altgeld's attitude is fully corroborated. After it was all over, even railroad owners privately admitted that "Governor Altgeld had done more to protect railroad and other property than any of his predecessors," that he "absolutely prevented the destruction of property outside of Chicago during the Pullman strike . . . and would have performed the same service within the city limits had not the municipal authorities stubbornly refused to appeal to him."[39] As for the official records, both Federal and state, they tell the same story, as do the contemporary newspaper accounts, if studied closely.

On July first alone, as shown by the Governor's letter-book, there were sent the following telegrams—potent evidence of Altgeld's vigilance:

"Springfield, July 1, 1894.
"To the Sheriff of Macon County, Decatur, Ill.:
"I have a dispatch purporting to come from passengers now detained

at Decatur because trains are obstructed and they ask for assistance. Wire me the situation fully. Are railroad officials making proper efforts to move trains and are you able to furnish the traveling public the necessary protection and to enforce the law?

JOHN P. ALTGELD, Governor"

"Springfield, July 1, 1894
(Later)

"To the Sheriff of Macon County, Decatur, Ill.:

"Have ordered troops to your assistance. They should reach you before sunrise. See that all trains unlawfully held are released at once.

JOHN P. ALTGELD, Governor."

"Springfield, July 1, 1894

"W. H. Lyford, General Counsel, C. & E. I. RR. Co.:

"We can furnish assistance promptly if the civil authorities show that they need it. Thus far there has been no application for assistance from any of the officials of Vermilion County, either sheriff, coroner, mayor of town or the county judge.

J. P. ALTGELD, Governor

"Springfield, July 1, 1894.
(At the same time)

"To the Sheriff of Vermilion County, Danville, Ill.:

"Officials of the Eastern Illinois Railroad complain that their trains have been tied up and that they cannot get sufficient protection to move them. Please wire the situation fully. Can you enforce the law and protect the traveling public with such force as you can command.

J. P. ALTGELD, Governor."

"Danville, Ill., July 1, 1894.

"Governor J. P. Altgeld:

"Your message received. Send me one hundred rifles and ammunition, and I will try to protect the railroad's men and property. As to the situation, there are from 300 to 700 men on the ground and oppose the movement of any and all trains or cars, except mail cars. They are usually quiet and duly sober, but are very determined. I will advise if I am not able to afford protection.

J. W. NEWTON, Sheriff."

"Springfield, July 1, 1894.

"To J. A. Newton, Sheriff, Danville, Ill.:

"We have not got 100 stands of arms left here, but from information we get we consider situation serious at Danville, and therefore have sent you troops. They will be there early in the morning. All those trains unlawfully held should be moved before noon.

J. P. ALTGELD, Governor."[40]

In brief, Altgeld was demonstrating that the state of Illinois was able and willing to maintain law and order within its borders, and never so definitely as at the very time Attorney General Olney was heading to the White House to tell Cleveland that Federal troops must be dispatched to Illinois, that no other authority could cope with the situation that he professed to believe existed there.

9

Earlier that day, President Cleveland had called a special cabinet meeting to discuss Olney's previous suggestions about the army. Daniel Lamont, the war secretary, had opposed using the troops. So did General Nelson A. Miles, commander of the western department. Likewise, Walter Q. Gresham, then secretary of state, voiced opposition. He had changed his mind about labor questions since 1877 when, as a federal judge in Indiana, he had issued injunctions against railroad strikers and was all for using the army.[41] In fact, Gresham, whom the Chicago *Tribune* boomed for president in 1888, had reached the point where he felt corporation lobbyists were "as dangerous to the government as the Haymarket anarchists."[42]

But when Olney waved his second Chicago telegram, Cleveland decided to follow his Attorney General's advice. It would be published by one of Cleveland's apologists (with Cleveland himself later giving the same impression) that Cleveland first "requested Governor Altgeld to see that the mails were not interfered with [but] Altgeld replied in effect that the affairs of the State of Illinois were exclusively his own business." So wrote Senator A. B. Farcquhar, with the ghostly assistance of Samuel Crowther, [43] and such is the impression given by many historians. But nothing of the kind happened. It was pure fairy tale.

At 3:30 P. M. on July third, War Secretary Lamont, at Cleveland's command, ordered all troops at Fort Sheridan to repair at once to Chicago. The soldiers arrived, ironically, on the morning of Independence Day, infantry, cavalry, and artillery, and set up camp on Chicago's lake front. If nobody else was, the blue-uniformed soldier boys must have been bewildered, for they found Chicago wholly quiet.

But if conditions in Chicago were peaceful—and they unquestionably were except for hysterical accounts in the *Tribune* and similar papers—there was one place in Illinois where intense excitement prevailed when word of Cleveland's startling action came there. This

was in the Executive Mansion at Springfield. Never had the governor
of a supposedly sovereign state been so openly and studiedly insulted,
nor with less reason, than Governor Altgeld was by President Cleveland's action. In after years, Olney would write, rather airily, that
"the advent of the . . . troops in Chicago amounted, of course, to a
reflection upon Governor Altgeld and his performance of his duties."[44]
A man of even less strong nature than Altgeld's would have reacted
profoundly.

On July fifth, Grover Cleveland heard from John Peter Altgeld.

CHAPTER TWENTY-NINE

THE PROTEST

1

AT THAT, considering Altgeld's temperament and the enormity of the personal affront for which President Cleveland was responsible, the message telegraphed from Springfield to Washington on July fifth was fairly mild—coming from Altgeld. In phraseology, that is. But in content it was distinctly Altgeldian, a bristling state paper deserving to rank with his Haymarket pardon.

"Executive Office, State of
Illinois, July 5, 1894
"Hon. Grover Cleveland, President of the United States, Washington, D. C.
"Sir: I am advised that you have ordered Federal troops to go into service in the State of Illinois. Surely the facts have not been correctly presented to you in this case, or you would not have taken this step, for it is entirely unnecessary and, as it seems to me, unjustifiable.

"Waiving all questions of courtesy, I will say that the State of Illinois is not only able to take care of itself, but it stands ready to furnish the Federal government any assistance it may need elsewhere. Our military force is ample, and consists of as good soldiers as can be found in the country. They have been ordered promptly whenever and wherever they were needed. We have stationed in Chicago alone three regiments of Infantry, one Battery and one troop of Cavalry, and no better soldiers can be found. They have been ready every moment to go on duty, and have been and are now eager to go into service, but they have not been ordered out because nobody in Cook County, whether official or private citizen, asked to have their assistance, or even intimated in any way that their assistance was desired or necessary.

"So far as I have been advised, the local officials have been able to handle the situation. But if any assistance were needed, the State stood ready to furnish 100 men for every one man required, and stood ready to do so at a moment's notice. Notwithstanding these facts, the Federal Government has been applied to by men who had political and selfish motives for wanting to ignore the State government."[1]

So Altgeld began his protest to President Cleveland. The facts he gave there—even to the statement that the President had been incorrectly advised (as Olney's conduct reveals)—were incontrovertible. Subsequent independent investigations have shown this many times. Especially was this true of the all-important point that state troops had been ordered out by Altgeld in connection with the Pullman strike "whenever and wherever they were needed." For Altgeld had conducted himself as he had during the previous coal strike, and so advised Cleveland. Some details of this point have been given, but there should be noted a significant paragraph in Altgeld's message that followed:

"In two instances the United States Marshal for the *Southern* District of Illinois applied for assistance (of the state) to enable him to enforce the processes of the *United States court*, and troops were promptly furnished him, and he was assisted in every way he desired. The law has been thoroughly executed, and every man guilty of violating it during the strike has been brought to justice. If the Marshal of the *Northern* District of Illinois (including Chicago) or the authorities of Cook County needed military assistance they had but to ask for it in order to get it from the State."

In other words, in that paragraph Altgeld immediately laid bare the peculiar circumstance that the Federal government was making an untenable distinction between the southern and northern districts—that the state was recognized in the former but ignored in the latter.

He continued by admitting that "some of our railroads are paralyzed." But this was "not by reason of obstruction, but because they cannot get men to operate their trains," a fact, he stated, that was being kept from the public. The railroads, he added, "are making an outcry about obstructions to divert attention." He cited two examples showing how he had been asked for troops supposedly because of "obstructions," only to have the militia discover that the trouble of the railroads was not violence, but simply that none of the railroad workers would work.

In the first case, Altgeld revealed, "we were obliged to hunt up soldiers who could run an engine and operate a train." He described for Cleveland's benefit the other case as follows:

"Again, two days ago, appeals which were almost frantic came from the officials of another road stating that at an important point on their line trains were forcibly obstructed, and that there was a reign of anarchy at that place, and they asked for protection so that they could move their trains. Troops were put on the ground in a few hours' time, when the officer in command telegraphed me that there was no trouble, and had been none at that point, but that the road seemed to have no men to run trains, and the sheriff telegraphed that he did not need troops, but would himself move every train if the company would only furnish an engineer. The result was that the troops were there twelve hours before a single train was moved, although there was no attempt at interference by anybody."

He continued by conceding there had been some infractions of the law. But "all these troubles were local in character and could easily be handled by the State authorities. The newspaper accounts have in many cases been pure fabrications, and in others wild exaggerations." He went into that in such detail, he explained, "to show that it is not soldiers that the railroads need so much as it is men to operate the trains," and that conditions were not such as to bring the situation within the meaning of the Federal statute on which Cleveland presumably acted. That statute "in reality a war measure," he observed, "authorized the use of Federal troops in a State whenever it shall be impracticable to enforce the laws of the United States within such States by the ordinary judicial proceedings." Such a condition, he reiterated, "did not exist. . . . Federal troops can do nothing that the State troops cannot do." Next Altgeld addressed himself to a fundamental principle of American government which, he believed, Cleveland's action had violated:

"I repeat that you have been imposed upon in this matter, but even if by a forced construction it were held that the conditions here came within the letter of the statute, then I submit that local self-government is a fundamental principle of our Constitution. Each community shall govern itself so long as it can and is ready and able to enforce the law, and it is in harmony with this fundamental principle that the statute authorizing the President to send troops into States must be construed; especially is this so in matters relating to the exercise of the police power and the preservation of law and order.

"To absolutely ignore a local government in matters of this kind, when the local government is ready to furnish assistance needed, and is amply able to enforce the law, not only insults the people of this State by imputing to them an inability to govern themselves, or an unwillingness to enforce the law, but is in violation of a basic principle of our institutions. The question of Federal supremacy is in no way involved. No one disputes it for a moment, but, under our Constitution, *Federal supremacy and local self-government must go hand in hand, and to ignore the latter is to do violence to the Constitution.*"

His conclusion was a firm, though respectful, demand on Cleveland to withdraw the troops.

"As Governor of the State of Illinois, I protest against this, and ask the immediate withdrawal of the Federal troops from active duty in this State. Should the situation at any time get so serious that we cannot control it with the State forces, we will promptly ask for Federal assistance, but until such time, I protest, with all due deference, against this uncalled for reflection upon our people, and again ask the immediate withdrawal of these troops. I have the honor to be,
Yours respectfully,
JOHN P. ALTGELD, Governor of
Illinois."

2

In sending that message, Altgeld revealed the same trait of political courage that has been ascribed so fulsomely to Grover Cleveland. It took courage because he knew that all of the principal organs of public opinion, Democratic as well as Republican papers, would be against him. He knew, too, that in any dispute between a president of the United States and a governor, popular support almost invariably will be with the holder of the chief office in the land. Moreover, this President was a member of his own party, and not long before had been re-elected by the greatest endorsement ever given a candidate up to that time.

It was plain to him, too, that the newspapers, notoriously the *Tribune* in Chicago, had been successful in convincing the country, even friends of labor, that "anarchy" prevailed in Chicago, that the strike was in reality a "revolution," that the issue was not and never had been the Pullman workers' wage question, but a contest between "law and order" and "lawlessness and anarchy." Above all, he was aware of the inferences which would be drawn about his position, no matter how right legally and morally he might be, from the fact that only a year before he had pardoned the Haymarket men. Proof that Altgeld was an Anarchist! So he expected the press to shriek.

The press did not disappoint him. "The floodgates of abuse were opened upon him. His critics treated his constitutional objections as flippancy and to the country at large (to discredit him) grossly exag-

gerated the degree of disorder." So, in astonishment, recorded Claude
G. Bowers, outstanding historian, ambassador to Spain under President Franklin D. Roosevelt, a commentator who could not be accused of anti-Cleveland bias.[2] Incredibly, the abuse of the press, immediately and for weeks thereafter, exceeded even that following the
Haymarket pardon.

Again, the Chicago *Tribune* led off—but with the eastern papers
soon in step. Under headings such as "Dastardly Altgeld!" and the
general, almost standing, editorial caption, "The Anarchist Governor
of Illinois," the *Tribune* fumed:

"The real fact in this case might as well be stated without reserva-
tion. This lying, hypocritical, demagogical, sniveling Governor of
Illinois does not want the laws enforced. He is a sympathizer with
riot, with violence, with lawlessness and with anarchy. He should be
impeached, even if the Legislature has to meet on its own motion to
do it. . . . His 'law' is worthless. . . . Those who know Altgeld are not
astonished. He is perverting facts and misstating the law deliberately
and intentionally . . . because he is an Anarchist opposed to all law. . . .
He has put Illinois to shame. . . ."[3]

Column after column of such matter filled the *Tribune* for days.
When its own supply of invective ran low, it filled in by quoting liber-
ally of similar sentiments in other newspapers. That supply was in-
exhaustible. The Aurora, Illinois, *Beacon* as one example declared
that "the Government should fill the state with Federal troops if
necessary, and if Altgeld makes any noise or attempts to interfere a
company of regulars should be sent to Springfield to watch the Herr
Most of Illinois and keep him quiet."

Around the country the story was the same. The Philadelphia
Telegraph published a classic item:

"A sausage-maker from Wurttemberg, or some other locality, permitted by the strange folly of the people of Illinois to be made governor of that State, has had the insolence to offer a gross and outrageous
affront to the President of the United States—an affront more abomin-
able than any indignity since the degradations submitted to by James
Buchanan at the hands of the Southern secession. . . . This foreign
adventurer. . . . This gubernatorial friend and defender of anarchists. . . ."[4]

The New York *Evening Post* epitomized the views of the press of
that metropolis in commenting: "It should surprise nobody that

Governor Altgeld of Illinois has come to the rescue of Debs and his fellow law-breakers. . . . He is the Executive who pardoned the Anarchists . . . and it is only natural that he should sympathize with Anarchists who have not yet been sent to prison. . . ."[5]

To which the New York *Commercial Advertiser* concurred:

"There is one man in Illinois just now who needs to be suppressed quite as much as the fellow Debs. . . . He is the half-criminal fool whom, in a spasm of vindictiveness and spite a number of otherwise reasonable men assisted the Democrats and Anarchists of his State to put in the Executive chair. His name is John P. Altgeld. . . ."[6]

Even the southern newspapers, which might have been expected to see Altgeld's point about Federal interference in a state, generally stood with the northern press. Thus the Memphis *Commercial*:

"We have been wondering that the loud yip-yap of the blatant Anarchist, John P. Altgeld, was not heard in the land. We could not imagine what Altgeld was doing with his mouth while the forces of anarchy and violence he had done so much to promote were holding their carnival and celebrating their jubilee within his blessed jurisdiction. Perhaps Altgeld has been too full of pleasurable emotion to wreak his happy thought upon expression. At last, however, Altgeld has emerged. . . . He is about as fit to control the situation as a firebrand is to protect a powderhouse."[7]

3

So—again—the press of the nation. From then on Altgeld was the special whipping-boy of a press enraged over the Pullman "outrage." Just as it had happened in connection with Haymarket that not the anarchists but the man who freed the survivors was the victim of the storm, so now Altgeld took precedence over even "Dictator" Debs as a target for the worst blasts of hate. An almost singular exception among the journals of the country was the tottering Chicago *Times*, which alone in Chicago supported the strikers, and for which Willis J. Abbott was permitted to write:

". . . It was the right thing, said at the right time to the right person. There can be no contravention of the broad principles of constitutional law laid down by the Governor. . . . It was true patriotism for Governor Altgeld to courageously protest. . . . The snarling pack of mercenaries yelping at his heels will have gone into oblivion long before his ringing letter . . . loses place as an epoch-making state paper."[8]

A few major public officials stood by Altgeld. Governors Hogg of Texas, Lewelling of Kansas, Pennoyer of Oregon and Waite of Colorado bravely supported him, even sending similar protests when Federal troops were sent or planned for their states. But the press dismissed them as Populists or "Anarchists like Altgeld."

Even Senator John M. Palmer raged against Altgeld. And this was curious, because Altgeld actually had, as a precedent, Palmer's own action during the Chicago fire of 1871, when Palmer was governor of Illinois and President Grant sent troops into the state. Palmer then voiced a protest similar to Altgeld's. But in 1894 Palmer garrulously gave out interviews seeking to show there was no similarity between the cases. Thus did the aging office-holder get revenge for Altgeld's part in the schemings of the 1891 senatorial contest.

Olney rushed to the press a statement defending the Federal intervention. "The soil of Illinois is the soil of the United States and, for all United States purposes, the United States is there with its courts . . . and its troops, not by license or comity, but as of right," he declared. Altgeld's message was a "manifesto" of "false premises and illogical non sequiturs." It was "hardly worth while to discuss at length." But Olney discussed it at length, although sneering at it as a "campaign platform [which] it is a safe prediction that the author will be . . . the only person to stand upon it." That would be a prediction that Mr. Olney came to regret for his reputation as a political prophet. "The paramount duty of the President of the United States is to see that the laws of the United States are faithfully executed and in the discharge of that duty, he is not hampered or crippled by the necessity of consulting any Chief of Police, Mayor or even Governor," Mr. Olney added.[9]

Aside from its drastic reversal of accepted Democratic doctrine since the formation of the party, as well as its variance with what was the accepted legal doctrine up to that time, Attorney General Olney's statement was especially interesting for two reasons. He had evaded Altgeld's main point, that Federal supremacy and the matter of states' rights were not involved—Altgeld specifically said so—but rather the right of the Federal government to invade a state with a military force when the state was able and willing to enforce all laws, Federal and state.

More striking were two facts brought out by Altgeld in connection with Mr. Olney. The first was that the Attorney General had executed a complete somersault from his own position taken less than a month before when he advised the Federal Judge at Springfield to ask Altgeld for troops to move mail trains stalled by coal strikers. The second was that Olney had turned turtle from the ideas he had expressed on almost the only occasion he had been in the public eye before Cleveland appointed him to his cabinet. This was in 1874 when the nation was aroused by President Grant's action in sending Federal troops into the state of Louisiana in connection with an election controversy. A protest meeting was held at Faneuil Hall in Boston on January 15, 1875, against that Federal interference in a state, even though the legislature of Louisiana had asked for the troops, and Mr. Olney was one of the speakers, so Altgeld revealed.

None other than Mr. Olney was among the "most distinguished men of Boston" who made speeches at that meeting denouncing the action of the Federal government in Louisiana, Altgeld continued.

"Mr. Olney among other things said: 'Apparently the administration meant to assert that the President might enter a state with troops to suppress disorder and violence at his own discretion upon his own view of the exigency and without waiting for the request or consent of the State itself. No more glaring attempt at usurpation can be imagined. If successful it would revolutionize our whole governmental system and clearly annihilate the right of local self-government by a State.'"[10]

In that same address, Olney had called President Grant's action "utterly subversive of our present system of government." "Be the confusion, anarchy, disorder in a State what they may, the Constitution does not permit the General Government to interfere and restore order, and put down insurrection, except upon the invitation of the State itself."[11] Altgeld, of course, had Olney there—cold, and Mr. Olney never answered.

4

And Cleveland's reactions to Altgeld's message? Supremely conscious always of a great sense of self-rectitude, as egotistical in his way as Altgeld was in his way, the President appeared abashed at first that the Governor of Illinois, a member of his own party, should dare challenge an act of his. Not that Cleveland meant to back down— any more than Altgeld would. Not even if he possibly suspected that Olney had misled him as to the facts. But that he was shaken temporarily, unmistakably jittery, appears clear from the panicky atmosphere in the White House that developed after Altgeld's telegram arrived that evening. The President summoned a special meeting of the Cabinet. First to come running was Olney. Postmaster General Bissell soon followed, apparently to assure Cleveland that the mails really were being obstructed. On his heels General Schofield dashed in. There was much scurrying about by lesser officials and the lights of the White House blazed long after midnight.

"Nothing created so much excitement in the little group as the communication from Governor Altgeld," the Washington correspondent of the Chicago Tribune related.[12] In short, Altgeld's protest would be treated flippantly or scornfully for public consumption, but it was taken seriously enough by the bigwigs themselves. Ignore it? This, it was decided, could not be. And so Cleveland placed his signature on an answer:

"Executive Mansion, Washington, July 5, 1894.
"Hon. John P. Altgeld, Governor of Illinois, Springfield, Ill.:

"Sir:—Federal troops were sent to Chicago in strict accordance with the Constitution and laws of the United States, upon the demand of the post office department that obstruction of the mails should be removed, and upon the representations of the judicial officers of the United States that the process of the Federal courts could not be executed through the ordinary means, and upon competent proof that conspiracies existed against commerce between the States. To meet these conditions, which are clearly within the province of Federal authority, the presence of Federal troops in the city of Chicago was deemed not only proper, but necessary, and there has been no intention of thereby interfering with the plain duty of the local authorities to preserve the peace of the city.

GROVER CLEVELAND."[13]

In even that brief reply, Cleveland had introduced some new and not substantiated angles. The "demand" of the post office department, for example. When had that been made, and to whom? The record up to that time did not show. Was it made that very night by Postmaster General Bissell? Again, what was the "competent proof" that "conspiracies existed"? The statement of Marshal Arnold, twisted from him by Olney?

However, with its emphasis upon the right of the Federal government to maintain interstate commerce and the movement of the mails, Cleveland's answer was supposed to squelch the upstart Governor of Illinois. The press believed it would have that effect. It was jubilant over Cleveland's "bold stand."

But Altgeld was not squelched. Back from Springfield came another telegram, more vigorous even than the first. Again Altgeld demanded withdrawal of Federal troops. His second telegram to Cleveland is worth noting in full.

"Executive Office, State of Illinois,
Springfield, Ill., July 6, 1894.
"To the Hon. Grover Cleveland, President of the United States, Washington, D. C.

"Sir:—Your answer to my protest involves some startling conclusions and ignores and evades the question at issue—that is that the principle of local self-government is just as fundamental in our institutions as is that of Federal supremacy.

"FIRST—You calmly assume that the executive has the legal right to order Federal troops into any community of the United States, in the first instance, whenever there is the slightest disturbance, and that he can do this without any regard to the question as to whether that community is able to and ready to enforce the law itself, and, inasmuch as the executive is the sole judge of the question as to whether any disturbance exists or not in any part of the country, the assumption means that the executive can send Federal troops into any community in the United States at his pleasure, and keep them there as long as he chooses.

"If this is the law, then the principle of self-government either never did exist in this country or else has been destroyed, for no community can be said to possess local self-government, if the executive can, at his pleasure, send military forces to patrol its streets under pretense of enforcing some law. The kind of local self-government that could exist under these circumstances can be found in any of the monarchies of Europe, and it is not in harmony with the spirit of our institutions.

"SECOND—It is also a fundamental principle in our government that except in times of war the military shall be subordinate to the civil authority. In harmony with this provision, the State troops are ordered out to act under and with the civil authorities. The troops you have ordered to Chicago are not under the civil authorities, and are in no way responsible to them for their conduct. They are not even acting under the United States Marshal or any Federal officer of the State, but are acting directly under military orders issued from military headquarters at Washington, and in so far as these troops act at all, it is military government.

"THIRD—The Statute authorizing Federal troops to be sent into States in certain cases contemplates that the State troops shall be taken first. This provision has been *ignored* and it is assumed that the executive is not bound by it. Federal interference with industrial disturbances in the various States is certainly a new departure, and it opens up so large a field that it will require a very little stretch of authority to absorb to itself all the details of local government.

"FOURTH—You say that troops were ordered into Illinois upon the demand of the post office department, and upon representations of the judicial officers of the United States that process of the courts could not be served, and upon proof that conspiracies existed. We will not discuss the facts [Altgeld had done so in his earlier telegram], but look for a moment at the principle involved in your statement. All of these officers are appointed by the executive. Most of them can be removed by him at will. They are not only obliged to do his bidding, but they are in fact a part of the executive. If several of them can apply for troops, one alone can; so that under the law, as you assume it to be, an executive, through any one of his appointees, can apply to himself to have the military sent into any city or number of cities, and base his application on such representations as he sees fit to make.

"In fact, it will be immaterial whether he makes any showing or not, for the executive is the sole judge, and nobody else has any right to interfere or even inquire about it. Then the executive can pass on his own application—his will being the sole guide—he can hold the application to be sufficient, and order troops to as many places as he wishes and put them in command of any one he chooses, and have them act, not under the civil officers, either Federal or State, but directly under military orders from Washington, and there is not in the Constitution or laws, whether written or unwritten, any limitation or restraint upon his power. His judgment, that is, his will, is the sole guide, and it being purely a matter of discretion, his decision can never be examined or questioned.

"This assumption as to the power of the executive is certainly new, and I respectfully submit that it is not the law of the land. The jurists have told us that this is a government of law, and not a government by the caprice of an individual, and further, instead of being autocratic, it is a government of limited power. Yet the autocrat of Russia could certainly not possess, or claim to possess, greater power than is possessed by the executive of the United States, if your assumption is correct.

"FIFTH—The executive has the command not only of the regular forces of all the United States, but of the military forces of all the States, and can order them to any place he sees fit; and as there are always more or less local disturbances over the country, it will be an easy matter under your construction of the law for an ambitious executive to order out the military forces of all of the States, and establish at once a military government. The only chance of failure in such a movement could come from rebellion, and with such a vast military power at command this could be readily crushed, for, as a rule, soldiers will obey orders.

"As for the situation in Illinois, that is of no consequence now compared with the far-reaching principle involved. True, according to my advices, Federal troops have now been on duty for over two days, and although the men were brave and the officers valiant and able, yet their very presence proved to be an irritant because it aroused the indignation of a large class of people, who, while upholding law and order, had been taught to believe in local self-government and, therefore, resented what they regarded as unwarranted interference.

"Inasmuch as the Federal troops can do nothing but what the State troops can do there, and believing that the State is amply able to take care of the situation and to enforce the law, and believing that the ordering out of the Federal troops was unwarranted, I again ask their withdrawal.

JOHN P. ALTGELD."[14]

5

The "old states' rights heresy!" now cried the northern papers, taking their cue from Olney. "Altgeld Breaks Loose Again!" said the Chicago *Tribune.*[15] "Hair-splitting and quibbling!" shouted the press in general.

Cleveland agreed that Altgeld's attitude was hair-splitting. The points raised by Altgeld about local self-government were to him "rather dreary discussion"—strange reaction from the then titular head of the party of Jefferson, Andrew Jackson and Stephen A. Douglas. Moreover, Altgeld·was simply supplying additional "annoyances," while he, Cleveland, was "saving the nation."[16] "I think Altgeld ought to be whipped!" wrote one of Cleveland's intimates at just that time, after a private audience with the President, and it appears he was echoing Cleveland's own sentiments toward Altgeld.[17] And so, with his "patience strained," Cleveland sent the following curt response:

"Executive Mansion, Washington, D. C., July 6, 1894.
"While I am still persuaded that I have neither transcended my authority nor duty in the emergency that confronts us, it seems to me that in this hour of danger and public distress, discussion may well

give way to active efforts on the part of all in authority to restore
obedience to law and to protect life and property.

GROVER CLEVELAND.

"Hon. John P. Altgeld
Governor of Illinois."[18]

From Cleveland's standpoint, his reply to Altgeld was perfect. It
had the virtue of brevity. And naturally, all "law and order" people
applauded the appealing sentiment that the times called for action,
not "discussion." Bravo, Grover! paeaned the press. "President
Cleveland's method of dealing with Gov. Altgeld is a model one," declared *The Nation*. "He wastes no time in arguing with him or in
defending himself against his attacks, but in a few terse sentences sets
him before the country in his true light as the friend and champion
of disorder."[19] . . .

"The most respectable document that President Cleveland has
signed," said the New York *Commercial-Advertiser*, adding an idea
that, if carried out, probably would have been as wildly applauded:
"He may have to sign still another in relation to John P. Altgeld before the end comes!"[20]

But Cleveland did not follow advice to place Governor Altgeld
under military arrest—nor did he hear from Altgeld again. Not, that
is, until the immediate cause of the controversy was over. For the
situation at Chicago had suddenly changed, even as Cleveland im-
patiently pondered Altgeld's second message.

CHAPTER THIRTY

STRIKE'S END

1

Up to Cleveland's receipt of Altgeld's second protest even Washington knew that no serious disorder had occurred in Chicago as yet. This was what made the appearance of Federal troops so mysterious to persons of an inquiring mind. But now there really was violence. Vindication of Grover Cleveland? It seemed so, at the time, and to certain astigmatic historians for years later. Actually, the new development vindicated Altgeld.

In stationing Federal troops in Chicago *before* any serious outbreaks, Cleveland in effect had assumed responsibility for maintaining order thereafter over the heads of the local authority. Yet, when real violence occurred, it was stamped out by Altgeld's militia and the police of Chicago. Cleveland's troops were well-nigh helpless and generally ineffective and useless.

In short, the subsequent events proved Altgeld's point, that Illinois was able to take care of itself. Almost everyone who has written of the Pullman affair has ignored that significant point. Yet this was the fact, as shown by study of the newspapers and official reports, and corroborated by the report of President Cleveland's own commission to investigate the strike.[1]

From the beginning of the strike until July sixth, damage done to property by "anarchistic mobs" in Chicago amounted to less than $6,000, according to records of the Chicago Fire Department, which kept an account of all strike damage. It was reported officially that "during the first three days of the month of July no efforts were made to damage the property of Corporations." On July fifth, however, menacing crowds had gathered in several sections, notably the stockyards district. They were dispersed in the main by local police. The Federal troops? Of their effectiveness, there is this illuminating section in the study made by Howard Barton Myers:

"On this day [the fifth] the whole stockyards force of the Federal

army, consisting of almost a thousand men, together with a considerable force of policemen and a large number of deputy marshals, tried,
all day to move a cattle train out of the Yards. 'Every time the engine
moved, the bell was rung, and every time it rang, a hundred more
strikers and their sympathizers came to see what the railroads and
the soldiers were attempting.' The mob completely blocked the track
ahead of the train by overturning cars and spiking switches. After
sitting in one spot for two hours, listening to the exceedingly uncomplimentary remarks of the assembled women of the neighborhood, the soldiers 'marched back to Camp Dexter to the tune of the
Rogues March, which was whistled by the boys perched upon the
fences and buildings along the line. As a result of the whole day's
work, they had moved the train six blocks. There it was abandoned
to the mercy of the mob."[2]

On the next day, a regiment of Cleveland's soldiers, responding to a
call over similar trouble, not only was no more effective, but the regiment became lost in the city and had to ask help to find the stockyards. But on that day—the sixth—the trouble was clearly beyond
control of both the local police and Cleveland's troops. That night
hundreds of freight cars were ablaze, also several buildings remaining
from the Columbian Exposition. It was not so bad as had been
painted, for the total damage was around three hundred thousand
dollars rather than the "millions" reported, but it was bad enough.

2

In Springfield, Altgeld kept closely in touch with the situation
through regular reports from his militia officers in Chicago. Before
the wild events of the sixth occurred, he had heard "rumors of an extension of the strike." Yet no call for assistance came to him either
from the Mayor of Chicago, democratic John P. Hopkins, or the
Sheriff of Cook County, Republican James H. Gilbert. Either because they felt they could handle the situation, or for other reasons,
those officials refrained from appealing to Altgeld. Until they did
so, or until he knew from responsible sources that laws were being
violated beyond control of the local authorities, Altgeld intended to
follow the policy that he had established more than a year before the
Pullman trouble.

"On the morning of the sixth of July," Altgeld recalled afterward,
"the president of the Illinois Central railroad telegraphed me that the
property of his road was being destroyed by a mob and that he could

not get protection. I wired him at once to get some one of the local authorities who are authorized to ask for troops to do so, and that if all should refuse, to wire me that fact, and that we would furnish protection promptly." He explained that he "took the position as a matter of law, that if the local authorities failed to protect property and enforce the law, and refused to apply for State aid while property actually is being destroyed, and the peace is being disturbed, that then the Governor of the State not only has the right, but it is his duty to see that order is restored and the law enforced."[3]

But still no word from Mayor Hopkins or the Sheriff. Altgeld now, however, went into action on his own initiative. When he telegraphed his response to the president of the Illinois Central, at the same time he sent another telegram "to a friend in Chicago requesting him to at once see Mayor Hopkins and tell him that it seemed to me the situation was serious, and that he had better apply to the State for aid."[4] That "friend" was his cousin, John Lanehart.[5]

This was "untold" history at the time, but the Chicago *Tribune*, in its issue of July seventh, carried on Altgeld's version, by reporting:

"Mayor Hopkins consulted with his advisors until 11:30 a. m. Then he wired Gov. Altgeld demanding [sic!] five regiments of militia. Altgeld *at once* [italics not the *Tribune's*] ordered out the First and Third Brigades. . . . The militia were advised by Altgeld to report to Hopkins to aid the mayor in suppressing riots, keeping the peace and enforcing the law."

And Altgeld, to resume his account, spoke the truth when he related:

"Never were troops moved with greater celerity. They at once got the situation under control and stopped the rioting. . . . Within twenty-four hours after the State troops arrived on the ground, the rioting was suppressed. There were still a few cases, during the following days, of stealthy incendiarism, but no more forcible resistance. . . ."[6]

He spoke the truth, too, corroborated inferentially by General Schofield himself, when he said that the Federal troops "accomplished nothing." Altgeld wrote:

"The federal troops and their officers were no doubt brave men and good soldiers, but they . . . were occupying an anomalous position, and were therefore under a disadvantage. . . . So far as can be learned, their persistence did not prevent the burning of a single freight car in Chicago . . . yet during all this time the impression was made on the country that President Cleveland and the federal troops were saving Chicago!"[7]

He could have boasted that the only serious encounter between soldiers and rioters was the one that occurred on July seventh, an affair in which seven rioters were shot to death—not by Federal troops, but by militia whose commander-in-chief was the "anarchist Altgeld." But, as Brand Whitlock dryly observed, "perhaps Governor Altgeld was willing to forego any 'credit' for any act, which, however necessary to the preservation of order, demanded so many lives."[8] As much as anything, that incident of seven men killed quelled the disorder—more effectively even than President Cleveland's excited and doubtfully necessary "proclamation" issued on July eighth banning all unlawful assemblages in Chicago.

As for the strike, it was broken once and for all on July seventh when Eugene Debs and all his union lieutenants were arrested by Federal marshals for contempt of Mr. Olney's injunction and, vaguely, for "conspiracy." From his cell, Debs advised the Pullman Company that the union would call off the strike officially if the company would agree to another request for arbitration. But again the Pullman Company said there was nothing to arbitrate.[9]

And this time, referring to the strike, the company was right.

3

Before passing on, one other point concerning the violence which erupted in Chicago on July sixth should be examined. As he indicated in the last paragraphs of his second protest to Cleveland, Altgeld apparently believed at the time that this violence happened primarily because of indignation caused by appearance of Federal troops. It was a fact that Debs theretofore constantly warning his followers against disorder, had declared in a speech after the troops came that "the first shots fired by the regular soldiers at the mobs here will be the signal for a civil war. . . . Bloodshed will follow." Those were intemperate words, and many believed that they helped cause what happened.

But was the violence a product solely of such indignation? Or were there other and more sinister causes? Many competent observers and investigators believe there were. They point to the rôle of the some 3,600 men whom Attorney General Olney authorized the United States Marshal at Chicago to deputize as agents of the Federal government. Pertinent, too, is the observation of Harry Thurston Peck, already noted, that violence broke out "singularly" after it first became plain to the railroad operators that Debs was winning, had won, so long as all was peaceful. Was it planned that way? Were the deputy marshals told to incite violence? Those are questions that will not down in view of certain facts known about the deputy marshals enrolled in behalf of the railroads.

Concerning the status of those Federal deputies, there is this paragraph in the report of Cleveland's own investigating commission:

"They were armed and paid by the railroads and acted in the double capacity of railroad employes and United States officers. While operating the railroads they assumed and exercised unrestricted United States authority when so ordered by their employers, or whenever they regarded it as necessary. They were not under the direct control of any government official while exercising authority."

To which the government commission added:

"This is placing officers of the government under the control of a combination of railroads. It is a bad precedent that might well lead to serious consequences."[10]

As a matter of fact, there was considerable evidence that this "bad precedent" did lead to "serious consequences" at the time.

Item one: Testimony of Police Superintendent Brennan of Chicago at the hearing conducted by Cleveland's strike commission, that his police were forced to arrest a number of the deputy marshals for highway robbery committed while they were supposedly acting for the government.[11] In his official report to the City Council of Chicago, Chief Brennan characterized the main body of the marshals as "thugs, thieves and ex-convicts."[12]

Item two: Report of Chicago Fire Department officials that when they were trying to extinguish the flames in the railroad yards on the night of the sixth, "they caught men in the act of cutting the hose and that *these men wore the badges of deputy marshals.*"[13] In this same connection, police officers reported catching the Federal deputies "instigating violence and acts of incendiarism."

Concerning the sudden outbreak of violence after Altgeld's protest was received by Cleveland, it should be noted that a good many persons, when Altgeld's first protest was published, while not approving, expressed the view that perhaps Cleveland should have permitted Altgeld to show that he was able to put down trouble if any occurred. Nor was the point overlooked that no serious trouble had as yet occurred. Was that violence engineered, in part at least, by the railroads themselves, to save President Cleveland's face and also their own hides? Admittedly, that is a serious charge. Yet, there was precedent for such conduct in the railroad strikes of 1877, especially in Pennsylvania. It was learned then that the burning of a few freight cars (preferably old and worn ones) had the double advantage of bringing troops to break the strike and furnishing the basis for collecting large indemnity from the taxpayers.[14]

4

Bearing on this point is the interesting notation in Henry D. Lloyd's notebook:

"Strike of 1894—E. W. Bemis (University of Chicago professor) was told that Mayor Hopkins before leaving office procured forty affidavits showing that the burning of freight cars was done by railroad men; that the railroad men moved cars outside of fire limits, then burned them, inciting bystanders to participate. Hopkins, fearing these affidavits might be destroyed by some subsequent mayor, took certified copies before leaving office. . . ."[15]

It would not have been difficult to "incite" such "bystanders" as the United States deputy marshals who were constantly in the yards. In addition to Police Chief Brennan's testimony concerning them, there was similar testimony from newspaper reporters.

Ray Stannard Baker, then on the Chicago Record, testified:

"From my experience with them [the marshals] it [their character] was very bad. I saw more cases of drunkenness, I believe, among the United States deputy marshals than I did among the strikers."[16]

Malcolm McDowell, reporter on the same newspaper:

". . . Everybody who saw them knew that they were not the class of men who ought to be made deputy marshals. . . . They seemed to be hunting trouble all the time. . . . I saw more deputy marshals drunk than I saw strikers drunk. . . ."[17]

And Harold I. Cleveland, of the Chicago *Herald*:

"I was on the tracks of the Western Indiana fourteen days. . . .I saw in that time a couple of hundred deputy marshals. I think they were a very low, contemptible set of men."[18]

There was more such testimony, leading the report of Cleveland's commission to hint strongly that the Chicago violence actually was inspired by the railroads themselves. As for the chairman of the investigation committee, Carroll D. Wright, he gave a Boston magazine editor basis for flatly asserting:

"Col. Wright would tell our . . . newspapers that not even hoodlums instigated the burning of the mass of cars, but that it was instigated by the railway managers themselves as the surest way to bring the Federal troops and defeat the strike."[19]

To which might have been added: "and to discredit Altgeld."

5

It should be stated that if such suspicions concerning the Chicago freight-car burnings are based upon fact, Attorney General Olney does not appear mixed up in that phase. Certainly President Cleveland was not aware at the time of the kind of men being deputized as Federal marshals—nor even of other facts. But even if he were, one wonders if he would have acted much differently. Cleveland's magazine article on the strike, written in 1904, when all the facts were available, does not show that he repented anything. He ignored completely the report of his own strike commission, and told the story as if the situation actually was as Mr. Olney and the newspapers pictured it at the time. It is noteworthy, however, that both Cleveland and Olney found it expedient in later years to justify their conduct almost solely on the undoubted necessity of preventing obstruction to the United States mails. Played down was the matter of disorder in Chicago, also the point concerning interruption of interstate commerce.

But were the mails interrupted in Illinois to such an extent as to warrant the action taken? Even this is highly questionable—and it was the only point that in any way justified the use of Federal troops. During even the heat of the strike, when undoubtedly pressure was brought from Washington upon the Superintendent of Mails at Chicago to report "obstructions," that official was exceedingly vague and contradictory in his statements.[20] And later, Altgeld would bring to light two significant documents.

One was the message that Superintendent of Mails Lewis L. Troy sent to Washington on June thirtieth, the day Olney went into action. That message was:

"No mails have accumulated at Chicago so far. All regular trains are moving nearly on time with few slight exceptions.
                    LEWIS L. TROY, Superintendent."

The other document was a signed statement by Superintendent Troy summarizing the whole effect of the strike on mail at Chicago.

"With the exception of some trains that were held at Hammond, Ind., Washington Heights, Danville and Cairo, Ill., the greatest delay to any of the outgoing and incoming mails probably did not exceed from eight to nine hours at any time.
                    LEWIS L. TROY, Superintendent."[21]

It was then, for "eight or nine hours' delay" in the mails, that Grover Cleveland permitted surrender of the government to the railroads to crush the strike of Debs's men. While condemning his conduct, Professor Allan Nevins in his book *Grover Cleveland—A Study in Courage* appears to feel that Cleveland is to be excused as having been duped by Mr. Olney.[22] Unquestionably, that was true to a great extent. Yet, does it exculpate the President completely? Doubtless Olney duped Cleveland concerning the extent of the violence and on the legal situation.

But on the matter of going over the head of a governor, a different question arises. Grover Cleveland had been a county sheriff, a mayor and also a governor before he was made president. In those other offices, he knew well the accepted procedure for suppressing disorders, that first the local authorities are to act, then the state authorities, and only after both have failed and called for help does the national government enter the picture. Yet he disregarded that procedure ruthlessly, without conducting any investigation of his own. The conclusion appears inescapable that Cleveland was wholly in sympathy with Olney's attitude—that he, too, wished to "smash" the Pullman strikers.

Cleveland had never possessed sympathy for organized labor, although he professed to have for political purposes. His true attitude appears shown in a letter published after his death. In 1884 Orestes Cleveland had suggested, in connection with Grover Cleveland's first presidential campaign, that he include in his letter accepting the nomination a polite reference to trade unions. To Daniel S. Lamont, Cleveland wrote: "I don't like the suggestion of Orestes Cleveland to say in my letter that I am in favor of aggressive organization of labor. . . ."[23] In short, Cleveland on labor appears to have been pretty much akin to Judge Gary on labor.

No wonder, then, Cleveland supposedly confided to a political crony that, of all the acts of his two presidential administrations, he felt that breaking the Pullman strike was one of the best moves he ever made.[24] Nearly everyone at the time seemed to agree with Cleveland— especially the Republicans. For his action in Illinois, they were willing even to forgive his heresies on the tariff. Chauncey Depew, president of the New York Central, as worthy a spokesman for the Republicans as any, was jubilant. Why, he advised the London *Times*, the strike, despite the "enormous losses," was destined "to prove of incalculable benefit to the country," thanks to Grover Cleveland. "The national idea has been strengthened. . . . Safe anchorage has been found for persons and property. . . . Every vested interest is more secure. . . ."[25]

6

Best of all, to many, was the absolute conviction that Altgeld— that "dastardly anarchist"—was now definitely done for. Cleveland had thoroughly discredited him. Altgeld was through, absolutely. Thank God!

No wonder this was the belief, considering that respected historians in after years would carry on the distorted picture that the press of 1894 painted of Altgeld's conduct in that strike. Thus, Historian James Ford Rhodes, as late as 1913, wrote:

". . . The President [Cleveland] and law-abiding citizens were hampered by the attitude of the Governor of Illinois, who was called 'the friend and champion of disorder'; anarchy was threatened and the police of Chicago under the mayor and the militia under the Governor, remained powerless to avert it. Had the Governor been like the state executives of 1877, he would have called upon the president for troops, who would have been sent under the constitutional provisions, but not only did he *decline* to make any such request, but even protested against the sending of . . . troops. . . . To Cleveland and to Olney we, in this country of reverence for just decisions, owe a precedent of incalculable value."[26]

More surprising, considering the source, was the comment of another respected historian:

"The Governor of Illinois had not asked for his [Cleveland's] aid, had not even called out the militia of the State to maintain order and protect property—sympathized, indeed, with the strikers and resented interference. . . ."[27]

The author of that "historical" judgment was a Princeton professor known as Thomas Woodrow Wilson, later, with the aid of Bryan and a platform pioneered by that same Governor of Illinois, to be known as President Woodrow Wilson.

But was Altgeld done for? Ahead was the campaign of 1896, first definite rumblings of which were heard after that British government action respecting the mints of India.

BOOK SEVEN

THE REVOLT

CHAPTER THIRTY-ONE

THE NEW ALTGELD

1

THREE MONTHS after the Pullman strike, Altgeld summoned George Schilling to his office and sprang the suggestion that Schilling make plans immediately for a trip to New York City on a "secret mission." The mission was explained by a letter of introduction that Schilling was to take along. It was addressed to the "Hon. David B. Hill, New York, N. Y."

"Dear Sir: This will introduce Mr. George Schilling, the Secretary of the Board of Labor Statistics of the State of Illinois. He is a man of wide acquaintance and influence with the leaders of organized labor and absolutely reliable. He visits your state at my suggestion to do what he can to secure democratic triumph and to render you personally any service in his power.

"Assuring you of my high regard and wishing you a success commensurate with the unparalleled and magnificent fight you are making, I am

Very respectfully yours,
JOHN P. ALTGELD."[1]

This letter represents a singularly remarkable Altgeld document. Senator David B. ["I am a Democrat"] Hill of New York then and thereafter stood for Tammany—at its worst. He was antithetical to Altgeld in every respect. For one thing, he was a pronounced reactionary; on the floor of the United States Senate only a few weeks before he had denounced the income tax measure of 1894 as "revolutionary, western populism." Altgeld shared the opinion of most political observers that Hill also was a corruptionist.

Yet, there he was, in the letter of introduction, assuring Hill of his "high regard," and instructing Schilling to "see Samuel Gompers and the other labor people in New York" to urge that they support Hill in his campaign for governor of New York. Strange business for Altgeld, this. Aside from furnishing additional evidence of Altgeld's ability to play the political game and also "to sling the buncombe," as one person would say, what did it mean?

It meant two things. First, Altgeld had determined to play a rôle in national politics—without waiting for his senatorial ambitions to be realized. Second, he had declared war upon Grover Cleveland aggressively and relentlessly. From now on, his principal objective in public affairs was to drive Cleveland and "Clevelandism" from the party of Jefferson and Jackson. Later it would be found ironical that his first move in that direction should have been an effort to help Senator Hill. For all of his plans for destroying Clevelandism had as the final objective reading Cleveland out of the party at the national Democratic convention in 1896—and in that convention the leading spokesman for both Cleveland and Clevelandism would be—Senator Hill! But in 1894, Hill and Cleveland were personal enemies, struggling for control of the New York Democracy. If Hill won the governorship of New York that year, the result would be a personal defeat for the President. It was for this that Altgeld stepped out of his rôle as merely a local Illinois politician to enter the New York political picture.

But how could Altgeld reconcile support for Hill with his personal political standards? Scratching his head over his assignment, George Schilling raised that question.

"I believe," said Altgeld, "that Hill represents the lesser of two evils. Of course, he is a damned crook, but the people will soon get tired of him and he will do no permanent harm to the country. It is the Clevelands, the men who put up respectable fronts, who are the real dangers."[2]

As it turned out, Hill was defeated. The New York labor leaders "simply could not stomach him," Schilling later told Altgeld. But Altgeld merely smiled. After all, there was plenty of time. He recognized, too, that the Middle West and the South formed the real battle ground in the fight against Cleveland.

2

Ominous for Cleveland was the fact that John Peter Altgeld was a changed man after the Pullman strike episode. Up to now in purely political matters he had been something of a compromiser. That was how he had won the governorship and how he hoped to garner the senatorship. But his day of weasel-words, of cautious utterances, was over. He would speak straight now—and clear. Up to now, too, he had been on the receiving end of abuse and vituperation. When he had answered at all before, it was generally on the defensive. Perhaps the Pullman strike opened his eyes more clearly to a number of things.

One was that under Cleveland the Democratic party was under the control, so he would say, of a "small band of schemers in New York, who have not a drop of Democratic blood in their veins, whose sympathies are entirely with the great corporations, who have not even a conception of a Democratic principle, but treat the American republic as a foraging ground."[3] Another was a realization that the Tory die-hards, while slightly more subtle than in the 'seventies and 'eighties, remained in the 'nineties just as uncompromising in their animosity toward Labor. The trusts and all forms of "monopoly" were becoming more entrenched and more arrogant than ever. If he intended ever to fill his destiny as a Voice, he would have to speak more firmly.

Still another eye-opener was clear evidence that the press had no intention of dealing either fairly or rationally with either him or his policies. A fight was being waged against him in which no holds were barred, no rules observed. Well, he could fight that way, too.

3

First to squirm under the bolts released by the "new" Altgeld was George M. Pullman. On August 19, 1894, while the sleeping-car magnate was congratulating himself on the victory over the American Railway Union, a startling communication came to Altgeld at Springfield.

"Kensington, Ill., August 17, 1894.
"To His Excellency, the Governor of the State of Illinois:
"We, the people of Pullman, who, by the greed and oppression of George M. Pullman, have been brought to a condition where starvation stares us in the face, do hereby appeal to you for aid in this our hour of need. We have been refused employment and have no means of leaving this vicinity, and our families are starving.
"Our places have been filled with workmen from all over the United States, brought here by the Pullman Company, and the surplus was turned away to walk the streets and starve also. There are over 1,600 families here in destitution and want, and their condition is pitiful. We have exhausted all the means at our command to feed them, and we now make this appeal to you as a last resource. . . .
THE STARVING CITIZENS OF PULLMAN
F. E. Pollans, L. J. Newell,
Theo. Rhode, Committee."[4]

Altgeld recognized that behind that communication was exactly the kind of situation he had warned against in his first statement on labor back in 1886. It was the tragedy of Spring Valley all over again, this time enacted in the city of Chicago itself—if the communication related the truth. In the case of the starving miners of Spring Valley, no government official had yet acted; only Henry Demarest Lloyd had taken up their plight. But Altgeld meant to do something in this case. First, he dispatched a telegram to George M. Pullman. Then, he took a train for Chicago to make a personal inspection of conditions in Pullman. He minced no words in his telegram to Pullman.

"Sir:—I have received numerous reports to the effect that there is great distress at Pullman. Today, I received a formal appeal. . . .

"Now, these people live in your town and were your employes. Some of them worked for your company for many years. . . . Many of them have practically given their lives to you. . . . Assuming they were wrong and foolish [in striking] they had yet served you long and well and you must feel some interest in them. . . . The State of Illinois has not the least desire to meddle in the affairs of your company, but it cannot allow a whole community within its borders to perish of hunger.

". . . Unless relief comes from some other source, I shall either have to call an extra session of the Legislature to make special appropriations, or else issue an appeal to the humane people of the State to give bread to your recent employes. . . ."

He added the pointed suggestion that the decent thing for the Pullman Company to do would be "to relieve the situation yourself, especially as it has just cost the State upwards of fifty thousand dollars to protect your property. . . ."[5]

4

George Pullman, who was so unnerved by the strike that during it all he locked himself up as "ill" at his summer estate in the East, made no reply. But the next morning, Vice-President Thomas H. Wickes of the sleeping-car company showed up at the Unity Block. He had no suggestions for relief, but he was "glad" to act as the Governor's "guide" on his tour of the town. His purpose was to "assist" Altgeld in "making essential discrimination," so Pullman later explained in criticizing Altgeld for candidly observing to Wickes that he "doubted the wisdom of going under any one's wing."[6] However,

Altgeld let Wickes accompany him, and on his tour he found at Pullman conditions that corroborated the letter of the committee of "starving citizens." There was starving—with deaths reported a little later.[7] Even the *Tribune* admitted the acute distress. With the spectacle of the Governor of the state, even if his name was Altgeld, visiting the homes of the poor, "rapping at doors, climbing staircases and asking questions of astonished men, women and children," it was forced to turn the light of publicity on the conditions in Pullman. A *Tribune* headline frankly declared: "Hunger Is Their Plight."[8] As for the Pullman Company executives, they could not deny actual conditions seen either. But when those on the ground were asked by Altgeld if they "had anything to suggest," they stood mute.

5

The next day another communication from Altgeld went to fidgety George Pullman.

"Sir:
"I examined the conditions at Pullman yesterday, visited even the kitchens and bedrooms of many of the people. . . .
"Something must be done at once. . . . I repeat now that it seems to me your company cannot afford to have me appeal to the charity and humanity of the State to save the lives of your old employes. Four-fifths of these people are women and children. No matter what caused this distress, it must be met. . . ."

He made two practical suggestions. Let the company, he said, forego its rent collections from its workers since the previous October first. If it had shut down its plant at that time, as the company itself claimed it should have because of slack business, it would not have collected the rents anyway, and so "would be just as well off." Then let the company stagger its jobs, putting double the number of men employed on half-time "so that all can at least get something to eat for their families [and thus] give immediate relief to the whole situation."

"I will be at the Unity block for several hours, and will be glad to see you if you care to make any reply.
                    Yours respectfully,
                              JOHN P. ALTGELD."[9]

To be certain that Pullman received the letter, Altgeld instructed Assistant Adjutant General Hugh Bayles of the National Guard to deliver it in person. Refused admission to Pullman's office at first, Bayles donned his full military uniform, pistols and all, and literally forced his way past startled clerks into Pullman's inner sanctum.[10] Pullman found the letter a hard one to answer, and afternoon reporters saw the magnate "pacing the floor, just like any other man who is dictating to a typewriter."[11]

6

Finally, Mr. Pullman finished his dictating. He was "honored" to acknowledge the Governor's letter. But he was pained that the Governor did not appreciate the offer to have Vice-President Wickes escort him about the town of Pullman. He had the "best reason for believing that the husband of a wife who is published as representing her family to you yesterday as in need of help drew more than $1,300 of his savings . . . for buying lots." That, he implied, was just an "indication" of how the Governor opened himself to misrepresentation by not being properly escorted by company officials.

Still, Mr. Pullman did not "doubt that there are many cases of need." But was the Pullman Company at fault? Oh, no. The trouble actually was occasioned because the workers involved refused to go back to their jobs, forcing the company to bring in new workers. Nevertheless, continued Mr. Pullman, he admitted that the situation is one "which must be dealt with without regard to what has caused it." He would give it the "consideration which is due from the company." But as for Altgeld's suggestions, they were imperiously rejected by Pullman. Canceling rents would do no good "if their needs are as pressing as you suppose them to be." Staggering the work? That, said Mr. Pullman, was tried before. The result was that the public received "an erroneous impression with reference to the sufficiency of the rate of the wages." Therefore, "the policy of the company now is to employ only as many men as it is possible to furnish work for on full time." It would not be changed.[12] In short, Mr. Pullman had learned nothing—yet—from the strike. Even his newspaper advocates admitted as much.

Altgeld responded immediately. First, a sharply worded reply to Pullman's letter.

"I see that your company refuses to do anything toward relieving the situation. If you make the round I made . . . you will be convinced that none of them had $1,300 or any other sum of money only a few weeks ago. . . . I cannot enter into a discussion with you as to the merits of the controversy between you and your former workmen. I assume that even if they were wrong and had been foolish, you would not be willing to see them perish. . . ."[13]

Next, Altgeld issued an official proclamation addressed to "The People of Illinois and Especially Those of the City of Chicago." In it, he told of conditions in Pullman, but with remarkable restraint. The proclamation concluded:

"We cannot now stop to inquire the cause of this distress. The good people of this State cannot allow women and children by the hundreds to perish of hunger. I therefore call upon all humane and charitably disposed citizens to contribute what they can . . . to the Pullman relief committee at Kensington, Ill. . . .
JOHN P. ALTGELD, Governor."[14]

From all parts of the state money poured in. The *Tribune* discovered it expedient to assist Altgeld in raising a fund to swell the sum collected as a result of his appeal. It was an Altgeld personal triumph, and a blow at the prestige of the Pullman Corporation in many respects worse even than the effect of the strike on the public mind. Nor was Altgeld finished.

7

In the following month, he directed another thunderbolt at the corporation. He had noted that on the witness stand before the committee named by President Cleveland to investigate the Pullman strike, Mr. Pullman was forced to give some interesting figures on the wealth of his company. Its paid-up capitalization was $36,000,000, upon which dividends of eight per cent had been paid regularly. The corporation had in its treasury, as surplus profits, "something like $25,000,000."[15] Thus, by his own figures the corporation was worth at least $61,000,000. Altgeld wondered how much taxes the corporation was paying. He sent for the figures, and discovered that the corporation, for capital stock tax purposes, was being assessed on the basis of a valuation of $1,695,500!

On September 25, 1894, George Pullman did some more squirming on discovering that Altgeld made those facts public in an official communication to the State Board of Tax Equalization.

"It was apparent," said Altgeld, "that the Pullman Company had for many years been annually defrauding the public out of from $640,-000 to $800,000 per year, and that consequently it had now in its possession several million dollars that in justice belonged to the public."[16]

In the beginning the only result of this was the public exposure. "I was subsequently told," Altgeld related afterward, "that the only effect was to cause some of the members of the [tax] board to raise their price and force the Pullman Company to come and see them."[17] But in the end, when the corrupt state board of equalization was replaced by another body (fruit of agitation begun by Altgeld) the Pullman Corporation saw its assessments raised considerably. In the end, too, the corporation was forced to give up all its real-estate holdings except those actually needed for factory purposes, for litigation pressed by Altgeld caused the Illinois Supreme Court to find that Pullman's "model town" was illegal from the beginning.

Thus did the "new" Altgeld in part even the scores of the Pullman episode, insofar as the company itself was concerned.

8

Two days after Altgeld had struck at the Pullman Company with his extraordinary proclamation of starvation, his attention was called to an address delivered before the American Bar Association convention at Saratoga. The speaker was the great Judge Thomas M. Cooley of Michigan, whose treatise Constitutional Law then as now was a standard legal text. An old man by then, Cooley devoted his address, as president of the association, to fulsome praise of President Cleveland for sending troops to Chicago and to vigorous denunciation of Altgeld. He scoffed at the constitutional objections raised by Altgeld. They were, he said, "not even plausible. . . ." Altgeld's protest was "not only unwarranted, but . . . revolutionary." Then, straying from the legal sphere, Cooley declaimed that "such a protest from the executive of a great state must necessarily tend at any time to still further excite the passions of those who in a mad way are defying the lawful authorities."[18] Judge Cooley was, of course, applauded by the lawyers at Saratoga to the echo. But he was to hear from Altgeld.

Altgeld conceded Judge Cooley's reputation based upon his book Constitutional Law, but felt that "Judge Cooley's reputation is liable to have an injustice done it unless the people will discriminate between the real Cooley and the later Cooley."

"In addressing the bar association he was in the position of a fashionable preacher who, if he wished to be popular with his audience, must cater to its tastes. The American Bar Association is a small body of men, most of whom have corporations for clients. They are shrewd and able men who know where fat fees come from. A lawyer whose clients are poor could not afford to go to Saratoga and have a good time and attend a bar meeting. Judge Cooley's utterance there must be taken with some others recently made, and the question is, how much importance attaches to them simply because they came from Cooley?"

Then he went after Cooley in the most effective manner possible. He quoted from Cooley's famous book to show that the Judge, himself, had warned against "the constant danger that free institutions are in from the encroachment of a central power through the agency of a standing army."

But, Altgeld declared, since writing that book, Cooley "made himself so obnoxious" as a judge in Michigan by decisions favoring corporations, that the people of Michigan "arose and put an end to his career in that state." President Cleveland, Altgeld added, then named Cooley as a member of the Interstate Commerce Commission. Of course, Altgeld said, Mr. Cooley feels "grateful" to Cleveland, and Altgeld hoped that Mr. Cooley's former "bright reputation" would "not be clouded by utterances that are born of a grateful dotage."[19]

Probably the good Judge, accustomed to the greatest reverence in his declining years, never did recover from that verbal lacing.

9

Chauncey Depew, whose charming after-dinner speaking manner had covered up from the general public his large-scale corporation lobbyist activity over several decades of financial piracy, was another victim of Altgeldian invective about this time. In April, 1895, Depew made a speech at the Auditorium in Chicago designed to make an end, once and for all, of Altgeld, "the anarchist." He served up all of the charges concerning Altgeld's alleged shirking of his duty in the Pullman affair. Altgeld, he said, is "an iridescent human humbug."[20]

Had Altgeld read Mr. Depew's speech? reporters in Springfield inquired.

"No, I have not," said the Governor. "Some years ago I listened to Mr. Depew for two hours and came to the conclusion that so long as the Lord insisted on limiting human life to about threescore and ten years, two hours was all the time that the average man could afford to spend . . . on Depew."

But when he was given a synopsis of Depew's remarks, he said that the speech "was in harmony with Depew's philosophy of life."

"How is that, Governor?"

"Well," Altgeld answered, "he is the most conspicuous product of the doctrine 'do evil that good may come of it' that this country has ever seen." Depew, he declared, was the man who reduced the business of buying up legislators for the railroads to a "science" so that "whenever the New York Central Railroad wished to buy a legislator they . . . simply put him on the scales and weighed him." This, he said, "was the beginning of that flood of corruption which is today washing the foundations from under our whole governmental fabric." He added: "No man could be a dealer in this leprosy without soiling his fingers, and I am told that since that time Mr. Depew has never been seen without gloves!"

"Then, why has not Mr. Depew been sent to prison?" inquired the reporters.

"Oh," said Altgeld. "That would have been vulgar and Mr. Depew would not do so vulgar a thing as go to prison. On the contrary he made of all this a stepping-stone to greatness. He wrapped the stars and stripes about him. He became a red, white and blue orator. He changed his calendar so as to make the Fourth of July embrace 365 days, leaving but six hours for the remainder of the year—and then he started for the White House."[21]

Even hostile newspapers agreed that Mr. Depew had met his match in the "iridescent human humbug" at Springfield. "A new scalp has been added to the collection which adorns the East wall of Governor Altgeld's office," the *Times-Herald* observed with amusement. "The scalp suggests a man of great culture, and visitors are puzzled to decide to whom it originally belonged. Private Secretary Dose vouchsafes no information on the subject, but many people are satisfied that it is the *late* Chauncey M. Depew of New York."[22]

10

Altgeld was in the same hard-hitting mood when the time came for him to report on "conditions of the state" in his biennial message to the Illinois Legislature that convened in January, 1895. Nothing like his message in its fierce denunciation of "vested interests" and in its bold challenge to the control and manipulation of government by the "privileged few" had ever come from an American governor before. Where his inaugural message of 1893 had been conciliatory, soft and sweetly reasonable, giving assurance of apparent conservatism, this document of 1895 was uncompromising, harshly plain-spoken and acidulous. Deleted of routine state matters, its content was more presidential than gubernatorial, for the problems he attacked were of national significance.

A week before, the *Tribune* got wind of the kind of message Altgeld was preparing and announced that he had "dipped his pen in gall" to prepare a document "full of hot shot." It would make "more of a sensation in politics than did DuMaurier's *Trilby* among literary folk."[23] This was accurate prophecy, for the *Tribune* itself was to receive some of the "hot shot."

CHAPTER THIRTY-TWO

"Government by Injunction!"

1

But the labor problem was the principal topic of the message. Once again he voiced the ideas which characterized his first essay on labor disputes in 1886, but more forcibly now. Machinery for arbitration was no longer a matter for theoretical discussion; it was now a necessity. The recent strikes in coal and rails proved this. If compulsory arbitration was not possible, compulsory *investigation* of labor disputes was, and the state must take action on that type of legislation. It was especially important that the state deal with situations such as the refusal of the Pullman Company to adopt a decent policy toward its former workers displaced by new men brought in to break the strike.

Certainly this was true of conditions typified by Spring Valley. For, at last, a governor of Illinois officially took up the shameful story of that mining community which Henry D. Lloyd had told so dramatically in *The Strike of the Millionaires against the Miners*, and which had sequel after sequel. Declaring for legislation to prohibit the importation into the state of "labor by squads" to displace workers already on the ground, Altgeld placed on the official state records the story of Spring Valley.

"Some years ago a number of non-resident capitalists bought large tracts of coal lands at Spring Valley. . . . Several thousand miners were induced to move there, a very large per cent of whom were Americans, many of whom were induced to buy lots of the company.

"The company then pursued so greedy and unconscionable a course toward its employes, through truck stores and other devices, that the men became restless. Thereupon it displaced almost every American laborer with foreigners. . . . By degrees the new men, finding themselves reduced to intense poverty by the exactions and greed of the company, became sullen and discontented, and last summer the public heard much about the dangerous foreigners at Spring Valley. Last year the company employed a large number of negroes, who

332

are displacing that many of the former employes, who now find themselves without work and without bread."

That situation in Spring Valley, he observed, illustrated the necessity for the government to change from an attitude of *laissez faire* to one of active intervention.

"This company has been a curse and a bill of expense to the State from the time it commenced operations. Almost every administration for a number of years has had to send a military force there to preserve order and protect the property of this concern that was really causing the trouble. . . . While we welcome every honest enterprise and industry, we cannot allow our State to become merely a foraging ground for wolfish greed. *We want no more enterprises of this character.*"[1]

When, it may be asked, had a governor talked that way to labor-exploiting corporations?

2

He continued by linking the labor question to what he called "the marked feature of this age"—capitalistic consolidation, "the large concerns swallowing the small ones or destroying them." The great struggle, he observed, was between combinations of wealth on the one hand and combinations of labor on the other. The "trusts," he declared, possessed the upper hand. "The Scotch brigands never had more effective weapons," he said, with reference to the power of the "trusts" to fix prices and wages.

Having in mind the Pullman strike specifically, he lashed directly at the Federal courts for the rôle they had been playing in the unequal struggle. Anticipating the great court issue of the Franklin D. Roosevelt administration in 1937, he declared:

"In recent years the Constitution seems to have become an insurmountable barrier to every measure intended for the protection of the public, while its most plainly expressed provisions for the protection of the liberty and the personal rights of the citizen are blown away with a mere breath."

This was a definite reference to the imprisonment of hundreds of Pullman strikers by Federal judges for contempt of court, without trial by jury—as happened notably to Debs in Chicago. Next he took up the cry of "anarchy" raised against strikers.

"At present the status seems to be this: Combinations by capital against the public and against labor have succeeded, no matter by what means, and the men who accomplished it are now patriots; while combinations among laborers for self-protection have failed, and the men who advocate it are enemies of society (i.e., 'anarchists').

". . . For several years there has come from certain classes a loud cry of anarchy intended to cover every man who protested against the destruction of American liberty with obloquy. It was a cry of 'Stop thief!' by a class that apparently wished to direct attention from what it was doing. Even if we had anarchists in our country, they could accomplish nothing, for men in rags never yet destroyed a government. They can sometimes destroy some property, but never a government."

The danger lies in another direction, he continued. The danger comes not from "anarchists," nor even trade unionists, but "from that corruption, usurpation, insolence and oppression that go hand in hand with vast concentration of wealth, wielded by unscrupulous men." These would produce "the worst form of government known to man," a "corrupt oligarchy." Moreover, he declared, Big Business was injuring itself and fighting labor unions. The result would be to destroy the purchasing power of the masses, upon which business depends, and also to create so much ill-feeling that vast sums had to be spent for watching property in times of unrest. He added: "Russianizing a government is an expensive business and has never yet succeeded—not even in Russia."[2]

3

Most significant of all in his message was his bold raising, for the first time in America by any figure of importance, of a new national issue: "Government by Injunction." For the next forty years the rôle of the courts, both Federal and state, in issuing injunctions would be the most controversial of all the controversial aspects of the Capital-Labor struggle. In 1932, the national Congress passed the Norris-LaGuardia Act, removing from the Federal courts the power to issue injunctions in labor disputes, and this was the fruit of agitation which Altgeld began on an effective scale in his message of 1895. He did this in connection with a long review of the Pullman strike.

The courts, in issuing their injunctions against labor unions, he declared, are guilty of an "usurpation of power . . . which is destroying the very foundations of republican government."

"During the last two years," he said, "the people of this country have repeatedly witnessed the operation of an entirely new form of government, which was never before heard of among men in either monarchy or republic, that is, *government by injunction.* . . ."

And how does this "new form of government" come into being? It arises when a "federal judge, not content with deciding controversies brought into his court, not content with exercising the judicial functions of government, proceeds to legislate and then administrate." Here, said Altgeld, is the way the system operates:

"He [the judge] issues a ukase which he calls an injunction, forbidding whatever he pleases and what the law does not forbid, and thus legislates for himself without limitation and makes things penal which the law does not make penal, makes other things punishable by imprisonment which at law are only punishable by fine, and he deprives men of the right of trial by jury when the law guarantees this right, and he then enforces this ukase in a summary and arbitrary manner by imprisonment, throwing men into prison, not for violating a law, but for being guilty of contempt of court in disregarding one of these injunctions. . . ."

He added:

"These injunctions are a very great convenience to corporations when they can be had for the asking by a corporation lawyer, and these were the processes of the court to enforce which the President sent the federal troops to Chicago!"

With uncommon clarity and perception, he explained to the legislature how "government by injunction" had developed out of the almost universal practice of placing railroads in Federal court receivership, not for liquidation, but for operation by the court, technically speaking. An "astounding fiction" was developed, he observed. When a railroad is in receivership, "the dignity and sacred presence of the court is supposed to extend over the whole road, and the road is said not to be in the hands of the receivers, as other property is in the hands of the owner, but in the actual possession of the court." And the result?

"If you commit an offense against a railroad that is in the hands of its owners, you will be prosecuted in the county where the offense is committed, tried by jury, and, if proven to be guilty, may be sent to the penitentiary. But if you tread on the grass or throw a stone onto a railroad that has been robbed by speculators and then put into the hands of a receiver to freeze out some stockholders, you will be guilty of a contempt of some court sitting several hundred miles away, and you will be liable to be arrested and carried to where it is, there to be tried, not by a jury or disinterested tribunal, but by that court whose awful dignity you have offended. . . ."

Where such injunctions are outside the law, they are "usurpations," he declared. Even when within the law, they are wrong, "for the Constitution has created other machinery to enforce the law." As for their need, he added, the nation grew great without such legal forms.

"If both the Constitution and our past experience are now to be disregarded, and the federal courts are to be permitted to set up this new form of government, then it will be equally proper for the State courts to do so, and we shall soon have government by injunction from head to toe. All of the affairs of life will be regulated, not by law, but by the personal pleasure, prejudice or caprice of a multitude of judges."[3]

4

Then he gave the legislature in official form his views of the use of Federal troops against the Pullman strikers and his story of his protests to President Cleveland.

"The placing of United States troops on active duty in Chicago under the conditions that existed there last Summer," he declared, "presents a question of the most far-reaching importance, and should receive the most serious consideration of every patriot and of every man who believes in free institutions. . . . The old doctrine of State rights is in no way involved. . . . Federal union and local self-government . . . have for a century been regarded as the foundation upon which the glory of our whole government fabric rests. One is just as sacred, just as inviolable, just as important as the other. Without federal union there must follow anarchy, and without local self-government there must follow despotism. . . . The great civil war settled that we should not have anarchy. It remains to be seen whether we shall be destroyed by despotism. . . .

". . . We grew great and powerful and won the admiration of the world while proceeding under a different form, and if we are to go in the same line, then the American people must arrest and rebuke this federal usurpation. . . . We will have a rapidly increasing central power controlled and dominated by class and by corporate interests. . . ."[4]

In short, he had not backed down a whit from his stand the previous summer, despite the denunciations of the press and of the Cooleys and Depews. If anything, he was more belligerent. Moreover, he had poured salt on the wounds of the Tory class by his spectacular reference to "government by injunction."

The newspapers, of course, howled at him once more. Would that "anarchist" stop at nothing? It was bad enough when he criticised the President. But this insolence in also criticising the Federal courts! Soon this man would be attacking—perish the thought!—the highest court in the land.

As it turned out, Altgeld shortly did direct philippics publicly against the Supreme Court of the United States. For on April 8, 1895, the Supreme Court of the United States rendered a surprising decision.

5

For generations, the Supreme Court had upheld the validity of a Federal income tax. Without such a tax the Civil War could not have been financed. Consequently, when Congress in 1894 adopted the Wilson-Gorman tariff bill with a rider providing restoration of a Federal tax on incomes, scarcely anyone seriously believed that the tax was other than constitutional. Yet, in the decision written by Melville W. Fuller, the Chicago attorney for Marshall Field and other large interests, whom Cleveland picked for Chief Justice, the court now found such a tax unconstitutional.

It was not a unanimous decision. And it was delivered midst ugly rumors of a packed court and the supposed sudden change of mind by one of the justices, but the Tories were none the less pleased. The country had been saved from communism—no less! Had not the great barrister, Joseph H. Choate, so declaimed to the court that this was the case? Incredibly, Mr. Choate was seriously listened to by the justices when he declaimed:

"The act of Congress which we are impugning [the income tax law] . . . is communistic in its purposes and tendencies, and is defended here upon principles as communistic, socialistic—what shall I call them—populistic as ever have been addressed to any political assembly in the world."[5]

Altgeld was scathingly sarcastic in his public comment on the decision. "The Supreme Court," he declared, has "come to the rescue [of] the Standard Oil kings, the Wall Street people, as well as the rich mugwumps." They had been bitter over passage of the income tax act, now they are "again happy. But," he said, "the great business and producing classes do not share their joy. . . . Their burden is made a little heavier and the whip has made a new welt on their backs, but what of it? In fact, what are they for, if not to bear burdens and to be lashed?"

He went on to observe that "this decision is radically defective in a number of particulars." It should have contained a "panegyric on the majesty of the law and the exact character of eternal justice." Also, "it should have contained a stinging rebuke to the growing discontent of the times." But he added it would be "unreasonable" to expect the court to think of everything. "It will have other opportunities from time to time to solidify our institutions and to teach patriotism by coming down with terrific force upon some wretch whose vulgarity and unpatriotic character will be proven by the fact that he is poor." Still, he continued, the decision "suggests a most important question to the American people." The judges of the Supreme Court wear large black gowns, "to impress the people with their infallibility."

"Now, as these gowns are not very thick, and as some people might be able to see through them and be unpatriotic enough to question the justice of having to bear the burdens of government while the rich escape, and as there is danger that some of these men may doubt the infallibility of the court, would it not be well to have each judge wear two gowns for a while, until the storm blows over?"[6]

Even for the "new" Altgeld that was strong language to apply to the highest tribunal of the land, but a few weeks hence he was to use even stronger. The following June the Supreme Court gave its decision in the case entitled "*In Re Debs, Petitioner*." This was on an appeal taken from the jail sentence given Eugene Debs by Judge Woods for alleged contempt of court in connection with the Pullman strike. With Lyman Trumbull, Clarence Darrow and S. S. Gregory defending Debs, arguments similar to the position taken by Altgeld against "government by injunction" were presented to the court. It was maintained especially that Debs under the constitution was entitled to a trial before a jury, instead of being simply tried by the very judge whose order he was accused of violating. Likewise, the right of the court to issue an injunction at all was vigorously attacked. But the Supreme Court, unanimous this time, upheld every act of the Federal government and the courts in connection with the Pullman episode. The court even went out of its way to approve the use of Federal troops, although this point was technically not at issue. In short, President Cleveland and Mr. Olney won a complete victory. Newspaper reporters wondered if Altgeld had anything to say now. He had plenty, he said.

6

First he observed that the Debs case decision "marks a turning point in our history, for it established a new form of government never before heard of among men, that is government by injunction." Then he paid his respects to the court.

"For a number of years it has been marked that the decisions of the United States courts were nearly always in favor of corporations. Then it was noticed that no man could be appointed to a federal judgeship unless he was satisfactory to those interests. Over a year ago The New York World talked about a packed court, and that court has within a few days rendered two decisions which unfortunately tend to confirm this charge. A [month] ago it did violence to the Constitution and the laws of the land by holding that the government has no power to tax the rich of this country. Now it has stricken down trial by jury and has established government by injunction."

He compared the condition of the country to pre-slavery days and observed: "Forty years ago the slave power predominated; today it is capitalism." He quoted George William Curtis' description of the slavery period as a time when "slavery sat in the White House and made laws in the capitol; courts of justice were its ministers and legislatures were its lackeys." It was only necessary, he said, to substitute the word, "capitalism" for "slavery" to make Curtis' comment fit the present day.

"Just see what a brood of evils has sprung from the power of capitalism since 1870.

"1. The striking down of over one-third of the money of the world, thus crushing the debtor class and paralyzing industry.

"2. The growing of that corrupt use of wealth which is undermining our institutions, debauching public officials, shaping legislation and creating judges who do its bidding.

"3. Exemption of the rich from taxation.

"4. The substitution of government by injunction for government by the Constitution and laws.

"5. The striking down of trial by jury."

To which he added:

"Never has there been so much patriotic talk as in the last twenty-five years—and never were there so many influences at work strangling Republican institutions."[7]

Once again, from coast to coast, the newspapers called for his head. The New York *Times* suggested that "the people of Illinois should ascertain whether the Governor has clearly violated the laws" as "an inquiry about this matter might disclose some ground upon which they could get rid of him."[8] In Chicago, the *Tribune*, as usual, let loose blast after blast. It printed approvingly a "letter to the editor" which called Altgeld "an Aaron Burr without his brains—a Johann Most without his decency—a Eugene Debs without his courage. . . ."[9]

7

This time, however, Altgeld scarcely could complain about the attitude of the *Tribune* toward him. For, in accord with his new character, he had struck back. He did this first in his message to the Legislature. In that message he discussed the general taxing system in the state, which he branded as a "giant of injustice" in that "owners of small and moderate sized properties are forced to bear nearly all the burdens of government." Then he deliberately singled out the Tribune Company as an example of a large corporation permitted apparent special tax privileges.

"For example," he wrote, "one of the oldest daily morning newspapers of Chicago has for very many years annually earned net profits amounting to upwards of $250,000, which would be large dividends on between $3,000,000 and $4,000,000. During last summer the owners of this paper refused to accept a cash offer of $3,000,000 for that property, thus showing that they valued it at a still higher figure. Yet the company which owns this paper pays taxes on an assessment of only $18,000."[10]

Having stuck his lance thus far into the *Tribune*, he gave it a twist, continuing:

"The publishers of this great paper assume the right, almost, to dictate to the community upon every public question. They assume the right to denounce whomsoever they please. They are in a sense above and beyond the law, for a poor private individual has no practical remedy against an unjust attack upon its part, and yet they manage to throw the burden of supporting our government upon the shoulders of others."[11]

He admitted, of course, that the *Tribune* was not alone. "There are thousands of men in this State who have great fortunes invested in stocks, bonds and other forms of personal property upon which they do not pay a dollar [in taxes], yet they enjoy all . . . of the advantages of government." To which he added, sarcastically: "Curiously enough, these are very often the men who have the most to say about patriotism and the duties of citizenship."[12]

Then, in March he followed with an even stronger attack on the *Tribune*. In a special message to the Legislature, he called attention to ownership of valuable land in downtown Chicago by the Chicago School Board and to the fact that this land is leased to private companies, one of which was the Tribune Company. He flatly charged that rentals assessed by a public board were out of line with real values, hence the lessors were profiting at the expense of the public. He asked emergency legislation "to compel the payment of such rental in the future as the ground is worth."

The *Tribune* was cited by him as a major offender. "In comparison with what other property in the same locality is paying, it is clear that the *Tribune* lot is worth nearly three times the rent it now pays." This means, he asserted, that "the owners of the *Tribune* have for a number of years been pocketing in the neighborhood of $25,000 a year that should have gone to the school fund."

Nor was this all that he had to say about the newspaper in the special message. There was the matter of its capital stock taxes mentioned in his general message of January ninth. He advised the legislature that if the Tribune Company were assessed for taxes "on the same basis as other property," it would be forced to pay approximately $40,000 a year, instead of about $1,500. "This," he said, "added to what should have gone to the school fund, makes over $60,000 a year that has been diverted from the public into the hands of private individuals in this one instance."

As a final thrust, he concluded:

"As these newspapers have much to say about patriotism and higher citizenship, they should set a better example. Waving the flag with one hand and plundering the public with the other is a form of patriotism that is getting entirely too common and is doing infinite harm to our country."[13]

8

For three days, the *Tribune* pondered. Then came the predictable scorching editorial: "Altgeld's Ignoble Revenge." Governor Altgeld had "paid the *Tribune* an unusual compliment by making it the subject of a special communication to the Legislature." The *Tribune* "inferred" from the "bitter declamation" that the Governor did not like that newspaper, although it did not see why anybody else should be "interested." Then it entered a blanket denial of all the direct or implied charges Altgeld had voiced, although observing his statements "are so pitifully false and puerile that they are scarcely worthy to be dignified by a serious answer." Yet it was answering because "there are many persons who delight in imputing bad motives to others and would rather believe evil than good of their neighbors."

It was true, said the *Tribune*, that it leased some school land, but the land was not nearly so valuable as the Governor professed to believe. The *Tribune* had offered to sell its leasehold three years before "and could get no responsible bidder for it." If it were not tied to the land by ownership of its improvements, it would "gladly move elsewhere." The Governor was in error about the taxes it paid, for actually the *Tribune* paid $5,800 more than the Governor stated, counting the taxes on its improvements. The Governor in declaring it should be assessed at $3,000,000 meant it should be taxed on its good will.

"Well," said the editorial, "we thank the Governor for his appreciation of the esteem in which the *Tribune* is held by the people who read it." If the esteem of its readers was worth $3,000,000, "presumably $2,900,000 of it arises from the fact that they have as little sympathy with Altgeld's peculiar doctrines as the *Tribune* has. . . ." If good will is taxes, it added, "Altgeld would be entirely exempt, while the *Tribune* would be mulcted in a heavy sum simply because it does not approve of his conduct."

And its final retort:

"Vale, Altgeld! Hail and Farewell! You have contributed to the innocent gaieties of the Lenten season. . . . But you have not deceived the world, the flesh or the devil. They all know you for what you are and claim you as their own, not better, not nobler, not fairer than other men, but if anything a trifle more malicious, a shade more unscrupulous, and far more revengeful than the average of mortals."[14]

9

But the *Tribune's* "*vale*" was uttered too soon. Within a few weeks it was to hear from Altgeld again—and more viciously than before. This time Altgeld used his pardoning power to further his "war" against the newspaper. In 1893, one Louis A. Hilliard was sentenced to prison as an embezzler and given a four-year term. The complainant was the Chicago *Tribune*, which had employed him as assistant cashier. Hilliard confessed an embezzlement of $13,000. Early in 1895, friends of the cashier filed a petition for a pardon, holding that he had been punished sufficiently, had made restitution of some of the money he had taken and that they would see that he obtained employment to assure full restitution and his proper return to society. On April twenty-eighth, Altgeld issued a pardon for Hilliard.

When the *Tribune* first heard of the pardon, it reported the fact as simply a matter of news, observing that "the pardon was not accompanied by the usual statement assigning the reasons for the exercise of executive clemency." But the next day the *Tribune* learned that there was a statement of reasons filed with the Secretary of State. The reaction of the *Tribune* editors to the statement was plainly indicated by its headlines on May first:

HE VENTS HIS SPITE

J. P. Altgeld Pardons Hilliard to Spite "The Tribune"—Utter Meanness and Littleness of the Governor of the Great State of Illinois Shown by His Use of An Executive Prerogative to Gratify A Personal Enmity—Embezzler Let Out of Prison in the Face of a Protest from His Wronged Employers—Governor's "Reasons."

10

There was a good deal of basis for those *Tribune* headline declarations. For after stating that he was assured that the prisoner had been punished enough and that he felt the ends of justice did not require Hilliard, in view of his previous record, to remain longer in prison, Altgeld declared in the pardon statement:

"There is another point suggested by this case and that is, how far the integrity and sense of right of young men employed in some large money-making establishment is undermined and weakened by a knowledge of the fact that their employers are gaining large sums of money which, while not always obtained by criminal means, nevertheless in equity and good conscience do not belong to them.

"This young man had charge of the financial department of the Tribune Company. He knew that the Tribune Company rented ground in the Chicago school fund and instead of paying a fair cash annual rental on it, had managed to get things so fixed that it pocketed in the neighborhood of $25,000 a year of money which ought to have gone to the school fund. He also knew . . . that it annually pocketed in the neighborhood of $40,000 which should have gone into the public treasury as taxes if the Tribune Company had paid the same proportion of taxes on its property that other people paid on theirs.

"In other words, he saw that the Tribune Company annually pocketed upwards of $60,000 of money which, in equity and good conscience, should have belonged to the public treasury, and he saw that notwithstanding this fact the owners of The Tribune were eminent and highly respected citizens. The natural effect of all this was to weaken the moral force of the young man, as well as his sense of integrity. There is no question that similar conditions exist in other large offices and, while this cannot be any excuse for the commission of crime by employes, it is a fact that is to be deplored and some remedy should be found."[15]

In the case of that pardon statement Altgeld's admirers probably must concede that the Tribune was justified in directing bitter criticism at him. There was a degree of pettiness in combining his antipathy for the Tribune with the exercise of his pardoning function, even though the pardon itself may have been justified. But could the Tribune have said that it did not abuse its own powers in a similar way?

In time, the Tribune editors "forgave" the pardon of the anarchists and also Altgeld's position in the Pullman strike. At least, its criticism of those acts was much tempered. But the Hilliard pardon never was forgotten or forgiven. It was a rare day after that when the name of Altgeld appeared in the Tribune except abusively. Yet not the Tribune nor the Cooleys nor the Depews figured in Altgeld's mind as the chief target of the counter-attacks he launched in this second half of his governorship.

The President of the United States was the man for whom he was really gunning.

CHAPTER THIRTY-THREE

National Leadership—and Revenge

1

WHEN Mr. Justice Brewer, he who had compared Altgeld to Jefferson Davis, cleared his throat on the bench of the United States Supreme Court to intone the decision in the Debs case, Grover Cleveland believed with great self-satisfaction that the court was voicing the "concluding words" in the controversy between himself and Altgeld in the Pullman matter.[1] But Cleveland was wrong.

Still to be heard from was the Democratic party—and the party at just that time was showing marked symptoms of open revolt against the man who had been its standard-bearer in three presidential campaigns. This revolt against Cleveland had been brewing from the beginning of his second term. It started when he resisted immediate action to revise downward the scandalous McKinley tariff—this despite the definite platform and personal commitments. When instead Cleveland called Congress into special session to repeal the Sherman Silver Purchase Act, the rebellion flared openly and fiercely. No matter how sound his economics might have been at the time, the President had committed the scarlet sin where large sections of his party were concerned. At best, the Sherman Act had been a mere sop to the silverites and the currency expansionists, for while it was supposed to atone for the "Crime of '73" it did not actually remonetize silver at all. Yet, sop that it was, even this was now removed. By ending government purchase of silver bullion, Cleveland had emulated in effect the British action in India and placed the nation upon the single gold standard!

Wall Street praised him. He had saved the nation from calamity. Republicans, save those from the silver mine states and other sections of the West, cried hallelujah. The "old guard" of the Democracy lauded him, chiefly those of the East. But the rank and file of the Democracy—the cotton growers of the South and the farmers of the West—the voters who had placed Cleveland in the White House again, these felt outrageously betrayed. They did not understand

345

then, nor later, the financial mysteries involved in the various monetary standards. But they did understand, from personal knowledge, that money was scarce and dear. And there was Cleveland, by a policy which the plutocrats hailed so joyously, making money even scarcer and dearer. So they felt.

Out of that sense of betrayal was born a new major political issue—and a new slogan. The issue was silver, and the slogan "Sixteen to One!" Since the early 'eighties, that issue and to a lesser extent the slogan had been heard in the political arena, but only in undertones. Now, thanks to Cleveland, it suddenly became the foremost political topic in the land. "Silver Dick" Bland of Missouri, "Pitchfork Ben" Tillman of South Carolina, the Populist leaders of the West and the young Nebraska Congressman William Jennings Bryan wore out their lungs on a thousand stumps to make it so.

Not since the Abolition days had any cause so inflamed the masses. In Kansas, the farmers roared approval when an amazing woman orator, one Mary Elizabeth Lease, a veritable political amazon, toured the state declaiming: "Kansas had better stop raising corn and begin raising hell!"[2] The "poor whites" of the South similarly cheered fiery one-eyed Ben Tillman when he promised to "stick my pitchfork into Grover Cleveland" if he were sent to the United States Senate. He was sent. When an energetic lawyer named William Hope Harvey in 1894 published an economic oddity entitled "Coin's Financial School," an allegorical argument for free silver, the pamphlet swept the nation. Its sales finally reached 2,000,000.

As the movement grew, it took on aspects of religious frenzy. Passionate hatreds were stirred, with Cleveland, to Altgeld's intense satisfaction later, the object of most of the hatred. "I have bin a Democrat always but would not now voat for Cleaveland Again for President to save him from the hangman," wrote a southern farmer, who felt that "with a few million Airs contracting the money in use to be able to buy too dollars worth of property with one dollar, this is no longer A free country."[3] His was a typical sentiment.

2

And Altgeld? In the beginning, he appears to have taken no more than an academic interest in the money question, although he must have studied it. He "never cared much about the money question," a close associate would recall.[4] There was some truth in that, and it explains why he was remarkably restrained in expressing his views prior to 1894. His restraint on the issue—he did not so much as mention it in his governorship campaign—was, in fact, so marked as to cause even close political associates to doubt if he was sincere when he finally emerged as a foremost advocate of free coinage of silver.[5] But in this they were wrong.

He had always been something of a bimetallist, even though rather passively so. At least, he never strayed far from the Granger economics that he had picked up in his Missouri days and spouted during his campaign for prosecuting attorney in Savannah. In Grangerism "cheap money" was integral. Thus, when repeal of the Sherman Act was under consideration, he voiced the idea that it should be replaced by an act providing for use an even greater volume of currency. In a statement given to the New York *Herald* on July thirty-first, 1894, he argued that money in the business world performs the same function as blood in the human body "and seems to be governed by similar laws."

Insufficient supply of either, he said, produces weakness. "Before the circulation of the blood was understood," he wrote, "bleeding was the universal treatment. When a patient was already weak, the doctor at once bled him. So with our money doctors. When the world is suffering because the volume of money is insufficient . . . all the remedies these learned doctors can prescribe is to take a little more blood out of the patient."[6]

Again, in October, 1893, writing for the St. Louis *Republic*, he expressed dissatisfaction with the quantity of money in circulation, although he then offered no definite cure. The following month, when asked for his explanation for Democratic reverses suffered in the elections that year, he criticized repeal of the Sherman law and adoption of a single gold standard. This statement was especially significant in that Altgeld, then for the first time, openly assailed Cleveland, blaming him for the party defeats. "The country had spoken on the subject of tariff reform," he declared, "but instead of acting on this decision, Mr. Cleveland, with sublime self-sufficiency, ignored it, and went chasing after the deceiving swamp light of a single gold standard." This, he said, meant that "the eastern and foreign manipulators seemed to have gotten complete control of the financial policy of the government."[7]

It should be noted that those remarks about Cleveland were made six months before the Pullman strike. Thus it was untrue, as many believed, that Altgeld's break with Cleveland was based solely upon Cleveland's action in the Pullman matter. The seeds were there already, going back, indeed, to his bolting the Democracy in his Missouri days, for Cleveland was the direct descendant of the Tilden Democracy of 1876.

3

Yet there is reason to believe that if the Pullman controversy had not arisen, Altgeld might have played only a minor rôle, if any, in the great silver uprising. For one thing, he was by no means yet wedded to the silver cause as such. In an address at Mattoon, Illinois, as late as October, 1894, he declared that while he favored expanding the currency, he had "nothing to say for silver or for any other kind of money."[8] He was simply interested in enough of any kind of money, gold if it were plentiful. Later, he would make it clear that he did not share the belief that there was anything sacred in the ratio of sixteen to one; any other practical ratio would satisfy him.

More important, his health was such that he seriously hoped to retire from active politics. It is certain that he did not want to go through another campaign for that reason alone.

Again, by the middle of 1894, his personal finances were in wretched shape, for he, too, was a victim of the depression and convinced that if he were to save himself from financial ruin it was vital that he soon begin to devote full time to his personal business. That very fall, his financial affairs had led to an extremely embarrassing situation. Needing to borrow relatively large sums because of the Walsh "treachery," he was accommodated by Rufus N. Ramsay, a banker at Carlyle, Illinois, who was elected state treasurer with him in 1892. He and Ramsay had been on intimate terms and apparently Altgeld had full confidence in the banker. It seems certain that Altgeld believed that Ramsay was loaning him money from the Ramsay bank, for which Altgeld signed notes or put up Unity Block stock as security.

In November, 1894, State Treasurer Ramsay died suddenly, after which it was discovered that he was short some $300,000 in state funds. The treasurer had been lending out the state money and it was from this source that he had accommodated Altgeld. In the state treasury itself, in fact, were found the notes that Altgeld had given Ramsay for loans totaling about $50,000.

That was a predicament! To leave the notes in the vault would produce just the kind of scandal his opponents would relish most. To remove the notes, and replace them with cash, meant committing a technical violation of the law. The law was that when a vacancy in the treasury occurred, the vaults must be sealed and kept sealed until a successor is appointed. Altgeld chose to commit the technical violation, and then was faced with the problem of getting the money to make the replacements. Hectic hours passed. The story was that "Buck" Hinrichsen came to his aid with a hurried trip to several sections of the state to borrow funds from various bankers. Hinrichsen later denied the story, but it seems to be true.[9]

After that close call—public exposure might have been disastrous even though the state lost not a penny because of Altgeld's arrangement with Ramsay—Altgeld had the problem of paying back the new loans. In Chicago, the only bankers who would lend "that anarchist governor" any money were the owners of small private banks, like that operated by E. S. Dreyer. He found himself driven by desperation to another technically questionable procedure—borrowing from downstate bankers who had on deposit funds of various state institutions. He made certain now that the money did belong to the banks, but the act gave the *Tribune* occasion to editorialize, when some of the loans became known, that "gentlemen who wish to keep their reputations free from the shadow of suspicion do not act as the governor has acted."[10]

The Unity Block, of course, was responsible for his fix. If he were ever to get out of it, he would have to be able to operate as a private individual—unless he wished to use the governorship for raising money in ways truly questionable. He had such opportunities, as will be noted later. And John W. Lanehart was not averse to having him take some such opportunities. But while Altgeld would commit minor technical breaches to save himself, he would go no farther. For every selfish reason, then, he ought to have foregone any more active politics, least of all the kind of politics certain to antagonize the financial interests still further. Standing for free silver, for example.

4

But after the Pullman episode, he threw himself into politics with even greater vigor than at any time in his career—and on the side of free silver. Here was an issue—fortunately one in which he could honestly believe—that promised to be the means by which he could even scores with the man in the White House, and also at last enable him to realize his major political ambition of "modifying the political machinery of the nation." Once that was clear to him, the silver cause had no more vigorous champion. By sheer industry in reading and digesting all the literature, he made himself the outstanding authority on the silver side, certainly the most learned in the political world. For, while the Bryans and Tillmans uttered phrases and slogans, Altgeld's utterances were characterized by logic, facts and figures.

Yet, despite the high scholastic caliber of his declarations on the money question, it must be stated that when it came to dealing with Cleveland personally, he was anything but academic. Hatred, as much as sincere political conviction, swayed him there. The Chicago *Daily News* once observed:

"The governor's hatred of the President now has reached the stage . . . where it is quite uncontrollable. If the name of Cleveland is mentioned in his presence he goes off into a fit. . . . The general fact of his affliction should be borne in mind and whenever he is invited to appear in public, other guests should be warned against mentioning Cleveland, federal troops, capital or any of the other topics which excite him into convulsions."[11]

That was caricature—but it had a basis.

Upon any and every occasion, he devoted himself to the work of destroying Cleveland's hold on the party. Typical was his response when he was invited to a dinner of the Democratic Iroquois Club in Chicago in April, 1895, to commemorate the birthday of Thomas Jefferson. Because the main speeches would be delivered by Cleveland supporters, he refused to be present, holding that the occasion would be converted into "a kind of Cleveland love-feast." "To laud Clevelandism on Jefferson's birthday," he declared, "is to sing a Te Deum in honor of Judas Iscariot on a Christmas morning!" Cleveland, he thundered, was the exact antithesis of Jefferson.

"Jeffersonism was the first-born of the new age of liberty and human progress, while Clevelandism is the slimy off-spring of that unhallowed marriage between Standard Oil and Wall Street. Jeffersonism brought liberty, prosperity and greatness to our country because it gave its benediction to the great toiling and producing masses, while Clevelandism has put its heel upon the neck of our people, has increased the burdens and the sorrows of the men who toil, and has fattened a horde of vultures that are eating the vitals of the nation. . . . Jefferson's eye took in the continent from the Atlantic to the Pacific. Cleveland is today ignorant of the fact that there is a country west of the Alleghenies. Jefferson belonged to the American people; Cleveland to the men who devour widows' homes. Jeffersonism is an illumination on the American firmament; Clevelandism merely a swamp-light floating around in the Standard Oil marsh."[12]

So Altgeld on Cleveland, until the President in fact was read out of the party.

5

In the struggle within the Democratic party in the developing days of the silver question, as also later, Altgeld's position could be the controlling factor, providing he played his cards right. Both sides of the furiously contending forces recognized this. For after New York and Pennsylvania, the Prairie State had the greatest number of votes in the national convention and in the electoral college. Just as important, Illinois was the key state in the real battleground—the Middle West. The central and far western states were counted certain for silver—just as the eastern states were certain for gold. The South wavered at first, although the odds favored silver. If Illinois went silver, the chances were that other middle western states would follow. Then the southern silverites would be encouraged and strengthened—and the trick would be turned. Such was the geographical-political picture.

There was the factor, too, that, more than any other figure in public life, Altgeld could influence the labor vote—not only in Illinois but through the nation. Unlike the farmers, industrial wage-earners were on the fence where the currency was concerned. But if anybody could swing labor to free silver, it was Altgeld, worshipped as he was by labor everywhere for his stand in the Pullman strike and also for his Haymarket pardon. A reflection of this was "Altgeld for president" booms started by labor unions in several parts of the country. In Georgia, labor groups seriously discussed finding a way of electing him president despite his foreign birth. He was, they said, their "ideal statesman."[13]

It was certain that where he led, laboring men by the thousands would follow. As would be stated by the Chicago Record, the working-men, even if lukewarm on silver, "appear willing to give him at least passive support on any monetary policy which he may choose to advocate" because they have "come to believe in Altgeld."[14]

6

He lost no time in contriving to consolidate the Illinois Democracy behind the silver cause. After the first year of his term, his office had been singularly free from the atmosphere of open politics. Things were more, as Brand Whitlock would relate, on the side of "intellectual culture." When he was not occupied with administrative matters, he would spend his evenings reading or discussing books—the novels of Meredith, Howells and Tolstoi mainly—with Mrs. Altgeld or with Brand Whitlock and Private Secretary Dose, who were frequent dinner guests. Once in a while he would read poetry aloud to Mrs. Altgeld and a "dreamy look would come over his face."[15] But now the Governor's quarters at the capital and mansion took on the appearance of campaign headquarters. He endlessly interviewed key leaders, dictated letters, went over the texts of agitation pamphlets and prepared speeches, all to fan the silver sentiment.

Speed was the essence of his strategy. Put the party in Illinois on record immediately, without waiting for the state and national conventions in 1896—such was the plan. Strike while the silver agitation was at its height—thus offset the danger of off-stage manipulation of delegates when convention time came around. Cleveland held the party machinery, controlled most of the national committeemen. And so, as he said to Governor Stone of Missouri, "it was absolutely necessary to build a fire, and a big one, in the rear of those committeemen."[16]

7

The "fire" ignited in April, 1895. Controlled by Altgeld, the state Democratic committee that month sensationally took the irregular step of calling a special party convention on the currency question to meet in Springfield on June 5, 1895. A howl went up from the Cleveland Democrats. The convention was unnecessary. It was illegal. It would split the party. Moving heaven and earth to prevent the gathering, they enlisted President Cleveland himself in their maneuvers. From the White House, on April thirteenth, the President dispatched a long letter to the so-called Honest Money League of Chicago in which he sought to discredit the silver movement as fallacious and dangerous to the nation.[17]

But instead of the clarion call which the Chicago Goldbugs expected, Cleveland's letter was a "long lecture . . . verbose and ponderous" (Professor Nevins' characterization).[18] Altgeld ripped into it caustically. "If it had any other name than that of the President signed to it, nobody would give it any attention. If I had signed such a document, it would be ridiculed all over the country. . . . Its weakness almost excites pity." If, he added, it was written to start a gold-standard boom, "the boomlet will be 'such a little one' that it will not reflect upon the virtue of its mother."[19]

As it turned out, Altgeld had sized up exactly the effect of Cleveland's epistle on silver. It proved, not a boom-starter, but a boomerang. As Bryan would say, looking back on the '96 campaign, Cleveland's letter proved "unexpected aid" to the silver cause.[20] One sentence alone proved fatal if Cleveland's idea was to hold the party together. In Illinois as elsewhere, thousands of Democrats were silverites but hesitated at disavowing their party leader. Yet Cleveland had written: "Disguise it as we may, the line of battle is drawn between the forces of safe currency and those of silver monometallism."[21] What did that mean if not that Cleveland was disavowing the silverites, inviting them to stand against him? They took the invitation.

The Illinois silver convention of 1895 was a complete triumph for silver—and for Altgeld. The night before, hundreds of delegates marched to the Executive Mansion for an impromptu serenade to the Governor. When Altgeld showed himself on the porch, the cheering awoke the sleeping town of Springfield. Cries of "Altgeld! Altgeld! Altgeld!" blended with martial strains of the popular Cook County Marching Club band. It was a scene which brought a pleasurable flush of color even to Altgeld's pale face as he bowed to the throng in acknowledgment of their plaudits.[22] From the Mansion porch, Altgeld in a short extemporaneous speech voiced the sentiment which would prove the basis for the ultimate victory of the silver forces over Clevelandism. "No alliances and no compromise!" And that evening, with "Bathhouse John" Coughlin, Chicago's famous alderman, as cheerleader, the Democracy learned a new war cry:

"Rah! Rah! Rah! Sixteen to One!"

That scene was duplicated at the convention the next day. Even the *Tribune*, which previously had been assuring its readers that the Illinois Democracy was "sick of Altgeld and wished he would get out,"[23] admitted that his appearance on the convention platform was the signal for an outburst of cheering "which lasted fully five minutes" and left no doubt that the party was wholly under his control.[24] His address set the keynote of the gathering:

"The time has come when the Democratic party must again stand for Democracy, and no longer for plutocracy!"[25]

8

Repercussions of the Illinois currency convention were national in scope. To silverites everywhere Altgeld had shown the way for committing the party to the silver cause in advance of the '96 convention. In quick succession, special silver conventions assembled in other states. In a single week, Texas, Mississippi and Missouri followed Illinois' lead, all declaring for silver at sixteen to one. In August, a national free silver committee was organized in Washington, composed chiefly of anti-Cleveland members of the United States Senate, a group later to be known as the "Senatorial Clique" of the Chicago convention.[26] With these senators Altgeld worked in close rapport. By the following spring, with the national convention only a few months away, it was already plain that the silver forces of the Middle West, the South and the West were likely to win complete control of the party despite all that Cleveland and his administration leaders were doing to check the avalanche.

And Cleveland was doing much. It was no secret that the Federal patronage was being used in efforts to stem the tide, this to an extent in some states that reached scandalous proportions for all of Cleveland's undoubtedly honest devotion to the civil service principle.[27] But he looked upon the silver "lunacy" as far more vicious than spoils could be. Ohio was narrowly saved by such tactics. Similarly Michigan was held partially in line. Especially did Cleveland concentrate upon the Solid South, making personal efforts to raise a special campaign fund to educate the southern Democracy on the fallacies of free silver. In October, 1895, he injected himself into the southern picture by attending the Cotton States Exposition at Atlanta, taking along the cleverest politicians of his cabinet to assist in missionary work, and making an address which was interpreted as an effort to keep the South in line. But when Altgeld followed Cleveland to Atlanta the next month, heading an official Illinois delegation to the exposition, he found himself a hero to the southern masses, and boldly struck at Cleveland in his characteristic fashion. In effect, he succeeded in counteracting Cleveland's trip.

9

President Cleveland and Banker Walsh were on friendly terms[28] and this may (though not necessarily) explain a peculiar and revealing incident that happened to Altgeld in the spring of 1896 in connection with the silver fight.

One of Walsh's associates, Fred L. Blount, had called on Altgeld in the fall of 1894 and inquired "in a friendly sort of way," as related later by Altgeld, how the Governor was getting on. Altgeld answered that he was "hard up" and pointedly mentioned that this was because of Walsh. Blount dropped the suggestion that it might be a good idea for Altgeld to see Walsh, that perhaps the banker would redeem the original Unity Company agreement. Altgeld accepted the suggestion—foolishly as it turned out, for it had all the earmarks of bait to ensnare him once more in Walsh's web.

He found Walsh surprisingly amiable, which probably should have warned Altgeld. But he was desperate, and took Walsh's word for it when the banker indicated that he was ready to make amends. Walsh declared that he would float another bond issue on the Unity Building for $400,000, the new bonds to be substituted for the old. He specifically assured Altgeld that he would buy the additional $100,-000. "I will take the $100,000, and then you will be in the same position as you would have been had we not canceled the old $100,000," he said.[29]

Altgeld was jubilant. But after the new bonds had been issued, he found Walsh slow in carrying through his new promise. Walsh asked for "more time," not once but several times. Finally, Altgeld made a strong appeal to the banker. "Mr. Walsh, I am carrying that $100,000 and it is breaking me down!"[30] But the banker again asked more time. In the end, Walsh declared that he could not take the $100,000 after all, but he would have his bank advance Altgeld $35,000 as a personal loan on Altgeld's note, until a more favorable time for issuing the bonds.

Altgeld was forced to agree. The note was for sixty days. Before its expiration, Altgeld again saw the banker. He wanted to know if the bonds could then be sold, for he could not pay the note.

"Oh, renew it!" Walsh said. "It ain't troubling you any. Renew it. Let it run." By then, Altgeld was worried. He recalled to Walsh that not only had he failed to buy the additional $100,000 bonds, but had taken no steps to substitute new bonds for any of the old, in accord with their new agreement. "I told you I would take care of it," said Walsh. "Why are you troubling yourself about it?" By then it was clear to Altgeld that he had been trapped again. But what was Walsh up to? Altgeld found out in the spring of 1896, when the free silver issue was nearing a head. He had again called on Walsh about renewal of the note. Once again Walsh gave his approval for the extension. But as Altgeld prepared to leave, the banker stopped him. "By the way, you are governor," Walsh began. "You can help get the Democratic party to take the right position on this money question that is coming up this summer. We have got to have a declaration for 'sound money.'"

Altgeld looked the banker in the eye. He had not come to discuss politics, he said. "I have come here to fix up a business matter. Besides, on this money question, I have got pretty strong convictions, and I have expressed them to the public. I could not shift my position on that without stultifying myself, and I could not do it!"

On hearing that, Walsh "got very angry," so Altgeld later testified. "Well! We have that note of yours. I want it paid. We want the money and be done with this thing!"

Altgeld reminded him of his earlier willingness to approve a renewal. He pointed out that the whole present arrangement was at Walsh's suggestion, that he would not have been dealing with him again at all if Walsh had not brought up the matter. "No difference!" growled Walsh. "Pay the bank!"[31]

Altgeld left, with the necessity of immediately raising $35,000 on top of all of his other borrowings—either that or "stultify" himself. Fortunately, he still had a bit more property left, including his home, and managed to get a loan from the Illinois National Bank to cover the Walsh note. He was worse off then than before.

10

But he pulled no punches on the free silver issue. Instead, he hit harder than ever. In April, 1896, Cleveland dispatched John G. Carlisle, his secretary of the treasury and the most able opponent of free silver in the Cleveland camp, to Chicago for an address. Carlisle was to counteract Altgeld's influence and win labor to the gold standard. The Kentuckian gave an able address. It was called unanswerable. But Altgeld answered it a few weeks later in the same auditorium, giving his notable "Non-Partisan Speech on the Money Question."[32] Most devastating of all was his revelation that the Secretary of the Treasury while a member of Congress in 1878 had voiced views on the money question identical with those of the free silverites. He quoted Carlisle as branding the demonetization of silver in 1873 as "the most gigantic crime of this or any other age," a scheme that "would ultimately entail more misery upon the human race than all the wars, pestilence and famine that ever occurred in the history of the world."

Just as devastating, Altgeld went after the *Tribune* in that address, showing that the paper which now was referring to the silver advocates as "lunatics," "liars," "hypocrites" and "scoundrels" had likewise formerly just as vociferously denounced the demonetization of silver. Editorial after editorial from the *Tribune*, all for silver, were quoted by him, including one that declared: "The folly of advocating the single gold standard of money must be obvious to everyone not blind as a bat in the daylight."[33] Who was now "blind as a bat"? The audience yelled its delight.

Through many such addresses, interviews and letters, Altgeld kept the silver sentiment in Illinois at fever pitch in preparation for the regular state Democratic convention in June, 1896. Until that convention met, the Cleveland forces believed there was still hope to "save" the party. With the nation eyeing it, the 1896 Illinois state convention assembled at Peoria on June twenty-third. Could Altgeld repeat this triumph of the currency convention the year before? Keen observers saw that there was only one answer. As stated prior to the session by the independent Chicago Record, it was plain that "the Peoria convention [would] be more absolutely under the control of Governor Altgeld than was the [national Republican] convention at St. Louis under the domination of Mark Hanna."[34] This was an accurate forecast. Without a hitch, Altgeld had all of the state's forty-eight delegates pledged to silver, and made himself chairman of the delegation.

For Cleveland, the news from Illinois plainly was the beginning of the end. He knew this. It was an embittered and sulking Cleveland who left Washington a few days later for the solitude of his home at Coral Gables. There closeted even from friends, he awaited the inevitable news from the national convention.

11

About the same time, a triumphant Altgeld entrained from Springfield to Chicago for the convention. In his shrewd brain were stirring plans which, if Cleveland had known of them, would have made the President a hundred times more bitter than he was. "With his success [at the Peoria convention] Altgeld becomes one of the most important of the factors that are to figure in the national party," observed the Chicago Record a week before the convention. "He will have a big part in naming not only the issue, but the candidate to be selected here next month. Much of the influence leading the other state conventions to adopt free silver will be ascribed to the Illinois Democratic organization, and that organization just now represents what Altgeld wants."[35]

All of which was true. Consigned to political oblivion exactly three years before for his action in the Haymarket case, vilified, hooted at and spat upon ever since by the so-called dominant elements everywhere, he was on his way to the Chicago convention unquestionably in the rôle of the biggest single individual in the national Democratic party.

Every word he uttered now was national news, respectfully treated and featured. The metropolitan newspapers of the East clamored for interviews, peppered him with questionnaires. What did he think of this and that? Whom would he support for president? Would he be downhearted if Cleveland bolted the party and supported McKinley? Would there be any compromise on silver? Candidates for the presidential nomination and their managers showered him with appeals for support. From the powerful Governor Hogg of Texas, unaware of Altgeld's foreign birth, came the suggestion that Altgeld himself be the nominee of the party.[36] Nor was Hogg alone in that thought.

"Altgeld," announced Governor Stone of Missouri, "Silver Dick" Bland's manager, "holds the key!"[37]

CHAPTER THIRTY-FOUR

Victory

1

Historians who treat the memorable '96 convention of the national Democratic party solely in terms of Free Silver and Bryan miss the essential significance of that revolutionary episode in American politics.

Had Bryan never appeared and the delegates been spared enthralment by his silver tongue, the course of that "revolution" would not have been changed. His nomination was an accident, albeit one carefully planned on his part. As for Free Silver, it was important but not overwhelmingly so from the historic standpoint. For generations both major parties had flirted with bimetallism after a fashion and it was in the cards that one or the other would take it up seriously.

What was of lasting importance in the Chicago convention is the fact that it meant demarcation of an era in American politics in terms of economics and social attitudes. From the reign of Andrew Jackson until the Chicago convention of 1896, there had been no distinction between the major parties on these issues. The party of Tilden and Cleveland was as conservative, avowedly so, as the party of Blaine and Mark Hanna. But by the action of the Chicago convention the party of Tilden and Cleveland was doomed. The Democracy was returned to Jefferson and Jackson, although in terms of industrialism rather than the disappearing agrarianism. And for the first time since the rise to dominance of industrialism, of monopolies and of corporations and corporation finance, one of the major parties took a clear stand on the basic economic issues which were dividing the nation between the "haves" and the "have-nots."

It was this return on a modern economic basis to the Jefferson-Jackson principles—the causing of the party to stand for "the people" rather than the "classes"—which constituted the revolutionary character of the '96 convention. This was its historical significance. But it was the platform as a whole, not the Free Silver plank alone, nor Bryan, that symbolized what was done.

The pronouncements on labor, on the courts, on injunctions, on civil and personal liberties and notably on that "communistic" thing, the income tax—these were the items of the platform which indelibly stamped a new character upon the party. These were what the conservative minority had in mind in characterizing the platform "extreme and revolutionary of the well recognized principles [hitherto] of the party."[1] And for that achievement, more than to any other leader of the time, the credit goes to—John Peter Altgeld.

His was the brain and the will; his the dominating force behind the platform. It was he who "laid out the program of the convention, dictated the platform and impressed his personality upon the policy adopted."[2]

2

To find the proof of Altgeld's domination of that platform one needs only to read the document itself. It is an Altgeld composition, in all its essential aspects—so much so that he well might have included it among his other papers in *Live Questions* and affixed to it the signature "John P. Altgeld." For that platform takes on meaning as a whole only when it is considered in relation to Altgeld. Incredibly, he had made of it a personal thing.

"We, the Democrats of the United States in national convention assembled, do reaffirm our allegiance to those great essential principles of justice and liberty, upon which our institutions are founded, and which the Democratic party has advocated from Jefferson's time to our own—freedom of speech, freedom of the press, freedom of conscience, the preservation of personal rights, the equality of all citizens before the law, and the faithful observance of constitutional limitations."

So the '96 platform began, summarizing all that followed. Ordinarily, such sentiments as were there expressed could be dismissed as political extravagance. But this was Altgeld speaking, unmistakably so. For in that paragraph was summarized the essence of his personal political philosophy, a philosophy now engrafted upon the national party. It could be concluded that this was so even without the last phrase—"the faithful observance of constitutional limitations." But with that phrase included, there could be no mistake. It was a reference to his personal quarrel with Grover Cleveland.

That such was the case is brought home by the second paragraph of the platform:

"During all these years the Democratic party has resisted the tendency of selfish interests to the centralization of governmental power, and steadfastly maintained the integrity of the dual scheme of government established by the founders of this Republic of republics. Under its guidings and teachings the great principle of local self-government has found its best expression in the maintenance of the rights of the States and in its assertion of the necessity of confining the General Government to the exercise of the powers granted by the Constitution of the United States."

Had the platform contained nothing else, those words alone constituted an amazing triumph for Altgeld. Here was the national party in effect approving the basic arguments he had raised in his telegrams to Grover Cleveland. Just as amazing, this was done before so much as a word had been uttered in the platform on the issue of Free Silver or any other question. Nor was this the full extent of Altgeld's achievement.

After the inevitable Free Silver plank—"We demand the free and unlimited coinage of both silver and gold at the present legal ratio of 16 to 1 . . . "—the platform returned to its opening thesis with even greater vigor. Thus, as the seventeenth paragraph, there was the following:

"We denounce arbitrary interference by Federal authorities in local affairs as a violation of the Constitution of the United States and a crime against free institutions. . . ."

To which was added:

"And we especially object to government by injunction as a new and highly dangerous form of oppression by which Federal judges, in contempt of the laws of the States and the rights of citizens, become at once legislators, judges and executioners. . . ."[3]

No mistake could be made about the source of that startling plank—nor its political meaning. Altgeld had "appealed" from the Supreme Court to Cleveland's party and had won a crushing victory. He had dealt Cleveland the bitterest blow of his career, and scored for himself the greatest personal political coup of any man of his time.

3

When it is realized that in 1894 Altgeld stood virtually alone in voicing the ideas of that plank, that the Supreme Court had upheld

Cleveland's action and also the judicial acts that Altgeld called "government by injunction," and, above all, that the issues involved were then to a great extent personal in character, the magnitude of this triumph over Cleveland scarcely could be exaggerated. On an issue which was almost wholly his own, he had contrived to drive from the party the man who had been the most powerful and popular leader of the Democracy since Jackson, for clearly that is what his planks amounted to even more definitely than the Free Silver plank. In addition, insofar as it may be considered possible for a major political party to do so, he had overruled not only the President of the United States but the Supreme Court itself! And, as it turned out, he had caused the resultant campaign to evolve around *his* planks and *his* political views quite as much as around Free Silver—at times more so.

When had any American more impressed national affairs?

And there was even more to his conquest. A plank placing the party definitely on record for arbitration of labor disputes concerning interstate commerce—this, too, was Altgeld's influence. So also the general labor plank of the platform with the conclusion, wholly Altgeldian in phraseology, that "as labor creates the wealth of the country, we demand the passage of such laws as may be necessary to protect it in all its rights." And similarly, the most important plank in the document after the declarations on Free Silver and on Cleveland's actions in the Pullman episode—the income tax plank. For this plank committed the Democratic party for the first time to the principle of the income tax, and lashed at the Supreme Court decision of 1895 in language identical with that used by Altgeld at the time.

In short, despite some meaningless academic discussion as to whether *Altgeld* literally wrote *all* of the Chicago Platform, the actual story about the platform was stated by a Chicago newspaper six years later. "John P. Altgeld wrote the Democratic platform of 1896—the Chicago Platform—wrote all there was in it that made it a platform."[4]

Not a handful of the convention delegates realized at the time what the revolting Democracy had done. They had come to Chicago to adopt a Free Silver platform. They believed they had adopted a Free Silver platform. But what they actually had adopted, to influence the party for generations to come, was an *Altgeld* platform! No wonder Cleveland admitted to friends that he was "dazed."[5] He not only had suffered the humiliation of absolute repudiation by the party that heretofore had acclaimed him as its idol, but worse still, he saw, as did a writer in *Leslie's Weekly*, that "Governor Altgeld . . .

comes very near to taking the President's place in the regard of the Democratic masses. From perhaps the most unpopular man in the United States [Altgeld] is now very nearly the recognized master of the Democratic party."[6]

4

It is doubtful if Altgeld himself had anticipated so great a triumph. But he could not have been on the ground long before it was clear to him that he occupied a controlling position among the leaders gathered for the convention. With New York and Pennsylvania in the gold camp, the forty-eight Illinois convention votes that he carried in his vest pocket made him the most powerful single individual among the silver leaders in that respect alone. But there was more to his influence. In sheer intellectual force, political sense and will power he towered over all the others. None there compared with him in those qualities. Perhaps only Senator Hill of New York came up to him, yet Hill's influence in this affair counted not at all, his strength pulverized by the silver storm. And so Altgeld was the natural leader. Ostensibly, the "senatorial clique," notably Tillman of North Carolina, Jones of Arkansas, Vest of Missouri and Daniel of Virginia, was running the show. But shrewd observers noted that they made no vital decision without consulting Altgeld, that his rooms in the Sherman House were the real control spot of the gathering, that "Altgeld was the ruling power in this seething mass."[7] It was so at least until he had obtained the platform that he wanted.

The chief contribution of his leadership was a formula: "No compromise!" Born out of his intense personal hatred for Clevelandism, he would have followed that formula himself regardless of the other silver forces. But in making it the guide for the others as well, he assured all that followed. Without hope of controlling the convention, the Cleveland-Gold Democrats concentrated on winning concessions. "Do not split the party." "You cannot win without the East." "If you must have a silver platform, at least name a sound money man for President." "Why antagonize Cleveland needlessly?" Such were the arguments, and others like them, that filled the hotel lobbies. Presidential ambitions were played against each other shrewdly. As usual, divide and conquer was the strategy. And there was wavering in the silver camp. But Altgeld stood firm—and held the others in line.

And the initial victory of the silver side, paving the way for all the others, came from his formula. Altgeld himself invoked it a few hours before the convention was called to order when the leaders of the opposing forces gathered at a secret meeting. The question was: Would or would not the regularly constituted National Democratic Committee be permitted to designate the temporary chairman of the convention? Precedent favored the committee. It would be "discourteous" to ignore the committee recommendations, so the gold men argued. The silver leaders listened—then Altgeld's low, slightly rasping voice was heard. Coolly facing Senator Hill, William C. Whitney and the other gold leaders, Altgeld flatly informed them that precedent would be tossed overboard—Free Silver had the delegates and Free Silver would rule from the beginning.[8] And so it turned out—the most strategic move of the convention, for when Senator Hill was rejected for chairman and Senator Daniel installed in his place, the battle was all but over. It meant, as stated by Edgar Lee Masters, who was on the ground, "an Altgeld platform and an Altgeld nomination. . . . His hour had come."[9]

5

Yet, in the main, he worked more in the background, impressed his views on the convention through the private caucuses. He shunned posts on any of the committees, intended no speech. However, when the delegates insisted upon hearing him the first day, he responded with a powerful extemporaneous speech in which, as in all the caucuses, he hammered at his "no compromise" theme. The "enemy" was using shrewd methods, he said. Only a few weeks before, the gold standard crowd talked of controlling the convention. But what were the arguments now heard "around the hotels and at your headquarters? 'Get together and agree upon something that we can all accede to and endorse,' is what they now say." And what do they mean?

"We are asked to do as we have done in the past. We are asked to adopt a declaration of principles which will mean one thing to one man and another to another man; which will mean one thing in one section of the country and another thing in another section, and which will enable these people to maintain a single gold standard in the end."

What the gold forces want, he summarized, was to put the Democratic party in the position of the steer "which jumped part way over the fence and could neither hook before nor kick behind." Well, that time was past. "Our people are in earnest. They will have neither straddling on platform or straddling on candidate. . . . Those prudent, cautious, wise gentlemen who have to consult the tin roosters every morning to see what their convictions should be during the day can have no show in this convention."[10]

More definitely than any other utterance before the convention, that speech by Altgeld expressed the true spirit of the revolting Democracy. But, while "greeted with yells of unrestrained delight,"[11] it was not *the* speech of the convention. The "young man from Nebraska," William Jennings Bryan, would make that.

6

For his curious prominence in the history of American politics, Bryan owed thanks to two principal facts. One was his amazing oratorical ability—nobody of his time could so sway an audience. The other was Altgeld's birth in Germany. But for this accident of nativity, there seems no doubt that Altgeld would have crowned his platform success by winning for himself the presidential nomination. All that happened at the convention bears out that conclusion— as Professor Nevins, among other keen students of that episode, has attested.[12]

Altgeld realized the price he paid for his German heritage. When the convention was over, "Buck" Hinrichsen complimented him on his influence. Altgeld responded with a "bitter smile." "Yes, I did everything but nominate myself; that was prevented by an accident of birth and a clause in the constitution."[13]

As it was, Altgeld's final approval made Bryan the nominee.

But he had wanted Richard Parks Bland of Missouri. Whether or not a different outcome in the subsequent election would have resulted had Altgeld's first choice for president been accepted is, of course, one of those impossible "if's" of history. Yet there is considerable basis for assuming that Altgeld's choice was the wiser one, that the Democratic party cheated itself out of victory at the polls when Altgeld's cool reason was overwhelmed by the excitement of Bryan's "Cross of Gold." True, Bland had none of Bryan's flair for oratory. Yet who knows how many votes Bryan lost in the end because sober-minded citizens finally determined that an older, more experienced head was preferable to a silver-tongued platform performer? As one of Bryan's biographers remarked: "Bryan suffered from the same disadvantage as Cicero. When people heard him speak, they said, 'How well he speaks,' and then they voted for McKinley. . . . When they got home they felt as if they had been to a restaurant and instead of dinner had been served nothing but sentimental songs."[14]

In the end, too, Bryan's youth, which so impressed the oratory-intoxicated convention delegates, was against him. It did him no good politically to be referred to as the "Boy Orator of the Platte," to have the Republican orators declaim that he was still in his thirties, to observe that he was an unsuccessful lawyer and with only one term in Congress on the credit side of substantial achievement. Thousands were prompted to believe, once Mark Hanna's propaganda mills got into action, that his true profession was acting. "Did America want a cheap actor in the White House?" Because he was so little known before the Chicago convention to the nation at large, it was possible for the Hanna propaganda machine to create serious discussion as to Bryan's mental capacities. The New York *Times*, for example, solemnly discussed the inane theory that Bryan really was insane, that his oratorical ability actually stemmed from a mental deficiency variously labeled as "querelent logorrhea," "graphomania" and "oratorical monomania."[15]

None of those side issues could have been injected into the campaign had Bland been the candidate. A successful lawyer in Missouri when Altgeld first tramped into Savannah, Bland had served as a representative and then as United States senator from 1872 until 1894. Few political figures were better known to the nation or commanded such widespread respect. There was about his appearance and bearing the same solid qualities that made McKinley attractive to substantial citizens. More important, Bland's nomination undoubtedly would have held the campaign to the one issue, the issue which Mark Hanna feared above all else, Free Silver. For he had espoused the silver cause while Bryan was yet a mere schoolboy, and had to his credit the Bland-Allison Act of 1878 by which silver temporarily was restored as legal tender after the "Crime of '73." As Bryan himself admitted, Bland was the "foremost champion of bimetallism" of the Democratic party.[16] Millions who had never heard of Bryan in 1896, for years had known the Missourian, admiringly, as "Silver Dick."

Altgeld believed those facts made Bland a winner. And besides, he respected his intellect. The same could not be said concerning Bryan. He conceded Bryan's ability as an orator, envied him in that respect, but otherwise considered him "somewhat superficial in make-up," did not feel that Bryan really comprehended the fundamentals of the money question.[17] In later years, though always loyal to Bryan politically, on one occasion more loyal to what had come to be known as Bryanism than Bryan himself—he had a sort of patronizing contempt for the "peerless leader." To Altgeld, among his intimates, the great William Jennings Bryan was just plain "William Bryan."[18] However, Bryan was sincere about Free Silver and, in an emotional way, stood for "the people." Also, he was against Cleveland—and so he was acceptable to Altgeld as second choice.

7

At least a year before the convention, Altgeld was aware of Bryan's presidential ambitions. The young ex-Congressman had begun a quiet, though persistent campaign in behalf of himself long before his "Cross of Gold" speech, this despite the legend that his nomination was all accident. He had called on Altgeld at Springfield during the World's Fair year of 1893.[19] Ostensibly his visit then was to get Altgeld's views on silver, yet later events indicate that his real purpose was to get the Governor's views on—Bryan.

As part of his campaign to impress Altgeld, Bryan made it a point to be on hand for a speech at the Cook County silver convention in May, 1895. Judge McConnell, who presided, had never heard of him. When told that "a Mr. Bryan of Nebraska was in the hall and would like to have an opportunity of addressing the convention," he permitted him to be on the program to fill in. When the state silver convention gathered at Springfield, Judge McConnell, again presiding, felt a tugging at his sleeve. It was Bryan "crashing" the meeting again.

"Judge," he pleaded, "are you going to give me a chance to address the convention?"

"Of course," said McConnell sarcastically, "the convention will need entertainment."[20]

Afterward, Bryan would tell of having been "invited" to address the Illinois conventions.[21]

Yet within a year Bryan had made such headway that he felt the time was ripe for a direct appeal to Altgeld in a letter in which he enclosed some speeches he had been giving in the hinterlands. Altgeld thanked him "a thousand times" for the speeches. They would "give you a much more enduring and brilliant fame than has been made by most presidents."[22] But not a word about Bryan's hopes!

However, Bryan was not to be put off easily. Especially not when he had just received word from an agent in Texas that made it more important than ever to get Altgeld's endorsement. "Write me just what attitude Altgeld is going to assume . . . whether he will be favorable to your nomination. . . . In case he is . . . it would go a considerable way in helping me here," so he had been advised from Texas.[23] Desperate, he soon showed up at the Unity Building to plead his case in person. F. D. P. Snelling, a young man in the office, witnessed part of the interview, saw Altgeld patting Bryan on the shoulder: "You are young yet," Altgeld was telling him. "Let Bland have the nomination this time. Your time will come." Altgeld also tossed out the suggestion that Bryan might be named for vice-president.[24]

But the pat on the shoulder and the remark about the vice-presidency did not call Bryan off. Altgeld finally felt it advisable to resort to an appeal to the Nebraskan's loyalty to the silver cause. He sent Bryan the following telegram:

"Since seeing you I have canvassed presidential situation. Find everywhere great admiration for you but an almost unanimous sentiment that you are not available for President this time. All feel you should be in new cabinet if we succeed. Now situation looks dangerous because of possible divisions among silver men. . . . We must practically nominate before convention meets or we may yet be defeated. The enemy will try to divide and conquer. I would like to have consultation and will pay expenses if you could run over."[25]

Bryan came. Probably Altgeld believed he had succeeded at last in talking Bryan out of his ambition, for about that time Bryan advised newspaper reporters that he was not a candidate for president "in any sense of the word."[26] Yet four days later, when the Illinois delegation held a caucus at the Sherman House, there he was, "button-holing all of the delegates," to Altgeld's intense disgust. "Buck, tell Bryan to go home—he stands no more chance of being nominated for President than I, and I was born in Germany!" Altgeld finally snapped to "Buck" Hinrichsen.[27]

However, Bryan stayed, never gave up hope. Two days later he persuaded Willis J. Abbott to speak to Altgeld in his behalf because "the Governor thinks a lot of you." "Tell Bryan," Altgeld said to Abbott, "that he's young enough to wait a few years. Dick Bland has earned this nomination and shall have it, if I can influence this convention." Altgeld thought Bryan might not get a chance even to speak at the convention because "the program is pretty well completed."[28]

8

But Bryan did speak. All of the other addresses in the debate on the platform had been acrid and argumentative. Bryan was antiphonal. Among the bearded veterans of the party, he glowed with youth, his "raven locks" gleaming, his face and manner electric. And almost his first words cast the spell he had hoped for.

"The humblest citizen in all the land, when clad in the armor of a righteous cause, is stronger than all the hosts of error. I come to speak to you in defense of a cause as holy as the cause of liberty—the cause of humanity. . . ."

No matter that he had used most of this before, that it was carefully rehearsed. The delegates and the spectators in the galleries responded as if they were hearing a voice from above, a messiah come to the Chicago Coliseum. And how they yelled when he came to the passage in which he spoke for the West against the East.

"We do not come as aggressors. Our war is not a war of conquest; we are fighting in the defense of our homes, our families, and posterity. We have petitioned, and our petitions have been scorned; we have entreated, and our entreaties have been disregarded; we have begged, and they have mocked when our calamity came. We beg no longer; we entreat no more; we petition no more. WE DEFY THEM!"

Speaking of silver, he was the spirit of embattled agriculture personified when there came from his throat:

"You come to us and tell us that the great cities are in favor of the gold standard; we reply that the great cities rest upon our broad and fertile prairies. Burn down your cities and leave our farms, and your cities will spring up again as if by magic, but destroy our farms and the grass will grow in the streets of every city in America!"

And now for his conclusion:

"Having behind us the producing masses of this nation and of the world, supported by the commercial interests, the laboring interests, and the toilers everywhere, we will answer . . . demands for a gold standard by saying to them:

"YOU SHALL NOT PRESS DOWN UPON THE BROW OF LABOR THIS CROWN OF THORNS, YOU SHALL NOT CRUCIFY MANKIND UPON A CROSS OF GOLD!"

Even Altgeld, despite his prejudice against Bryan, was very nearly swept off his feet by the sheer impact of that speech. As the hall turned into a bedlam of cheering, whistling, clapping, singing, pounding of seats with canes and throwing of hats into the air, he did not applaud, but he did turn to Judge McConnell and say: "Judge, I had rather be able to make a speech like that than be president of the United States."[29] However, when members of the Illinois delegation attempted to carry the Illinois banner into a snake-march for Bryan, Altgeld held it firm. He was still for Bland. The next day he remarked to Clarence Darrow: "It takes more than speeches to win real victories. . . . I have been thinking over Bryan's speech. What did he say anyhow?"[30] Years later Darrow thought Altgeld also had commented something to the effect: "Wasn't Bryan a damn fool?"[31]

9

But Bryan had said enough to weaken Altgeld's hold on the convention, even on his own delegation. Many of the Illinois delegates wanted to cast their votes to Bryan for president on the very first ballot. They showed traces of mutiny at once. Nor was this solely because of Bryan's speech. The Nebraskan on his trips to Illinois to woo Altgeld, had made a conquest of "Buck" Hinrichsen. The chairman of the state central committee appears to have been working secretly for him all the while, although professing to be with Altgeld. Moreover, Bryan had a big advantage over Bland by being on the scene. Foolishly, Bland purposely stayed away from Chicago—for reasons of "dignity." What this meant was well summed up by Judge McConnell.

"In any political convention, two-thirds of the delegates are in expectation of official appointment if their nominee is successful. This convention was full of men who wanted to be collectors, postmasters, etc., and naturally, they would argue, they would stand a better chance with a man who knew them than with one they had never seen. I believe this factor . . . did more to promote [Bryan's] nomination than his speech."[32]

In Bryan's favor, too, was Altgeld's physical condition. Everyone who saw him at that convention was struck by his paleness. "His pallor startled one Republican watcher."[33] Masters noted that he was "sick—and showed it." Had he been otherwise, it seems probable that he might have stood out to the end against the pressure placed upon him to switch Illinois to Bryan, and if so, it is doubtful that

Bryan would have been nominated. As it was, he exhibited tremendous will power in attempting to ride out the stampede.

When his delegation threatened a revolt in the very beginning,
Altgeld faced the rebels down. "We are not political coquettes," he
said. "We are here for business and not for political play. We are
Democrats and we are for Bland and free silver."[34] And so Illinois'
forty-eight votes went for Bland on the first ballot. And Bland with
223 votes was high man on that initial vote. Yet there was Bryan,
second man, leading Governor Boies of Iowa and Senator Tillman.

On the second ballot, a noticeable switch to Bryan at the expense
of various favorite sons occurred. The Illinois delegates became even
more impatient. As a concession Altgeld finally agreed that if a majority of the delegation asked for a caucus, he would allow one to be
held to consider, but only consider, a switch from Bland. Such a caucus was held after the first ballot. Editor Clendenin, a Bryan man,
has described the results:

". . . the delegation retired to an ante room. Governor Altgeld
opposed changing our state vote. He gained his point. [But] Bryan
continued to gain. Another caucus of our delegation was called.
Altgeld held the caucus firm. Caucus after caucus was called as the
balloting proceeded. Altgeld was dismayed but still insisted on
having his way. I saw this caucusing must not continue. Secretary of
State Hinrichsen agreed with me and said that if we kept fooling with
the buzzer, Bryan would be nominated before Illinois would do its
duty. . . ."[35]

Altgeld held out for Bland until after the fourth ballot, the ballot
in which Bryan for the first time topped Bland's total. He had been
pulled from his chair by excited Bryan men.[36] He had been shouted at
by milling delegates from other states. "Vote for Bryan! No Crown
of Thorns. No Cross of Gold!" An effort was made to tear the Illinois
banner from his taut fingers. But he kept firm, and Illinois for the
fourth time announced "no change." Just before the fifth ballot, another caucus by his delegation was requested.

All eyes were on Altgeld as the Illinoisans filed from the hall. The
whole convention seemed to sense that the crisis was near. If Altgeld
had continued to stand for Bland, who knows what would have happened? The Bryan boom might have collapsed then as suddenly as it
had developed, or both Bryan and Bland been deserted for a third man.
Already Senator Hill had made overtures to Altgeld concerning "Hori-

zontal Bill" Morrison.[37] "For God's sake, stand by Mr. Bland!" cried an Arkansas delegate who clutched at Altgeld's arm as the Governor walked out. Altgeld's face was "white as death."[38] He made no reply. He knew then that he had reached the point in his leadership when, if he wished still to lead, he must follow.

When the convention clerk reached Illinois on the fifth ballot roll call, Altgeld stood up. The eyes of the twenty thousand in the galleries and the sixteen hundred delegates on the floor—the eyes of all America—were fixed upon his squat frame, the peculiar patch of hair on top of his head and the close-clipped black beard that came to a point at his chin, features which caricaturists soon were to make familiar in every hamlet of the land. For once, the galleries were silent. The delegates were tense—even to the Goldbug delegations who had steadfastly refused to participate in the balloting at all.

Nobody marched now. No bands played. The noisiest convention in history was suddenly as quiet as a cathedral. Had Altgeld taken that opportunity to make a speech, to explain what he was about to do, unquestionably the scene, the moment and the man would have formed an unforgettable episode. But he had not come to make a speech—so he had declared in his talk the opening day. He had come to make a platform and nominate a president. He already had done the former. Now, in one sentence, he would do the latter.

"Illinois casts its forty-eight votes for William Jennings Bryan of Nebraska!"

It was over then. "The hall shook under the cheers." All order was at an end. Delegates and audience arose to their feet. Bryan was in. No question about that, for Altgeld's words were the signal for state after state to switch from Bland to Bryan. The Illinois delegation led a march around the hall, chanting:

> "Bryan, Bryan, William J. Bryan,
> Bryan, Bryan, William J. Bryan,
> Bryan of Nebraska,
> and the State of Illinois!"

But Altgeld remained where he was, outwardly calm and contemplative as his pale blue eyes surveyed the scene that he had wrought. Strictly speaking, Bryan's nomination was a defeat for him. Yet—was it? Here was Senator Jones, the new chairman of the National Democratic Committee, running up to him, obviously bewildered, turning to Altgeld for guidance. "What shall we do now?" Altgeld told him.

And so he was still "key man." And there was this consideration also: Had Bland been nominated, he could doubtless have been expected to stand more on his own feet in the event of election. But this boy from Nebraska—if he should be elected . . . would not the *real* president be Altgeld . . . ? Who else was there to come up to the man who personified the platform on which Bryan would run, the man who had crossed swords with and vanquished Grover Cleveland?

CHAPTER THIRTY-FIVE

"THE FIRST BATTLE"

1

But Bryan lost. A theory has been advanced that the spirit of victory was not in Bryan, that even the Cross of Gold speech, seemingly so aggressive, actually was a speech not of triumph but of failure.[1] There is something in that theory. For in the campaign Bryan permitted himself to be placed in the position of constantly defending the Chicago Platform. He would deny that the platform was "anarchistic." He would deny that the platform expressed contempt for the Supreme Court. He would deny that any real harm was meant to the big interests.

Mark Hanna could not have wished for better tactics in view of the political axiom that a smart politician never denies, but makes another charge against the enemy, as Altgeld always did. Yet had the election been held that summer unquestionably Bryan would have been victorious. The Republican high command realized this. Private letters of key Republicans reveal that they were terrorized by the hold Bryan had upon the masses everywhere except in the financial centers of the East.[2] His dramatic nomination and his oratory cast the same spell upon crowds wherever he went during July and August. As for his Republican opponent, William McKinley, he was so poor a match for Bryan in arousing mass enthusiasm that Mark Hanna determined the best strategy throughout the campaign would be to keep him at his home in Canton, Ohio. There McKinley delivered innocuous "front porch" greetings to Republican "pilgrims," whose "pilgrimages" were mainly paid for out of the Republican campaign fund. He was very nearly a "forgotten man" until his election.

Hanna had one especially excellent reason for keeping McKinley in the background. With the campaign starting off on the issue Gold Standard v. Free Silver, McKinley was in the unfortunate position of having put himself on record as an out-and-out bimetallist. As a congressman he had delivered strong speeches against the single gold standard. In 1891 he had attacked Cleveland's "sound money" views

374

as violently as any Free Silver Democrat did after Cleveland's election.[3] Obviously it was much better to keep him quiet.

As a substitute for a visible, active candidate, Mark Hanna developed something better, a "campaign of education." It was based upon the biggest campaign fund ever collected and expended in American history up to that time—no less than three and a half million dollars, with some estimates placing the true figure closer to sixteen million dollars.[4]

The Democratic party had less than $600,000.

2

In that memorable campaign Altgeld would have preferred to play only a minor rôle. It was against his real personal desires that he stood for re-election as governor. There was considerable scoffing in the press when he told the state convention, which renominated him by acclamation, that he preferred to retire to private life immediately. In his speech to the state Democracy, he had said:

"My health has been so badly broken that it is necessary for me to get out of the intense strain I have been under for several years. Again, at the time of my election I had large property interests, but was greatly in debt. . . . This, added to the fact that I have had to neglect my affairs to some extent, has reduced me to a situation where I am not financially able to make a campaign and where justice to my creditors requires that I should give my time to my own affairs rather than to the public. . . .

"I am not unmindful of the honor the Democratic party has conferred on me, and I am ready to do what I can to serve my country, but I must ask that some one of the many able and patriotic men in the party be placed at the head and that I be permitted to retire."[5]

Practically none believed his remarks were anything but "shrewd politics." The Chicago Daily News gibed: "Governor Altgeld seems to have accepted a nomination by declining one." "He knew his men and played Caesar with good dramatic effect," the New York Tribune commented cynically.[6] But Altgeld actually was talking from the heart. Only a few weeks before, he had earnestly begged Judge McConnell to take the nomination for governor. "He said he was tired," McConnell observed.[7]

It is certain that, physically he was in no condition to make an active campaign. If he was "nerve-wearied" when Nellie Bly interviewed him in July, 1894, he was more so in 1896. Moreover, he had learned as early as September, 1894, that he was afflicted with the dread disease locomotor ataxia, first signs of which were a peculiar shuffle in his walk. With characteristic frankness, he even announced that fact to the press in New York after a noted New York specialist, Dr. Spitzka, had examined him. Apparently, he was not at all alarmed, for that evening he dined in style at Delmonico's.[8] When he returned to Illinois, he issued a crisp denial of the locomotor ataxia statement—probably on Mrs. Altgeld's advice. "Bosh," he said.[9] But it was true.[10] It did not affect him mentally, notwithstanding a remark uttered thirty-three years after Altgeld's death by Carter Harrison the Younger,[11] but it was an added burden on an already weakened constitution.

As for his personal finances, he had not understated his position, for his affairs had gone from bad to worse. True, Lanehart was making valiant, though not always wise, efforts to recoup the losses. There were schemes in his shrewd head which might well have succeeded, and one of which will soon be examined. But a week after the Democratic national convention, John W. Lanehart came down with violent stomach pains. Two days later, on July sixteenth, Altgeld was called from Springfield to learn that Lanehart, then thirty-nine, had died from appendicitis. Lanehart's death was a hard blow to Altgeld, both personally and in a business way. He had been deeply fond of his handsome cousin. And with Lanehart gone, his business affairs more than ever demanded his personal attention.

However, he threw himself into the campaign with all the energy that he could command. But it was Bryan's election, not his own, that drove him on, for now none was more loyal to Bryan than Altgeld. If Altgeld did not enter into a zealous fight for Bryan and the Chicago Platform, the platform that so definitely was his, who would? And then he had another reason, one that Mark Hanna gave him.

Hanna did not relish a fight on the silver issue alone, for even he wondered if the masses could be properly "educated." And so he looked for another issue. He found it in Altgeld. What better bogeyman than the Illinois Governor existed for frightening the property-owning classes into the McKinley camp? And so Altgeld personally was made a leading—much of the time the leading—issue of the campaign, with the cry of "anarchy!" now resounding across the nation. He was forced by that alone to enter the lists.

3

There were days when he literally risked his life as the fight raged. Dizzy spells overcame him after several speeches and he was deathly ill for hours. Still he kept on, making as many as seven and eight speeches a day. "He was so sick," related the Chicago *Tribune* concerning one of his tours through Illinois, "that he remained in bed in the sleeping car between stations, raising himself from bed by sheer will power to deliver another speech a short time later."[12]

Fortunately, he had the good sense to go to Colorado Springs with Mrs. Altgeld for a rest before the campaign was on in earnest. On his way, the train was stopped long enough for Bryan to come aboard at Lincoln, Nebraska, to pay his respects and discuss the campaign.[13] Then for three weeks he put politics aside to bask in the Colorado sunshine and ride horseback with Mrs. Altgeld along the mountain trails near Pike's Peak. Often he enjoyed earnest conversations with children of other guests at his hotel resort.

One such conversation has been preserved. A boy and his sister were near a high hedge, so dense that a horse could not crash through, and the girl wondered what the boy would do to get free if he found himself completely enclosed in such a hedge. "I don't know," the boy said.

"Couldn't you try something?" interjected Altgeld. "Here, try this." He proceeded to break off one twig, then another, then another. "See, you could break a twig at a time, until there was an opening. That's the way to get by obstacles unless—unless you can sweep them away like this." With his arm, he described a broad half-circle. . . .[14]

4

When he returned to Springfield on August twenty-sixth, he found the campaign seething, himself the center of the cauldron not only in the key-state of Illinois but throughout the East and West. Much to Mark Hanna's glee, the Goldbug Democrats showed the way to damn the Democratic ticket by damning Altgeld, and all that they claimed he stood for—"free riot," "national dishonor," "destruction of our bulwark, the United States Supreme Court," and, finally, "anarchy." Henry Watterson, "Marse Henry" of the southern Democracy, had let out a scream of protest through his Louisville *Courier-Journal*. "Both liberty and order are assailed by the platform of the Chicago convention . . . and in that regard it is distinctly a concession to the exactions of Governor Altgeld and Senator Tillman!" Another ticket is "our only hope," he said.[15] Through Watterson's initiative, the so-called National Democratic ticket was put in the field. Mark Hanna chortled when John M. Palmer was selected to head it. Thus did the aged Senator complete the circle of his political mugwumpery and seek final revenge upon Altgeld—getting, however, less than 9,000 votes in Illinois and scarcely more than 100,000 in the nation.

Opening the Republican oratorical campaign, Ex-President Benjamin Harrison directed his fire squarely against Altgeld. The Chicago convention was "surcharged with the spirit of revolution. Whenever our people elect a president who believes that he must ask of Governor Altgeld . . . permission to enforce the laws of the United States, we have surrendered the victory the boys won in 1861."[16] Quickly this became the leading theme. Bryan was not to be feared. It was Altgeld who threatened the nation.

In July, Leslie's Weekly carried a full-page cartoon entitled "The New Master of the Democratic Party." It showed a vicious-looking, bearded figure standing over the bodies of Cleveland, Senator Hill and other Democrats. The figure, labeled "Altgeld," carried a banner labeled "Anarchy" and a flaming torch. Harper's Weekly featured similar cartoons by W. A. Rogers. That magazine's final contribution was a drawing showing Altgeld with a torch labeled "Anarchy," a torn copy of the Constitution in one hand, and behind him the shadowy figure of Charles Guiteau, slayer of President Garfield, who was drawn to resemble Altgeld. The caption: "1881-1897: Guiteau was a Power in Washington for One Day. Shall Altgeld be a Power There for Four Years?"[17]

Editorially, Harper's Weekly pontificated:

"Governor Altgeld . . . is the brain and inspiration of the movement for which Mr. Bryan stands. . . . It is he who chose Mr. Bryan in preference [sic] to Mr. Bland. . . . Governor Altgeld preferred the impulsive, susceptible, imaginative, yielding Mr. Bryan . . . who would be as clay in the hands of the potter under the astute control of the ambitious and unscrupulous Illinois communist. . . . To Governor Altgeld the passage of a law establishing free coinage of silver would be but a step towards the general socialism which is the fundamental doctrine of his political belief. . . . He seeks to overturn the old parties, the old traditions, and the essential policies which have controlled the government since its foundation."[18]

5

And the Republicans really feared Altgeld, not because they believed the nonsense about his revolutionary ideas, but because of his political position in the Middle West.

"The distinction for so many years enjoyed by New York—that of being the pivotal State in the quadrennial contests for supremacy between the two great parties—seems this year to have been transformed to Illinois. This, the most important of the Middle Western states—important in population and wealth no less than geographical position—will furnish the battle ground. . . . Here, too, it is that probably one of the ablest, most versatile and resourceful politicians stands ready to lead what to a candid and unprejudiced observer of the field looks like a 'forlorn hope.' . . ."[19]

So the New York *Tribune* discussed Altgeld's position. Mark Hanna apparently agreed with that diagnosis, for he directed the greatest concentration of oratorical talent into Illinois witnessed in any state of the nation. Robert G. Ingersoll, Carl Schurz, Bourke Cochran, Chauncey Depew, Theodore Roosevelt, Albert J. Beveridge, the biggest oratorical guns of the generation—they were all sent there to pound away at Altgeld. Shrewdest of all on Hanna's part was the enlistment of Carl Schurz in the anti-Altgeld campaign. Like Ingersoll, he was of a past generation, but Germans everywhere idolized him. Schurz, who had bolted the Republican party in 1884 because he could not stomach James G. Blaine, was none too impressed by the ideals of Hanna. But he had agreed to make one speech as an opponent of Free Silver, and it was determined that this thunderbolt should be directed against Altgeld, if only in an effort to undermine his hold on the German voters. Schurz was pleased, for he recognized in Altgeld a worthy opponent, viewed him as "by far the strongest of the silver men in purely intellectual debate."[20]

6

Looking more like an ancient prophet than ever, Schurz delivered his speech in Chicago on September 5, 1896, before the Hanna-financed "American Honest Money League." He confined himself to the money question. It was a dignified and powerful address, very nearly coming up to the advance advertisements that it would be the strongest utterance of the campaign in behalf of the Gold Standard. He presented, according to Schurz's biographers, "an annihilating assault upon the historical, economic and political bases of the free-coinage platform."[21]

But Altgeld declined to be annihilated. On September nineteenth, in Chicago's Central Music Hall, before an audience larger even than turned out for Schurz, he answered the other great German-born statesman. In the whole campaign combat, Altgeld made the two most important addresses, and his answer to Schurz was one of these. Both sides recognized that the Schurz address and Altgeld's answer represented a dramatic high-point of the battle, one that brought together the leading intellectuals of the opposing parties. When Altgeld answered Schurz the hall was so crowded that he had difficulty getting to the platform. Thousands stood outside. He received an ovation. "Men and women rose in their seats, waved their hats and handkerchiefs and yelled. . . . No man could have asked for a more flattering reception"; so a McKinley paper reported.[22] And he was as dignified as Carl Schurz and, granting his premises, just as "annihilating."

He, too, went into history, tracing the effect of the demonetization of silver in '73, citing the statements of leading financial authorities in Europe and America, giving statistic after statistic to bolster his interpretations. He boldly challenged figures given by Schurz, asserting that the older statesman had misrepresented some facts and withheld others. It was not true, he said, that there was enough money in circulation. Government reports, prepared under a gold-standard administration, proved this. It was not true that there was overproduction of silver. "Fortunately, this is not a matter that we need to speculate about. We have history, experience and accurate data upon this subject." It was not true that silver had fallen in value. "Silver occupies the same relation to the products of the earth and to labor today that it did before. It is gold that has gone up. The law striking down the competition has given gold a monopoly. It protects gold against competition. Practically the gold dollar is a 200-cent dollar."

He argued that the single gold standard placed a double burden upon the producing classes, making it necessary for laborers and farmers to produce twice as much "to get a gold dollar and pay debts or taxes." This, he went on to say, destroyed purchasing power, injured business and occasioned unemployment. "It was no comfort to tell a laborer that if he had a gold dollar, it would buy twice as much as it used to, for if there were no purchaser for what he made, there was no way to get any kind of dollar." And this, he said, explained the business depression of the 'nineties. He argued that free coinage of silver would cure the business "paralysis" by increasing the amount of money in circulation. But, he declared, no remedy at all for the depression is offered by the gold standard advocates.

". . . The substance of the[ir] whole argument is that we will be better off and suffer less if we keep quiet and that the remedy proposed by the Chicago platform would only make matters worse instead of better, or, as Mr. Schurz puts it, the application of this remedy would be jumping out of the frying pan into the fire. . . . If he is correct in this then the only question which is left for the consideration of those of our people who are dying in the frying pan is whether they would be any worse off in the fire."[23]

Most of his talk dealt with economic theory, necessarily dry, but for more than two hours he held his audience spellbound—not by charm of oratory, for he had none, but by sheer force of logical presentation, directness and crispness. And so it was a night of triumph for him, even to his handling of a heckler in the audience. Obviously drunk in preparation for his rôle, the heckler stood up and shouted: "You old anarchist, you!" Quick as a flash, completely composed, Altgeld shot back with a sardonic smile:

"Our friend there seems to have imbibed too much at 16 to 1!"[24]

There was a roar of laughter—and no more heckling.

The most impressive tribute of all came to him from Carl Schurz. Altgeld had got under the old statesman's skin. Forgetting his resolve to make only one speech, Schurz turned up with another at Peoria, Illinois, on October twenty-fourth. It was devoted solely to answering Altgeld. Governor Altgeld, said Schurz, "had furnished to the campaign on the silver side the only plea that has the appearance of serious reasoning. . . ."[25]

Unfortunately for enlightenment of the electorate on the silver issue, Altgeld did not make a rejoinder and the "debate" with Schurz came to an end. Probably he would have answered, but the campaign by then had veered from Free Silver—to Altgeld and his controversy with Cleveland. In part this was planned by the Republicans. Yet Altgeld himself was responsible, for on October 17, 1896, he went to New York City to deliver his second major address of the campaign. The place was Cooper Union, made famous by Emerson and Lincoln, and the subject, "The Chicago Riots—Government by Injunction—Federal Interference."

7

It was against Altgeld's better political judgment that he made that Cooper Union talk, for unquestionably it had the effect of playing into the hands of the enemy. When Schilling and Darrow said they believed he should go into the East and tell the story of the Pullman episode, he raised objections. "It would be like digging up last year's bird nest."[26] But about that time Henry George came to Springfield to see Altgeld. Between George and Altgeld a profound mutual respect had developed. In many respects they were kindred spirits, even though, as noted, Altgeld had made his fortune through methods denounced by George in his great book. While Altgeld never fully subscribed to the Single Tax theory, he was tolerant toward it. He lent the dignity of his office to a Single Tax meeting held in Springfield during 1895, by presiding and introducing the lecturer, Louis F. Post. He also permitted Schilling to engage Post to write the famous tax report issued by the Illinois Bureau of Labor and Statistics in 1896,[27] a document heavily loaded with facts that lent themselves to Single Tax propaganda. And for George personally, Altgeld felt tremendous admiration. "It was like entering a morning in June to meet the quiet, unpretentious and sincere Henry George," he felt.[28] Moreover, he was grateful to him because, when all the world was against him in the controversy with Cleveland, George, up to then a Cleveland man, organized a mass meeting in New York City to uphold him.[29]

Henry George had visited Springfield especially to urge that Altgeld go to New York for a speech on the Chicago Platform planks against Federal interference and government by injunction. The charges of anarchy against Altgeld were proving dangerous to Democratic success, George said. He felt that a good speech by Altgeld himself would counteract this. Coming from George, this advice was persuasive, and so a few days later, Altgeld sent Joe Martin to New York to make arrangements for a meeting in Cooper Union. He did not have much time to prepare a speech and was forced to lift whole sections from other statements he had made on his controversy with Cleveland, notably his 1895 message to the legislature. He even included in toto his telegrams to Cleveland. As a result, the speech was unpardonably long.

Yet Altgeld made an unforgettable impression upon New York— far exceeding in favorable effect the impression that Bryan made there at the opening of the campaign. Long before the hour of the meeting, Cooper Union was filled to capacity. Thousands were massed around the hall, stopping all traffic for blocks. "They came from far and near, representing all classes and creeds," said the New York Times. "Their one desire was to hear and see that famous citizen of Illinois who has been called everything from an anarchist to a statesman."[30]

The same newspapers that three years before had called him a nonentity and confidently predicted his disappearance from the political scene sent corps of reporters to clamor for interviews and report on his every word and act. In spite of themselves, the New York editors found it necessary to print complimentary references to him. Thus the New York *Tribune*, while squeezing in a statement that "descriptions which have likened him to Guiteau are not far out as such descriptions go," conceded that "with all his apparent fragility of frame, there is an alertness in his movements that betokens vitality of an unusual order."[31] His dignity of manner, his precise diction, his self-control, all were remarked upon. For days he received more newspaper attention than any other figure in the campaign, not excepting the candidates themselves.

The New York correspondent of the strongly McKinley *Times-Herald* in Chicago explained how this had happened.

"Eastern papers had habitually represented him as snorting thunder and crying for blood. They painted him in the reddest hue of the red flag. They were prepared for wild talk of revolution, for indecent raving about the rights of mankind, for a riot of oratorical madness. New York was disappointed. . . . He had neither hooks nor horns nor tail. He looked and acted very much like any other dignified gentleman. He spoke with vigor and adroitness. He argued with the acumen of a trained lawyer. He made an elaborate, closely reasoned defense of the Chicago platform. It is conceded that he made the ablest presentation . . . that has been offered to the public. . . . He proved to be an orator of ability, a man of power. . . ."[32]

The audience that jammed Cooper Union went wild over him. Not a few, it was plain, were there not so much because of the campaign but to pay their respects to the man who had pardoned the men of Haymarket. When he appeared on the platform, the audience "stood up as one man." They waved flags on which his name was printed, and cheered until their throats were hoarse. Henry George, Mary Lease, Congressman (later Governor) William Sulzer and other notables were there. But the crowd was Altgeld's. "We love you for the enemies you have made! We love you for the enemies you have made! . . . " So chanted the throng when he stood to begin his talk.

8

It was a fighting speech, in sharp contrast to most of Bryan's. The nation, he declared, was confronted by a "quartette of blighting sisters" in addition to the gold standard. These, he said, were the "modern Eumenides": "Federal Interference in local affairs," "Government by Injunction," "Usurpation by the United States Supreme Court," and "Corruption." Nor were these "blighting sisters" to be considered apart from the monetary issue.

"All four are clothed in phariseeism and pretense, and all recognize the gold standard as their natural or foster mother . . . blighting sisters whose smile means paralysis and whose embrace means death. . . . This campaign is to decide, not only whether we shall perpetuate the experiments of this English financial system, but also whether we shall permanently adopt these four sisters into our household and make them the ruling members of the family."

In short, he left no doubt that he considered the other planks of the Chicago Platform fully as important as the silver plank—and he made no secret of this feeling. After giving his side of the Pullman affair, he launched into a bold discussion of the plank criticising the Supreme Court decision in the income tax case. He frankly admitted that the Chicago Platform "denounces the peculiar conduct of the Supreme Court." Well, such criticism was in line with precedent set by Jefferson, Jackson and also Lincoln. If the Chicago Platform is "subversive," so were those statesmen.

"I say that there cannot be in a republic any institution exempt from criticism, and that when any institution is permitted to assume that attitude, it will destroy republican government. . . .
"The Supreme Court cannot by mere decision upon a constitutional question rob the people of the powers of self-government nor prevent the American people from deciding for themselves, through the properly constituted machinery whether they will accept the Supreme Court decision as being final or whether they will refuse to accept it as a rule of action. As Mr. Lincoln said, 'It does not necessarily become a rule of political action!' . . ."

In discussing corruption as one of the great questions of the campaign which go "to the foundations of free government," he declared that the voters must decide "whether we shall dissolve on boodle, bribery and corruption . . . whether we shall declare scoundrelism is in the end the loftiest form of patriotism."

"It is a remarkable fact that those men and those influences whose slime is dissolving our institutions are all helping Mr. Hanna. Everything within their reach is being prostituted. Where they can, they degrade the religious press and defile the pulpit. They have dragged the American flag in the mire by using it as an advertising sheet for McKinley and Hobart. . . . Wave the flag and plunder the public is the gospel of McKinleyism!"[33]

In the heart of enemy country he was fighting hard, hitting hardest, when another might have attempted a conciliatory tone. Perhaps the conciliatory tone would have been better politically. For the very vigor of his challenging address brought down upon his head the full force of the Hanna propaganda machine. The New York *Times* epitomized the reaction when the next day it assured its readers that Altgeld's Cooper Union talk stripped at last the "mask" from the Bryan campaign. Silver was not the issue at all. The issue was "Altgeld's anarchistic policies."[34]

9

Two days before, in Chicago, a newcomer in national politics already had discovered that issue. Listen to him the evening of October 15, 1896, before the "American Republican College League" in the Chicago Coliseum. He is speaking in the polished accents of Harvard, living up to his label of the "scholar in politics." It is Theodore Roosevelt's first important political speech, and Altgeld is his theme.

"For Mr. Bryan we can feel the contemptuous pity always felt for the small man unexpectedly thrust into a big place. But in Mr. Altgeld's case we see all too clearly the jaws and hide of the wolf through the fleecy covering.

"Mr. Altgeld is a much more dangerous man than Bryan. He is much slyer, much more intelligent, much less silly, much more free from all the restraints of public morality. The one is unscrupulous from vanity, the other from calculation. The one plans wholesale repudiation with a light heart and bubbly eloquence, because he lacks intelligence . . . the other would connive at wholesale murder and would justify it by elaborate and cunning sophistry for reasons known only to his own tortuous soul. For America to put men like this in control of her destiny would be such a dishonor as it is scarcely bearable to think of."

The reference to "conniving at wholesale murder" was, of course, Theodore Roosevelt's interpretation of Altgeld's Haymarket pardon.

Ten years earlier he had expressed the wish to lead his New York policemen against the radicals of Chicago—and he had not changed.[35]

Theodore Roosevelt continued:

"Mr. Bryan and Mr. Altgeld are the embodiment of the two principles which our adversaries desire to see triumph; and in their ultimate analysis these principles are merely the negation of the two commandments, 'Thou shalt not steal' and 'Thou shall do no murder.' . . . Mr. Altgeld condones and encourages the most infamous of murders and denounces the federal government and the Supreme Court for interfering to put a stop to the bloody lawlessness which results in worse than murder. Both of them would substitute for the government of Washington and Lincoln, for the system of orderly liberty which we inherit from our forefathers and which we desire to bequeath to our sons, a red welter of lawlessness . . . as fantastic and as vicious as the Paris commune itself."[36]

Such was the tenor throughout of Roosevelt's address. And he believed his vicious misrepresentation of Altgeld, or thought he did. When about that time Willis J. Abbott offered to introduce him to Altgeld, Roosevelt reared up and in a strident voice, heard through the Pullman car in which they were riding, announced he would not meet Altgeld socially—"Because, sir, I may at any time be called upon to meet the man sword to sword upon the field of battle. . . . The sentiment now animating a large proportion of our people can only be suppressed, as the Commune in Paris was suppressed, by taking ten or a dozen of their leaders out, standing . . . them against a wall, and shooting them dead. I believe it will come to that." When his remarks were published later, Roosevelt denied making them—but he had made them.[37]

After that Chicago speech, Roosevelt wrote his sister, Mrs. Cowles, "I did my best at Altgeld. . . ." By that speech, he brought himself into such favorable esteem by the Republican big-wigs that McKinley named him assistant secretary of the navy, thus starting him on the career which made him president of the United States—so that later he could stamp on his party policies pioneered by the man who "connived at wholesale murder."

10

Just as ironical was the part played two weeks after Roosevelt's talk by another up-and-coming young Republican—Albert J. Beveridge of

Indianapolis. To him fell the opportunity to make the closing speech of the national campaign, an address to be delivered at Chicago. Ex-President Harrison had been opportuned to make the talk, but declined and suggested the younger Hoosier. Altgeld and Altgeld's Cooper Union address was Beveridge's theme. The campaign, he frankly declared, was to decide if Altgeld's theories on government were to prevail.

Preservation of American institutions was at stake, he orated. The question was "if these American institutions as Hamilton designed them, as Marshall defined them, as Lincoln consecrated them, shall continue . . . or whether they shall be changed, corrupted and disrupted along the lines that John C. Calhoun marked and John P. Altgeld has re-surveyed!"[38]

That attack upon Altgeld did for Beveridge what Theodore Roosevelt's address did. Looking back upon this speech and its effect in later life, United States Senator Beveridge was convinced that it paved the way to the Senate two years later, so his biographer, Claude Bowers, writes.[39] Two years later he was still winning plaudits by assailing Altgeld, declaring that the height of inconsistency would be "an Altgeld speech on the Fourth of July."[40]

11

Altgeld did not bother to answer either Roosevelt or Beveridge, for by then the national campaign was over. In the last days, he concentrated on efforts to hold the city of Chicago in line. He literally dragged his weary body from meeting to meeting. After one appearance, he stumbled from the stage, slumped into a chair and for nearly an hour was in a sort of semi-coma. Added to the strain of his platform appearances was the endless business of conferring with other party leaders, going over last-minute campaign plans. One evening he sent word to Adolf Kraus, asking for an invitation to dine at the Kraus home. And that was strange, because Kraus was a leader among the Gold Democrats. Altgeld explained why he wanted to be with a "Goldbug" that night. "I have not had a minute's peace since the campaign started. All day long a line of politicians is in my office. When I leave the office, they come to my home . . . I cannot stand it much longer. I had to go to some place where they would not be likely to look for me."

One of Lawyer Kraus's small sons came up to him that evening.

"Are you the President of the United States?" the boy asked.

"No," said Altgeld. "I am only the Governor of Illinois."

"Well," said the boy. "You don't look like it!"[41]

Altgeld laughed. He didn't feel much like a governor, or anything else, so weary he was. But he kept on, all the while pleading for Bryan, scarcely ever mentioning his own contest with John R. Tanner, the Republican candidate against him for governor. "If there are Republicans . . . who feel they must in part support their ticket, then I say in all earnestness of my soul, go into the booth and vote for Mr. Tanner for Governor. Then think of your families; think of the future of your children; think of the future of our great country and cast a vote for Bryan and for humanity."[42]

To the end, he was still fighting. On the last day, at the request of reporters, he issued a statement, claiming victory for Bryan and also striking at the flag-waving campaign staged by the opposition. "The people's welfare vs. corporate aggrandizement has been the issue. . . . Mark Hanna saw three months ago that his party was hopelessly beaten on the financial issue. He then adopted a panic policy and now runs for protection behind the flag which he is shamelessly prostituting in the interest of a discredited cause."[43]

Yet even then, he probably knew it would be a miracle if Bryan were to win. Reports reached him of Republican tactics much more effective than speech-making, or the cry that "Altgeld is an Anarchist." Workingmen all over the nation were being told that if Bryan won, there would be no need for them to return to the factory the next day. Some plants already were shut down and notices posted which, in effect, were: "This plant will re-open if McKinley is elected. It will remain closed if Bryan is elected." And while those tactics were used in the cities, insurance agents and bankers were bringing similar pressure upon the farmers. Did they wish their mortgages extended? Well, they would be extended if McKinley won. But if Bryan won, it would mean foreclosure. Champ Clark sought to cash a check at a bank for $10, but was refused when it was learned he needed the money for transportation to make a speech for Bryan.[44]

And then, early in October, there was the effect of happenings in India—India which, in 1893, had given unexpected impetus to the silver issue. Its own wheat crop had failed, and suddenly India began buying American wheat in huge quantities. Slowly, the farmers of the Middle West began finding themselves prosperous once more. Wasn't it better, then, many felt, to line up with Mark Hanna after all?

12

Altgeld received the first discouraging returns while lying on a leather sofa in a suite he had engaged for himself and Mrs. Altgeld at the Palmer House. He was all in, but in a light mood. To reporters, he declared that he had no intention of staying up all night to get the results. They would be the same in the morning—and he needed his sleep. Clarence Darrow came to the hotel to chat awhile. His heart ached at the idea that Altgeld had been defeated along with Bryan but Darrow believed he ought to appear optimistic for Altgeld's sake, and spoke vaguely of victory. Then Fred D. P. Snelling came to the room bearing a batch of telegrams for Altgeld. Altgeld asked him what he had heard.

"We are hopelessly lost."

"I felt the same way," said Altgeld. "But Darrow here thinks we are going to win. He thinks I had better be guarded because there will be a terrible commotion over our victory." He smiled.

"You will be perfectly safe, Governor," said Snelling. "There will be no commotion."[45]

"I thought so," Altgeld said. Soon he was left alone with Mrs. Altgeld, who read to him until he fell asleep.

BOOK EIGHT

THE YOUNG OLD MAN

CHAPTER THIRTY-SIX

No Regrets!

1

And no victory "commotion" disturbed his slumber that night. In the Union League Club, staid bankers played leapfrog because McKinley had won and Altgeld was defeated, but the Democrats who had not gone to bed were gathered in little mournful groups. Below Altgeld's room, in the Palmer House bar, Darrow and Schilling were in one such group. In the eyes of a woman with them there were tears. "I could forgive the workingman for defeating Bryan, but to think of letting Altgeld be defeated . . . I can never forgive them for that!" She echoed the sentiment that Florence Kelley had written earlier to Henry D. Lloyd. "If the workingmen allow Altgeld to be defeated now, in the face of his record, surely they deserve to have no other friend. . . ."[1]

In New York, Henry George shook his head sadly. "Oh, what did it matter about Free Silver. Too bad, too bad! The people lost again!"[2] . . . And Tom Johnson of Ohio thought: "What they feared was not free silver—but free men!"[3]

For some in Illinois there was slight comfort in the fact that Altgeld, despite all the fury over his Haymarket pardon and the Pullman episode, had run ahead of Bryan by ten thousand votes. That was something, although not much. Even so, the defeat held promise of compensation for Altgeld. Perhaps he could have some peace now, and also an opportunity to rebuild his fortune. But neither his own restless nature, nor his enemies would permit that yet.

That very next morning, even before all of the returns were in, Joseph Medill's *Tribune* carried an editorial heavily laden with all the old-time hatred for Altgeld. "Exit Altgeld!" It gloated that "John Pardon Altgeld" had been defeated by a bigger majority than had made him governor in 1892. Then for nearly a column it went on to rake him for "his cynical misconduct, his criminal sympathies, his anarchistic tendencies, his fostering of evil, his industrious, sedulous efforts to breed social discord . . . his patronage and protection of Debs-ism, free riot and state sovereignty . . . all the essential doctrines of Jeff Davis and Herr Most."[4]

2

That would hold him! So Joseph Medill must have believed. But Altgeld, even in defeat, had some fight left in him. From the Palmer House he issued the most widely quoted statement of that campaign. It showed that he was already thinking of another battle, that he was far from vanquished—or chastened.

"Consider that only six months ago our great party lay prostrate. It had been betrayed into the hands of jobbers and monopolists by President Cleveland . . . Yet under these sore conditions . . . it arose with new energy, it cut loose from the domination of trusts and syndicates, it repudiated the men who betrayed it . . . it drove out the political vermin and with a new inspiration it again proclaimed democratic principles and espoused the cause of toiling humanity. Although it was obliged to reform while under the fire of the enemy, it made the most heroic political fight ever seen in this country.

"It was confronted by all the boodle that could be scraped together on two continents; it was confronted by all the banks, all the trusts, all the syndicates, all the corporations, all the great papers. It was confronted by everything that money could buy, that boodle could debauch or that fear of starvation could coerce. . . . It was confronted by a combination of forces such as had never been united before and will probably never again be, and worse still the time was too short to educate the public."[5]

He could have observed that while Bryan was overwhelmed in the electoral college, he would have won had less than 20,000 votes been distributed differently. By so narrow a margin did Hanna's millions of dollars win over Bryan's thousands.[6] Thus, despite the kind of opposition that defeated Bryan, Altgeld declared that he believed "at the next general election of the people, the Democrats will triumph." To Bryan, three days later, he expressed the same idea. "You have done a work for humanity which time will not efface and while we were not able to batter down all the fortified strongholds of plutocracy and corruption in our fight, I am convinced that another assault will drive them from the land."[7]

The Tribune was thrown into a fit of anger by Altgeld's post-election statement. "Viper Altgeld Gnaws A File!" "Altgeld after election is the same viperous Altgeld as before election, only a little more so!" His statement proved this, the newspaper argued, because of its "violent . . . anarchistic tone."[8]

3

In other large cities the newspapers were scarcely less rancorous toward the "Viper." The New York *Tribune* opined that defeat of "Altgeld the Anarchist" was "cause for national rejoicing," although "burglars, bomb-throwers, murderers, robbers . . . and all anarchists and criminals in general" would mourn him. Bryan? He was only a "puppet in the blood-imbued hands of Altgeld." The New York *World* expressed itself similarly, while the St. Louis *Star* asserted that "Altgeld's defeat is of more consequence even than the election of McKinley, because the Republican party and the people of the United States might have survived the defeat of the sound money cause, but the triumph of Altgeldism would have meant the destruction of the most sacred principles. . . ."[9] *Harper's Weekly*—"The Journal of Civilization"—agreed, calling Altgeld "the most dangerous enemy to American institutions of all the ruffianly gang which has broken out of the forecastle of the ship of state and attempted to occupy the quarter-deck and seize the helm."

4

To the very end of his governorship, which had two months more to run, he was treated with the same kind of abuse and hatred. The very last day produced a typical incident. In accord with custom, Altgeld on that day had escorted his successor to the House of Representatives for the inaugural. Earlier, he had sent Governor-elect Tanner a polite and cordial note offering the use of his carriage and any assistance that he and his wife could give, for, on that occasion at least, he forgot political enmities. But Tanner could not forget. Even as Tanner was walking with Altgeld to the inaugural chamber, the new governor licked his chops in anticipation of a last devastating insult planned at Altgeld's expense.

Every other retiring governor had been permitted to deliver a farewell message at his successor's inaugural. That custom had been adhered to by Altgeld in 1892 in the case of Governor Fifer. Altgeld was led to expect the same courtesy, in fact had released his message to the press that morning. But the inauguration committee, controlled by Tanner and doubtless egged on by the *Tribune*, secretly determined that Altgeld would not be permitted to make his talk. And so it was. He was left sitting, his speech in his pocket. "Illinois has had enough of that anarchist!" Governor Tanner is supposed to have declared.

Except the *Tribune*, which applauded, even Republican papers felt ashamed later of that treatment of Altgeld on his last day at Springfield. Especially was this so when the text of the talk that Altgeld prepared was published. For he had planned nothing but words of good will for his successor. "While politically divided, we are all Illinoisans and the greatness and grandeur of this State rise above all considerations of persons or party. . . . To [Governor Tanner] who is to stand at her head, I extend the most cordial greeting and hearty good wishes. Loving Illinois as I do, I shall applaud his every act that tends to her advancement. . . ."

Such was the tenor of the talk that he was not permitted to give.[10] And so, his last day as governor was marred by vindictiveness of his enemies exceeding any he had ever displayed.

5

But he took it philosophically. It was a relief to be done with Springfield. "Well, we are rid of this, anyway!" he had observed to Brand Whitlock a day or two before. The lifting of the load of administrative detail gave him a lightness of spirit that made even Tanner's insult seem unimportant. On the morning of Tanner's inaugural, Altgeld appeared to be in the best humor since his arrival in Springfield four years before. As he busied himself with last minute correspondence, it was noticed that when he went from one office to another it was with "a hop, skip and a jump." He joked with newspapermen who called on him. "All I need now," he told the reporters that morning, "is a rich uncle to pay some of my bills. Otherwise, I expect to do all right."[11]

And his very last contact with Springfield, despite the Tanner insult, was a pleasant one. With Mrs. Altgeld, he had slipped quietly away to the Alton depot. He expected to be unnoticed. But at the station, there was a regiment of militia among several that had been called out to add pomp to Tanner's inaugural. Some of the militia members recognized Altgeld as he helped his wife on the train. Soon the militia regiment was shouting three cheers for him, and the soldiers waved their hats. It was a spontaneous tribute, from the "common people," for that was the class that the militia members, farmers and laborers from small towns, represented. Altgeld appreciated it and bowed cordially.

Then the train took him toward Chicago. He was a private individual once more.

6

Alone with Mrs. Altgeld on that six-hour trip northward across the prairies that separated the state capital from Chicago, he had an opportunity to let his mind dwell upon the events that had happened since that other January, four years previous, when he was heading in the opposite direction on that same railroad route bound for his own inaugural. It should not be difficult to reconstruct the thoughts that passed through his head. First of all, there was the Haymarket matter.

No regrets there! Not one. In a little while he would be telling his faithful friend Schilling that if the state should ever erect a monument to him, because he had been governor, the theme should be his pardon of those three men, Fielden, Schwab and Neebe.[12] Best of all about that pardon, he had been wrong in assuming that his act meant his political suicide. Grover Cleveland, if nobody else, knew better!

Recollection of some other pardons may have flickered across his mind. The Tribune's nick-name, "John Pardon," was based on the claim that he had freed more criminals from the Illinois prisons than any other governor. That was untrue, as he had proved in statements more than once,[13] but it was true that he had exercised his pardoning power a good many times.

"Many of the pardons he granted were the result of sympathy for a mother, wife, sister or daughter of the condemned, and in such cases he used to laugh at the criticism of the press. I remember one day an old woman came to the State House to plead for a pardon for her son, a worthless, vicious youth, who had been sentenced to prison for larceny. She was a Pole . . . and spoke only imperfect English. The Governor was absent, but I met her in the corridor and she told me her pitiful story. When the Governor returned, I sent her to him. Half an hour later, having some business with him, I entered his office without knocking, and I found him and the old lady weeping together. He was trying to comfort her and had ordered a pardon for her scamp of a son. He seemed somewhat ashamed of his emotion, and said in half apology: 'It is a bad law that punishes a parent for the sins of a child!' "[14]

So "Buck" Hinrichsen related. Yet, study of many pardon matters reveals that justice prompted him to act as much as sympathy—justice and that strong feeling for the under-dog. There was the case that Judge Hardin Masters of Lewistown, Illinois, father of Edgar Lee Masters, brought to his attention. It concerned a ne'er-do-well resident of Masters' town named Weldy. Lewistown was "dry" and Weldy had the habit of going to the near-by village of Havana to get drunk. On his return one day, the town marshal, John Logan, a crusading "dry" who had already killed two men, saw him reeling toward his home. Marshal Logan knocked Weldy to the ground with a lead-knobbed cane, then proceeded to beat him mercilessly. Weldy had a pistol and killed the marshal. He was given life imprisonment, and later many prominent townsmen, including both the prosecutor and the judge, felt that Weldy had been dealt with too harshly. Judge Masters brought many papers to Altgeld on the case, then told him the story. "Altgeld listened . . . and, without looking at the papers, granted an immediate pardon to Weldy, saying that Weldy had a right to kill Logan for such uncalled-for brutality."[15]

Ex-Governor Fifer came to Altgeld with another case that resulted in one of the most curious of Altgeld's pardons. Back in Bloomington for the practice of law after Altgeld defeated him, Fifer represented a young man who was charged with manslaughter. The youth had walked across a farmer's land as a shortcut to his home. The farmer went after him with a gun and there was a scuffle. The farmer struck his head against a fence and the blow killed him. In one trial the jury disagreed, but a second trial resulted in a conviction. Fifer saw Altgeld immediately, bringing with him letters from both judge and prosecutor to the effect that a miscarriage of justice had occurred. The result of Fifer's visit became apparent on the day that sentence was to be passed. As the sheriff prepared to escort the youth to prison, Fifer pulled from his pocket a document. It was a pardon from Altgeld—granted in advance![16]

Two "Jean Valjean" cases came to his desk in 1895. One Harry Steel had been sentenced, incredibly, to serve fourteen years for stealing a pair of shoes from a secondhand store in Chicago—to sell them, Altgeld was advised, to buy food. And one James B. Miller, a family man out of work, had been sent to prison for five years for stealing a slab of bacon for his family. Altgeld pardoned them both, insisting that in each case the punishment failed to fit the crime.[17] And in 1896 a labor case was involved. During the coal strike of 1894, a riot had occurred at the Peter Little mine near Peoria. Two men were killed in a clash between strikers and "scabs." As a result, four union leaders, including a former member of the legislature, John L. Gehr, were placed on trial for murder and convicted. Altgeld discovered the following about that case:

(1) Not the union men, but the "scabs," had done the killings, but the union leaders were prosecuted on the theory that they had started the riot; (2) the county employed all of the lawyers in the district for the prosecution, forcing the defense to bring in lawyers from the outside who were looked upon with suspicion; (3) whenever any witness was produced to testify in behalf of the defendants, the witness was "arrested on some trumped-up charge of riot and he was at once thrown into jail."[18]

It was not surprising, therefore, that Altgeld intervened.

In the case of a physician of Sidell, Illinois, Dr. Willis B. Cauble, Altgeld granted a pardon very promptly. The physician was Catholic, and there was considerable anti-Catholic prejudice in the community. Altgeld was informed that when a charge of forgery was brought against Dr. Cauble, a prominent member of the anti-Catholic A. P. A. announced that if he were on the jury, he would vote to send "that Catholic to prison for ten years." And, lo, the A. P. A.-er was on the jury, and the physician was given a ten-year sentence, even though there were mitigating circumstances in the doctor's favor.[19] Did Altgeld recall the bloody anti-Catholic riots of his boyhood when he freed the physician?

A pardon that especially offended the "respectable" elements involved two Democratic poll watchers who had been accused of violating the election laws in a Chicago election. The Civic Federation of Chicago had made an issue of the case and assisted in the prosecution as part of a crusade for clean elections. Altgeld acted when he discovered that the defendants had pleaded guilty with the definite understanding they would be let off with fines, only to have the judge hand them prison sentences. The *Tribune* and the Civic Federation let out a roar of protest when he pardoned the pair. In that case, Altgeld answered, in a letter to a member of the Civic Federation.

First, he stated that he granted the pardons "because on my judgment, justice required it, and my course in this case is based upon the same principles that have guided me in everything else . . . to do what is right and never for a moment ask whether my act will meet with the approval or disapproval of any man or organization of men." Then he took cognizance of the fact that the Civic Federation, representing Big Business in Chicago, accused him of fostering political corruption by his pardons.

"This is foreign to the subject [he wrote] but as you have introduced it, let me ask, who caused this . . . corruption? Not the poor, not the great masses of the people. It was the corrupting hand of unscrupulous wealth, which no matter how infamous its work, always wore the glove of respectability. . . . If you will look over the list of subscribers to [the Civic Federation] you will find there the names of some men who are stockholders in various corporations which spent money in Chicago and at Springfield to defeat legislation . . . to corrupt public officials in order to gain an unjust advantage, and which then paid to its stockholders the fruits that were obtained by bribery and corruption. If your association desires to right some of the great wrongs . . . why do you not look occasionally into the source of the evil?"[20]

It was no wonder, then, that so much abuse was heaped upon him for his pardon record, aside from the Haymarket case. And if he made mistakes they were "on the side of the angels." Nor could it be said that he was always swayed by too much sympathy. The week after "Buck" Hinrichsen saw him weeping with the Polish mother, he had before him the case of a man condemned to hang for choking his mistress to death. Lawyers argued that their client was not a person of murderous intention. "He had frequently choked his mistress without serious injury to her." But no evidence of any injustice was presented, and Altgeld closed an all-day hearing by observing: "He choked her once too often!"[21] And there was the fact that out of all the criminals he had released, not more than one or two was ever in trouble again. Even Weldy of Edgar Lee Masters' home town gave up drinking and became an industrious citizen.

7

He must have given a thought, too, to the Pullman episode. Some day, perhaps, he must have felt, the facts would come out to show how right he was. And if he gave a thought to the strikers, the men who followed Eugene V. Debs in that sacrificial strike, it was with a profound feeling of sympathy. Poor devils! Thousands of them had been blacklisted, unable to get other railroad jobs. Well, he had helped a few, putting them on state jobs where he could, when George Schilling brought them to his attention. Debs had expressed to

Schilling (Altgeld had not yet met Debs) his gratification for that help by Altgeld. Later Debs would refer to Altgeld as "one of the great souls of this sordid age,"[22] and perhaps had this matter in mind as much as anything.

A more pleasant phase of his term to dwell upon concerned the University of Illinois. When Altgeld became governor, the state university at Champaign-Urbana was known as a "cow college." It had good facilities for training in agriculture, some for engineering, but scarcely any facility for anything else. Fewer than 800 pupils attended the institution, and in educational circles the university was a subject for scorn. The reason was not hard to find. The politicians were not interested in appropriating money to be expended by professors. When a display of "economy" was called for, the university usually was the goat. In 1891, the legislature felt it was dealing generously with it when it appropriated $132,700 for the "cow college" for two years' operation.

But Altgeld brought to the governor's post a vision of his state possessing a university second to none in the country. So he addressed the State Legislature.[23] It took a battle to do it, but he forced through an increase in appropriations for the biennium to $295,000 in 1893, and to $424,000 in 1895. He was motivated by a general Jeffersonian attitude on education in a democracy, and also by a motive that in later years appeared ironic.

At the time he became governor, John D. Rockefeller had begun pouring millions into the University of Chicago. Altgeld feared that, as a result, the "Rockefeller university" in Chicago would reflect the viewpoint of the Standard Oil Corporation on social issues. He believed a strong state university was necessary to neutralize the influence of the University of Chicago, never dreaming that the University of Chicago would become the leading center of progressive thought in the Middle West while the University of Illinois nearly always has remained a conservative force.

Fortunately for Altgeld's plans for the state institution, Dr. Andrew Sloan Draper became president in 1894, for Draper had also a vision of greatness for the school. Altgeld gave the principal address at the installation of Dr. Draper, and then had a heart-to-heart talk with the new college head.

"He talked of the things he wanted done; they were good things to do and showed that his sympathies were genuine and that he had given not a little thought to an involved and rather depressed situation.

He wanted more buildings, more teachers, more students, more carrying of liberal learning to all the people and all the interests of the State, and much more money to do things with. It was a little surprising to hear a live Governor talk like that!"

So Dr. Draper recalled his interview with Altgeld that day.[24] The University of Illinois really became a university as a result, for Altgeld saw to it that the "cow college" added a department of medicine, a law school, a dental school, a graduate school, a pharmacy school, and was strengthened immeasurably in the liberal arts. In short, as Allan Nevins, the historian of the university, wrote, Altgeld "was the first state executive to realize that the interests of the people were bound up with making the University powerful and comprehensive."

One incident involving the university probably provoked a sardonic smile. In an outburst of patriotism the General Assembly of 1895 (known as the most corrupt in the history of the state) passed a bill compelling the display of the American flag at all schools. In 1896, Altgeld learned that he, the governor of Illinois, had been indicted by the grand jury of Champaign County because the University of Illinois had violated the flag law. It had the flag on its main building, but not on the subsidiary buildings—such was the "crime." Politics, of course, and the Republican sheriff of Champaign county announced he intended to arrest Altgeld at the Executive Mansion. "Don't come after me unless you are prepared to take on the state militia!" Altgeld answered, half in jest. The sheriff changed his mind and finally the case was dropped when even Republican newspapers saw its absurdity. It was a case that illustrated his point when he was once asked how to advise young men ambitious to become millionaires. "Rely on yourself—keep your manhood—keep your own counsel—do your own errands and look ahead. . . . But if you wish to get rich very quickly, then bleed the public and talk patriotism!"[25]

8

Some other matters during his term were of a nature to inspire some quiet chuckles. In May, 1894, he received an invitation to attend the commencement exercises of Northwestern University. He was not asked to speak, but only to "sit on the platform." He could not resist replying that if he had been asked to speak, he would be forced to decline for lack of time to prepare, "but inasmuch as you simply ask me to sit upon the platform, a request which as I understand it involves no labor except what may be necessary to swell out to a reasonable degree of importance and look wise, I accept. . . . It strikes me that this is a new use to make of Governors, but if they can render this country valuable service in that way, why, I shall be delighted. . . ." How the *Tribune* did howl when that bit of facetiousness was made public! "Altgeldian humor," it called it.[26]

Then there was the look on the faces of the pompous glass manufacturers when he turned down their request that he exempt their factories from enforcement of the new law against child labor. They had said that if they could not employ children, they would shut their factories and put up signs reading "Closed Because of Pernicious Legislation in Illinois." "I do not object to a sign," said Altgeld. "But I suggest that your signs read: 'Closed Because the Governor of Illinois Will Not Allow Us to Employ Babies!' "[27]

His friend John W. Yantis of Shelbyville told him an amusing story about the 1895 session of the legislature. Altgeld had vetoed what were known as "The Eternal Monopoly Bills," legislation wanted by Charles T. Yerkes, the traction "baron." Unquestionably considerable "boodle" had been distributed among members of the legislature to pass the bills. After his veto, an effort was made to re-pass them. Yantis, as secretary of the Railroad and Warehouse Commission, was working with Altgeld to hold the legislature in line behind the veto. Altgeld had him talk to a certain leader in the Assembly. "You are not going to vote against the Governor, are you?" Yantis asked the legislator. "It is going to pass, anyway, and ten thousand dollars looks good to me!" "But how are they going to get enough fellows?" said Yantis. "They can't afford to pay that kind of a price to get enough fellows." "Oh," said the legislator, "they've got a lot of cheap skates lined up."

And that, as he later told Altgeld, gave Yantis an idea. He looked up another legislator, who admitted that he was voting for the bills. "What are they giving you?" "Two hundred dollars." "Don't let them make a sap out of you," said Yantis. "They are paying as high as ten thousand dollars!" The second legislator was indignant. "Why, the crooks told me that two hundred was the top!" He passed the word to several other legislators who had been "swindled" similarly. "They became incensed . . . and refused to vote for the bills, and it failed by one vote to override the Governor's veto."[28]

9

If Altgeld thought of that amusing incident in connection with the "Eternal Monopoly" bills, he also thought of the more serious phases of that legislation. The full story, never before adequately or correctly told, involves the brazen "financiering" of Charles T. Yerkes, a rumored "million dollar" bribe attempt, a desperate effort by John W. Lanehart to make a financial killing, the supposedly infamous Ogden Gas Company "deal"—and Altgeld's beloved Unity Block.

It was known by a few persons at the time that Altgeld could have made one fortune during the 1895 session of the Legislature if he had wanted to accept from Yerkes, who controlled the Chicago traction companies, a "gift" ranging in estimate from $100,000 to $1,000,-000. The money could have been his for doing exactly nothing at all, for the "Eternal Monopoly" bills had been passed by a tremendous majority, and he had only to let them become a law automatically. He could have stated later that there would have been no sense in attempting a veto inasmuch as the bills had the votes of three-fourths of the legislators and thus could reasonably be expected to be passed again over a veto.

After Altgeld's death, thousands of persons knew of his refusal to be bribed, for doing nothing at all, and that he did it at a time when he needed money in the worst way, when accepting the "gift" meant saving his Unity Block and ending all the financial worries into which he had been plunged. Ironically, it was the *Tribune* that told the story of the Yerkes bribe offer—after both Altgeld and Joseph Medill had passed on. It was told in an article by Forrest Crissey, in a series of political reminiscences entitled *Tattlings of a Retired Politician*.

Fictitious names were used in that *Tribune* story—the Governor was "Cal Peavey," the Unity Block was "The Empire Building," Lanehart was referred to as "Mike Boylan" and so on. But there was no doubt in anyone's mind that the *Tribune* was telling the story of Altgeld's refusal to be bribed by Yerkes, especially not when, in describing "Governor Cal Peavey," the *Tribune* story carried a paragraph that read:

"Almost the whole press of the state was against him and he was hounded as an anarchist, a calamity howler and a general enemy of society, capital, vested rights and a whole lot of other sacred and civilized things. But Cal kept his nerve and continued to talk right out in meeting. The harder they pounded, the more he showed his teeth and stuck out his bristles."[29]

Then the story went on to relate that the "anarchist Governor" was in a bad way financially because of his sky-scraper, and that this was exactly at that time the legislature passed certain franchise bills wanted by "United Traction." While Governor "Peavy" was studying the measures in Springfield an agent of "United Traction" walked into the "Empire Building" in Chicago and asked "Mike Boylan" to accompany him to the safety vaults. There the agent counted out a million dollars, locked the money in the vault, then returned to "Boylan's office."

Suddenly, he dropped the key to the vault on "Boylan's" desk and said: "You know what to do with this!" When the Governor learned of the matter, he told "Boylan": "Young man! I'd advise you to take better care of that damned scoundrel's money than you ever did of any money in your life!" And "that night the Governor wrote a veto message that fairly scorched the rails of the line."

Such was the story of the "million dollar bribe," as revealed in the *Tribune*, during the legislature of 1895. Was it based on fact? It was, for all the essentials of that story were true. F. D. P. Snelling was in the Unity Block office the evening, just before closing time, when an agent for Yerkes entered with a bag. The man asked for Lanehart, who was talking in his office with Joe Martin. Altgeld then was in Springfield. The Yerkes man saw Lanehart, and together they left for the safety vault room of the Unity Building. They came back, had a few minutes more conversation, then the Yerkes man departed.

All this was seen by Snelling, and later Lanehart told him enough for him to guess that a large sum of money had been left for Altgeld if he chose to do what Yerkes wanted.[30] Only the exact amount of the sum offered Altgeld is unknown. It was at least $100,000, but more probably a half million dollars. The half-million dollar figure was given by Altgeld himself years later when Judge Edward F. Dunne (later Governor) brought up the subject[31] and George Schilling recalled that Altgeld mentioned that amount to him.[32]

At least it was enough to have freed Altgeld from all the financial worries that were then "breaking him down." Unquestionably, Yerkes knew of those worries, for he and Banker Walsh worked together on many "deals." Up to then, Yerkes probably had not encountered any man in politics who could not be bought off, if the price were high enough. That was how he had lifted himself, practically by his bootstraps, to control of the vast traction properties in Chicago. It was his stock in trade and it had never failed him before. Probably Yerkes got the shock of his life when he found that Altgeld could not be bribed, even with bankruptcy staring him in the face. No wonder Yerkes would say about that time, concerning Altgeld: "I admire that man!"[33]

As indicated, the story of the Yerkes bribe effort had become well known, thanks largely to the story in the *Tribune*. Scarcely known at all, however, is the fact that Altgeld in his veto of the Eternal Monopoly Bills of 1895 tossed away, not one fortune, but two fortunes. The other had to do with the Ogden Gas Company "deal."

10

For forty years, "Ogden Gas" has been an example *célèbre* in the history of politico-financial corruption that from time to time has marked municipal affairs in Chicago and other large cities. The number and the prominence of the men who were skyrocketed to great wealth as a result of Ogden Gas has become legendary. The scheme— as it turned out finally—followed a familiar pattern. The city council had the power to grant franchises to public utilities, such as electric· light companies, telephone companies—and gas companies. If a company already was established, it was to its benefit that no other franchises in the same field be granted. When other franchises were granted, the established company usually tried to buy out the newcomer—as cheaply as possible. Aldermen were familiar with that situation—and so were others high up in politics with the ability to influence aldermen. And so it had become a great American custom in large cities for aldermen to vote franchises, not for the purpose of establishing actual companies, but to use them as a means of shaking down utility companies for large sums. Ogden Gas turned out, finally, to be one of the most lucrative of such schemes—for those in on the deal at the end.

Not until 1935 had anyone recalled that Altgeld was connected in any way with the Ogden Gas episode—yet he was, through his cousin, John W. Lanehart.[34] Heretofore, the assumption always has been that Roger Sullivan, later "boss" of the Illinois Democracy, John P. Hopkins, then mayor, were the originators of the Ogden Gas Company. The truth, however, is that John Lanehart devised the scheme and associated Sullivan and Hopkins with him in order to put it over.[35]

Another assumption has been that the Ogden Gas Company was organized with no idea except for "shaking down" the existing Chicago Gas Trust, that is, to get a franchise for operating a gas company from the city council simply to force the Gas Trust to buy the franchise later. In other words, it has been believed that there was never any intention to operate a gas company. Now, it seems clear that the men taken in on the plan by Lanehart may have had only that idea. But

Lanehart appears to have intended a legitimate company—at least this was so after he had a certain unpleasant interview with Altgeld. And there is the fact that the Ogden Gas Company, usually pictured as a mythical creation, did build a plant and for several years was engaged in the actual production and distribution of gas.[36]

Yet, the Ogden Gas Company was a creation of "boodle." Was Lanehart, in this episode, a "boodler"? The answer is, he was, not as a recipient of "boodle," but as a distributor. Unquestionably, graft was distributed among members of the Chicago City Council to induce passage of the ordinance granting the Ogden company a franchise. Supposedly, the stock was divided into eleven blocks. One list shows that four aldermanic leaders received a block each; Mayor Hopkins, two blocks; Roger Sullivan one block; Levy Mayer, as attorney,[37] one block; Patrick Sexton, a financier, one block; Lanehart, one block, with the remaining block set aside for "chicken feed," i. e., miscellaneous corruption.[38] Lanehart directed a good deal of the distribution of the stock. For Lanehart was "a very practical man . . . who played politics in a practical way. He knew what was necessary if he were to get the franchise passed."[39]

11

And Altgeld? Did he know what his cousin, at that time known as his business partner, was up to? The answer is no—not until the ordinance was passed on February 25, 1895.[40] Altgeld learned from the newspapers. And when the scandal broke, he made a hurried trip to Chicago. F. D. P. Snelling was in Altgeld's office when the Governor arrived at the Unity Block. He saw that Altgeld was "blazing with indignation" and heard him summon Lanehart. When Lanehart arrived, he went into Altgeld's private office and they were together for some time.

"I could hear the Governor talking pretty loud. He was evidently giving it to Lanehart. When Lanehart came out later, I spoke to him. 'Well, I guess the Governor let you have it,' I said. Lanehart smiled and said, 'Yes, but I was able to fix things all right. I think I was able to convince him that we were all right.' "[41]

So Mr. Snelling recalled that occasion.

How did Lanehart convince Altgeld that he was "all right"? It appears certain that he did this by convincing Altgeld that the Ogden Gas Company was not to be a mere dummy corporation. A plant was to be constructed and gas was to be sold, at a lower price than the Gas Trust charged.[42] And this, Lanehart could have observed, was directly in line with views often expressed by Altgeld, that it is necessary to have competitive companies in the utility field to prevent gouging of the public.

Long before Lanehart had thought of organizing a gas company, Altgeld, while a judge, had talked of competitive gas companies in an address before the Sunset Club of Chicago on October 23, 1890. In that talk, a discussion of corruption in city government, he had said:

"Take the matter of gas. . . . If there had been a general law to the effect that by applying to the Department of Works any responsible party could, under general regulations, put down gas pipes and supply the people, would we not have had more competition and cheaper and better gas?"[43]

Well, the Ogden ordinance provided that it would supply gas at 90 cents a thousand, whereas the Trust then charged $1.25. What, then, was wrong with the plan except the fact that the ordinance had to be "boodled" through the council? But how did the Gas Trust get its franchises? And how could anyone get into the gas field in Chicago without paying for a franchise? And who was doing the howling over the ordinance, if not the Gas Trust crowd, the group that was always fighting Altgeld anyway?

Those were persuasive arguments. If Altgeld raised the point that the company was pictured as having been organized merely for the purpose of being sold later to the Gas Trust, Lanehart had a ready answer. The ordinance specifically provided that the company could not be sold to another gas company without approval of the city council.

There was the point, too, that if the company were successful, it would mean that Lanehart would have the means to get them both out of the hole into which they had been plunged by the Unity Block. At that time, Lanehart was involved in the Unity matter almost as disastrously as Altgeld, for they seemed to have pooled their joint resources.

12

Up to that point Altgeld's sole connection with the Ogden Gas matter was in his private capacity and that only because he was a cousin of Lanehart. But in the following May he found himself concerned as governor, when the three "Eternal Monopoly" bills came to his desk from the legislature. Two of the bills were those desired by Yerkes, Senate Bills 137 and 138. They permitted the Chicago city council to grant traction franchises for a term of ninety-nine years, whereas the limit had been twenty years. The third bill, House Bill No. 618, related to gas. Its chief provision seemed to be innocent enough, for it simply provided that before a city council could grant a franchise to a new gas company, the new company must have written permission from owners of a majority of the frontage on each block in which it proposed to lay pipes. The practical effect of that provision was to prevent issuance of any further gas franchises in Chicago.

Now, if the ninety-nine-year traction franchises were worth millions to Mr. Yerkes, House Bill 618 similarly was worth millions to the Chicago Gas Trust—and to the Ogden Gas Company. Those two companies would have a monopoly, forever. Altgeld saw that. He saw, too, that his cousin Lanehart stood to profit tremendously even though he may not have been involved in that phase of the boodling.[44] If Lanehart made a killing, it would mean financial relief for Altgeld too. Who would be harmed, except the Gas Trust crowd? Well, the people would be harmed, for that gas bill meant legalizing monopoly. And Altgeld was against monopoly. It was a problem, a harder one morally than was presented by Yerkes' bribe offer.

As Altgeld pondered that problem, his friend Judge McConnell came to visit him at Springfield. Yerkes had called on McConnell and somehow convinced him that his traction bills would be advantageous to Chicago, especially because they would permit consolidation of all lines and thus make possible better service. He persuaded McConnell to urge Altgeld to sign them, knowing, of course, their friendship. McConnell went to Springfield.

"I found the Governor sitting on the lawn of the Governor's mansion. After initial cordial greetings I told him of my mission. I began by saying that I was not there as a friend, but as an attorney representing a client. He said, 'Go ahead.' . . .

"After I had finished, he said, 'Well, Judge, you have made the best argument in favor of the bills that I have heard. He went on to say that he felt convinced that a consolidation of the lines would prove of advantage to the public. [But, he said,] 'I am the leader of the Democratic party and in every platform of that party for twenty-five years there has been a declaration against monopolies. Can I, without being a traitor to my party, sign a bill creating a monopoly?' Then turning to me directly, he said, 'I have been offered a hundred thousand dollars

to withhold my veto. Now, I ask you, what would you do?' I answered,
'I would veto the damn bills!' "[45]

On May fourteenth, Altgeld did veto the Yerkes bills—and also the
gas bill.[46]

13

Any regrets there? Probably he was not altogether certain when he
thought of it from one point of view. For one thing, it was as clear
as noonday that his successor, Governor Tanner, would let Yerkes
and the Gas Trust have what it wanted. (So it turned out.) Hence,
his personal sacrifice to prevent fastening a utility monopoly upon
Chicago would be only a temporary victory for the people. And so, all
he had gained by throwing away two fortunes was the maintenance of
his self-respect. Was that sufficient? Yes, that was sufficient, for he
really believed the statement he made a little later that "tainted dollars . . . the getting of something for nothing . . . leads to moral
death."[47]

And yet, he may have had some misgivings anyway on that ride back
to Chicago. There was his wife, sitting quietly next to him. How
loyally she had stood by him! How tremendously she had helped him!
And now she was none too well, mainly from worry over him. If
something should happen to him, would he even be able to leave her
enough so that she could maintain herself, after all the money he had
made? It was doubtful, for, barring a miracle, he was returning to
private life a bankrupt—thanks to Banker Walsh. Certainly that
would be the case if all his obligations came due at once.

Yet, would he have to be a bankrupt after all? John Lanehart, beloved cousin despite his faults, had done a thing that might prevent
that eventuality after all—if Altgeld could bring himself to profit by
it. For after Lanehart died in 1896, it was found that he had left a
will that reflected his love for Altgeld. After providing that Mrs.
Lanehart should receive his personal belongings and $15,000 in lieu
of dower rights, Lanehart's testament, dated November 11, 1895,
read:

"All the rest . . . I give . . . to my cousin, John P. Altgeld, but I desire that my said estate so bequeathed to him shall not be subject to
the payment of any of *his* debts or obligations existing at the time of
my decease. . . . I intend that he shall have my property . . . for his own
benefit."[48]

That was Lanehart's way of attempting to help Altgeld get out of the fix into which the Unity Block venture had placed him. And so the Ogden shares, Lanehart's block of "one eleventh," became Altgeld's. Even then, in 1896, there was inside talk "on the street" that in a little while there would be another "Ogden deal," and when that happened, Lanehart's holdings would be worth hundreds of thousands of dollars, perhaps a cool million. And that money could be Altgeld's, if he wanted to stay in the Ogden arrangement along with Hopkins, Sullivan and Levy Mayer. Did he want to stay? He would have to give some thought to that. Perhaps that was on his mind as he reached Chicago that night.

14

No crowds met him at the station. Only Joe Martin was there. But Joe Martin was enough. No matter what happened, Altgeld knew he could count on the man who had been a gambler. Had not Joe turned down a good deal of money in connection with those same "Eternal Monopoly" bills, not because Joe had any scruples about taking the money, but because he felt it would reflect upon Altgeld?[49] Until his death, Joe Martin would show the same kind of loyalty to Altgeld, for, as he once told Adolf Kraus, he loved Altgeld "more than any other man who ever lived." And now, he knew, Altgeld needed such loyalty as his more than ever.

CHAPTER THIRTY-SEVEN

More Storm

1

The four violent years at Springfield, his financial troubles, his grave concern for the health of his wife, and his own illnesses had left their mark upon Altgeld. Heavy lines of worry showed in his face. On entering the governorship he had been a man who held himself erect, and there was a sparkle in his blue eyes. Now there was a sag in his broad shoulders and a lack-luster in his eyes except when something stirred him a great deal. Because of his short legs, he always seemed a shorter man than he really was for his five feet six and a half inches of height. Now he seemed a smaller man than ever. He had lost between ten and fifteen pounds, and it showed in the bagginess of his clothes.[1] Then, too, that peculiar shuffle in his walk was becoming accentuated.

He had become, in fact, an old man—at forty-nine. If only he could have peace now! But there was no peace. Even the Unity Block was now a source of pain for he was forced to perform some unpleasant tasks when he resumed active direction of the Unity Block management. Old friends had taken offices there, and some of them were many months behind in their rents. Previously, he had ordered that they not be disturbed. But now he was forced to approve sending out notices of eviction. DeWitt C. Cregier, whom he had elected mayor in 1889, was among those on the list.[2] It hurt to do that, but the year 1899 stared him in the face. A large block of the Unity bonds would come due then, and unless the payments were met it meant losing his favorite "child"—to Banker Walsh! He found, too, that debts for operating the building had piled up; $35,000 owing for coal alone. Suits against him were threatened. Joe Martin came to his aid there, advancing the $35,000 personally. Joe took a note, probably knowing even then that he would tear it up later.

2

Worse trouble was ahead. A few weeks after his return to Chicago E. S. Dreyer's bank failed. It was discovered that the man who had

412

carried the Haymarket pardons to Joliet prison had wrecked the bank with unwise investments and was headed for Joliet now as a prisoner himself. Caught in the crash was considerable state money, for Dreyer had been treasurer for the state home for the blind and kept its funds in his own institution. The *Tribune* made much of that fact, pointedly emphasizing that Dreyer was an appointee of Altgeld. It also brought out prominently that a number of shares of Unity Company stock were found among the assets of the bank, evidence of Altgeld's borrowings. A short time later it was found that a state grain inspector at Chicago was short in his accounts. He was appointed during the Altgeld administration, and again Altgeld was blamed. The *Tribune* growled that such happenings probably were typical of all of Altgeld's administration.

But those incidents were mild compared to happenings in April, 1897. For on April fifth the Globe Savings Bank closed its doors. Altgeld had been an original director of that bank and later second vice-president. It appears that Lanehart induced him to enter that venture, for Lanehart was a close friend of Charles W. Spalding, the Globe president, with whom he had been friendly at Dartmouth College. On becoming governor, Altgeld resigned from the bank, having no further connection with the Globe, except as a borrower and through the fact that Lanehart was the attorney for the bank.

At first it looked as though the failure of the Globe was simply a result of the business depression. Spalding announced that "everything is all right; nobody will lose anything." But little by little the true picture became known. The bank had been gutted because of peculations by President Spalding. Scarcely anything would be left for the depositors. Worse still, Spalding was treasurer of the University of Illinois and, as such, had in his possession nearly $400,000 worth of university securities. He had used those securities for his own purposes, even obtained a personal loan from the First National Bank by putting up university holdings as collateral.

The *Tribune* had been waiting for just such an episode. Even people who agreed with the *Tribune's* political views were saying that Altgeld, after all, was an honest man—and that was something. Now the *Tribune* saw a chance to smear the old "anarchist" with the tar of financial dishonesty. And so it displayed prominently the fact that Altgeld "directly or indirectly" was a heavy borrower from the Globe. It submitted a list showing that between himself and Lanehart, whose debts Altgeld had guaranteed, Altgeld owed the Globe $59,600. He had put up as security Unity Company stock which, said the *Tribune* "is not regarded, however, as of full value."[3]

Who then, was responsible for wrecking the Globe? Altgeld! So the *Tribune* was insinuating, and not too subtly. It gloated when certain Globe depositors among those who had formed a protective organization announced that they wanted to "lynch Altgeld" or send him to the penitentiary "with Spalding and the rest of the gang!" No mention was made that Mrs. Altgeld had an account in the bank and that her brother Charles J. Ford, then Altgeld's business associate, had made a large deposit in the Globe the day before it closed, all of which was lost.[4]

For days the *Tribune* hammered away at him—in many respects more viciously than it had after the Haymarket pardon and the Pullman episode. Some of the facts unearthed by the *Tribune* looked damaging to Altgeld with respect to the losses of the university. The newspaper produced a letter he had written to the University of Illinois trustees that looked as if Altgeld had insisted upon Spalding's appointment as treasurer against the inclinations of the trustees. (The other candidate was Walsh.) Another letter was produced to show that Altgeld had helped Spalding to get more of the university funds in his bank than the banker might otherwise have received. It was true that Altgeld had done that. But his reason was good. The money would earn interest and, in connection with his expansion program, he wanted the university to have the benefit. However, the *Tribune* implied that he was working hand-in-glove with Spalding to help the treasurer "loot" the university.[5]

Never had Altgeld been in such a predicament. A grand jury investigation was called. It was certain that Spalding, already under arrest, would be indicted for embezzlement, for he had confessed, splattering the memory of John W. Lanehart as he did so, insisting that it was Lanehart who had advised him to borrow on the university securities.[6] Altgeld was subpoenaed.

Would he be indicted too? The *Tribune* was working to bring that about. That would be revenge! On April twenty-ninth, it editorialized:

"Whatever Altgeld touched, he destroyed or blasted or cursed. In the case of the rotten Globe Savings Bank, he has landed his man in jail because of his friendship, while he himself borrowed $57,000 of the bank's funds. What else could be looked for from an anarchist?"

And for days Altgeld lived in fear that this time the *Tribune* would overwhelm him, that he would be forced to undergo a criminal prosecution. He betrayed his fears by arranging with Colonel Patrick Sexton to have a large sum of money ready in case he should need bail.[7] Fortunately, his story satisfied the grand jury, despite the *Tribune* hounding. But the case was not yet over. The *Tribune* now demanded a state legislative investigation and again Altgeld's name was smeared across the newspapers day in and day out, although no evidence incriminating him existed.

Nothing in his career had cut him so deeply, so it is shown by a letter he wrote to his friend Judge Lambert Tree in May, after the storm had quieted a bit.

"Personally [he wrote] I have what the parrot described to its mistress as a 'hell of a time.' During my whole public career I have never been pursued with so much venom as during the last four or five months. I had long been used to facing the frown of the Fates, but this time they assume the aggressive and I have felt the sting of their irony.

"You know I took pride in having my administration honest. Well, the grain inspector whom I appointed in Chicago was $4,500 short in his accounts and for political effect has been made the subject of senatorial and grand jury investigation, and an effort has been made to besmirch an entire administration.

"Then the failure of some banks has tied up some public funds. Worst of all, Mr. Spalding, the President of the Globe Savings Bank and the treasurer of the State University at Champaign, has failed and it looks as if the institution would lose several hundred thousand dollars.

"Of course, all these things are charged to me, and while I am in no way responsible and do not mind the abuse, I am nearly heart-broken over the loss to the University. I had done more for that institution than all the other Governors put together. . . . I would as soon have been paralyzed as to have had anything happen to this institution."

He was pouring out his heart there, the first and almost the only time that he showed signs of feeling truly beaten. Yet he had no intention of giving up.

"But I am alive and am going steadily on. [He concluded his letter to his friend.] I confess I do not have any philosophy that fits the case. To say that 'there is no peace for the wicked' does not seem broad enough, and I do not feel at liberty to say that 'whom the Lord loveth He chasteneth', for I do not see His Finger in the affair. I conclude that it is simply a case of having been mistaken in men."[8]

Yes, he had been mistaken in men. But that was not the whole story. Perhaps he forgot how much of a politician he had been in "patronage" matters when he entered upon his governorship. Now those errors were coming home to roost, with a vengeance.

3

The pity of it was that he might have spared himself nearly all of that heartbreaking Globe Bank episode if only he had let himself compromise just a bit with his ideas of public righteousness. For the Ogden Gas Shares that Lanehart had left him represented a gold mine. No matter by what means Lanehart had got them, Altgeld had come by them honestly enough, through Lanehart's will. And Lanehart obviously had intended that Altgeld have the benefit of them.

Yet they ate at his conscience and he could not bring himself to use them to get out of his financial fix. In February, he went to see Adolf Kraus. "I have these Ogden shares," he said. "They will be worth a great deal, but I do not want that kind of money. Still, I cannot afford to throw them away entirely. Get me someone who will buy them, and I will take any amount offered."[9] Lawyer Kraus interested Jacob Franks. And on March 3, 1897, Altgeld appeared in the Probate Court of Cook County for permission as executor of Lanehart's estate, to sell his Ogden shares to Franks for $35,000.[10]

He applied all of the money to paying debts left by Lanehart. And he paid all of Lanehart's debts, even some that could have been ignored. For example, the records show that Lanehart had received $5,000 from a Chicago alderman "to be invested . . . in the Ogden Gas Company."[11] Now, that particular alderman had voted against the Ogden ordinance. It seems unlikely that the alderman would have brought up that Lanehart loan, yet Altgeld paid him off, with interest.

Everything that Lanehart left went in the same way, Altgeld keeping nothing for himself, despite the terms of Lanehart's testament. And he lived to see what his sacrifice of the Ogden shares meant, for in 1901 Lanehart's gas company was secretly sold to the Chicago Gas Trust.[12] That new deal meant that Jacob Franks obtained at least $666,666 for the shares that Altgeld let him have for $35,000. All the more ironical, John R. Walsh squeezed into Ogden Gas, too, and profited along with the others.

4

Nothing that Altgeld did in those first years after his return to Chicago turned out much better for him. On the day before the

Globe Bank failure, Chicago held a mayoralty election. Still recognized as the leader of the Democratic party, Altgeld personally selected the Democratic candidate for mayor. A number of prominent Democrats had been urged, but Altgeld designated a young man with a great name: Carter H. Harrison II.

Young Carter Harrison would not have been considered except for Altgeld.[13] And after nominating him, Altgeld threw his personal prestige behind Harrison's campaign. "I believe that Mr. Harrison has more manhood and honesty of purpose in his little finger than you will find in a regiment of those pharisees who fill the air with pretense of righteousness and then help to foster iniquity." So Altgeld spoke of Harrison in the campaign.[14] He especially urged his German following to vote for "young Carter." And Harrison was elected.

Altgeld was pleased, for he felt that in politics, at least, the Harrison victory showed that the people had not forsaken him. He was especially happy because the election was interpreted as a victory for Free Silver, despite the McKinley triumph a few months back. Harrison had been known as a Bryan man and had supported Free Silver as part owner of the *Times*, which he inherited from his father. "It looks as if he would make a good mayor and I hope all will be well," Altgeld wrote to Lambert Tree a month later concerning Harrison.[15]

5

But young Mr. Harrison began acting in ways Altgeld thought peculiar. He appointed numerous "Goldbug" Democrats to key jobs. He brought enemies of Altgeld into his administration. For example, he appointed Robert A. Waller as his comptroller, knowing that Waller was entirely distasteful to Altgeld. Waller was one of the Lincoln Park trustees removed by Altgeld in 1894. Worst of all, he had been one of the few Chicago Democrats who had sided with Cleveland against Altgeld in the Pullman controversy. And so Altgeld's re-entry into politics turned sour, too. Well, he was not much interested in municipal politics, anyway. And for a time, he kept his peace.

But he was interested in national politics. He was looking ahead to 1900. The "Goldbugs" all over America were planning to oust men like Bryan and Altgeld from control of the party, if they could. The '96 campaign had left Altgeld with a passion for Free Silver and all the rest of the Chicago Platform that meant anything. Any democrat who did not stand foursquare on the Chicago Platform was anathema to him. Probably he could have forgiven young Carter

Harrison's objectionable appointments, but events that happened later turned the disappointment that he felt in Harrison to doubts about his stand on Free Silver.

First, there was Harrison's reaction to a pleasantry tossed off by "Marse Henry" Watterson of the Louisville *Courier-Journal*. Watterson had declared that if young Carter Harrison kept on, he would be a logical Democratic candidate for the presidency in 1900. Harrison was pleased—and that annoyed Altgeld. For he remembered that it was Watterson who had led "Gold" Democrats in their fight against Bryan in '96. He added that incident to Harrison's appointment of men like Waller—and got four.

Perhaps he was wrong, for Harrison had insisted that he was loyal to the Chicago Platform. Yet in the fall of 1897, Altgeld saw what appeared to him to be additional evidence that young Harrison was attempting to lead the Democracy back to Clevelandism. In New York City, Henry George had entered upon another mayoralty campaign, this time as a "Jeffersonian Democrat." There was no question as to where George stood on Free Silver and all of the other planks of the Chicago Platform. But there was grave question as to where Tammany Hall under Richard Croker stood. It was all too clear that Croker and his Tammany Democrats might pay lip-service to Free Silver on occasion, but would stab it and Bryan at the first opportunity. Free Silver Democrats in New York City lined up behind Henry George, and Tammany became frightened for its candidate Judge Robert Van Wyck. "Boss" Croker had an idea, one that concerned the young man recently elected mayor of Chicago. "There was a flirtation and a correspondence. . . . The Tiger saw a chance to have the western democracy again led into his rear yard," so Altgeld described the sudden friendship that developed between Croker and young Harrison.[16]

In October, 1897, the results of Croker's plan became apparent, for Mayor Carter Harrison of Chicago was invited to New York City to make a speech in the election campaign there in behalf of Tammany. And against Henry George. "His [Harrison's] Chicago friends urged that by going he could pave the way to secure [New York's] votes in the next national convention [for President]," declared Altgeld later. "So he went—went to fight the men who stood by our platform and help the men who repudiated it."[17]

Croker's purpose appears to have been plain enough. Young Carter Harrison had been elected mayor of Chicago only a few months before—as an Altgeld man and as a Silver man. His election had captured the imagination of the country. .What better way existed to cut into Henry George's Free Silver support than by having the "Free Silver" Democrat from Chicago back the Tammany man? From Altgeld's standpoint, Harrison's acceptance of Croker's bait was unforgivable. Moreover, something unforeseen happened that made it seem even worse to him.

In appearing before Tammany that night of October 28, 1897, Harrison delivered a speech that smacked strongly of the kind of super-patriotism to which Altgeld had been subjected all during his governorship. In attacking Henry George, Harrison quoted a speech in which George had said:

"For the republic which we now have, I care nothing. It is the new republic which is coming to which I bow. Not a republic of millionaires and tramps. A republic where one man has the power of the Czar, where women faint and little children go hungry, is not worthy of the name! But a republic of God, a republic of America, a republic such as was founded by Thomas Jefferson!"

Harrison felt that those words of Henry George proved that Henry George "was unworthy of being entrusted with any share of American government." So he told the Tammanyites, who cheered him to the rafters. Then Harrison had more to say. "This republic of ours is good enough for you; this republic of ours is good enough for me. If it is not good enough for Mr. George, let us say to him: 'The world is wide, and there are daily sailings of steamers from the port of Greater New York!' "[18]

Altgeld's indignation over that slur against Henry George's patriotism may be imagined. But what made Harrison's remarks against Henry George burn forever in Altgeld's heart was the coincidence that within forty-eight hours after Harrison in such "flapdoodle" fashion had invited Henry George to leave the country, Henry George left the world, dying in the midst of the campaign. After that, Altgeld declared war on his former protégé with bitterness.

6

From the standpoint of personal political prestige, Altgeld's war on young Carter Harrison probably was a mistake, for it led him into becoming a candidate for mayor himself in 1899 and he was badly beaten. Yet it was good for Altgeld's spirit. Up to his fight with

Harrison he had been listless, for he foresaw that soon he would lose the Unity Block. He impressed Clarence Darrow as being "dazed and lifeless." According to Darrow, he once declared that "he would be content to crawl under a sidewalk and die," that "he had lived his life." And he no longer cared to practice law, even though it was clear that he could have many clients.[19] But the Harrison fight put new life into him.

When Harrison came up for re-election, Darrow and others urged Altgeld to become an independent candidate against him. In December, 1898, Altgeld agreed. "I have said to a great many who have importuned me," he wrote in a public statement, "that I refuse to run for mayor because I was governor and that there was no reason why I should allow myself to be dragged through the mud of this city for an office I do not want, but finally I have said to them that if there was no other way of rescuing the Democratic party from the treachery of the City Hall, I would run for mayor—or even constable if necessary!"[20] By "treachery" he referred to his reading of Harrison's position on Free Silver, and also on monopoly.

Traction had become a leading issue in Chicago, for soon Yerkes' old franchises were expiring. Yerkes professed to want an extension of fifty years. Altgeld came out with the demand that no franchise at all be granted that did not provide finally for public ownership of the streetcar lines. And Harrison, while opposing Yerkes' fifty-year scheme, announced he favored a twenty-year franchise, saying the time was not ripe for municipal ownership, although he favored it in principle. The result was that Altgeld felt Harrison was playing into Yerkes' hand, and Harrison felt Altgeld was doing the same, and both appear to have been sincere. It became a major issue of the campaign, and led to the most absurd charge ever made against Altgeld, that he was "battling for Yerkes."

Carter Harrison the Younger probably believed that. For one thing, stories came to him that Yerkes had put up campaign funds to help Altgeld. Curiously enough, there appears to have been some truth in that. Yerkes had no liking for Harrison, yet he admired Altgeld. In fact, Yerkes once claimed that he had cast his own vote for Altgeld for governor although he threw the support of his personal machine for Tanner.[21] Perhaps, too, Yerkes believed that by encouraging a split in the Democratic party between Harrison and Altgeld, neither of whom would do his bidding, a more tractable Republican administration could be placed in office. At any rate, Clarence Darrow has indicated (though not in so many words) that money did come from Yerkes to pay for Altgeld's campaign expenses in 1899,[22] although Darrow also indicated that Altgeld did not know the source. Even if he did, any suggestion that Yerkes later could have caused Altgeld to change his views on traction must be put down as utterly fantastic.

7

The campaign was a bitter one. From the size of the crowds that gathered to hear Altgeld on the stump, it appeared to even veteran politicians that Altgeld would win—without a payroll machine. Concerning one Altgeld meeting, even the *Tribune* declared that "both as regards size and character, the meeting was a big surprise to the City Hall politicians, and demonstrated . . . that the Altgeld movement is not a thing to be sneered at. . . . It was the largest indoor political meeting the West Side ever knew."[23] It was so in all parts of town.

But the political observers overlooked one aspect of those crowds not readily apparent. The people who followed Altgeld, no matter where he might lead, wanted to hear him every night, and so the same people showed up at every meeting, North Side, South Side or West Side.[24] The vote was Harrison 148,496; Zina R. Carter (Republican) 107,437; Altgeld, 47,169.

However, Altgeld was not downhearted. Forty-seven thousand votes in a Chicago municipal election at that time were not to be sneezed at. They meant, or so it was interpreted, that he held a balance of power in any serious fight between the Democracy and the Republicans or on questions of policy within the party. More important for his larger purposes, the showing that he made without any payrollers was destined to have an important effect upon the then beginning struggle within the national Democratic party.

Democratic leaders throughout the nation had watched the Altgeld-Harrison fight. They noted that in Chicago alone, the second leading Democratic city in the nation, a large block of the party's voting strength would refuse to compromise on Free Silver. That was the national significance of Altgeld's showing. One more important result of that campaign was to bring Altgeld's name back into the political arena at the appropriate time before the 1900 national conventions. Free Silver Democratic groups all over the nation swamped him with requests for platform appearances. He accepted many, including engagements at St. Louis, Omaha, Louisville, Philadelphia and Detroit.

He found that he had lost none of his old-time power to sway audiences. He was still Altgeld, leader in the national party! In June, 1899, an influential liberal journal pointed out that fact. "That John P. Altgeld will be as influential in the next Democratic convention as he was in the last, even his enemies now admit. They thought him politically dead when a peanut politician with no higher ambition than office-getting and aided by ward heelers . . . from both parties defeated him for mayor of Chicago. But he has risen from his ashes. . . ."[25]

8

Once again he began conferring with the other national leaders, Senator Jones, chairman of the national committee, Governor Stone of Missouri, Senator Tillman—and William Jennings Bryan. Once again he mapped out the program for the national convention. And it was the same program that carried the day against Cleveland in 1896—"No compromise!" He admitted that new issues had developed. Imperialism was one, after the Spanish-American War had happened. He was for the war—to free the Cubans—but against imperialistic colonial expansion. But the next Democratic platform, regardless, must reiterate the 16-to-1 plank. So he felt.

There were those in the party—nor were they all eastern Gold Democrats—who did not agree. Many Free Silver men of 1896 were arguing for a vague declaration in the 1900 platform to the effect that the party "re-affirm" the platform of 1896. They wanted no direct mention of 16 to 1. They wanted to win in 1900, and they believed 16 to 1 was a Jonah. And so the silver issue again stirred the Democracy, with Altgeld in the thick of it. And he was happy, for the first time since his return to Chicago. The excitement of the approaching convention probably eased greatly the pain of losing the Unity Block and the fact that Banker Walsh had double-crossed him for the third time. That happened in May, 1899.

Just before the Unity bonds became due, Altgeld went to see Walsh. He admitted that he could not pay. However, he hoped to avoid an out-and-out foreclosure.

"I went to Mr. Walsh and told him if foreclosure proceedings were begun it would give the building a black eye, that I had carried the building through the panic and borrowed the interest for keeping it up. I suggested turning the building over to a trust company and let them collect the rents. He thought that was eminently the right thing to do, and there was an express understanding between Mr. Walsh and me that there should be no steps taken immediately toward foreclosure."[26]

Thus Altgeld described his last interview with Banker Walsh, one that he sought in an effort to at least save his building from the stigma of failure. The arrangement to have a trust company take over the management was adopted. No sooner had that been done than Banker Walsh broke his word and brought foreclosure proceedings. Alone, Altgeld walked into court to protest the action, but the law was against him. After that he could not bear to even rent an office in the Unity Block, and it was not long before he had moved into the Ashland Building.

9

All his property was gone then, all except a home on middle-class Malden Street on the Northwest Side—and even that, it turned out, was heavily mortgaged. But the national political scene buoyed him up. He noticed, moreover, that a change had come over the press in its treatment of him. Even the *Tribune* now was much less spiteful, for Joseph Medill had died in 1897 and the *Tribune* became more of a newspaper and less of a personal organ.[27] Still more remarkable was the change in front made by *Harper's Weekly*. Just before Altgeld lost the Unity Block, Henry Loomis Nelson, editor of *Harper's Weekly*, was visiting in Chicago. He told Francis Fisher Browne, editor of *The Dial*, that the one man in particular he wanted to meet was Altgeld. Browne arranged the meeting. "Altgeld greeted [the editor] in that cordial way he had, saying, in a half-quizzical, half-sarcastic voice, 'Ah!—*Harper's Weekly*, a Journal of Civilization!' . . . Not once in the interview did Altgeld refer to *Harper's Weekly's* personal abuse." Afterward, Editor Nelson exclaimed to Editor Browne: "How in the world did such a man as that come to be so misrepresented before the public?" "Ask yourself, Mr. Nelson: surely your journal has done its full share." Editor Nelson was silent, and then: "Yes, I suppose we have; but of course, we got it from the Chicago newspapers."[28]

Always after that, *Harper's Weekly* treated "the Illinois communist" with the greatest respect. In November, 1899, it told the nation that "it will not do to under-rate this leader. . . . He is head and shoulders above all the other Bryan and Free Silver leaders. The men who nominated Bryan—and also are to control the next Democratic convention—unless the bosses of the stripe of Croker, Goebel and McLean control it—will always listen respectfully to the advice of Altgeld. He will ever remain the man upon whom they must depend if they are ever to attempt to meet the arguments of the strong men of the Republican party. Perhaps even if the bosses and their machines capture the convention . . . Altgeld will nevertheless remain the brains of the new Democracy. . . ."[29]

The new Democracy! That was what he had been fighting to bring about—and now one of his erstwhile enemies was conceding that it had happened at last. Yes, that was something to make up for much that had happened since '96.

And he was to have another triumph at the 1900 Democratic convention in Kansas City. The Harrison crowd kept him from going as a delegate, as punishment for his independent mayoralty race, but he was there nevertheless. And once more Bryan was nominated, and once more the platform contained the 16-to-1 plank. Harrison, as head of the Chicago delegation, fought against that plank.[30] But Altgeld's views prevailed over the man who had vanquished him in 1899. And it was Altgeld's old flair for strategy that did it, as testified by Governor Charles S. Thomas of Colorado, chairman of the platform committee.[31]

10

In that second Bryan campaign, Altgeld was nearly as active on the stump as in '96, and he seemed to be in even better physical condition. One speech that he made must have awakened memories of long ago. He made it at Fort Scott, Kansas, where in 1870 he had worked as a section hand on the M. K. & T. railroad just before he came down with his illness that sent him northward for Savannah, Missouri. By a strange coincidence, he became ill at Fort Scott on that speaking tour, suffering a sore throat that made him "wince with agony" as he spoke. But he went on with his speech.[32] Through much of that campaign, he trailed the leading Republican orator, Theodore Roosevelt, then candidate for the vice-presidency that was destined to make him president. Roosevelt was still talking about the "lawless elements" in the Democratic party, still thinking of Haymarket and Pullman—and Altgeld. And Altgeld gave back as good as he took, in his old pungent way.

But again Bryan lost, probably because prosperity again had come to America with, or perhaps because of, the war with Spain. This time the triumph of McKinley meant that Altgeld's active political career was done, entirely so. And, anyway, the dawning of the new century, the 1900's, had made the things that he had represented seem suddenly so very ancient. Haymarket? Pullman? Government by Injunction? Free Silver? How long ago all those matters appeared as America leaped forward industrially and commercially after the war! Nor could there be any question about prosperity. There was so much prosperity that even the laboring legions were getting what appeared to be enough, in some cases. Serious talk was heard about America's never knowing labor-capital strife again. A good many persons believed it, including labor leaders who once were assailed as radicals. Hence Altgeld's day seemed to be fading.

CHAPTER THIRTY-EIGHT

PEACE

1

AFTER that second Bryan campaign, when he was approaching fifty-three, Altgeld returned seriously to the practice of law. At least, it was as serious as his new attitude toward life would permit. Gone now, forever, was the ambitious man, the politician, the seeker of power. A sort of serenity of spirit had settled over him. He had had money, and it had brought him nothing at all in the end, and so now his sole financial interest was merely in getting a few dollars to apply on his remaining debts, and to keep Mrs. Altgeld from knowing how very bad off he really was financially. Not until the last did she learn that all his fortune had been swept away with the Unity Block.

He had his own law office for a while. Then Clarence Darrow persuaded him to come into the firm of Darrow and Thompson, for by 1901 Darrow had developed a lucrative practice. As a gesture of respect, Darrow designated Altgeld as senior member of the firm. In June, 1901, Altgeld wrote to Henry D. Lloyd, on the stationery of Altgeld, Darrow and Thompson: "You will see from the heading of this letter that I have gone to work and am trying to make an honest (?) living—although I have a deep conviction that a reformer ought not to have to work."[1]

But he forced himself to hold up his end of the partnership, and it was not long before all his old-time legal shrewdness came back to him. The junior member of the firm, William O. Thompson, marveled years later at the sheer brilliance that Altgeld displayed in handling technical legal questions. "Altgeld's ability to analyze a case was remarkable," Mr. Thompson recalled. "This was due not only to his knowledge of the law, but also to his ability to understand the essential elements in the case." He cited an instance.

"One morning, a few minutes past nine, a man came into the office and wanted to engage our firm to represent him at a hearing that morning at ten o'clock before a certain judge upon an application by the complainants in the case for an injunction against him. . . . We were left with only a little over a half hour before we had to appear. . . .

"The other side . . . had their case briefed and supported with the citation of many authorities. While they were talking, Altgeld sat there as silent as the sphinx. . . . It seemed unfair that we should have to meet an elaborately prepared case upon such short notice, but there was no help for it. When the complainant's attorney had finished Altgeld rose, went to the bar and told the Judge that . . . we had had no chance to prepare our defense. With that he launched into an analysis of the complainant's case and the authorities cited in such a way I had not often heard even when there had been ample time for preparation. When Altgeld had finished, there was nothing left of the complainant's case, and after a reply from the complainant's attorney, the court denied the injunction."[2]

There were other such instances. That year of 1901 William Randolph Hearst and the editors of Hearst's Chicago American were cited for contempt of court for a cartoon lampooning Judge Elbridge Hanecy in a utility case. The judge had indicated that he would send the editors to jail, and Altgeld was retained as defense counsel. Later it was determined that another law firm also should be brought in, that of Adolf Kraus and Levy Mayer, then known as the cleverest lawyers in Chicago. A conference of the legal battery was held, and the other lawyers offered suggestions as to how the Hearst editors should be defended. But it was Altgeld who mapped out the course that won the day.[3]

2

And so he began earning enough to live on. However, he continued taking an interest in public affairs—although no longer as a combatant, but rather as something of an "elder statesman," giving counsel from a position above the field of battle. When a group of liberal-minded lawyers began a movement to organize another bar association in Chicago, he encouraged the movement, for he felt, according to Clarence Darrow, that the existing Chicago Bar Association, of which Goudy had been first president, "was one of the many aids to monopoly," controlled as it was by corporation-minded lawyers.[4] Edgar Lee Masters, then practicing law in Chicago, was active in abortive effort to organize the Cook County Bar Association and had been commissioned to prepare the constitution and by-laws. He went to Altgeld's office to show him the draft that he had prepared.

As he entered the office, Masters saw Altgeld standing at the window "absorbed in reflection." Altgeld heard Masters come in, but did not turn away from the window at once. Masters did not interrupt his reverie, but waited until Altgeld voluntarily turned away from the window. It was then that Masters had his first good glimpse of Altgeld's eyes. "They were the bluest that I ever saw, child-like, gentle, and radiant." Altgeld read the manuscript that Masters brought to him. "This is excellent. Excellent," he said. Then taking out a pencil, he added, "But we can condense it a little. This word can go out, and this one."[5]

He had come a long way, then, since the days when, at about Masters' age, he had been forced to borrow Edward Osgood Brown's dictionary in order to be certain that he was using words correctly.

3

The newspapers still came to him for interviews on important public events. In May, 1901, the United States Supreme Court rendered a decision on the status of Porto Rico and the other possessions acquired by the United States as a result of the war with Spain. The decision held that the new territories were subject to all the laws of the United States. It was a decision that was wanted by Big Business. Altgeld felt that the war had been fought to give freedom to the former Spanish colonies, and that the Supreme Court once more had "struck a blow at liberty." Once again, then, he lashed at the court.

"The syndicates for many years have controlled the Supreme Court of the United States, and from time to time get it to render such decisions as they want. Several years ago, when Congress passed a new income tax law, the syndicates wanted it destroyed . . . and got the majority of the court to hold it void. . . . Now, with regard to our insular possessions, the syndicates want to exploit, not only the United States, but these islands, by means of tariff laws and other measures whereby they can catch the coon 'a-coming and a-going.' They have gotten the court to render such a decision as they wanted, and in the future they will get such other and further decisions as their rapacity may demand."[6]

And so Altgeld continued fighting for his old principles. His chief interest now was in battling monopoly, the syndicates, and he began giving speeches reminiscent of nothing so much as the talks that he made back in Savannah, Missouri, when he was running as the

Granger candidate for prosecuting attorney. An Anti-Monopoly Conference was held in Chicago, with progressive leaders from all parts of the nation attending, and he was a principal speaker. In September, 1901, he went to Brooklyn, New York, to deliver a labor address, with monopoly as a principal theme. The syndicates, he said, were a product of "a wave, rather a deluge, of thought that has enveloped the earth and is threatening our civilization—this is the deluge of commercialism." The harvest now is being reaped, he declared, "a harvest of corruption, a harvest of bribery, a harvest of moral decay." Yet he felt that "a new morning will dawn radiant with the splendors of freedom, and the children of toil will come into their inheritance."[7]

At Brooklyn on that occasion a young man named Herbert S. Bigelow, of Cincinnati, Ohio, had made a talk just before Altgeld was presented. Afterward, Altgeld made a point of going up to the young man and complimenting him. Later Herbert S. Bigelow became the spearhead of a great liberal movement in Ohio, one that resulted in the famous Ohio Constitutional Convention, and that also had its effect on the development of the Theodore Roosevelt-Progressive movement in the Republican party. "Governor Altgeld's personal expressions to me after the Brooklyn meeting . . . and his prediction of a useful future for me, made a deep impression on me. . . . His words spurred me on." So Herbert S. Bigelow later recalled.[8]

That same year of 1901 saw a great struggle in St. Louis between the forces of monopoly and public ownership advocates. Lee Meriwether was a candidate for mayor on a platform pledged to public ownership of utilities. He was a Democrat, but the machine Democrats had disowned him to stand with the utility companies. Altgeld went to St. Louis to make an address for Meriwether, despite protests by the regular Democratic organization in Missouri. He was accused of "splitting" the party. He denied that, asserting that Democrats who favored monopoly were not Democrats. The crowd that turned out for him made the meeting "one of the largest ever held in the city of St. Louis."[9] Did he think of the time when St. Louis had no place at all for him, when he nearly starved there, back in '69, before he found that chemical plant job?

4

That was the year, too, when a young man named Leon Czolgosz, who called himself an anarchist, was swept by a great insanity to do a terrible act—shoot and kill President McKinley. Only a short time before, Prince Kropotkin, the great "philosophical" anarchist, had visited Chicago and had discussed anarchy with Altgeld at a luncheon arranged by Graham Taylor. The Prince was saying that there were times when violent deeds were necessary in order to rid the world of tyrants. But Altgeld disagreed, "filed exceptions to any justifications for such conclusions in America."[10] And so Altgeld, of course, deplored the assassination of McKinley as profoundly as any. Czolgosz' act caused the newspapers to refer once again to the Haymarket case. And once more there was a national hysteria over anarchists. A law was introduced in Congress to close the country to immigrants who held political views that were deemed "un-American." Because of his connection with the Haymarket case, Altgeld might well have kept silent.

But he had been raising his voice against all movements that tended to violate his Jeffersonian ideas on liberty, and in December, 1901, he boldly struck out against the proposed anti-immigrant legislation in an address before the Good Government Club at the University of Michigan.

"Of course," he said, "if any law can be passed that will make human life more secure amongst either the high or the low, it should be done." However, he insisted that "the American people, of all other people in the world, should not lose their heads . . . and should not adopt measures to prevent assassination and to suppress anarchy which, in other times and in other countries, have themselves produced the things that we seek to prevent."[11]

In short, he was still the Altgeld who had written *Our Penal Machinery and Its Victims* seventeen years ago. About the same time the *Tribune* asked him for an article on the proposed laws to suppress anarchy. He wrote: "We have lunatics, we have criminals, and we have desperate men, just as the world always has, but the anarchist bogey-man has been greatly over-worked."[12]

For the first time such ideas as those failed to bring down upon his head a storm of abuse. Was it because he was no longer feared, or was he being understood at last? Perhaps it was the latter. Only a little while before, the editor of the Detroit *News*, a newspaper that had called him a "menace" in the old days, heard him give a talk in Detroit. The editor went away with a deep sense of guilt for what had been printed about Altgeld. "It is pretty nearly time," he finally wrote in an editorial, "to turn to the wall that popular picture of Altgeld, painted by unscrupulous political enemies in Illinois, in which he is represented as the arch-enemy of republican institutions."[13]

His speeches kept him busy, but something else occupied him in 1901. Oratory had been his "first love," so he once declared, and now in his spare time he had been writing down his thoughts on oratory. In his early days he had hunted in libraries for books that would help a man learn how to speak well, and none had satisfied him. And so he was writing one himself. In May, 1901, the fruits of his labor in that field became public with the publication of *Oratory: Its Requirements and Its Rewards*.[14] It was a tiny volume, just sixty-five pages long, but men like Newton D. Baker have called it a "classic."[15] And it gave Altgeld more pleasure than almost anything else he did in those days. When Henry D. Lloyd wrote him how much he enjoyed Altgeld's *Oratory*, Altgeld answered: "Many thanks for your kind words about my little book. I cannot tell you how sweet they are to me. It is one of my children that the world is not frowning upon."[16]

In talking to a newspaper reporter, he likewise referred to the book as his "child." William H. Stuart of Hearst's *American* had come to his office in search of political news.

"Politics is petty," Altgeld answered. "Political things pass with the day. I am not interested in politics, but I am interested in a new-born child."

"A child?" gasped Reporter Stuart.

"Yes," Altgeld said. "Here it is." And he displayed a copy of *Oratory*. "There is something," he said, "that will live after me. It will be remembered long after everything I did in politics is forgotten."[17]

After the book on oratory was published, he began working on another literary work. This was to be a philosophical work, a collection of little essays that he intended calling *The Cost of Something for Nothing*. The essays were to express his own philosophy, culled from all the things that had happened to him, a synthesis of the ideas that he had expressed in all of his speeches and writings hitherto. Running through all the essays was one theme: The cost of getting something for nothing is too great a price for any man to pay. It is "moral death." In one essay he wrote:

"If the reader cares to make the investigation, he will find that many of the very rich of our country are supported by dollars that are tainted by injustice, and they are slowly but surely destroying the people who have them. They are a heritage of death. Instead of envying them, or trying to emulate them, the young man starting in life may well thank God if he has no tainted dollars to blight his career."[18]

Was he thinking of his own career—and perhaps also of Banker Walsh, who even then was indulging in schemes with his banks that in 1906 would send Walsh to the penitentiary?

He labored over the little essays at every free moment, but he was not destined to see them published.[19]

5

In the early weeks of 1902, he was never so active with his platform appearances and with his law practice. He seemed in good condition. W. E. Ford of Mansfield, Ohio, who had helped him do his sums as they studied above the carpenter shop and tannery, visited him in February and found him enjoying what Ford thought was excellent health. Altgeld enjoyed that visit, and also another about the same time with his old Savannah chum, Ben Holt. Ben had come to Chicago with a load of cattle. He did not believe Altgeld could have the time to see him, and so he simply left a message that he was in town. Not see Ben Holt! Altgeld made the trip that evening to the Stockyards Inn and stayed until after midnight chatting about the old days in Missouri.[20]

Probably it was about this time that there occurred an incident that must have taken him back in memory to the days when he visited the police courts in Chicago to gather material for *Our Penal Machinery and Its Victims*. He had been walking in North Clark Street on a Saturday night when he noticed a street fight. Two or three "ruffians," as he later called them, were pummeling several other young men. The police arrived, but Altgeld saw the police arrest, not the "ruffians," but their victims. He protested to the officers that they were arresting the wrong persons, but to no avail. On the Monday following, Altgeld appeared at the police court. He walked up to the clerk and asked about the case. "I told those young men I would be down to be a witness for them, and I am here for that purpose," he said. The court clerk could not find the case.

The clerk looked over his docket again. "Oh, I remember that case. We didn't try it. Those young men were gentlemen and we didn't have any trial. They were discharged." Altgeld was disgusted, and he showed it. "Oh, they were *gentlemen*, were they! . . . They should have been tried just the same as anybody else!" Then he stomped out, indignant that he did not have the chance to show that the police, as in the old days, apparently were still jailing the wrong people.[21]

In the first week of March he traveled to Buffalo, New York, to fill a speaking engagement he had made with the Independent Club. "Shall the People Own the Monopolies?" was his subject. He delivered a talk up to his old-time standards. The Democratic party, he argued, must stand for public ownership of monopoly industries, or be untrue to its basic principles.

"I hear men talk about following in the footsteps of Jefferson. Why, Jefferson was the great radical of his day! He referred everything back to the people; he wanted everything left in the hands of the people. . . . Jefferson indeed did say that that government was best which governed least; that was when he was speaking of those governments that are distinct from the people; that are a constant menace to the people; that are a convenience for the powerful in plundering the people. But that is a very different proposition from having the people manage their own affairs, from having them control and own those things upon which their comfort, their happiness, their health and their very lives depend. Were Jefferson alive today, his voice would be heard from ocean to ocean demanding that the people themselves must own the monopolies."[22]

6

He returned to Chicago to find himself wanted as attorney in a case involving the issue that as early as 1894 he had called the greatest menace to American institutions: government by injunction. The hackmen's union was engaged in a strike against the Pennsylvania Railroad. The railroad had obtained an injunction against the union, and Altgeld was asked to defend the workers. How he relished that case! He argued it before Judge C. C. Kohlsaat on March 11, 1902. It was an all-day session. And he was obviously tired when court adjourned. His doctor had frequently warned him against tiring himself out. Knowing this, some of his friends urged that he give up the idea of filling a speaking engagement that night at Joliet. But he insisted that he would go, for he had promised, and then, the subject interested him. The meeting at Joliet was called by sympathizers of the Boers to protest against the war that Great Britain was waging against the little country in Africa. The upper-dog against the under-dog—and Altgeld went to Joliet to add his voice on the side he always defended.

Among a group of his friends a secret pact had been made that Altgeld was never to be permitted to travel alone. Charles A. Williams, later a judge, was supposed to go with Altgeld that evening, but could not, and so Joe Martin was called and he went. On the train, Altgeld admitted that he felt very tired. Then he remembered that in the excitement over the injunction case he had neglected to eat any lunch, and he usually consumed a heavy one, almost always ordering two pieces of pie.[23] In the train diner, he ate a big steak—in violation of the rule he had set down in his book on oratory that a speaker should never eat much before going on the platform. However, he said he felt a good deal better.

But when he arrived at Joliet, he again complained of feeling tired. He was to stop at the Hotel Munroe. A special room had been reserved for him, but was not yet ready for him to go in and he was asked to wait "because it was the best room in the house." "I am so tired," he confessed, "that I'd rather have any kind of a room than have to stand around waiting for the best one."[24] After he was finally settled in a room, he prepared to rest, only to be disturbed by a request for an interview by a newspaper editor. It sapped more of his strength.

7

The scene of his speech that night was a theater in which he had opened the formal speaking campaign of his governorship race in 1892. Ex-Mayor P. C. Haley of Joliet presided and began introducing Altgeld immediately. Someone told Haley that the program called for some choral singing to precede Altgeld's speech, and Haley intended to conform, but Altgeld whispered to him: "Don't change that. I want to speak and have it over with!"

He spoke for forty-five minutes, vigorously denouncing the treatment of the Boers by Great Britain. It was noticed that he seemed in distress. He perspired greatly and continually wiped his forehead with a handkerchief. Once or twice he seemed to be unsteady on his feet. But he kept on. He referred to world conditions in general. Everywhere the strong seemed to be taking advantage of the weak, he said. But in his closing he struck a note of optimism.

"I am not discouraged. Things will right themselves. The pendulum swings one way and then the other. But the steady pull of gravitation is toward the center of the earth. Any structure must be plumb if it is to endure or the building will fall. So it is with nations. Wrong may seem to triumph. Right may seem to be defeated. But the gravitation of eternal justice is upward toward the throne of God. Any political institution if it is to endure must be plumb with that line of justice."[25]

He sat down as the crowd applauded, and wiped his forehead again. Another speaker began talking, and just then Altgeld turned to the chairman and whispered: "I feel dizzy." He got up and walked toward the wings of the stage. But before he stepped off the stage he began to stagger. Two members of the choral society saw this and helped him into the wings. Then he was seized with a violent attack of vomiting, as had happened to him at Flag Springs in Missouri.

He lay there on the stage an hour before it was felt advisable to move him to the hotel. The Illinois Medical Society was holding its annual banquet that night in Joliet and a request for a doctor was sent there. At least a half dozen responded. He had been in a coma, but revived as the doctors worked over him. He recognized one as Dr. M. B. Cushing, whom he had appointed physician at one of the state institutions when he was governor.

"How do you do, Cushing?" he said. "I am glad to see you."

It was decided to remove his clothes. He had revived sufficiently to help himself at that, but some of the doctors worked at his shirt. One tried to unbutton it from the back. Altgeld gave him an amused look. "My shirt, sir," he said with mock annoyance, "unbuttons in the front!" There was laughter, in which he seemed to join, and it was suggested that "the Governor was all right, after all."

But he wasn't, for soon the doctors had confirmed their worst fears. He had suffered a cerebral hemorrhage. After a while, newspaper reporters came to the room. He saw them, and asked that as a "personal favor" they say nothing about his illness, because he did not want his wife to know. "I've got to be careful of her, you know," he said.[26]

Those were very nearly his last words, for then he lapsed into a deep coma. At midnight word was sent to Clarence Darrow in Chicago that he had better come to Joliet. Then at a quarter of four the next morning, March twelfth, Dr. James B. Herrick of Chicago made the announcement that caused tears to well in the eyes of Joe Martin, the supposedly hard-boiled little ex-gambler.[27] At last his "little Dutchman" was at peace.

8

Now all of the newspapers, the *Tribune* among them, had nothing but praise for John Peter Altgeld. Almost everyone agreed that a "great man" had passed. But afterward—he was forgotten entirely, so at least it was felt by the boy poet who had seen him while he was governor. For ten years Vachel Lindsay brooded over that feeling, and then, by his poetry, did his part to preserve the memory of the man who had become his "particular idol."[28]

"Sleep softly, . . . eagle forgotten, . . . under the stone,
Time has its way with you there, and the clay has its own.
Sleep on, O brave-hearted, O wise man, that kindled the flame. . . ."

THE END

NOTES

NOTES

CHAPTER ONE

[1]Altgeld's age on his arrival in America has been variously fixed, but he gave it as three months in a letter to Governor Hogg of Texas, June 8, 1896; in John Peter Altgeld, *Live Questions*, 1899 edition (Chicago: George S. Bowen and Co.). p. 525.

[2]See Louis Bromfield, *The Farm*, (New York: Harper and Brothers, 1933) for an accurate description of the countryside in which Altgeld grew from infancy to manhood.

[3]Cenia Pollock Valentine, interview, November 20, 1936. She was raised on an adjoining farm.

[4]Speech of Acceptance, *Live Questions*, 1899 edition, p. 229.

[5]R. P. Bishop, "Commoners in American Politics: Hon. John P. Altgeld," *The National Magazine*, XVI, April-November, 1892.

[6]William H. Hinrichsen, "Illinois Giants I Have Known," Chicago *Inter-Ocean*, March 16, 1902.

[7]*Ibid.*

[8]Quoted by George A. Schilling to author, February, 1937.

[9]New York *World*, July 17, 1894.

[10]Albert J. Beveridge, *Abraham Lincoln*, II, 353-4. Reprinted by permission of, and arrangement with Houghton Mifflin Company, publishers.

[11]Beveridge, II, 487.

[12]From *Altgeld of Illinois*, by Waldo R. Browne, copyright 1924, published by the Viking Press, Inc., New York, p. 9.

[13]Ohio Adjutant General Records.

[14]Chicago *Chronicle*, March 13, 1902.

[15]Browne, *op. cit.*, p. 8.

[16]Speech of Acceptance, *Live Questions*, p. 28. 1899 edition.

[17]Bishop, cited *supra*.

[18]Cenia Pollock Valentine, interview.

[19]W. E. Ford, quoted by his daughter, Mrs. Kitty Ford Neuman of Mansfield, to author, November 19, 1936. The family is distantly related to Mrs. Emma Ford Altgeld.

[20]New York *World*, July 17, 1894, Nellie Bly, interview.

[21]Bishop, cited *supra*.

CHAPTER TWO

[1]Edward Osgood Brown, *Biographical Sketch of Hon. John Peter Altgeld, Twentieth Governor of Illinois*, pp. 29-30 (Chicago Historical Society, December 5, 1905, pamphlet).

[2]Chicago *Daily News*, September 20, 1884.

[3]Edward Osgood Brown, *op. cit.*, p. 30.

[4]Altgeld campaign pamphlet (1892), *Judge John P. Altgeld, the Democratic Nominee for Governor of Illinois. His life. His speech of acceptance. The Platform on which he runs.*

[5]Chicago *Times*, October 19, 1884.

[6]Chicago *Inter-Ocean*, March 23, 1902, and Waldo R. Browne, *op. cit.*, p. 14.

[7]St. Joseph *Gazette-Herald*, March 13, 1902.

[8]Chicago *Inter-Ocean*, March 23, 1902, and St. Louis *Republic*, March 24, 1902.

[9]St. Louis *Republic*, March 24, 1902.

[10]Altgeld campaign pamphlet.

[11]Schilling to author, May 30, 1935.

[12]Related by Altgeld in a political speech near Flag Springs in 1874; John K. White, to author, Savannah, July 24, 1936.

[13]William Prentiss, in *Prominent Democrats of Illinois, a Brief History of the Rise and Progress of the Democratic Party of Illinois*, p. 138. (Chicago: Democratic Publishing Co., 1899). Judge Prentiss visited Savannah in the '90's.

[14]From *Altgeld of Illinois*, by Waldo R. Browne, copyright 1924, published by the Viking Press, Inc., New York.

[15]Cincinnati *Enquirer*, March 13, 1902.

CHAPTER THREE

[1]Sally Woodcock, of Savannah, granddaughter of Benjamin Holt, Sr., interview, July 24, 1936.

[2]Redmond S. Cole, of Tulsa, Okla., a grandson, letter August 6, 1936.

[3]Statement made to George A. Schilling, quoted in letter to Waldo R. Browne, November 17, 1922.

[4]Based on version of Sally Woodcock; cf. Browne, pp. 15-16.

[5]Mary E. Kent, daughter of Alexander Bedford, to Redmond S. Cole, October 15, 1936.

[6]*Ibid.*

[7]Redmond S. Cole, grandson, letters, August 1 and 6, 1936.

[8]Thomas B. Rea of Omaha to Justice J. P. Burns, December 9, 1936.

[9]Mrs. Alice Fry, daughter of Judge Rea, to author.

[10]From *Altgeld of Illinois*, by Waldo R. Browne, copyright 1924, published by the Viking Press, Inc., New York, p. 16.

[11]*Alley* v. *Gamelick*, 55 Missouri Supreme Court Reports 518; *Munkers* v. *K. C. St. J. and C. B. R. R.*, 60 *ibid.*, 334; *Buis* v. *Cook*, 60 *ibid.*, 391; *Woods* v. *Boots*, 60 *ibid.*, 546; 57 *ibid.*, 249; 62 *ibid.*, 577.

[12]60 Missouri Supreme Court Reports 391, and Browne, p. 16.

[13]Finley McFadden, the clothier, to T. H. Nicholas of Savannah, related to author by Nicholas, July 24, 1936.

[14]Andrew County *Republican,* April 27 and May 22, 1874, files in the office of the Savannah *Reporter.*

[15]Quoted in *Centennial History of Illinois,* IV, 89.

[16]From *Thorstein Veblen and His America,* by Joseph Dorfman, copyright 1934, published by the Viking Press, Inc., New York, p. 15-16.

[17]Buck, Solon J., *History of the Grange Movement.* (Cambridge: Harvard University Press, 1913).

[18]Andrew County *Republican,* August 28, 1874.

[19]*Ibid.*

[20]Andrew County *Republican,* September 18, 1874.

[21]Clipped in Andrew County *Republican,* September 24, 1874.

[22]Andrew County *Republican,* September 25, 1874.

[23]*Ibid.,* October 30, 1874.

[24]Andrew County *Republican,* October 30, 1874.

[25]*Ibid.*

[26]John K. White of Savannah, to author, July 26, 1936.

[27]Andrew County *Republican,* November 6, 1874.

[28]*In the Matter of Henry Alexander on petition for Habeas Corpus,* 59 Missouri Supreme Court Reports, 598.

[29]Thomas B. Rea, to Justice of Peace Burns, December 9, 1936.

[30]St. Louis *Republic,* March 24, 1902.

[31]Browne, letter to George A. Schilling, dated Wyoming, New York, November 7, 1922.

[32]Letter to author, June 12, 1936.

[33]Interviews with author, 1935-36; letter to Waldo R. Browne, November 17, 1922. "In the main I think this is true."

[34]Mansfield (O.) *Daily Shield,* March 14, 1902.

[35]New York *World,* Nellie Bly, interview.

CHAPTER FOUR

[1]Smith, Henry J. and Lewis, Lloyd, *Chicago, A History of Its Reputation,* p. 113. (New York: Harcourt, Brace and Co., 1929).

[2]Hayes, C. J. H., *A Political and Social History of Modern Europe,* II, 258. (New York: The Macmillan Co., 1916).

[3]Chicago *Tribune,* November 22, 1875.

[4]Willis J. Abbott, *Watching the World Go By.* pp. 63-64. (Boston: Little, Brown and Co., 1933).

[5]*Ibid.,* p. 80.

[6]Chicago *Tribune,* November 27, 1875.

[7]James Weber Linn, *Jane Addams,* p. 37. (New York: D. Appleton-Century Co., 1935).

[8]Nellie Bly, interview.

[9]Chicago *Tribune,* February 26, 1874.

CHAPTER FIVE

[1]Chicago *Chronicle,* March 13, 1902.
[2]Edward Osgood Brown, p. 27.
[3]J. Seymour Currey, *Chicago: Its History and Its Builders, a Century of Marvelous Growth,* II, 296. (Chicago: S. J. Clarke Publishing Co., 1912).
[4]Henry M. Walker memorandum, September 5, 1935, prepared for author.
[5]Sally Woodcock, interview.
[6]Edward Osgood Brown, p. 28.
[7]*Ibid.*
[8]Schilling, interview, May 10, 1935.
[9]Waldo Browne, *op. cit.,* p. 20.
[10]Walker memorandum.
[11]*Ibid.*
[12]Cook County Circuit Court Records, No. 21085.
[13]Circuit Court Records, No. 21133.
[14]Circuit Court Records, No. 21537.
[15]*Ibid,* No. 23759.
[16]Henry M. Walker, interview with author, March 23, 1937.
[17]Mrs. Adolph Heile, interview, April 12, 1937.
[18]Charles A. and Mary R. Beard, *The Rise of American Civilization,* II, 230. (New York: The Macmillan Co., 1930).
[19]Louis Adamic, *Dynamite,* p. 24. (New York: Viking Press, Inc., 1935).
[20]Matilda Gresham, *Life of Walter Q. Gresham,* pp. 379-408. (Chicago: Rand, McNally and Co., 1919).
[21]Chicago *Tribune,* July 12, 1877.
[22]William T. Hutchinson, *Cyrus Hall McCormick,* I, 615. (New York: D. Appleton-Century Co., 1935).
[23]Currey, *op. cit.,* II, 304.
[24]Quoted by Altgeld, "Reasons for Pardoning, etc.," in *Live Questions,* II, 374. (Springfield: Illinois State Register, 1894); *Harmonia Association* v. *Brennan,* Cook County Circuit Court.
[25]Quoted in Lewis and Smith, *op. cit.,* p. 154.
[26]Currey, II, 377.

CHAPTER SIX

[1]Marriage Affidavit and Record Book, Richland County, XII, 261.
[2]Ruth Ford Atkinson, letter to the author, July 6, 1936, and Faye Ford Betak, interview.
[3]William O. Thompson, memorandum, prepared for the author, October, 1935. Mr. Thompson was a member of the law firm of Altgeld, Darrow and Thompson.
[4]New York *Journal,* March 26, 1896, article on Mrs. Altgeld entitled "A

Brilliant Western Woman."

[5]Ruth Ford Atkinson, letter.

[6]New York *Journal*, March 26, 1896.

[7]Published in 1887 by Laird and Lee.

[8]Hinrichsen, *Inter-Ocean*, cited *supra*.

[9]Mrs. Adolph Heile, interview.

[10]Chicago *Daily News*, September 20, 1884.

[11]Ruth Ford Atkinson.

[12]Bishop, cited *supra*.

[13]Schilling, interview.

[14]F. D. P. Snelling to author, February, 1935.

[15]Browne, p. 32.

[16]Chicago *Daily News*, October 18, 1930.

[17]Henry George, *Progress and Poverty*, pp. 340-341. (New York: R. Schalkenback Foundation, 1935).

[18]Chicago *Morning News*, April 28, 1890.

[19]Interview, December, 1936.

[20]Clarence Darrow, *The Story of My Life,* pp. 107-08. (New York: Charles Scribner's Sons, 1932).

[21]Chicago *Tribune*, November 11, 1892.

[22]Mrs. Heile, interview.

[23]Herman Clark, "When Chicago Was Young," Chicago *Tribune*, April 19, 1936.

[24]Ruth Ford Atkinson.

[25]*People for use of D. S. Bolckhom* v. *Carl Affeld*, Cook County Circuit Court.

[26]Browne, p. 30.

[27]Mrs. Heile, interview.

[28]Ruth Ford Atkinson, and New York *Journal,* cited *supra*.

CHAPTER SEVEN

[1]Chicago *Tribune*, October 1, 1875.

[2]Chicago *Evening Post,* July 31, 1891; *Live Questions*, II, 289.

[3]Schilling, interview, May, 1935.

[4] Chicago *Daily News*, July 16, 1896.

[5]*Ibid.*, July 20, 1896.

[6]This account based on the autobiography of Louis F. Post, "Living a Long Life Over Again" unpublished, in Library of Congress, MSS Division, pp. 222a-226a. It is verified in conversations with Schilling and others.

[7]Adolf Kraus, *Reminiscences and Comments,* pp. 118-19. (Chicago: Rubovits, Inc., 1925).

[8]Louis F. Post, testimony, April 14, 1919, in *Martin* v. *Martin,* No. 331958, Superior Court of Cook County, Illinois.

[9]George Schilling, interview with author, May 30, 1935.

[10]Chicago *Times,* September 21, 1884.

[11]Chicago *Tribune,* August 3, 1884.

[12]*Ibid.,* September 21, 1884.

[13]September 20, 1884.

[14]September 21, 1884.

[15]October 28, 1884.

[16]Edgar Lee Masters, "John Peter Altgeld," *American Mercury,* Vol. IV, No. 14, February, 1929, pp. 161-74.

[17]S. P. McConnell, manuscript fragment in possession of author.

[18]Quoted by Allan Nevins, in *Letters and Journal of Brand Whitlock,* I, xxx. (New York: D. Appleton-Century Co., 1936).

[19]Darrow, *op. cit.,* p. 103.

[20]Notebook in Altgeld file, Illinois State Historical Library, Springfield.

[21]Pamphlet issued by Brown and Dunning, Ann Arbor, Michigan.

[22]Fremont O. Bennett, *Politics and Politicians of Chicago,* p. 322. (Chicago: Blakely Printing Co., 1886).

[23]Harvey Wish, "The Governorship of John P. Altgeld," Northwestern University Doctoral thesis, 1936, p. 13, quoting *Times-Herald,* November 20, 1895.

[24]Chicago *Tribune,* January 29, 1886.

[25]*In the Matter of Probate of the Will of Wilbur F. Storey,* 120 Illinois Supreme Court 244 (1887), and *The People* ex rel. *Eureka C. Storey* v. *Joshua C. Knickerbocker, Probate Judge,* 114 Illinois Supreme Court 539 (1885).

[26]Chicago *Journal,* April 27, 1892.

[27]Chicago *Times,* May 15, 1885.

[28]*Journal of the Senate of the 34th General Assembly of Illinois,* p. 754.

[29]Chicago *Times,* May 15, 1885.

CHAPTER EIGHT

[1]Chicago *Tribune,* March 24, 1879, quoted in *Centennial History,* IV, 125.

[2]Schilling, interview.

[3]Chicago *Tribune,* March 23, 1879.

[4]Chicago *Times,* May 26, 1878.

[5]Earl R. Beckner, *A History of Illinois Labor Legislation,* pp. 63-64. (Chicago: University of Chicago Press, 1929).

[6]Altgeld, "Reasons for Pardoning," *Live Questions,* II, 376-77.

[7]*Ibid.,* pp. 377-383.

[8]Chicago *Tribune,* May 7, 1885.

[9]*The Socialist,* Chicago, September 14, 1878.

[10]From *The History of the Haymarket Affair,* by Henry David, copyright, 1936, and reprinted by permission of Farrar & Rinehart, Inc., Publishers, pp. 121-122.

[11]Schilling, interview; also Melville Stone, *Fifty Years a Journalist,* p. 169. (New York: Doubleday, Doran and Co., 1921).

[12]Chicago *Tribune,* November 22, 1875.

CHAPTER NINE

[1]East St. Louis *Truth,* December 21, 1895.
[2]Reprinted in *Live Questions,* both Vol. I and the 1899 edition.
[3]*Live Questions,* p. 68.
[4]*Ibid.,* p. 183.
[5]*Ibid.,* p. 179. The italics are Altgeld's.
[6]*Ibid.,* p. 189.
[7]Chicago *Times,* September 20, 1884.
[8]Darrow, *op. cit.,* p. 41.
[9]*Live Questions,* p. 98.
[10]Chicago *Times,* May 7, 1886.
[11]*Life of Albert R. Parsons,* pp. 18-19. Compiled and published by his wife.
[12]Schilling, interview.

CHAPTER TEN

[1]Schilling, interview.
[2]*Ibid.*
[3]Official circular issued by Powderly in 1886, Schilling papers.
[4]Schilling, interview.
[5]*Live Questions,* I, 70.
[6]*Ibid.,* p. 17.
[7]*Ibid.,* pp. 14-15.

CHAPTER ELEVEN

[1]David, *The History of the Haymarket Affair,* p. 188.
[2]*Spies* et al v. *The People,* 122 Illinois 1, at 27 and 48.
[3]Chicago *Daily News,* May 3, 1886.
[4]*Ibid,* May 4, 1886.
[5]Chicago *Times,* May 4, 1886.
[6]*Ibid.,* May 4, 1886.
[7]*Abstract of the Record in the Haymarket Trial Before Judge Gary* (hereafter cited as *Abstract*), p. 298.
[8]*Ibid.*
[9]Chicago *Tribune,* May 5, 1886.
[10]*Abstract,* pp. 311-12.
[11]*Spies* v. *The People,* p. 29.
[12]*Abstract,* p. 299.
[13]Waller testimony, *Abstract,* pp. 4-6.

[14]*Abstract*, p. 306.

[15]Waller testimony, *Abstract*, p. 4.

[16]*Spies* v. *The People*, p. 158.

[17]Waller testimony.

[18]*Abstract*, p. 133.

[19]Testimony of Mayor Harrison, *Abstract*, p. 175.

[20]*Abstract*, p. 133.

[21]*Ibid.*, p. 178.

[22]Chicago *Daily News*, May 4, 1886.

[23]Michael Loftus Ahern, *Political History of Chicago, 1837-87*, pp. 249-50. (Chicago: Donahue, Henneberry Co., 1886).

[24]Testimony of Reporter G. P. English, *Abstract*, p. 134.

[25]Testimony of Reporter Edgar A. Owen, *Abstract*, p. 124.

CHAPTER TWELVE

[1]Chicago *Tribune*, May 5, 1886.

[2]*Abstract*, pp. 16, 126, 181.

[3]Chicago *Tribune*, June 27, 1886.

[4]Ahern, *op. cit.*, p. 242.

[5]*Abstract*, p. 322.

[6]Chicago *Tribune*, June 30, 1886.

[7]David, *op. cit.*, pp. 508-525, and Chicago *Tribune*, Nov. 15, 1887.

[8]David, p. 210.

[9]*The Spectator*, LIX, 605, cited in Russell Hugh Baugh, "Attitude of John P. Altgeld . . . Toward Problems of Labor as Shown Especially in the Pardon of The Anarchists, etc.," master's thesis, University of Wisconsin, 1926, p. 25.

[10]Chicago *Tribune*, July 18, 1886.

[11]Chicago *Times*, May 6, 1886.

[12]From *Fifty Years a Journalist*, by Melville E. Stone, copyright, 1920, 1921, by Doubleday, Doran & Company, Inc., p. 173.

[13]Chicago *Times*, June 11, 1886.

[14]*Life of Albert R. Parsons*, p. 229.

[15]*Live Questions*, II, p. 394.

[16]Schilling, interview.

[17]Ingersoll to Schilling, November 7, 1887, in Schilling papers.

[18]Caro Lloyd, *Henry Demarest Lloyd*, I, 89. (G. P. Putnam's Sons, 1912).

[19]Michael J. Schaack, *Anarchists and Anarchy*, p. 623. (F. J. Schulte and Co., 1889).

[20]*Life of Parsons*, p. 230, and Stone, *op. cit.*, p. 176.

[21]Chicago *Tribune*, Nov. 10, 1887.

[22]James R. Buchanan, *Story of a Labor Agitator*, p. 398. (New York: Outlook, 1903).

[23]Schilling, interview.

[24]From *Fifty Years a Journalist,* by Melville E. Stone, copyright, 1920, 1921, by Doubleday, Doran & Company, Inc., p. 177.

[25]David, p. 462.

CHAPTER THIRTEEN

[1]From *My Friend Julia Lathrop,* by Jane Addams. By permission of The Macmillan Company, publishers, p. 46.

[2]Lloyd, *op. cit.,* I, 101. Ironically, Mr. Bross provided that the children of the Lloyds should come into control of his *Tribune* holdings. Thus, William Bross Lloyd, not a liberal but a "communist," became part owner of the *Tribune.*

[3]*Tribune,* January 19 and 20, 1887. Nina Van Zandt "Spies" lived in Chicago until her death April 10, 1936.

[4]William Morris to Browning, Kelmscott House, November 7, 1887, in Sigmund Zeisler, "Recollections of the Anarchist Case," *Illinois Law Review,* V, xxi, November, 1926.

[5]Butler to William P. Black, February 14, 1888, in *Life of Parsons,* pp. 261-63.

[6]Chicago *Tribune,* November 9, 1887.

[7]Chicago *Times,* May 7, 1886.

[8]Schilling, interview, May, 1935.

[9]Chicago *Tribune,* September 10, 1886.

[10]Schilling, interview, May 30, 1935.

[11]Schilling, interview.

[12]Altgeld, *The Cost of Something for Nothing,* pp. 73-74. (Chicago: Hammersmark Publishing Co., 1904).

[13]Chicago *Tribune,* September 4, 1886.

[14]Chicago *Tribune,* September 16, 1886.

[15]Clipped in *The Knights of Labor,* Chicago, November 6, 1886.

[16]Schilling, interview.

[17]*Knights of Labor,* November 6, 1886.

[18]Schilling, interview.

CHAPTER FOURTEEN

[1]Hinrichsen, in the Chicago *Inter-Ocean,* cited *supra.*

[2]Mrs. Heile, interview.

[3]For example, *Birmingham Fire Insurance Company* v. *Pulver,* 126 Ill. 340 and *Baltimore and Ohio and Chicago Railroad* v. *Illinois Central Railroad,* 137 Ill. 34.

[4]For example, *C. & N. W. R. R.* v. *Mary A. Snyder, Adm.,* 128 Ill. 655 (1899) and *C. and N. W. R. R.* v. *Annie Dunleavy, Adm.,* 129 Ill. 139 (1899).

[5]*The People* v. *The People's Insurance Exchange,* 126 Ill. 466 (1889).

[6]Chicago *Tribune,* December 18, 1889. See Theodore Dreiser, *The Financier,* for the story of Yerkes' difficulty in Philadelphia. Frank Cowperwood, the hero in Dreiser's novel, is based upon Yerkes.

[7]Darrow, *op. cit.,* p. 97.

[8]Judge Charles A. Williams, interview.

[9]See *C. & N. W. R. R.* v. *Annie Dunleavy, Adm.,* 128 Ill. 139 (1889), and *Rollin P. Blanchard* v. *Lakeshore and Michigan Railroad,* 126 Ill. 416 (1888) as examples.

[10]New York *Times,* June 29, 1893.

[11]Chicago *Tribune,* June 23, 1888.

[12]Chicago *Times,* July 19, 1890.

[13]See, for example, *Timothy Grady* v. *People,* 125 Ill. 122 (1889) and *John Gundrat* et al. v. *People,* 138 Ill. 103 (1891).

[14]Chicago *Times,* January 15, 1888, and *Live Questions,* I, 74-79. (Chicago: Donahue, Henneberry Co., 1890). This statement, for no apparent reason, was omitted by Altgeld from his subsequent volumes of *Live Questions.*

[15]Nellie Bly, interview.

[16]Chicago *Times,* September 9, 1889, and *Live Questions,* I, 80-89.

[17]Wish, *op. cit.* pp. 23-24; also *Caro Lloyd,* I, p. 101.

[18]Chicago *Times,* February 23, 1890, and *Live Questions,* I, 122-46.

[19]Chicago *Morning News,* April 28, 1890, and *Live Questions,* II, 67-73.

[20]*Live Questions,* I, 144.

[21]Chicago *Herald,* March 10, 1889.

[22]Chicago *Journal,* March 10, 1889.

[23]Chicago *Tribune* and Chicago *Times,* May 5, 1886.

[24]*The Forum,* VIII, 684 (February, 1890).

[25]Chicago *Tribune,* March 4, 1890.

CHAPTER FIFTEEN

[1]Plaintiff's Brief in *City of Chicago* v. *John P. Altgeld,* Ser. No. 3155, Appellate Court, First District, Illinois, dated November 26, 1888, pp. 17-19.

[2]Altgeld to reporters, Chicago *Tribune,* June 23, 1888.

[3]Chicago *Times,* June 20, 1888.

[4]Chicago *Tribune,* June 27, 1888.

[5]Chicago *Daily News,* June 23 and 25, 1888.

[6]Chicago *Tribune,* June 23, 1888.

[7]*Ibid.*

[8]Edward Osgood Brown, p. 30.

[9]*Plaintiff's Brief in City of Chicago* v. *John P. Altgeld,* No. 3155, Appellate Court, First District, Illinois, dated November 26, 1888, pp. 17-19.

[10]*Live Questions,* II, 29.

[11]Judge Altgeld to Hon. Sherwood Dixon, February 12, 1889, *Live Questions,* I, 48-61.

[12]When the case was re-tried, Judge Altgeld's claim for damages was again upheld and he was awarded a final judgment of $15,000. Chicago *Tribune*, December 19, 1889 and *Circuit Court Docket Book*, 1888-89.

[13]*City of Chicago* v. *John P. Altgeld*, 33 Illinois Appellate, First District, 23 (1889).

[14]Altgeld to Judges Garnett, Gary and Moran, April 18, 1889; reproduced in the Chicago *Tribune*, June 29, 1893.

[15]Altgeld, *The Cost of Something for Nothing*, p. 28.

[16]Chicago *Herald*, February 8, 1889 and *Knights of Labor*, February 9, 1889.

[17]Chicago *Tribune* April 5, 1889.

[18]Chicago *Times*, April 6, 1889.

[19]Schilling, interview.

CHAPTER SIXTEEN

[1]Probably published at Altgeld's own expense. A collection of articles and letters, expanded in later editions (1894 and 1899).

[2]Chicago *Daily News*, March 2, 1891.

[3]Schilling, to the editor of *The Public*, Chicago, probably 1902. His letter, in possession of the author, was suppressed.

[4]Chicago *Times*, October 16, 1892.

[5]Chicago *Tribune*, October 15, 1892.

[6]Chicago *Tribune*, November 3, 1892; front-page story quoting Rep. Cockerell at length.

[7]Chicago *Evening Post*, Feb. 6, 1891.

[8]Cockerell, interview, Chicago *Tribune*, November 3, 1892.

[9]Wilbanks letter, reproduced in facsimile, in the Chicago *Tribune*, October 15, 1892. Underscoring Altgeld's statement.

[10]Chicago *Times*, October 16, 1892.

[11]Wilbanks affidavit, in the Chicago *Tribune*, October 15, 1892. Dated April 22, 1892, Galveston, Texas. While made for political reasons, this document is credible nonetheless.

[12]Chicago *Tribune*, March 12, 1892.

[13]October 15, 1892.

[14]*Live Questions*, II, 287.

[15]Nellie Bly, interview.

[16]Kraus, *Reminiscences*, p. 107-08.

[17]Appellant's Brief, *Unity Company* v. *McCormick*, Appellate Court, First Illinois District, No. 14126, p. 256.

[18]Snelling, interview.

[19]Chicago *Inter-Ocean*, August 11, 1891.

[20]Altgeld explained this gold clause in a speech at a meeting of Democratic Polish Jews in Chicago, November 2, 1896 (*Times-Herald*, November 3,

1896). It was a matter that embarrassed him politically all through his later career. The *Tribune* and Carter H. Harrison, (*Stormy Years*, p. 134) especially, used it as proof of Altgeld's "insincerity" on the gold question. It was nothing of the kind.

[21]Altgeld testimony in *Unity* v. *McCormick*, Brief of Appellant, Illinois Appellate Court, Case No. 14126.

[22]*Ibid.*, p. 257.

[23]Testimony of John M. Oliver, *ibid.*, p. 87.

[24]*Ibid.*, p. 65.

[25]Altgeld testimony, Supplemental Brief, *Unity* v. *McCormick*, p. 56.

[26]Browne, p. 31.

[27]Brentano to author, May 30, 1936.

[28]Chicago *Evening Post*, July 31, 1891.

CHAPTER SEVENTEEN

[1]Chicago *Inter-Ocean*, July 2, 1891.

[2]Chicago *Evening Post*, July 31, 1891.

[3]Chicago *Inter-Ocean*, August 31, 1891.

[4]Chicago *Daily News*, October 2, 1891.

[5]Chicago *Daily News*, December 30, 1891.

[6]Chicago *Herald*, March 5, 1892.

[7]*Ibid.*

[8]Chicago *Daily News*, April 21, 1892.

[9]*Ibid.*

[10]Schilling, interview, June 1, 1936.

[11]Chicago *Herald*, April 26, 1892.

[12]Altgeld campaign pamphlet cited *supra*. This is based on a stenographic report of his speech, the text differing somewhat from that included by Altgeld in his second volume of *Live Questions*.

[13]Masters, "Altgeld," *American Mercury*, p. 160.

[14]Abbott, *op. cit.*, p. 107.

[15]Whitlock, *op. cit.*, p. 48.

[16]Chicago *Daily News*, May 17, 1892.

[17]Chicago *Herald*, August 29, 1892. News "feature" written by Brand Whitlock.

[18]Chicago *Tribune*, April 28, 1892.

[19]Chicago *Daily News*, April 28, 1892.

[20]Chicago *Tribune*, September 22, 1892.

[21]Springfield *Journal*, clipped in *Tribune*, August 25, 1892.

[22]Chicago *Tribune*, August 7, 1892.

[23]Chicago *Daily News*, May 19, 1892.

[24]Chicago *Inter-Ocean*, August 13, 1892.

[25]Chicago *Herald*, August 28, 1892.

26August 29, 1892.

27Chicago *Tribune,* August 9, 1892.

28Allan Nevins, *Letters of Grover Cleveland,* p. 310. Reprinted by permission of, and arrangement with Houghton Mifflin Co., publishers.

29Chicago *Record,* July 27, 1892.

30*Laws of Illinois,* 1889, p. 237.

31*Centennial History,* IV, 184.

32Chicago *Tribune,* November 7, 1892. Statement by Mrs. Ada C. Sweet, chairman of education committee, Chicago Woman's Club; also, Goodspeed and Healy, *History of Chicago and Cook County,* II, 627.

33Schilling, interview.

34Joseph Kirkland and John Moses, *History of Chicago,* I, 251. (Munsell and Co., 1895).

35Chicago *Record,* July 11, 1892.

36The vote was Fifer, 402,672; Altgeld, 425,558.

37Chicago *Tribune,* November 11, 1892.

CHAPTER EIGHTEEN

1Mrs. Heile, interview.

2Chicago *Tribune,* November 21, 1892.

3William O. Thompson memorandum.

4Chicago *Tribune,* March 13, 1902.

5*Ibid.,* January 9, 1893.

6*Ibid.,* January 11, 1893.

7*Ibid.,* January 25, 1893.

8*The Public,* May 24, 1912, p. 494.

9Hinrichsen, cited *supra.*

10Victor Robinson, *The Don Quixote of Psychiatry: A Biography of Dr. Shoval Vail Clevenger,* pp. 107-08. (New York: Historico-Medical Press, 1919); also *Tribune,* April 19, 1893.

11Dr. Shoval Vail Clevenger, *Fun in a Doctor's Life,* p. 143. (Atlantic City: Evolution Publishing Co., 1909). Also Ethel L. Dewey, *Recollections of Richard Dewey, Pioneer in American Psychiatry,* pp. 147-152. (Chicago: University of Chicago Press, 1936).

12Robinson, *op. cit.,* pp. 120-22, quoting letter of Dr. Chapman V. Dean.

13Henry W. Clendenin, *Autobiography,* pp. 204-5. (Springfield: Illinois State Register, 1925).

14Altgeld to J. W. Babcock, Nov. 20, 1894, in *Live Questions,* 1899 edition, p. 457.

15Chicago *Herald,* February 8, 1895.

16Address to Trustees, November 28, 1893, *Live Questions,* 1899 edition, p. 359.

17*Ibid.,* p. 413.

18Darrow, *op. cit.,* p. 104.

CHAPTER NINETEEN

[1]Chicago *Evening Post,* July 31, 1891.
[2]Chicago *Tribune,* January 11, 1893.
[3]*Live Questions,* II, p. 250.
[4]*Ibid.,* p. 253-254.
[5]*Ibid.,* p. 250.
[6]*Ibid.,* p. 246.
[7]*Ibid.,* p. 249
[8]*Ibid.,* pp. 246-247. Italics supplied.
[9]Chicago *Tribune,* March 16, 1895.
[10]*Illinois Laws,* 1893, p. 76.
[11]Chicago *Tribune,* April 22, 1892.
[12]Altgeld Proclamation, June 3, 1893, in *Illinois Blue Book,* 1935-36, p. 693.
[13]*Ibid.,* p. 692.
[14]Chicago *Tribune,* June 11, 1893.
[15]*Ibid.,* June 17, 1893.
[16]Brand Whitlock, *Forty Years of It,* p. 924. (New York: D. Appleton-Century Co., 1914). Whitlock then was employed as a clerk in the office of the Secretary of State. Altgeld had asked him to become his private secretary, but Whitlock preferred the other job in order to have more leisure for studying law.
[17]Altgeld to legislature, in the Chicago *Tribune,* June 17, 1893.
[18]Schilling, interview.
[19]Chicago *Tribune,* June 11, 1893.
[20]*Ibid.*
[21]*Ibid.,* June 17, 1893.

CHAPTER TWENTY

[1]Darrow, p. 100.
[2]*Ibid.,* p. v.
[3]Schilling, interview.
[4]Darrow, p. 101.
[5]Segment of manuscript by Samuel P. McConnell; also his published article, "The Chicago Bomb Case, Personal Recollections of an American Tragedy," *Harpers,* May, 1934.
[6]Schilling letter, addressed to "Editor, *Public,*" original in possession of author.
[7]Chicago *Tribune,* March 20, 1893.
[8]Schilling, interview, May 2, 1935.
[9]Schilling, interview.
[10]Chicago *Times,* October 21, 1884.
[11]Zeisler, Zigmund, "Reminiscences of the Haymarket Case," in *Illinois*

Law Review, V, xxi, Nov., 1926, No. 3. Mr. Zeisler, later a prominent member of the Chicago bar, was one of the lawyers in the Haymarket case, for the defense.

[12]*Life of Parsons,* p. 222.

CHAPTER TWENTY-ONE

[1]*The Century Magazine,* XLV, No. 6, 802-837.
[2]Lloyd, I, 99.
[3]*The Century Magazine,* p. 809.
[4]Chicago *Tribune,* April 2, 1893.
[5]*The Cost of Something for Nothing,* p. 74.
[6]Chicago *Tribune,* June 24, 1886.
[7]Chicago *Tribune,* December 29, 1887; also in Lloyd, I, illustration facing p. 100.
[8]Gary, article in *The Century Magazine* cited *supra,* p. 837.
[9]*Ibid.,* p. 809.
[10]*Ibid.,* p. 830.
[11]*Live Questions,* II, 390-1.
[12]Swett brief, quoted in *Life of Parsons,* pp. 164-65.
[13]Gary, article in *Century,* cited *supra,* p. 809.
[14]*Ibid.,* p. 828.
[15]*Ibid.,* p. 829.
[16]See page 102, this book.
[17]Gary, p. 810. Italics supplied.
[18]*Ibid.,* p. 830.
[19]Schilling, interview.
[20]*Ibid.,* p. 834, and the Chicago *Daily News,* September 23, 1886.

CHAPTER TWENTY-TWO

[1]Chicago *Tribune,* April 3, 1893.
[2]Suppressed Schilling letter to *The Public.*
[3]*The Century Magazine,* p. 809.
[4]McConnell, in *Harpers,* May, 1934, p. 735.
[5]Albert J. Beveridge, *Lincoln,* II, 281-90.
[6]Schilling, interview, May 30, 1935.
[7]It should be emphasized that this explanation for Senator Trumbull's refusal was Schilling's "surmise." Trumbull may have had other reasons. Certainly in later years he acquitted himself magnificently of any suspicion of fearing the corporations, for he openly espoused the Populist party and volunteered his services in the Debs case.
[8]Suppressed Schilling letter.
[9]Chicago *Tribune,* January 12, 1893.

[10]Djmek affidavit, April 14, 1893, in *Live Questions*, II, 389.

[11]S. Philip Van Patten to Schilling, April 11, 1893.

[12]Asterisks indicate items used or referred to by Altgeld in his pardon statement.

[13]Notebook in Schilling papers.

[14]Schaack to Detwiler, May 4, 1893, in *Live Questions*, II, 382-3.

[15]*Live Questions*, II, p. 275.

[16]See p. 102, this book.

[17]Gary, p. 810. Italics supplied.

[18]*Live Questions*, II, 257-58.

[19]*Ibid.*, II, 263.

[20]*Ibid.*, II, 282.

[21]*Ibid.*, II, 282-83.

[22]Whitlock, *op. cit.*, pp. 74-75.

[23]Hinrichsen, *Inter-Ocean*, March 16, 1902.

[24]Whitlock, *op. cit.*, p. 74.

[25]August Spies, *Autobiography*. (Chicago: 1887). Preface by Nina Van Zandt, published by Nina Van Zandt. In John Crerar Library, Chicago. This was written while Spies was in Cook County jail awaiting execution of his sentence.

[26]Whitlock, *op. cit.*, p. 75.

CHAPTER TWENTY-THREE

[1]Edgar Lee Masters, *Tale of Chicago*, pp. 257-58. (New York: G. P. Putnam's Sons, 1933). Masters, however, applauded the pardon.

[2]Favor affidavit, November 7, 1887, in *Live Questions*, II, 344-45.

[3]*Live Questions*, II, 343.

[4]Favor affidavit.

[5]*Live Questions*, II, 346.

[6]*Ibid.*

[7]*Ibid.*, II, 353-54.

[8]*Ibid.*, II, 349.

[9]*Ibid.*, II, 355.

[10]*Ibid.*, II, 359-63.

[11]*Spies* et al. v. *The People*, 122 Illinois 1, at 258.

[12]*Ibid.*

[13]*Ibid.*, p. 263.

[14]*Ibid.*, p. 261.

[15]*Ibid.*, p. 262.

[16]*Ibid.*, p. 263.

[17]*People* v. *Coughlin*, Illinois 140 (1893). Justice Magruder's dissenting opinion appears on p. 189.

[18]Schilling, interview.

[19]*People* v. *Coughlin*, p. 182; also *Live Questions*, II, 364-65.

[20]*People* v. *Coughlin*, p. 179.

[21]*Ibid.*, p. 184.

[22]*Ibid.*, p. 186.

[23]*Live Questions*, II, 370.

[24]McConnell, in *Harpers*, p. 738.

[25]*Live Questions*, II, 370.

[26]*Ibid.*, II, 371.

[27]*Ibid.*

[28]*Ibid.*, II, 372.

[29]*Ibid.*

[30]*Ibid.*, II, 384.

[31]See p. 55, this book.

[32]See p. 79, this book, and note 7, Chapter Eight.

[33]*Live Questions*, II, 383-84.

[34]*Ibid.*, II, 385.

[35]*Ibid.*, II, 389.

[36]*Ibid.*, II, 390.

[37]*Ibid.*, II, 392.

[38]*Ibid.*, II, 394.

[39]*Ibid.*, II, 395.

[40]*Ibid.*, II, 396.

CHAPTER TWENTY-FOUR

[1]Chicago *Tribune*, June 27, 1893.

[2]Schwab to Frank A. Stauber, from Joliet, June 3, 1892, in Chicago *Times*, June 27, 1892.

[3]Enclosed by Schwab in letter to Schilling, July 5, 1893, in Schilling papers. Italics supplied.

[4]Schilling, interview.

[5]Schilling, interview, and Fielden letters to Schilling.

[6]Chicago *Tribune*, July 3, 1893.

[7]Chicago *Tribune*, July 5, 1894.

[8]Lloyd, *op. cit.*, I, 241.

[9]Schilling, interview.

[10]Brown to Schilling, June 28, 1893.

[11]Lloyd, I, 103.

[12]Swinton to Schilling, August 8, 1893.

[13]Darrow, *op. cit.*, p. 102.

[14]From *Twenty Years at Hull House*, by Jane Addams. By permission of The Macmillan Company, publishers, p. 207.

[15]Schilling, interview.

[16]Browne, *op. cit.*, p. 114.

[17]Chicago *Tribune,* June 27, 1893.

[18]*Ibid.,* June 28, 1893.

[19]*Ibid.,* June 28, 1893.

[20]*Ibid.*

[21]*Ibid.,* June 27, 1893.

[22]*Ibid.,* September 12, 1895.

[23]*Ibid.,* June 29, 1893.

[24]Chicago *Daily News,* June 29, 1893.

[25]New York *Times,* June 28, 1893.

[26]*Ibid.,* June 29, 1893.

[27]*Ibid.,* June 28, 1893.

[28]Chicago *Daily News,* June 30, 1893.

[29]Chicago *Tribune,* June 29, 1893.

[30]*The Nation,* LVI (1893), 464.

[31]Chicago *Record,* July 3, 1893.

[32]Cincinnati *Enquirer,* June 29, 1893.

[33]Cenia Pollock Valentine, interview.

[34]Chicago *Tribune,* July 5, 1893.

[35]*Ibid.,* June 29, 1893.

[36]*Ibid.,* December 10, 1893.

[37]*Ibid.,* May 23, 1894.

[38]*Ibid.,* June 9, 1894.

[39]New York *Tribune,* September 2, 1894.

CHAPTER TWENTY-FIVE

[1]Chicago *Tribune,* September 16, 1894.

[2]Darrow, *The Story of My Life,* p. 101. (New York: Charles Scribner's Sons, 1932).

[3]A. L. Bowen, "Personal Reminiscences of Joseph W. Fifer; an Interview with the Former Governor and a Description of His Times," in *Illinois Blue Book,* 1925-26, p. 305.

[4]Chicago *Sunday Tribune,* January 5, 1936.

[5]Bowen, cited *supra,* p. 304.

[6]John M. Palmer, *Personal Recollections of John M. Palmer, The Story of an Earnest Life,* pp. 463-64. (Cincinnati: Robert Clarke Co., 1901).

[7]Schilling, interview.

[8]Chicago *Times,* June 27, and July 25, 1892; also, minute book of The Amnesty Association kept by George A. Schilling.

[9]Chicago *Tribune,* August 7, 1893.

[10]*Live Questions,* II, 44-46. Italics supplied.

[11]Schilling, interview, and Chicago *Record,* June 27, 1893.

[12]*Live Questions,* II, 414.

[13]*National Union Building Association* v. *Bremer,* 41 Illinois Appellate 223 (1891).

[14]Chicago *Tribune*, November 8, 1893.

[15]*Ibid.*, November 5, 1893.

[16]Altgeld to Lloyd, June 3, 1890, in Lloyd, I, 115.

CHAPTER TWENTY-SIX

[1]W. O. Thompson memorandum.

[2]Whitlock, *op. cit.*, p. 75.

[3]Masters, *Tale of Chicago*, p. 258.

[4]Browne, p. 114.

[5]Darrow, p. 103-104.

[6]Wish, p. 128.

[7]Schilling, interview.

[8]Clipped in Chicago *Tribune*, November 4, 1893.

[9]Chicago *Tribune*, May 25, 1895.

[10]*Ibid.*, May 26, 1895.

[11]Schilling memorandum.

[12]Whitlock, p. 77.

[13]Chicago *Daily News*, June 30, 1893.

[14]*Ibid.*

[15]Chicago *Tribune*, June 30, 1893.

[16]David, Henry, *History of the Haymarket Affair*, p. 229.

[17]Chicago *Tribune*, August 31, 1893.

[18]New York *World*, July 17, 1894.

[19]Chicago *Tribune*, September 16, 1894.

[20]Lloyd, I, 106.

[21]From *Altgeld of Illinois*, by Waldo R. Browne, copyright 1924, published by The Viking Press, Inc., New York, p. 115.

[22]Bly, interview.

[23]Theodore Roosevelt, *An Autobiography*, p. 152. (New York: Charles Scribner's Sons, 1931).

CHAPTER TWENTY-SEVEN

[1]Chicago *Record*, October 27, 1893.

[2]*Live Questions*, II, 298.

[3]*Ibid.*, II, 298-302.

[4]*Ibid.*, II, 305.

[5]Quoted in Wish, *op. cit.*

[6]Chicago *Tribune*, December 11, 1893.

[7]*Ibid.*, June 12, 1894.

[8]*Ibid.*, March 5, 1894.

[9]Henry James, *Richard Olney*, p. 36-37. (Boston: Houghton Mifflin Company, 1923).

[10]*Report of Illinois Board of Labor Statistics for 1894*, p. 454.

[11]Bly, interview.

[12]Altgeld to August Luer, *Tribune,* March 17, 1894; also, *ibid.,* March 17 and 18, 1894.

[13]Edward O. Brown, Chicago Historical Society pamphlet, p. 31.

[14]Chicago *Tribune,* April 27, 1894.

[15]Wish, *op. cit.,* pp. 144-145.

[16]Chicago *Tribune,* May 28, 1894.

[17]*Live Questions,* 1899 edition, p. 927. Italics supplied.

[18]Altgeld, in 1895 General Message to General Assembly, in *Live Questions,* 1899 edition, p. 928.

[19]Father John F. Powers to Lloyd, May 30, 1894. In Schilling papers.

CHAPTER TWENTY-EIGHT

[1]Chicago *Tribune,* May 12, 1894.

[2]Graham Taylor, *Pioneering on Social Frontiers,* p. 112. (Chicago: University of Chicago Press, 1930).

[3]Currey, *Chicago: Its History and Its Builders,* III, 204. (Chicago: S. J. Clarke Publishing Co., 1912).

[4]Quoted in Currey, *op. cit.,* III, 207.

[5]Russell Hugh Baugh, "The Attitude of John Peter Altgeld Toward Problems of Labor," master of arts thesis, University of Wisconsin, 1930, p. 47, quoting John Lee, *Industrial Organization,* p. 20.

[6]Taylor, *op. cit.,* p. 115.

[7]See United States Strike Commission appointed by the President, *Report of the Chicago Strike of June-July, 1894,* Washington, Government Printing Office, 1895. (Hereafter cited as *U. S. Strike Report*), pp. xxiv and xxxviii.

[8]David Karsner, *Debs: His Authorized Life and Letters from Woodstock Prison to Atlanta,* p. 137. (New York: Boni and Liveright, 1919).

[9]*U. S. Strike Report,* pp. xxxix and 130.

[10]Eugene V. Debs, *The Federal Government and the Chicago Strike,* a pamphlet answering Grover Cleveland, p. 31. (Chicago: Charles H. Kerr and Company, 1910).

[11]Beer, *Mauve·Decade,* p. 78. (New York: Alfred A. Knopf, Inc., 1926).

[12]Beer, *Hanna,* p. 132. (New York: Alfred A. Knopf, Inc., 1929).

[13]*Ibid.,* p. 253.

[14]*U. S. Strike Report,* p. xxxi.

[15]New York *Comrade,* April, 1902, quoted in David Karsner, p. 176.

[16]Charles A. Ewing, "Compulsory Arbitration," in *Proceedings of Illinois State Bar Association,* 1895, p. 255.

[17]Ewing, *op. cit.,* p. 258.

[18]Peck, *op. cit.,* p. 379.

[19]Nevins, *op. cit.,* p. 618.

[20]Altgeld to a Boston newspaper, February 25, 1896, in *Live Questions,* 1899 edition, p. 527.

[21]James, *Olney,* p. 22.

[22]James, p. 22, and Nevins, *Cleveland,* p. 615. (New York: Dodd, Mead and Co., 1932).

[23]James, *op. cit.,* p. 205.

[24]*Ibid.,* pp. 36-37.

[25]*Ibid.,* p. 37.

[26]Nevins, *Cleveland,* p. 616; Debs, p. 8.

[27]James, p. 47. Italics supplied.

[28]In re *Debs,* 158 U. S. 570.

[29]*Ibid.,* 572.

[30]Nevins, *Cleveland,* p. 618.

[31]*Ibid.*

[32]*Ibid.,* p. 628.

[33]James, p. 48.

[34]Nevins, *Cleveland,* pp. 619-20. Italics supplied.

[35]James, p. 48.

[36]*Ibid.,* pp. 48-50. Italics supplied.

[37]Lloyd to Willis J. Abbott, in *The Pilgrim,* April, 1902; also, quoted in Caro Lloyd, I, 147.

[38]Lloyd interview, New York *Journal,* October 18, 1896; reprinted in Chicago *Labor Advocate,* October 24, 1896; in Caro Lloyd, I, 147-51.

[39]Cincinnati *Enquirer,* March 18, 1902.

[40]*Live Questions,* 1899 edition, pp. 653-54.

[41]Nevins, *Cleveland,* p. 621.

[42]Gresham, *op. cit.,* p. 799-801.

[43]A. B. Farcquhar, with Samuel Crowther, *The First Million the Hardest,* p. 271. (New York: Doubleday, Page and Co., 1922).

[44]James, p. 204.

CHAPTER TWENTY-NINE

[1]*Live Questions,* 1899 edition, pp. 668*ff.* Italics supplied.

[2]Claude Bowers, *Beveridge and the Progressive Era,* p. 60. Reprinted by special permission, and arrangement with Houghton Mifflin Company, publishers.

[3]Chicago *Tribune,* July 7, 1894.

[4]Clipped in Chicago *Tribune,* July 9, 1894.

[5]*Ibid.,* July 7, 1894.

[6]*Ibid.*

[7]*Ibid.,* July 10, 1894.

[8]Chicago *Times,* July 7, 1894.

[9]Chicago *Tribune,* July 7, 1894.

[10]Altgeld, Speech at Cooper Union, in *Live Questions,* 1899 edition, pp. 676-77.

[11]Boston *Post,* January 16, 1875, in Browne, *op. cit.,* p. 169.

[12]Chicago *Tribune,* July 6, 1894.

[13]*Live Questions,* 1899 edition, p. 670; Nevins, *Letters of Cleveland,* p. 360. Reprinted by special permission of, and by arrangement with Houghton Mifflin Company, publishers.

[14]*Live Questions,* 1899 edition, p. 671.

[15]Chicago *Tribune,* July 7, 1894.

[16]Grover Cleveland, "The Government in the Chicago Strike of 1894," *McClure's Magazine,* July, 1904.

[17]James A. Barnes, *John G. Carlisle,* p. 332. (New York: Dodd, Mead and Company, 1931).

[18]Chicago *Tribune,* July 7, 1894; Nevins, *Cleveland,* p. 361.

[19]*The Nation,* July 12, 1894.

[20]Clipped in the Chicago *Tribune,* July 10, 1894.

CHAPTER THIRTY

[1]See Howard Barton Myers, "The Policing of Labor Disputes in Chicago: A Case Study." A dissertation submitted for the degree of Doctor of Philosophy at the University of Chicago, 1929 (as yet unpublished), pp. 224-28; 261-68. Citing official U. S. Army reports and Federal Strike Commission report. Also see Gen. John M. Schofield, *Forty-Six Years in the Army,* pp. 647-690; also Altgeld, *Live Questions,* 1899 edition, "Cooper Union Address," and "General Message on Assembly of Legislature," 1895; also contemporary newspapers, including the Chicago *Tribune,* July 4, 1894.

[2]Myers, *op. cit.,* pp. 224-26.

[3]*Live Questions,* 1899 edition, p. 666.

[4]*Live Questions,* 1899 edition, pp. 664-65.

[5]Snelling, interview.

[6]*Live Questions,* 1899 edition, p. 665.

[7]*Ibid.,* p. 666.

[8]Whitlock, *op. cit.,* p. 92.

[9]*U. S. Strike Report,* p. xli.

[10]*U. S. Strike Report,* p. xliv.

[11]*Ibid.,* p. 356.

[12]Debs, *op. cit.,* p. 12.

[13]*Ibid.,* p. 27.

[14]Gustavus Myers, *History of the Great American Fortunes,* II, 204. (Chicago: Charles H. Kerr and Co., 1910).

[15]Caro Lloyd, *op. cit.,* I, 147.

[16]*U. S. Strike Report,* p. 370.

[17]*Ibid.,* pp. 366-77.

[18]*Ibid.,* p. 370.

[19]Lloyd, New York *Journal,* quoting *New England Magazine,* October, 1896, in Caro Lloyd, p. 152.

[20]Chicago *Tribune,* July 7, 1894.

[21]*Live Questions,* 1899 edition, p. 658.

[22]Professor Nevins in *Grover Cleveland—A Study in Courage* gives the best and most objective account of the Pullman strike by any historian who has written about the affair.

[23]Nevins, *Letters,* p. 40.

[24]Farcquhar, *op. cit.,* p. 272.

[25]Depew, quoted in Currey, *op. cit.,* III, 215-16.

[26]From *History of the United States,* by James Ford Rhodes. By permission of The Macmillan Company, publishers, VIII, 425-29.

[27]Woodrow Wilson, *A History of the American People,* IV, 40. (New York: Harper and Brothers, 1902).

CHAPTER THIRTY-ONE

[1]From original among Schilling papers, in possession of the author. Dated October 31, 1894.

[2]Schilling, interview.

[3]Altgeld, in newspaper interview, February 27, 1896, quoted in *Live Questions,* 1899 edition, p. 529.

[4]Chicago *Record,* August 20, 1894; also *Live Questions,* 1899 edition, p. 421.

[5]Chicago *Tribune,* August 22, 1894; *Live Questions,* 1899 edition, p. 421.

[6]Chicago *Tribune,* August 22, 1894.

[7]*Ibid.,* August 23, 1894.

[8]*Ibid.,* August 21, 1894.

[9]Chicago *Tribune,* August 22, 1894, and *Live Questions,* 1899 edition, pp. 422-23.

[10]Snelling, interview, December 10, 1937.

[11]Chicago *Tribune,* August 22, 1894.

[12]Chicago *Tribune,* August 22, 1894.

[13]*Live Questions,* 1899 edition, p. 424.

[14]Chicago *Tribune,* August 22, 1894.

[15]*U. S. Strike Report,* p. 569.

[16]*Live Questions,* 1899 edition, p. 427.

[17]*Ibid.*

[18]Chicago *Tribune,* August 23, 1894.

[19]*Live Questions,* 1899 edition, pp. 418-20.

[20]Chicago *Times-Herald,* April 18, 1895.

[21]*Live Questions,* 1899 edition, pp. 482-84.

[22]Chicago *Times-Herald,* April 18, 1895.

[23]The Chicago *Tribune,* January 6, 1895.

CHAPTER THIRTY-TWO

[1]*Live Questions,* 1899 edition, pp. 919-20.

[2]*Ibid.,* pp. 936-37.

[3]*Ibid.*, pp. 933-34.

[4]*Ibid.*, pp. 934-35.

[5]*Pollock* v. *Farmers' Loan & Trust Company*, 157 U. S. 532.

[6]Chicago *Tribune*, April 18, 1895, and *Live Questions*, 1899 edition, pp. 464-65.

[7]Chicago *Tribune*, June 3, 1895, and *Live Questions*, 1899 edition, pp. 459-61.

[8]Clipped in the Chicago *Tribune*, June 5, 1895.

[9]Chicago *Tribune*, June 8, 1895.

[10]He referred to capital stock, not real-estate tax.

[11]*Live Questions*, 1899 edition, p. 917.

[12]*Ibid.*, p. 914.

[13]*Ibid.*, pp. 938-40.

[14]Chicago *Tribune*, March 10, 1895.

[15]*Ibid.*, May 1, 1895.

CHAPTER THIRTY-THREE

[1]Cleveland, in *McClure's Magazine*, July, 1904.

[2]Peck, *Twenty Years of the Republic*, p. 452. (New York: Dodd, Mead and Co., 1906).

[3]Barnes, *John G. Carlisle*, p. 429. (New York: Dodd, Mead and Co., 1931).

[4]Samuel P. McConnell, "The Silver Campaign of 1895-96," unpublished MS.

[5]Chicago *Chronicle*, March 13, 1903, statement of John P. Hopkins; also New York *Tribune*, October 17, 1896.

[6]*Live Questions*, II, 54-62.

[7]*Ibid.*, pp. 412-17.

[8]*Live Questions*, 1899 edition, p. 432.

[9]See "open letter" of William S. Forman to Altgeld, August 22, 1896, in the Chicago *Record*, August 24, 1896, and other papers, for charges against Altgeld in this connection. Also open letter of William R. Morrison to Benjamin R. Burroughs of Edwardsville, Ill., October 19, 1896, in the Chicago *Tribune*, October 22, 1896. As enemies of Altgeld, Forman and Morrison insinuate that Altgeld knew he was getting state funds from Ramsay. There is no evidence that such was the case, although reason exists to believe the contrary. In the case of *Unity Company* v. *McCormick*, it was testified that M. F. Dunlap of Jacksonville lent Altgeld $15,000 in November, 1894, seeming corroboration of the part played by Hinrichsen, who lived in Jacksonville.

[10]Chicago *Tribune*, February 5, 1895. The *Tribune* insinuated (February 3 and 4, 1895) that Altgeld removed certain officials of state hospitals because they would not help him get loans from banks which were depositaries of state funds. It presented a damaging circumstantial case in two instances, but Altgeld issued a denial which stopped further attacks upon him on that score until the 1896 campaign, when his financial troubles were made a political issue.

[11]Chicago *Daily News,* December 2, 1895.

[12]*Live Questions,* 1899 edition, pp. 467-69.

[13]Chicago *Inter-Ocean,* November 12, 1895.

[14]Chicago *Record,* May 18, 1896.

[15]Hinrichsen, in the Chicago *Inter-Ocean,* cited *supra.*

[16]*Live Questions,* 1899 edition, p. 487.

[17]Nevins, *Letters,* p. 384.

[18]Nevins, *Cleveland,* p. 676.

[19]Chicago *Times-Herald,* April 16, 1895; *Live Questions,* 1899 edition, 471-73.

[20]William Jennings Bryan, *The First Battle,* p. 158. (Chicago: W. B. Conkey Co., 1896).

[21]Nevins, *Letters,* p. 386.

[22]C. R. Tuttle, *Illinois Currency Convention,* pp. 66-68. (Chicago: Charles H. Kerr and Co., 1895).

[23]Chicago *Tribune,* May 5, 1895.

[24]*Ibid.,* June 6, 1895.

[25]Tuttle, *op. cit.,* Chapter XII.

[26]Bryan, *op. cit.,* p. 162 and Nevins, *Cleveland,* pp. 681-82.

[27]Nevins, *Cleveland,* p. 683.

[28]See Cleveland letter to Lambert Tree, in Nevins, *Letters of Grover Cleveland,* 309.

[29]Testimony of Altgeld in *Unity* v *McCormick,* p. 17 of *Abstract* cited *supra.*

[30]*Ibid.*

[31]*Ibid.,* pp. 17-20.

[32]*Live Questions,* 1899 edition, p. 541

[33]These editorials were written by Henry Demarest Lloyd.

[34]Chicago *Record,* June 20, 1896.

[35]*Ibid.,* June 24, 1896.

[36]*Live Questions,* 1899 edition, p. 525.

[37]Chicago *Record,* June 23, 1896.

CHAPTER THIRTY-FOUR

[1]Minority Report, 1896 Convention, in Bryan, *op. cit.,* p. 198.

[2]Hinrichsen, in the Chicago *Inter-Ocean,* cited *supra.*

[3]Platform, 1896, in Bryan, *op. cit.,* p. 408.

[4]Chicago *Record-Herald,* March 13, 1912.

[5]Nevins, *Letters,* p. 447.

[6]*Leslie's Weekly,* July 16, 1896.

[7]Charles Warren, "A Manufacturer of History," *McClure's Magazine,* April 1900; also, Paxton Hibben, *The Peerless Leader, William Jennings Bryan,* p. 152. (New York: Farrar and Rinehart, Inc., 1927).

[8]Robert O. Law, *The Parties and the Men, or Political Issues of 1896,* a

History of Our Great Parties from the Beginning, pp. 422-27; Bryan, *op. cit.,* p. 188.

[9]Edgar Lee Masters, "The Christian Statesman," *American Mercury,* III (December, 1924).

[10]*Live Questions,* 1899 edition, pp. 585-90.

[11]Peck, *op. cit.,* p. 494.

[12]Nevins, *Cleveland,* p. 701; Melville Stone, *op. cit.,* p. 220; H. H. Kohlsaat, *From McKinley to Harding,* p. 49. (New York: Charles Scribner's Sons, 1923).

[13]Hinrichsen, in the Chicago *Inter-Ocean,* cited *supra.*

[14]M. R. Werner, *Bryan,* pp. 119-20. (New York: Harcourt, Brace and Co., 1929).

[15]*Ibid.,* p. 108.

[16]Bryan, *op. cit.,* p. 23.

[17]William Sulzer to W. R. Browne, 1923, cited by Wish.

[18]Mrs. Betak, interview.

[19]Whitlock, *op. cit.,* p. 80.

[20]McConnell, MS., "The Silver Campaign of 1895-96."

[21]William Jennings Bryan and His Wife, *Memoirs,* p. 101. (Philadelphia: John C. Winston Co., 1925); also Wayne C. Williams, *William Jennings Bryan,* pp. 126-27. (New York: G. P. Putnam's Sons, 1938).

[22]Altgeld to Bryan, June 9, 1896, Bryan Papers, Library of Congress.

[23]George A. Cardon to Bryan, June 8, 1896, in Marian Silveus, "The Antecedents of the Campaign of 1896," Ph.D. thesis, 1932, p. 206.

[24]Snelling, interview, June 25, 1935.

[25]Silveus, cited *supra,* p. 208.

[26]Chicago *Tribune,* June 26, 1896.

[27]McConnell MS.

[28]Abbott, *Watching The World Go By,* pp. 157-59. (New York: Dodd, Mead and Co., 1895).

[29]McConnell MS.

[30]Darrow, *op. cit.,* p. 91.

[31]Darrow, interview.

[32]McConnell MS.

[33]Beer, *Mauve Decade,* p. 85.

[34]Chicago *Daily News,* July 9, 1896.

[35]Clendenin, *op. cit.,* pp. 222-23.

[36]Law, *op. cit.,* p. 470.

[37]Franklin Daniel Scott, "The Political Career of William R. Morrison of Illinois," Master's Thesis, University of Chicago, 1924, p. 88.

[38]Law, p. 470.

CHAPTER THIRTY-FIVE

[1]Paxton Hibben, *The Peerless Leader, William Jennings Bryan,* p. 195.

[2]See, for example, Anna Roosevelt Cowles, *Letters from Theodore Roose-*

velt to Anna Roosevelt Cowles, 1870-1918. (New York: Charles Scribner's Sons, 1924).

[3]Peck, *op. cit.*, p. 467.

[4]*McClure's Magazine,* "The Strategy of the National Campaign," October, 1900, Vol. 40, No. 6, p. 494; also Werner, *Bryan,* p. 100.

[5]*Live Questions,* 1899 edition, pp. 584-85.

[6]New York *Tribune,* October 18, 1896.

[7]McConnell MSS.; also Chicago *Daily News,* May 2, 1895.

[8]New York *Tribune,* September 16, 1894.

[9]Chicago *Tribune,* September 18, 1894.

[10]Chicago *Chronicle,* March 13, 1902, other newspapers, also interviews with friends.

[11]Carter H. Harrison, *Stormy Years,* p. 172. (Indianapolis: Bobbs-Merrill Co., 1935).

[12]Chicago *Tribune,* March 12, 1902.

[13]Chicago *Record,* August 6, 1896.

[14]Denver *Post,* March 12, 1902.

[15]From *Editorials,* by Henry Watterson, copyright, 1923, by Doubleday, Doran & Company, Inc., p. 76-78.

[16]Benjamin Harrison, *Views of an Ex-President.* (Indianapolis: Bowen Merrill Co., 1901).

[17]See *Harper's Weekly,* October 24, 1896.

[18]*Ibid.,* October 18, 1896.

[19]New York *Tribune,* October 18, 1896.

[20]From *Reminiscences* by Carl Schurz, copyright, 1907, reprinted by permission from Doubleday, Doran & Company, Inc., p. 430.

[21]*Ibid.*

[22]Chicago *Times-Herald,* September 20, 1896.

[23]*Live Questions,* 1899 edition, pp. 612-47.

[24]Masters, "John Peter Altgeld," *American Mercury.*

[25]Chicago *Times-Herald,* October 25, 1896.

[26]Schilling, interview.

[27]Post, *op. cit.,* and Schilling, interview.

[28]*Live Questions,* 1899 edition, p. 779.

[29]Henry George, Jr., *The Life of Henry George,* p. 577. (Toronto: Poole Publishing Co., 1900).

[30]New York *Times,* October 18, 1896.

[31]New York *Tribune,* October 18, 1896.

[32]Chicago *Times-Herald,* October 18, 1896.

[33]*Live Questions,* 1899 edition, pp. 647-90.

[34]New York *Times,* October 18, 1896.

[35]Henry F. Pringle, *Theodore Roosevelt,* p. 589. (New York: Harcourt, Brace and Co., 1931).

[36]Chicago *Times-Herald,* October 16, 1896; also Pringle, p. 163.

[37]Pringle, p. 164 and Abbott, *op. cit.,* pp. 177-78.

[38]Chicago *Times-Herald,* October 30, 1896.

[39]Bowers, *Beveridge and the Progressive Era,* p. 62. Reprinted by special permission of and by arrangement with Houghton Mifflin Company, publishers.

[40]*Ibid.,* p. 74

[41]Kraus, *Reminiscences,* pp. 110-11.

[42]*Live Questions,* 1899 edition, p. 604.

[43]Chicago *Times-Herald,* November 3, 1896.

[44]Werner, *Bryan,* p. 102.

[45]Snelling, interview.

CHAPTER THIRTY-SIX

[1]Florence Kelley to Lloyd, October 1, 1896, in Lloyd papers.

[2]Beer, *Mauve Decade,* p. 88.

[3]Tom L. Johnson, *My Story,* p. 109.

[4]Chicago *Tribune,* November 4, 1896.

[5]*Live Questions,* 1899 edition, p. 691.

[6]Bryan, *The First Battle,* p. 607.

[7]Altgeld to Bryan, November 9, 1896, cited in Barnes, *Carlisle,* p. 488.

[8]Chicago *Tribune,* November 5, 1896.

[9]Clipped in Chicago *Tribune,* November 7, 1896.

[10]*Live Questions,* 1899 edition, 697-700.

[11]Chicago *Tribune,* January 11, 1897.

[12]Schilling to Johann Waage, Secretary of the Altgeld Monument Commission, October 15, 1913, Schilling papers.

[13]See, for example, his "Biennial Message to the General Assembly," January 6, 1897, in *Live Questions,* 1899 edition, p. 955.

[14]Hinrichsen, in the Chicago *Inter-Ocean,* cited *supra.*

[15]From *Across Spoon River, an Autobiography,* by Edgar Lee Masters, copyright, 1936, and reprinted by permission of Farrar & Rinehart, Inc., publishers, p. 95.

[16]Bowen, "Personal Reminiscences of Joseph W. Fifer," in *Illinois Blue Book,* p. 304-05.

[17]Chicago *Times-Herald,* March 10 and 12, 1895.

[18]Chicago *Tribune,* January 11, 1896.

[19]Chicago *Times-Herald,* March 12, 1895.

[20]*Live Questions,* 1899 edition, p. 516.

[21]Hinrichsen, in Chicago *Inter-Ocean,* cited *supra.*

[22]Debs, *The Federal Government and the Chicago Strike,* p. 32. (Chicago: Charles H. Kerr and Co., 1910).

[23]*Live Questions,* 1899 edition, p. 910.

[24]Allan Nevins, *History of the University of Illinois,* p. 154. (New York: Oxford University Press, 1917).

[25]*Live Questions,* 1899 edition, p. 476.

[26]Altgeld to Henry Wade Rogers, May 31, 1894, in Chicago *Tribune,* June 8 and 9, 1894.

[27]Schilling MS. fragment.

[28]John W. Yantis to author, through his son, Judge Aubrey L. Yantis of Shelbyville, Illinois. Memorandum, December 24, 1937.

[29]The *Tribune's* story on the "million-dollar bribe" was reprinted, with others, in a book entitled *Tattling Tales of a Retired Politician,* by Forrest Crissey, (Chicago: Thompson and Thomas, 1904). Illustrated by John T. McCutcheon. McCutcheon's drawing of Governor "Peavey" is a striking likeness of Governor Altgeld.

[30]Snelling to author. Joseph S. Martin told the same story to his son-in-law, Ralph G. Johansen of Chicago, who told it to author in 1936. Theodore Dreiser uses this incident in the second volume of his novel about Yerkes, *The Titan,* pp. 482-490. Mr. Dreiser informed the author (interview, 1935) that he investigated the bribe story carefully and found it was true. He related that Mr. H. H. Kohlsaat of Chicago, author of *From McKinley to Harding,* told him that he had documentary proof of the bribe attempt. It is also verified by a manuscript fragment written by Judge Samuel P. McConnell.

[31]Edward F. Dunne, *History of Illinois,* II, 219.

[32]Schilling, interview, June 23, 1935.

[33]Schilling, interview.

[34]The reference is to Carter H. Harrison. In his book *Stormy Years,* pp. 194-203, Mr. Harrison brings Altgeld's name into the story of Ogden Gas.

[35]See Chicago *Tribune,* February 27, 1895, and Chicago *Times-Herald,* May 15, 1895. F. D. Snelling in interview with author, May 6, 1937, stated positively that Lanehart conceived the plan for the Ogden Gas Company. Mr. Snelling was an original incorporator of the company, at Lanehart's request.

[36]See Chicago *Tribune,* April 24, 1897, also various financial directories of the period 1897-1906.

[37]Later counsel for the Illinois Manufacturers' Association.

[38]This list is given in Harrison, *Stormy Years,* p. 193. Interviews by author have tended to verify it.

[39]Snelling, interview, May 6, 1937.

[40]Mr. Snelling and others are very positive on this point. They are to be believed.

[41]Snelling, interview.

[42]As noted, that was done.

[43]*Live Questions,* II, 20

[44]Lanehart denied, in a public statement, that he was instrumental in getting House Bill 618 introduced. The *Times-Herald,* May 15, 1895, quoted Lanehart: "Speaking as the owner of a gas franchise [Ogden] I am willing to go into the field and compete and do not ask any such legislation. . . . I do not pose as a moralist or a reformer, but that is a step too far in the direction of a

monopoly to suit me." There is more reason to believe that the Chicago Gas Trust wanted the bill, as a means of stopping the formation of other gas companies after the Ogden franchise was granted. Robert Todd Lincoln, then president of the Gas Trust, was one of the few Chicagoans who denounced Altgeld's veto. *Times-Herald,* May 15, 1895. Nearly everyone else applauded, including the *Tribune.*

[45]McConnell MS. fragment. Copy in possession of author, original in possession of McConnell's widow. McConnell may have erred concerning the amount.

[46]Veto message in *Live Questions,* 1899 edition, p. 942. Also Chicago newspapers for May 15, 1895.

[47]Altgeld, *The Cost of Something for Nothing,* p. 44.

[48]Will of John W. Lanehart, in Probate Court of Cook County.

[49]Ralph G. Johansen and Schilling, interviews.

CHAPTER THIRTY-SEVEN

[1]Joseph S. Martin to George Keller, Hartford, Conn., October 15, 1913, in files of *Martin* v. *Martin,* cited *supra.*

[2]Snelling, interview. Mr. Snelling was agent for the building at this time.

[3]Chicago *Tribune,* April 15, 1897.

[4]Chicago *Inter-Ocean,* May 21, 1897.

[5]Chicago *Tribune,* April 10, 11, 14, 15, 16, 22, 24, 25, 30, 1897; May 24, 1897.

[6]*Ibid.,* May 2, 1897.

[7]Schilling, interview.

[8]Altgeld to Lambert Tree, May 11, 1897, quoted in Waldo Browne, pp. 300-1.

[9]Kraus to Schilling, told author by Schilling, June, 1936. Franks was the father of the boy killed by Leopold and Loeb.

[10]Lanehart Estate Records, Probate Court, Cook County. Note that Altgeld transferred his Ogden holdings in open court. Cf. with statement by Carter Harrison (*Stormy Years*) relating how Altgeld came to have the Ogden shares and his disposition of them, pp. 194 and 199.

[11]Note signed by Lanehart, November 6, 1895, in Probate Court file.

[12]Chicago *Tribune,* July 13, 1901.

[13]Harrison admits this inferentially in *Stormy Years,* pp. 77-84.

[14]*Live Questions,* 1899 edition, p. 731.

[15]Letter to Tree, cited *supra.*

[16]Altgeld to State Senator J. N. C. Shumway, January 20, 1899, in W. F. Cooling, *The Chicago Democracy, a History of Recent Municipal Politics.* (Chicago: Platform Publishing Co., 1899).

[17]*Ibid.*

[18]*Ibid.,* p. 44; see also Carter Harrison, p. 133.

[19]Darrow, *Story of My Life,* p. 107.

[20]Chicago *Record,* December 20, 1898.

[21]Schilling, interview.

[22]In interview with author, December, 1935.

[23]Cooling, *op. cit.,* p. 72.

[24]Darrow, p. 109.

[25]*The Public,* edited by Louis F. Post, later Assistant Secretary of Interior in Woodrow Wilson's administration, June 10, 1899.

[26]Altgeld affidavit, in *Abstract of Record, Unity* v. *McCormick,* cited *supra.*

[27]See James Weber Linn, *James Keeley, Newspaperman,* (Indianapolis: Bobbs-Merrill Company, 1937), for an excellent description of how the *Tribune* underwent a change after Medill's death.

[28]Francis F. Browne to Louis F. Post, quoted in Waldo Browne, *Altgeld of Illinois,* pp. 313-14. Waldo Browne is the son of Editor Browne of the *Dial.*

[29]*Harper's Weekly,* November 18, 1899.

[30]Harrison, 202.

[31]Waldo Browne, *op. cit.,* 319.

[32]Chicago *Record,* September 15, 1900.

CHAPTER THIRTY-EIGHT

[1]Altgeld to Lloyd, June 18, 1901, in Caro Lloyd, *op. cit.,* II, 112-113.

[2]William O. Thompson memorandum.

[3]*Ibid.*

[4]Darrow to John J. Meehan, January 30, 1934.

[5]Edgar Lee Masters quoted in Waldo Browne, *op. cit.,* p. 329.

[6]Edgar Lee Masters, *Levy Mayer and the New Industrial Era,* p. 144. (New Haven: Yale University Press, 1927).

[7]Newspaper release, Schilling papers.

[8]Letter to author, April 17, 1935.

[9]St. Louis *Globe-Democrat,* March 28, 1901.

[10]Graham Taylor, *Pioneering on Social Frontiers,* p. 317. (Chicago: Chicago University Press, 1930).

[11]Chicago *Tribune,* December 15, 1901.

[12]Chicago *Tribune* clipping, undated except for year 1901.

[13]*The Public,* March 10, 1900, p. 5.

[14]Published by Charles H. Kerr and Company.

[15]Nevins, *Letters and Journal of Brand Whitlock,* p xxxi. (New York: D. Appleton-Century Co., 1936).

[16]In letter to Lloyd cited *supra.*

[17]William H. Stuart, Chicago *Evening American,* December 10, 1919.

[18]*The Cost of Something for Nothing,* p. 41-42.

[19]They were finally published posthumously in 1904 by the Hammersmark Publishing Company, in which Clarence Darrow was a "silent partner" with Samuel Hammersmark. Darrow wrote an introduction to the essays.

[20]Sally Woodcock, interview.

[21]William Tracy Alden, attorney-at-law, to author, letter, September 28, 1937.

[22]Release for newspapers, Schilling papers.

[23]William O. Thompson memorandum.

[24]Chicago *Record-Herald,* March 13, 1902.

[25]Chicago *American,* March 12, 1902.

[26]Chicago *Chronicle,* March 13, 1902. Mrs. Altgeld lived until March 30, 1915, almost always an invalid after the death of her husband. Altgeld's friends raised a fund to provide for her when it was learned that he had died penniless. In 1903, the Illinois General Assembly voted her $5,000, to be used to lift the mortgage from her home.

[27]From Altgeld's death until his own fifteen years or so later, Joseph S. Martin devoted all of his time—literally—and nearly all of his money to activities for perpetuating the memory of Altgeld. He arranged and financed memorial meetings held in Chicago and elsewhere on the anniversaries of the birth and death of Altgeld. The portrait of Altgeld that hangs in the Chicago Historical Society collection was presented by Martin. When Martin died, it was discovered that he had provided in his will that $25,000 of his estate be used to erect a monument to Altgeld. That bequest, however, was made unnecessary by action of the Illinois General Assembly, when a new Democratic administration, under Governor Edward F. Dunne, appropriated the money for the Gutzon Borglum monument to Altgeld that now stands in Lincoln Park, Chicago. Martin's will also provided a fund for writing the story of Altgeld's life, which appeared in 1924, by Waldo R. Browne.

[28]*The Public,* May 24, 1912, p. 494.

BIBLIOGRAPHY

BIBLIOGRAPHY

PUBLISHED SOURCES

Abbott, Willis J., *Carter Henry Harrison, A Memoir* (New York: Dodd, Mead and Co., 1895).

Watching the World Go By (Boston: Little, Brown and Co., 1933).

Abstract of the Record in the Haymarket Trial before Judge Gary, filed with the Illinois Supreme Court in the case of *Spies* v. *People*, 122 Ill. 1.

The Accused the Accusers, Speeches of Anarchists in Court (Chicago: Socialistic Publishing Society, 1886 (?). At Chicago Historical Society.

Adamic, Louis, *Dynamite* (New York: Viking Press, Inc., 1935).

Addams, Jane, *My Friend, Julia Lathrop* (New York: The Macmillan Co., 1935).

Twenty Years at Hull House (New York: The Macmillan Co., 1910).

Ahern, Michael Loftus, *Political History of Chicago, 1837-87* (Chicago: Donahue, Henneberry Co., 1886).

Altgeld Campaign Pamphlet, 1892, "Judge John P. Altgeld, The Democratic Nominee for Governor of Illinois. His Life. His Speech of Acceptance. The Platform on Which He Runs."

Altgeld, John Peter, *The Cost of Something for Nothing* (Chicago: Hammersmark Publishing Co., 1904).

Live Questions, I (Chicago: Donahue, Henneberry Co., 1890); II (Springfield: Illinois State Register, 1894); 1899 edition (Chicago: George S. Bowen and Co.) includes Volumes I and II, and also new material.

Oratory: Its Requirements and Its Rewards (Chicago: Charles H. Kerr and Co., 1901).

Our Penal Machinery and Its Victims (Chicago: Janssen McClurg and Co., 1884). Reprinted in Volume I and in 1889 edition of *Live Questions.*

Andrew County *Republican* (Savannah, Missouri).

Baldwin, G. S., *Anarchy at an End* (1886). At Chicago Historical Society.

Bancroft, Frederick and Durrey, William, *Reminiscences of Schurz* (New York: Doubleday, Doran and Co., 1908), 3 vols.

Barnes, James A., *John G. Carlisle* (New York: Dodd, Mead and Co., 1931).

Beard, Charles A. and Mary R., *The Rise of American Civilization* (New York: The Macmillan Co., 1930), 2 vols.

Beckner, Earl R., *A History of Illinois Labor Legislation* (Chicago: University of Chicago Press, 1929).

Beer, Thomas, *Hanna* (New York: Alfred A. Knopf, Inc., 1929).

The Mauve Decade (New York: Alfred A. Knopf, Inc., 1926).

Bennett, Fremont O., *Politics and Politicians of Chicago, Cook County and Illinois, 1787-1887* (Chicago: Blakely Printing Co., 1886).

473

Beveridge, Albert J., *Abraham Lincoln* (Boston: Houghton Mifflin Co., 1928), 2 vols.

Bishop, R. P., "Commoners in American Politics: Hon. John P. Altgeld," *The National Magazine,* XVI (April-November, 1892).

Bowen, A. L., "Personal Reminiscences of Joseph W. Fifer, An Interview with the Former Governor and a Description of His Times," in *Illinois Blue Book,* 1925-26, p. 305

Bowers, Claude, *Beveridge and the Progressive Era* (Boston: Houghton Mifflin Co., 1932).

Bromfield, Louis, *The Farm* (New York: Harper and Brothers, 1933).

Brown, Edward Osgood, *Biographical Sketch of Hon. John Peter Altgeld, Twentieth Governor of Illinois* (Chicago: Chicago Historical Society, December 5, 1905).

Browne, F. F., "Altgeld of Illinois," *National Review* (London), XXVIII, 452.

Browne, Waldo, *Altgeld of Illinois* (New York: The Viking Press, Inc., 1924).

Bryan, William Jennings, *The First Battle* (Chicago: W. B. Conkey Co., 1896).

Bryan, William Jennings and Mary, *Memoirs* (Philadelphia: Winston Co., 1925).

Buchanan, James R., *The Story of A Labor Agitator* (New York: Outlook, 1903).

Buck, Solon J., *The Granger Movement, 1870-1880* (Cambridge: Harvard University Press, 1913).

Centennial History of Illinois; editor-in-chief, Clarence Walworth Alvord (Springfield: Illinois Centennial Commission, 1918-20), 5 vols.

Chicago *Chronicle*
Chicago *Daily News*
Chicago *Evening American*
Chicago *Evening Post*
Chicago *Herald*
Chicago *Inter-Ocean*
Chicago *Journal*
Chicago *Labor Advocate*
The Chicago Martyrs, Speeches and Reasons (San Francisco: Free Society, 1899). At Chicago Historical Society.
Chicago *Morning News*
Chicago *Record*
Chicago *Record-Herald*
Chicago *Times*
Chicago *Times-Herald*
Chicago *Tribune*
Cincinnati *Enquirer*
Clendenin, Henry W., *Autobiography of Henry W. Clendenin, Editor* (Springfield: Illinois State Register, 1925).

Cleveland, Grover, "The Government in the Chicago Strike of 1894," *Mc-Clure's Magazine* (July, 1904).

Clevenger, Shoval Vail, *Fun in a Doctor's Life* (Atlantic City: Evolution Publishing Co., 1909).

Coleman, McAlister, *Eugene V. Debs: A Man Unafraid* (New York: Greenberg, Inc., 1930).

Cooling, W. F.,*The Chicago Democracy: A History of Recent Municipal Politics* (Chicago: Platform Publishing Co., 1899). Crerar Library, Chicago.

Cowles, Anna Roosevelt, *Letters from Theodore Roosevelt to Anna Roosevelt Cowles, 1870-1918* (New York: Charles Scribner's Sons, 1924).

Crissey, Forrest, *Tattling Tales of a Retired Politician* (Chicago: Thompson and Thomas, 1904).

Croly, Herbert, *Marcus Alonzo Hanna* (New York: The Macmillan Co., 1912).

Cummings, Homer, *Federal Justice* (New York: The Macmillan Co., 1937).

Currey, J. Seymour, *Chicago: Its History and Its Builders; A Century of Marvelous Growth* (Chicago: S. J. Clarke Publishing Co., 1912), 5 vols.

Darrow, Clarence, *The Story of My Life* (New York: Charles Scribner's Sons, 1932).

David, Henry, *The History of the Haymarket Affair* (New York: Farrar and Rinehart, Inc., 1936).

Davis, Walter Bickford, and Durrie, Daniel Steele, *An Illustrated History of Missouri* (St. Louis: A. J. Hall and Co., 1876).

Debs, Eugene V., *The Federal Government and the Chicago Strikes*, a pamphlet answering Grover Cleveland (Chicago: Charles H. Kerr and Co., 1910).

Dennis, Charles H., *Victor Lawson* (Chicago: University of Chicago Press, 1935).

Denver *Post*

Dewey, Ethel L., *Recollections of Richard Dewey: Pioneer in American Psychiatry* (Chicago: University of Chicago Press, 1936).

Dorfman, Joseph, *Thorstein Veblen and His America* (New York: Viking Press, Inc., 1935).

Dreiser, Theodore, *The Financier* (New York: Boni and Liveright, 1927).
The Titan (New York: Boni and Liveright, 1914).

Dunne, Edward F., *History of Illinois* (Chicago: Lewis Publishing Co., 1933), 5 vols.

East St. Louis *Truth*

Ewing, Charles A., "Compulsory Arbitration," in *Proceedings of Illinois State Bar Association, 1895.*

Farquhar, A. B., and Crowther, Samuel, *The First Million the Hardest* (New York: Doubleday, Doran and Co., 1922).

Gary, Joseph E., "The Chicago Anarchists of 1886. The Crime, The Trial, and the Punishment. By the Judge Who Presided at the Trial," *The Century Magazine*, XLV, 802-37.

George, Henry, *Progress and Poverty* (Fiftieth Anniversary Edition; New York: R. Schalkenback Foundation, 1935).

George, Henry, Jr., *The Life of Henry George* (Toronto: Poole Publishing Co., 1900).

Goodspeed, Weston A., and Healy, Daniel D., *History of Chicago and Cook County* (Chicago: Goodspeed Historical Association, 1909), 2 vols.

Gresham, Matilda, *Life of Walter Q. Gresham* (Chicago: Rand, McNally and Co., 1919), 2 vols.

Harper's Magazine

Harper's Weekly

Hayes, C. J. H., *A Political and Social History of Modern Europe* (New York: The Macmillan Co., 1916), 2 vols.

Harris, Frank, *The Bomb* (New York: Robert Kerr, 1909).

Harrison, Benjamin, *Views of an Ex-President* (Indianapolis: Bowen-Merrill Co., 1901).

Harrison, Carter H., *Stormy Years* (Indianapolis: Bobbs-Merrill Co., 1935).

Hibben, Paxton, *The Peerless Leader, William Jennings Bryan* (New York: Farrar and Rinehart, Inc., 1927).

Hill, Frederick Trevor, *The Chicago Anarchists' Case* (New York: Harper and Brothers, 1907).

Hinrichsen, William H., "Illinois Giants I Have Known," Chicago *Inter-Ocean*, March 16, 1902.

Hull, Paul C., *Chicago Riot: A Record of the Terrible Scenes of May 4, 1886* (Chicago: Belford, Clarke & Co., 1886). At Chicago Historical Society.

Hutchinson, William T., *Cyrus Hall McCormick* (New York: D. Appleton-Century, 1935), I.

Illinois Appellate Court Reports
    City of Chicago v. *John P. Altgeld,* 33, at 23 (1889).
    City of Chicago v. *John P. Altgeld,* Ser. No. 3155, November 26, 1888.
    National Union Building Association v. *Bremer,* 41 at 223 (1891).
    Unity Co., v. *McCormick,* Appellate's Brief, No. 14126; also Supplemental Brief.

Illinois Blue Book, 1925-26; 1935-36.

Illinois Board of Labor Statistics, Report for 1894.

Illinois Supreme Court Reports
    Baltimore and Ohio and Chicago Railroad v. *Illinois Central Railroad,* 137 at 34 (1891).
    Birmingham Fire Insurance Co. v. *Pulver,* 126 at 340 (1888).
    Rollin P. Blanchard v. *Lake Shore and Michigan Railroad,* 126 at 416 (1888).
    Chicago and Northwestern Railroad v. *Annie Dunleavy, Adm.,* 129 at 132 (1889).

Chicago and Northwestern Railroad v. *Mary A. Snyder, Adm.*, 128 at 655 (1889).
De Wolf et al. v. *McGinnis*, 106 at 553 (1883).
Timothy Grady v. *People*, 125 at 122 (1889).
John Gundrat et al. v. *People*, 138 at 103 (1891).
People v. *Coughlin*, 144 at 140 (1893).
People v. *People's Insurance Exchange*, 126 at 466 (1889).
People ex rel. Eureka C. Storey v. *Joshua C. Knickerbocker*, 114 at 539 (1885).
Spies et al. v. *The People, 122* at 1 (1887).
Storey, Probate of Will of, 120 at 244 (1887).
Illustrated Graphic News, "Haymarket Riot Number," May 15, 1886 (Chicago). At Historical Society.
James, Henry, *Richard Olney and His Public Service* (Boston: Houghton Mifflin Co., 1923).
Johnson, Claudius, *Carter Harrison* (Chicago: University of Chicago Press, 1927).
Johnson, Tom L., *My Story* (New York: B. W. Huebsch, 1911).
Jones, Mother, *Autobiography* (Edited by Mary Field Barton: Chicago: Charles H. Kerr, 1925).
Journal of the Senate of the 34th General Assembly of Illinois.
Karsner, David, *Debs, His Authorized Life and Letters from Woodstock Prison to Atlanta* (New York: Boni and Liveright, 1919).
Kelley, O. H., *Origin and Progress of the Order of the Patrons of Husbandry in the United States, 1866-73* (Philadelphia: J. A. Wagenseller, 1875).
Kirkland, Joseph and Moses, John, *History of Chicago* (Chicago: Munsell and Co., 1895), 2 vols.
Knights of Labor
Kohlsaat, H. H., *From McKinley to Harding* (New York: Charles Scribner's Sons, 1923).
Kraus, Adolf, *Reminiscences and Comments* (Chicago: Rubovits, Inc., 1925).
Krock, Arthur, *Editorials of Henry Watterson* (New York: George H. Doran Co., 1923).
Lanehart Estate Records, Probate Court of Cook County.
Law, Robert O., *The Parties and the Men, or Political Issues of 1896, A History of Our Great Parties from the Beginning*, (1896). Probably Chicago.
Laws of Illinois (1889); (1893); (1895).
Leslie's Weekly
Lindsay, Nicholas Vachel, "The Altgeld Temperament," in *The Public* (May 24, 1912).
Linn, James Weber, *James Keeley, Newspaperman* (Indianapolis: Bobbs-Merrill Co., 1937).
Jane Addams (New York: D. Appleton-Century Co., 1935).

Lloyd, Caro, *Henry Demarest Lloyd* (New York: G. P. Putnam's Sons, 1912), 2 vols.

Lum, Dyer Daniel, *A Concise History of the Great Trial of the Chicago Anarchists in 1886*. Condensed from the official record. (Chicago: Socialistic Publishing Co., 1887). At Chicago Historical Society.

Masters, Edgar Lee, *Across Spoon River, An Autobiography* (New York: Farrar and Rinehart, Inc., 1936).

"The Christian Statesman," *American Mercury*, III (December, 1924).

"John Peter Altgeld," *American Mercury*, IV (February, 1929).

Levy Mayer and the New Industrial Era (New Haven: Yale University Press, 1927).

Tale of Chicago (New York: G. P. Putnam's Sons, 1933).

McConnell, Samuel P., "The Chicago Bomb Case, Personal Recollections of An American Tragedy," in *Harper's Magazine* (May, 1934).

McElroy, Robert M., *Grover Cleveland, The Man and the Statesman* (New York: Harper and Brothers, 1923).

Missouri Supreme Court Reports, (1872-76).

Myers, Gustavus, *History of the Supreme Court of the United States* (Chicago: Charles H. Kerr and Co., 1912).

History of the Great American Fortunes (Chicago: Charles H. Kerr and Co., 1910).

Nation

Nevins, Allan, *History of the University of Illinois* (New York: Oxford University Press, 1917).

Grover Cleveland: A Study in Courage (New York: Dodd, Mead and Co., 1932).

Letters and Journal of Brand Whitlock (New York: D. Appleton-Century Co., 1936).

Letters of Grover Cleveland (Boston: Houghton Mifflin Co., 1935).

New York *Journal*

New York *Times*

New York *Tribune*

New York *World*

Palmer, John M., *Personal Recollections of John M. Palmer: The Story of An Earnest Life* (Cincinnati: Robert Clarke Co., 1901).

Parsons, Lucy E., *Life of Albert R. Parsons* (Chicago: Mrs. Parsons, 1903).

Peck, Harry Thurston, *Twenty Years of the Republic* (New York: Dodd, Mead and Co., 1906).

Prentiss, William, article in *Prominent Democrats of Illinois: A Brief History of the Rise and Progress of the Democratic Party of Illinois* (Chicago: Democratic Publishing Co., 1899).

Pringle, Henry F., *Theodore Roosevelt* (New York: Harcourt, Brace and Co., 1931).

Rhodes, James Ford, *History of the United States* (New York: The Macmillan Co., 1928), VIII.

Robinson, Victor, *The Don Quixote of Psychiatry: A Biography of Dr. Shoval Vail Clevenger* (New York: Historico-Medical Press, 1919).

Roosevelt, Theodore, *An Autobiography* (New York: Charles Scribner's Sons, 1931).

St. Joseph (Missouri) *Gazette-Herald*

St. Louis *Republic*

Salter, William M., "What Shall Be Done with The Anarchists?" Lecture before the Society for Ethical Culture, Grand Opera House, October 23, 1887. At Chicago Historical Society.

Schaack, Michael J., *Anarchy and Anarchists* (Chicago: F. J. Schulte and Co., 1889).

Schofield, General John M., *Forty-six Years in the Army* (New York: Century Co., 1897).

Smith, Henry J., and Lewis, Lloyd, *Chicago: A History of Its Reputation* (New York: Harcourt, Brace and Co., 1929).

Spies, August, *Autobiography* (Chicago, 1887). In the John Crerar Library, Chicago.

Stone, Melville, *Fifty Years A Journalist* (New York: Doubleday, Doran and Co., 1921).

Sullivan, William L. (editor) *Dunne: Judge, Mayor, Governor* (Chicago: Windemere Press, 1916).

Swinton, John, *Striking for Life—Labor's Side of the Labor Question* (New York: American Manufacturing and Publishing Co., 1894).

Taylor, Graham, *Pioneering on Social Frontiers* (Chicago: University of Chicago Press, 1930).

The Philistine

The Pilgrim

The Public

The Socialist

Tuttle, C. R., *Illinois Currency Convention* (Chicago: Charles H. Kerr and Co., 1895).

United States Strike Commission, *Report of the Chicago Strike of June-July, 1894,* (Washington: Government Printing Office, 1895).

United States Supreme Court Reports
 In re Debs, 158 at 570 (1895).
 Pollock v. *Farmers' Loan and Trust Co.,* 157 at 532 (1894).

Warren, Charles, "A Manufacturer of History," *McClure's Magazine* (April, 1900).

Werner, M. R., *Bryan* (New York: Harcourt, Brace and Co., 1929).

White, Horace, *Life of Lyman Trumbull* (Boston: Houghton Mifflin Co., 1913).

White, William Allen, "Cleveland," in *McClure's Magazine*, XVIII (February, 1902), 322.

Whitlock, Brand, *Forty Years of It* (New York: D. Appleton-Century, 1914).

Williams, Wayne C., *William Jennings Bryan* (New York: G. P. Putnam's Sons, 1936).

Wilson, Woodrow, *A History of the American People* (New York: Harper and Brothers, 1902), 5 vols.

Zeisler, Zigmund, "Reminiscences of the Haymarket Case," in *Illinois Law Review*, XXI (November, 1926).

UNPUBLISHED SOURCES

Altgeld Collection, Illinois State Historical Society, Springfield.

Baugh, Russel Hugh, "The Attitude of John Peter Altgeld toward Problems of Labor," Master's thesis, University of Wisconsin, 1930.

Bryan Papers, Library of Congress.

Cleveland Collection, Library of Congress.

Holly, William H., "A Forgotten Governor," paper prepared for the Chicago Literary Society.

Labadie Collection, University of Michigan Library.

McConnell, Samuel P., "The Silver Campaign of 1895-96," unpublished Mss.

Myers, Howard Barton, "The Policing of Labor Disputes in Chicago: A Case Study," Doctor's thesis, University of Chicago, 1929.

Post, Louis F., "Living A Long Life Over Again," in Library of Congress, Mss. Division.

Schilling (George A.) Papers, in possession of author.

Scott, Franklin Daniel, "The Political Career of William R. Morrison of Illinois," Master's thesis, University of Chicago, 1924.

Silveus, Marian, "The Antecedents of the Campaign of 1896," Doctor's thesis, University of Wisconsin, 1932.

Wish, Harvey, "The Governorship of John P. Altgeld," Doctor's thesis, Northwestern University, 1936.

PERSONAL ACKNOWLEDGMENTS

PERSONAL ACKNOWLEDGMENTS

During the six years in which the author has been engaged in work on this book, mainly during leisure time, he has had the help and encouragement of many persons, both in the research and in the writing. Indeed, one of the pleasures experienced by the author has been his appreciation of the generosity of friends, acquaintances and complete strangers with their time to help bring out this work.

First of all, grateful acknowledgment is due to Mr. George A. Schilling of Chicago. In many respects, this book is also the story of this Grand Old Man of Chicago Labor. As will be learned from the text, the career of Altgeld was influenced tremendously by his friendship with George A. Schilling, in particular his action in the Haymarket case. Many were the hours that the author was privileged to spend with Mr. Schilling to get from him first-hand recollections concerning Altgeld in the 'eighties and 'nineties and also of the stirring events in the labor movement in which Mr. Schilling played a leading part. In addition, the author obtained from Mr. Schilling many documents of extraordinary interest and importance, most of which had not been available before.

Other friends and associates of Altgeld in Chicago were helpful also. The author acknowledges with deep gratitude interviews granted to him by the late Clarence S. Darrow (who likewise figures greatly in the story of Altgeld); Mr. Fred D. P. Snelling, who for a time was agent of the Unity Block by appointment of Altgeld; Mrs. Adolph Heile, whose husband befriended Altgeld during his lean years in Chicago; the late Henry M. Walker; Judge Charles A. Williams of the Superior Court of Cook County; Mrs. Julia McConnell Follansbee, daughter of the late Judge Samuel P. McConnell, and Mr. Ralph G. Johansen, son-in-law of the lovable Joseph S. Martin.

Mr. William O. Thompson, who was the junior member of the law firm of Altgeld, Darrow and Thompson, prepared for the author, through the courtesy of Dr. Paul H. Douglas of the University of Chicago, an exceedingly valuable memorandum based on his personal association with Altgeld during his last years. Special thanks are due to him. Acknowledgment is gratefully made also to Federal Judge William H. Holly of Chicago, who joined the law firm of Darrow and Thompson after Altgeld's death, for the loan of a paper that he prepared on Altgeld on the basis of conversations he had with Mr. Darrow. To the widow of the late Judge Samuel P. McConnell, the author is indebted for making available several manuscripts prepared by Judge McConnell.

In Richland County, Ohio, where Altgeld lived from infancy until he was twenty-one, the author interviewed a number of persons who had known him or knew of him. Among these, the author is grateful for time granted to him by Mrs. Cenia Pollock Valentine, who grew up on the farm adjoining the Alt-

483

gelds' in Little Washington; Mr. William E. ("Ed") Ford and Mrs. Kitty Ford Neuman, cousins of Mrs. Altgeld, and Mr. E. L. Wesson, an expert on Richland County history, all of Mansfield, Ohio.

Many were the persons interviewed by the author in Savannah, Missouri, where Altgeld became a lawyer before going to Chicago. Sally Woodcock of the Holt family, who remembers that Altgeld bounced her on his knee when she was eight or nine; Justice of the Peace John P. Burns, Charles Booher, Jr., and John K. White were some who contributed valuable reminiscences of Altgeld's life in Savannah. In addition, Mrs. L. T. Lee, the charming editrix of the Savannah *Reporter,* was of great help in making available the files of the old Andrew County *Republican,* from which a good deal of new material was obtained. Among others who helped to throw light on Altgeld's Missouri days, and to whom the author is grateful, are Mr. Redmond S. Cole of Tulsa, Oklahoma, a grandson of Alexander Bedford; Thomas B. Rea, attorney-at-law of Omaha, Nebraska, nephew of Judge David Rea, who started Altgeld on his career as a lawyer; Mrs. Alice Fry, daughter of Judge Rea, and Mrs. Mary E. Kent of St. Joseph, Missouri, daughter-in-law of Josiah Kent, the school trustee who made Altgeld the " 'tater teacher" of the Republican School in Andrew County.

Two nieces of Mrs. Altgeld were especially helpful in throwing light on Altgeld's personal life. They are Mrs. Ruth Ford Atkinson of Demarest, Georgia, who wrote several exceedingly interesting letters to the author and also lent some interesting photographs, and Mrs. Faye Ford Betak of Evanston, Illinois, who granted an interview to the author.

For letters containing interesting information, the author is indebted to Judge Aubrey L. Yantis of Shelbyville, Illinois, whose father, John W. Yantis, was a close political friend of Altgeld; Mr. William Tracy Alden, attorney-at-law of Chicago; Mr. C. R. Clendenin, vice-president of the State Register Publishing Company of Springfield, Illinois, whose father, the late Henry W. Clendenin, also was a close political associate of Altgeld, and Mr. Lee Meriwether of St. Louis. Through the courtesy of Mr. Samuel Hammersmark, the author had the opportunity of interviewing Mrs. Lucy Parsons, widow of Albert R. Parsons, who was one of the men hanged for the Haymarket affair, and the author expresses gratitude to both Mrs. Parsons and Mr. Hammersmark. Thanks are also due to Dr. William E. Dodd of the University of Chicago, for his attempt, while United States Ambassador to Germany, to unearth information concerning the Altgeld family in Germany.

In the research necessary for this book, especially that involving going through literally hundreds of volumes of bound newspapers, the author had the help of his brother-in-law, Mr. Bernard L. Helstien. His assistance was so intelligent and also indefatigable that the author's indebtedness to him is large indeed.

Help given by the libraries in Chicago and elsewhere was considerable and the author would consider himself derelict if he did not mention the numerous librarians, especially at the Chicago Public Library, the John Crerar Library in Chicago, the Chicago Historical Society, the Newberry Library in Chicago, the Library of Congress, the Cincinnati Public Library, the Mansfield (Ohio) Public Library and others, who gave of their time so willingly. Special mention should be given to Miss Agnes Inglis, who has charge of the Joe Labadie Collection in the library at the University of Michigan. The author also extends his thanks to Mr. Wiley W. Mills of Chicago for having made available his set of the bound volumes of *The Public*.

The author's indebtedness is, of course, great to numerous persons whose books he had consulted and from whom passages were excerpted. These are listed in the bibliography, but the author wishes here to express his thanks and appreciation to those writers, in particular Waldo R. Browne, Edgar Lee Masters and Allan Nevins.

In the writing of this book, the author was privileged to have the advice, freely given, of his friend, Mr. Louis Zara, the novelist. Mr. Zara was good enough to read nearly all of the manuscript and the author is indebted to him for many suggestions of value. The author absolves him, however, of any artistic flaws that probably exist. Mr. Albert Lepawsky of the University of Chicago Department of Political Science also read parts of the manuscript and the author likewise is indebted to him for valuable suggestions. To Miss Helen M. Mahoney and Miss Aila Hakala the author is indebted for certain technical assistance, given in leisure time, and he wishes here to express to them his real appreciation.

There are three persons in particular whom the author wishes to mention even though they had little or nothing to do with this book directly. In fact, they will read the story for the first time when it is published. Yet the author feels that the interest shown in him by Professor James Weber Linn, Professor Paul H. Douglas (while the author was a student at the University of Chicago and later) and Mr. Barnet Hodes, Corporation Counsel of the City of Chicago, has been such as to have made them important for the completion of this book, even though they may not be charged with any responsibility for it except that which results from a friendship treasured by the author.

Even though she will know that it is unnecessary, the author wishes to acknowledge the help of his wife. Her assistance is apparent both in the writing and in the research, but more important than that was her patience and her understanding in the face of that most difficult of all human relationships—living with a man engaged in a task such as this book represents.

INDEX